Ada for Software Engineers (Second Editio

WONG

Mordechai Ben-Ari

Ada for Software Engineers (Second Edition with Ada 2005)

Mordechai Ben-Ari, BSc, MSc, PhD
Weizmann Institute of Science
Rehovot 76100
Israel

ISBN: 978-1-84882-313-6 e-ISBN: 978-1-84882-314-3

British Library Cataloguing in Publication Data
A catalogue record for this book is available from the British Library

Library of Congress Control Number: 2009921268

First published 1998

Printed on acid-free paper

Springer Science+Business Media
springer.com

Preface

Albert Einstein once said everything should be made as simple as possible, but not simpler. Einstein could have been talking about programming languages, as the landscape is strewn with "simple" languages that, several versions later, have 500-page reference manuals!

The truth is that we expect a lot of our programming languages. We demand support for encapsulation and abstraction, type checking and exception handling, polymorphism and more. Ada, unlike other languages which grew by the gradual addition of features, was designed as a coherent programming language for complex software systems. *Ada for Software Engineers (ASE)* is written to equip you with the knowledge necessary to use the Ada programming language to develop software systems.

Although Ada never achieved the popularity of Java and the C-something languages, it remains the programming language of choice for reliable software. Every time you step on an airplane or a fast train, you are quite literally trusting your life to software written in Ada. Given the low level of reliability of much of the software we use daily, I can only regret that the use of Ada is not more widespread, and I hope that this book will encourage more software engineers to give Ada a chance.

Intended audience

The book is intended for software engineers making the transition to Ada, and for upper-level undergraduate and graduate students, including those who have had the good fortune to study Ada as their first programming language. No specific knowledge of Ada is assumed; the prerequisites are a basic knowledge of computer science and computer systems, and at least two years of programming experience. As the title implies, if you are a software engineer or training to become one, this book is for you.

Structure of the book

The complexity of modern programming languages leaves textbook writers with a painful dilemma: either gloss over the gory details, or write books that are heavy enough to be classified as lethal weapons. Is there another way? A concise description of Ada is freely available: the *Ada Reference Manual (ARM)* [7], which is the document defining the language standard. The *ARM* has a reputation for being ponderous reading meant for "language lawyers." Nevertheless, I believe that—with a bit of guidance—software engineers can learn to read most of the *ARM*. *ASE* is based upon two premises: (a) it is best to learn the individual language constructs within the context of actual programs, and (b) if the learning is based upon the terminology and concepts used in the language standard, you will be able to use the *ARM* as your primary reference manual.

The Ada language will be taught using a few relatively large case studies, rather than a large number of small examples each crafted to demonstrate a particular construct or rule. Experienced programmers know that the key to mastering a programming language is not to memorize the syntax and semantics of individual constructs, but to learn how to integrate the constructs into language-specific paradigms. We will need to gloss over details when explaining a case study; rest assured that everything will eventually be explained. Certain sections are marked with an asterisk and can be omitted during your initial study of Ada. This material is not necessarily more difficult, but you can't learn everything at once, and these are topics that can be left for your second reading of the book.

The chapters in the book can be divided into five parts and three appendices. The first two parts contain the core concepts of Ada and should probably be read first and in sequence (skipping the starred sections, of course). The others chapters can be read as necessary.

1. After an introductory chapter, Chapters 2–5 quickly cover elementary language constructs such as statements, subprograms, arrays, records and pointers that should be familiar from your previous programming experience.
2. The second part is based upon the progressive development of a case study demonstrating the Ada constructs for programming-in-the-large (including object-oriented programming): packages and private types (Chapter 6), type extension, inheritance, class-wide types and dynamic polymorphism (Chapter 7–8), and generics (Chapter 9).
3. Chapters 10–14 cover other topics and are more or less independent of the previous ones: exceptions, the type system in depth, access types (pointers), numerics and input–output.
4. The fourth part contains material on program structure (Chapter 15), the container library (Chapter 16), and interfaces (Chapter 17).
5. Chapters 18–22 include topics broadly covered by the term *systems programming*: multitasking, hardware interfaces, and real-time and distributed systems.

A special feature of the book is the comprehensive *Glossary* (Appendix A), which explains the *ARM* terminology with examples. In addition, discussions in the text always contain references to the relevant paragraphs in the *ARM*. The *Index of ARM Sections* will be invaluable when you begin to use the *ARM* as a reference manual.

At the end of each chapter are *Projects* and *Quizzes*. Projects are non-trivial programming exercises, many of which ask you to extend the case studies in the text. Quizzes are *not* routine exercises as the term is usually used; they are intended help you understand the finer points of the Ada language, and can be skipped until you have significant experience programming with Ada. Each quiz is a small Ada program; you are to examine it and decide what will happen when the program is compiled, and—if the program contains executable statements and compiles successfully—the result of the execution. Appendix B *Hints* refers you to the relevant clauses of the *ARM* from which you should be able to find the answers to the quizzes *before* looking at Appendix C *Answers*. (To save space, **with** and **use** clauses for `Ada.Text_IO`, `Ada.Integer_IO` and `Ada.Exceptions` are omitted.)

Supplementary material and links

All the case studies, quizzes and programs in the book were compiled and executed. The full source code is available in the software archive at:

- `http://www.springer.com/978-1-84882-313-6`.

The programs were developed using the GNAT compiler for Ada 2005. It is available in commercial, academic and free versions; see:

- `https://libre.adacore.com`.

There are two comprehensive websites on Ada:

- ACM Special Interest Group on Ada (SIGAda), `http://www.sigada.org`,
- Ada Resource Association (ARA), `http://www.adaic.com`.

From these websites you can download documents such as the *ARM*, and find links to compiler vendors, support software, relevant conferences, and other resources.

Ada 2005

This book was original written for the Ada 95 version of the language. That edition is out of print and I have used the occasion of the publication of a new version of Ada, Ada 2005, to expand and improve the book. Constructs of Ada 2005 are freely used, but sections that use them are annotated to indicate which constructs are new. The software archive for the previous edition of the book will remain freely available.

Acknowledgments

First edition: I would like to thank Michael Feldman, Kevlin Henney, Richard Riehle, Reuben Sumner, Tucker Taft and Peter Wegner for reviewing the manuscript, and Simon Plumtree of John Wiley for his support and assistance.

Second edition: I am grateful to Edmond Schonberg for his constant help as I learned Ada 2005. I am indebted to Robert Duff for his comprehensive review that enabled me to correct many bugs in the text. The staff at AdaCore has been extremely helpful answering my queries on the GNAT compiler. I would like to thank Beverley Ford and the staff at Springer for their friendly and efficient handling of the publishing issues that I raised.

Mordechai (Moti) Ben-Ari
Rehovot, 2008

Contents

Chapter 1
The Language for a Complex World

1.1 Programming or software engineering?

Computer science students often extrapolate from their demonstrated ability to write small programs and believe that the same methods and techniques will enable them to develop large software systems. Only later, when they gain experience and mature into competent software engineers, do they realize that the real world does not correspond to the ideal setting of a lab.

Modern software systems are built by tens, even hundreds, of software engineers. Inevitably, a large team will suffer from inconsistencies caused by growth and rapid turnover. Throw in human personality traits such as ambition and envy, and it is a wonder that a large system can even be built!

The work of a software engineer is often the most complex in the entire project. The reason is that the tasks that are implemented in software rather than hardware are precisely those that concern the entire system. Other engineers typically work on individual components and subsystems, which are then integrated into a software-controlled project. For example, a mechanical engineer who designs the landing gear of an airplane is less involved in systems engineering than a software engineer who writes the control program of the aircraft and who must understand the general principles of all the subsystems. Even in fields not traditionally considered engineering, the same situation holds: the software engineer working on a stock exchange must be familiar with the basic principles of the instruments being traded, together with the communications system and the requirements of the traders using the system. Software engineering is significantly more complex than just programming, and it should not be surprising that different tools are needed.

1.2 Reliable software engineering

The structure of the software market for personal computers has caused reliability to be consciously neglected. Software packages are compared by lists of features, performance, and price. Vendors feel pressured to bring new versions to market, regardless of the reliability of the product. They can always promise to fix the bug in the next version.

But word-processors, presentation graphics and interactive games are not the only type of software being developed. Computers are now controlling the most complex systems in the world: airplanes and spacecraft, power plants and steel mills, communications networks, international banks and stock markets, military systems and medical equipment. The social and economic environment in which these systems are developed is totally different from that of packaged software. Each project pushes forward the known limits of engineering experience, and delays and cost overruns are frequent, yet the cost cannot be recouped by selling more copies of the software. A company's reputation for engineering expertise and sound management can be more important in winning a contract than a list of features.

Above all, system reliability cannot be compromised: a bug in a medical system can lead to loss of life; the crash of a communications system can disrupt an entire economy; the failure of a spacecraft can cost hundreds of millions of dollars. In fact, all these have occurred because of software faults.

1.3 Programming languages for software engineering

Software engineering is the term used to denote the ensemble of techniques for developing large software projects. It includes managerial techniques such as cost estimation, documentation standards, configuration management and quality assurance procedures. It also includes notations and methodologies for the analysis, design and testing of the software itself.

In the end, however, a software system is successful if "it"—the "code"—executes reliably and performs according to the system requirements. The best-managed project with a superb design is a failure if the delivered code is no good. Managerial techniques and design methodologies must be supplemented by the use of a programming language that supports reliable programming.

The alternative to language support for reliability is "bureaucracy." The project manager must write conventions for interfaces and specifications of data representations, and each convention must be checked, possibly by software tools, but often manually in code inspections. The result is that all the misunderstandings are discovered at best when the software components are integrated, and at worst after the software is delivered. Why can't these conventions be formalized in a programming language so that they can be checked by the compiler and run-time system?

1.4 Ada for software engineering

The Ada language is complex because it is intended for developing complex systems, and its advantages are only apparent if you are designing and developing such a system. Then, and only then, will you have to face numerous dilemmas, and you will be grateful for the Ada constructs that help you resolve them. Here are some questions you face when developing a large system and the support in Ada for answering the questions:

- **Q:** How can I decompose the system?
  A: Into packages that can be flexibly structured to form the software architecture.
- **Q:** How can I specify the module interfaces?
  A: In a package specification that is separate from its implementation.
- **Q:** How can I describe the data?
  A: With a rich type system.
- **Q:** How can I ensure independence of the components of my system?
  A: By using private types to define abstract data types.
- **Q:** How can data types relate to one another?
  A: Either by composition in records or by inheritance through type extension.
- **Q:** How can I reuse software components from other projects?
  A: By instantiating generic packages.
- **Q:** How can I synchronize dozens of concurrent processes?
  A: Synchronously through rendezvous or asynchronously through protected actions.
- **Q:** How can I get at the raw machine when I need to?
  A: By using representation items.
- **A:** How can I ensure that scheduling deadlines are met in my real-time system?
  A: By specifying scheduling and queuing policies, and by enforcing the use of a subset of the language constructs whose execution time is predictable.
- **Q:** How can I make the most efficient use of my expensive testing facility?
  A: By testing as much of the software as possible on a host machine using a compiler that accepts the same standard language as the target machine.

1.5 The development of Ada

The Ada language was developed at the request of the US Department of Defense, which was concerned by the proliferation of programming languages for mission-critical systems. Military systems were programmed in languages not commonly used in science, business and education, and dialects of these languages proliferated. Each project had to acquire and maintain a development environment and to train software engineers to support these systems throughout decades of deployment. Choosing a standard language would significantly simplify and reduce the cost of these logistical tasks.

Though Ada was originally intended for military systems, it is now the language of choice for any critical system.

1.5.1 Ada 83

A survey of existing languages showed that none would be suitable, so it was decided to develop a new language based on an existing language (Pascal). The competition was won by a team led by Jean Ichbiah, and the language published as an ANSI/MIL standard in 1983 and as an ISO standard in 1987. There were several unique aspects of the development of Ada:

- The language was developed to satisfy a formal set of requirements. This ensured that from the beginning the language included the necessary features for its intended applications.
- The language proposal was published for scientific review *before* it was fully implemented and used in applications. Many mistakes in the design were corrected before they became entrenched by widespread use.
- The standard was finalized early in the history of the language, and facilities were established to validate compilers against the standard. Adherence to the standard is especially important for training, software reuse and host/target development and testing.

1.5.2 Ada 95

A decade later, a second round of language design was performed by a team led by S. Tucker Taft. This design followed the same principles as the previous one: proposals by the design team were published and critiqued, and finally accepted as an international standard in 1995. This language is called Ada 95 to distinguish it from the previous version called Ada 83. For the benefit of readers familiar with Ada 83, we summarize the major differences between that language and Ada 95:

- In Ada 83, derived types were of limited expressive power and not widely used. In Ada 95, *tagged* derived types are the basis for type extension and dynamic polymorphism, which are the constructs required for object-oriented programming.
- Packages in Ada 83 could be nested, but this introduced excessive dependences among the packages. *Child packages* in Ada 95 can be used to construct subsystems as flexible hierarchies of packages that share abstractions (private types).

- The rendezvous is an extremely successful construct for task-to-task communication, but it is rather inefficient for mutual exclusion. Ada 95 introduced *protected objects* that are far more efficient for simple synchronization.
- New numeric types were introduced: *modular types* for unsigned arithmetic and *decimal fixed point types* for financial calculations.
- In Ada 83, access types (pointers) were only allowed to point to data allocated on the heap. *General access types* were introduced in Ada 95; they enable the creation of pointers to static data or to data allocated on the stack by the normal declaration of variables. The concept of *accessibility levels* ensures that errors such as dangling pointers are detected.
- Ada 95 extended support for hardware interfacing, as well as for programming in a mixed-language environment. Data types are defined for machine words, as well as for objects shared with libraries and modules written in Fortran, Cobol and C.
- Libraries for character and string handling, and for mathematical functions are specified within the standard, and international character sets are supported.
- The language was divided into a core that must be supported by all implementations and into special-needs annexes that are optional. The core language is of a reasonable size; extensions which are of interest in specialized applications only can be implemented as needed. There are annexes for systems programming, real-time systems, distributed systems, information systems, numerics (scientific computation), and for systems with additional safety and security requirements.

The Ada Joint Project Office of the US Department of Defense was closed in 1998 and Ada no longer has any government connection. The *Ada Resource Association* composed of commercial companies who develop tools for Ada promotes the use of the language. Standardization of the language continues under the procedures of the International Organization for Standardization.

1.5.3 Ada 2005

The Ada Working Group (ISO/IEC JTC 1/SC 22/WG 9) has continued to work on interpreting, refining and extending the Ada language. In 2001, the standard was updated with *Technical Corrigendum 1*, reflecting clarifications to the Ada 95 language standard. Subsequent work led to the publication of *Amendment 1* containing modifications to the language; this version of the language is called Ada 2005 and the updated standard was published in 2007.

The changes from Ada 95 to Ada 2005 are much less extensive than those made in the transition from Ada 83 to Ada 95. The most significant changes are as follows:

- Ada 2005 supports a 32-bit character set (`Wide_Wide_Character` and `Wide_Wide_String`), in addition to the 16-bit character set (`Wide_Character` and `Wide_String`) introduced in Ada 95.

- The support for object-oriented programming has been enhanced; for example, the distinguished receiver syntax familiar from other languages is now allowed. *Interfaces*—which may be familiar to you from the Java language—are supported to enable a form of multiple inheritance without the complexity of full multiple inheritance as in C++.
- *Anonymous access types* enable greater flexibility when using pointers. In particular, anonymous access-to-subprogram types facilitate the use of iterators.
- Numerous standard libraries have been added to Ada 2005, most importantly, a *container library* that supports the data structures vectors, doubly-linked lists, ordered and hashed maps, and ordered and hashed sets. Libraries for real and complex vectors, including the basic operations of linear algebra, are supported within the Numerics Annex.
- The Real-Time Systems Annex has been enhanced with new methods of scheduling and new libraries. It also includes the *Ravenscar profile*, a specification of requirements and restrictions that ensures that the performance of a real-time system written in Ada is predictable.

1.6 The Ada Reference Manual

The Ada 2005 programming language is defined by a document called *Ada Reference Manual: International Standard ISO/IEC-8652:1995 with Technical Corrigendum 1 and Amendment 1: Language and Standard Libraries*. It is freely available online in several formats such as PDF and HTML, and is published in book form as [7]. Henceforth, we will refer to this document as the *ARM*. The *ARM* is intended to serve as a *contract* between software engineers writing applications in Ada and compiler implementors. If you write your program according to the rules in the *ARM*, the executable file generated by the compiler will execute as described in the *ARM* on any computer, running any operating system. In practice, the *ARM* does not specify every aspect of the language so as not to overly constrain the implementors of a compiler, but even this freedom is carefully documented.

The Ada approach of creating a standard as early as possible can be contrasted with the situation in other languages such as Fortran or C, which were extensively used before standardization. By then, quirks of the first implementations had become part of the language, and the spread of dialects made it extremely difficult to port existing programs. The danger of early standardization is that constructs that are of little use or are difficult to implement may be required by the standard. The development of both Ada 95 and Ada 2005 dealt with this danger by arranging for compiler developers and applications software engineers to study and test constructs before the standard was finalized.

For all versions of Ada, there is a document called the *Rationale* that presents the reasoning behind the design decisions that were taken. The *Rationale* for Ada 95 is still relevant for Ada 2005 because it describes in detail the design of the support for object-oriented programming and the Special Needs Annexes.

Finally, the *Annotated Ada Reference Manual* is a version of the *ARM* containing additional material that justifies the rules and explains obscure points or implementation aspects. This document is not normally needed by applications engineers.

Ada 95

The printed version of the *ARM* for Ada 95 is [6].

1.6.1 The structure of the ARM

The *ARM* consists of thirteen sections, fifteen annexes and an index. The sections are:

1. General
2. Lexical Elements
3. Declarations and Types
4. Names and Expressions
5. Statements
6. Subprograms
7. Packages
8. Visibility Rules
9. Tasks and Synchronization
10. Program Structure and Compilation Issues
11. Exceptions
12. Generic Units
13. Representation Issues

Sections 1, 2, 4, 5, 6, 11 are relatively straightforward and define the structures used for writing the declarations and statements of individual units. Section 3 Declarations and Types is quite complex because the entire Ada type system is defined in a single long Section. It is best read in parts as you learn the language. Sections 7, 8, 10, 12 describe the structures used to construct large and flexible software systems. Section 9 presents concurrent programming in Ada and Section 13 shows how to query and specify machine-dependent representations of Ada programs.

The annexes are:

A. Predefined Language Environment
B. Interface to Other Languages
C. Systems Programming

D. Real-Time Systems
E. Distributed Systems
F. Information Systems
G. Numerics
H. High Integrity Systems
I. (not used)
J. Obsolescent Features
K. Language-Defined Attributes
L. Language-Defined Pragmas
M. Summary of Documentation Requirements
N. Glossary
O. (not used)
P. Syntax Summary
Q. Language-Defined Entities

Annex A is quite long (about 160 pages) and contains the specification of the standard Ada libraries that any implementation must provide. Annexes B and J are also part of the *core* of Ada. Annexes C through H are *Special Needs Annexes* that need not be provided by an implementation; these annexes specify constructs that are only important for developing certain kinds of systems, such as real-time systems or numerical libraries. The other annexes are *informative* and summarize information given elsewhere.

Annex §A.1 specifies the package `Standard` that is the parent of all Ada units and contains the declaration of predefined entities like the type `Integer`. The other packages in Annex §A are child packages of a package called `Ada`. They include libraries for character and string handling, basic numerics libraries, input–output libraries, and libraries for working with the execution environment. It also describes the container library.

The sections and annexes of the *ARM* are divided into clauses and subclauses, which are in turn divided into numbered paragraphs. We use the notation §C(P) to refer to paragraph(s) P within clause or subclause C. Framed extracts from the *ARM* are identified by the clause number above the box and the paragraph number(s) within the text. An ellipsis (...) indicates omissions from a paragraph. These selective extracts are intended to simplify your initial understanding; be sure to read the full paragraphs from *ARM* when you start to program in Ada.

The numbering of clauses and paragraphs is consistent between Ada 95 and Ada 2005. When there was a need to add new paragraphs between existing ones, a decimal notation was used; for example, the **return** statement has changed, so paragraph 5 of clause 6.5 is now followed by eight new paragraphs labeled 5.1–5.8. If a paragraph was deleted, the sentence *This paragraph was deleted* is used to preserve the numbering scheme.

Changed paragraphs also have /1 or /2 following the paragraph number. The number 1 indicates that the change is associated with the 2001 Technical Corrigendum 1 (still Ada 95), while 2 means that the change is associated with Amendment 1 (Ada 2005). Since this information is primarily of historical interest, it has been omitted from the text. The *ARM* for Ada 2005 is available in an edition that highlights the changes from previous editions. This can be useful if you are familiar with the Ada 95 *ARM* and are learning Ada 2005.

Most of the text of the *ARM* is *normative*, meaning that an implementation must conform to the text. Annexes K–Q and the index are *informative*, meaning that they are not part of the contract. For example, Annex §K *Language-Defined Attributes* is a convenient list of all the attributes defined throughout the normative text. It is useful if you are searching for an attribute, but the rules of the language are determined by the normative text where the attribute is defined. In addition, the text contains *Notes* and *Examples*, which are informative. The Examples are usually too simple to be useful, but the Notes are quite important because they describe rules that are *ramifications* of other rules, meaning that they can be deduced from other rules, although it may be difficult to understand why this is so. For all practical purposes you will be not be led astray if you trust the Notes.

1.6.2 The terminology of the ARM

Like any contract, the *ARM* is written in very precise language, and the term "language lawyer" is used for people who are experts at interpreting the document. Like any legal contract, however, the rules are binding upon you, even if you don't exactly understand the text of the rule! Fortunately, many of the most difficult parts of the *ARM* are intended for compiler implementors, and you don't need to understand them in order to write applications. For example:

§3.2.2

> 8 A subtype_mark shall resolve to denote a subtype. The type *determined by* a subtype_mark is the type of the subtype denoted by the subtype_mark.

is a rule that only a language lawyer could love, but:

§2.4.1

> 6 An underline character in a numeric_literal does not affect its meaning. The letter E of an exponent can be written either in lower case or in upper case, with the same meaning.

is a rule which needs neither explanation nor paraphrasing.

The clauses and subclauses have a common structure §1.1.2:

Syntax The syntax of the constructs is given in BNF. The complete syntax is collected in Annex §P.

Name resolution rules These rules specify requirements on constructs within a certain context. They are also used disambiguate multiple possible interpretations. For example, the name resolution rule of an if-statement is:

§5.3

> 4 A condition is expected to be of any boolean type.

This means, first, that the condition must be of a boolean type; furthermore, if the condition in an if-statement is a function call `Func(X,Y)` and there are two such functions, one returning the type `Boolean` and one returning the type `Integer`, the compiler will select the one returning the type `Boolean`.

Legality rules These rules prescribe what it means for a program to be *legal*, that is, to compile successfully. For example, the statement:

```
case C of
  when 'A'      => Proc1(Z);
  when 'A'      => Proc2(Y);
  when others => null;
end case;
```

is not legal because:

§5.4

> 10 Two distinct discrete_choices of a case_statement shall not cover the same value.

Static semantics These clauses define the compile-time effect of a construct and are also used extensively for defining terms. For example, the rules for a for-loop statement include:

§5.5

> 6 A loop_parameter_specification declares a *loop parameter*, ...

In a for-loop:

```
for N in 1 .. 10 loop
  ...
end loop;
```

the loop parameter `N` is implicitly declared at the point where the statement is written.

A large part of Section §3 Declarations and Types consists of static semantics rules that define the compile-time properties of types.

Dynamic semantics These clauses tell you what a construct does at run-time. The following clause should come as no surprise:

§5.3

> 5 For the execution of an if_statement, the condition specified after **if**, and any conditions specified after **elsif**, are evaluated in succession (treating a final **else** as **elsif** True **then**), until one evaluates to True or all conditions are evaluated and yield False. If a condition evaluates to True, then the corresponding sequence_of_statements is executed; otherwise none of them is executed.

1.7 Case studies

Experienced software engineers know that it is relatively easy to learn the syntax and semantics of a new programming language. It is much more difficult to become a proficient programmer in a language, in the sense of learning and internalizing the way programs should be designed and written in the language. Learning Ada can be initially frustrating, because many rules seem to be arbitrary, but they were put there to make programs more reliable, as well as to make it easier to read and maintain a program.

I believe that the correct way to learn Ada is through the study of relatively long and reasonably realistic *case studies* that show the use of the language constructs *in context*. This facilitates learning the motivation behind the language rules and the tradeoffs involved in choosing among various constructs. The downside is that the presentation is not "linear" and "structured" with all the explanations pertaining to a certain concept or construct concentrated in a single section. The Glossary, the Subject Index, and the Index to *ARM* Sections will help you find your way around.

The case studies are displayed in numbered listings with the directory name containing the source code shown above a listing. The listings are interspersed with detailed explanations and the notation ‡n refers to line numbers in the listing.

All programs have been compiled and executed, and the full source code is available in the software archive. To save space, some of the source code has been omitted or reformatted. Hopefully, errors have not been introduced in this process, but in any case, the source code files should be considered more definitive than the text.

Chapter 2

First Steps in Ada

This chapter presents the basic concepts of Ada starting with a simple program.

2.1 Case study: country of origin

The following program reads the name of a car manufacturer and prints the country of origin. In this era of globalization, where cars are designed in one country and assembled in several others, the program is admittedly artificial and incomplete, but it will serve its purpose of presenting the basics of Ada.

Ada uses the term *subprogram* to refer to either a procedure or a function. The main subprogram §10.2(7), here `Country1`, is a subprogram that is not nested within any other unit:

country1

```
with Ada.Text_IO; use Ada.Text_IO;
procedure Country1 is
```

The first line of the program is a *context clause*, which is used to obtain access to the input–output library `Ada.Text_IO`.

A subprogram consists of a subprogram_specification, followed by a declarative_part and a handled_sequence_of_statements §6.3(2). The declarative part begins with declarations of the types `Cars` and `Countries`, followed by a declaration of the variable `Car`:

```
   type Cars is
     (Ford, Chevrolet, Pontiac, Chrysler, Dodge,
      Rover, Rolls_Royce,
      Peugeot, Renault, Citroen,
      BMW, Volkswagen, Opel,
      Honda, Mitsubishi, Toyota,
      Daewoo, Hyundai
     );
```

```
type Countries is (US, UK, France, Germany, Japan, Korea);

Car: Cars;
```

There is no required order for the declaration of entities, except that a declaration must appear before it is used.

The declarative part also includes the declaration of a function `Car_to_Country`:

```
function Car_to_Country(C: Cars) return Countries is
begin
  case C is
    when Ford | Chevrolet..Pontiac | Chrysler..Dodge
                                 => return US;
    when Rover | Rolls_Royce => return UK;
    when Peugeot..Citroen    => return France;
    when BMW..Opel           => return Germany;
    when Honda..Toyota       => return Japan;
    when Daewoo | Hyundai    => return Korea;
  end case;
end Car_to_Country;
```

The structure of the function declaration is the same as that of the main subprogram: a specification (here with a parameter and a return type), a declarative part (empty), and a sequence of statements (here, a single case statement).

The executable part of the subprogram is a sequence of statements, in this case a single loop statement with other statements nested within:

```
begin
  loop
    Put("Enter the make of the car: ");
    Car := Cars'Value(Get_Line);
    Put_Line(Cars'Image(Car) & " is made in " &
      Countries'Image(Car_to_Country(Car)));
  end loop;
exception
  when Constraint_Error => Put_Line("Car make is not recognized");
  when End_Error        => null;
end Country1;
```

The sequence of statements is followed by two exception handlers. The first, for the predefined exception `Constraint_Error`, is used to write an error message if the string entered in the input does not represent a valid make of a car; the second, for IO exception `End_Error`, is used to terminate the program when an end-of-file indication is encountered.

2.2 Library units and context clauses

Non-nested units such as subprograms are called *library units* §10.1.1. A *compilation unit* is a library unit, optionally preceded by a *context clause* §10.1.2, which lists packages that are imported into the unit. (A compilation unit can also be a subunit (Section 15.3).) Packages—the Ada construct for creating modules—will be discussed in depth in Chapter 6; until then we will only use a context clause to import input–output packages like `Ada.Text_IO` §A.10.

2.3 Input–output

There are no input–output *statements* in Ada. Instead, the standard libraries use general language constructs such as types and subprograms. The case study used `Get_Line` ‡29 and `Put_Line` ‡30, which are subprograms specified in §A.10.7 Input–Output of Characters and Strings. The output procedures have only one parameter, unlike the output statements in languages like C and Pascal, which can take an arbitrary number of parameters. This limitation can be overcome by the use of the operator `"&"` ‡30 for string concatenation §4.5.3(3–4).

Ada 95

The function `Get_Line` is new to Ada 2005. Previously, there was only a procedure `Get_Line` with two parameters §A.10.7(18–19), one a buffer into which the input string is placed and the other the index of the last character of the input. The program, therefore, needs two more variables:

```
S:       String(1..80);    --  Input string
Last:    Integer;          --  Last character of input string
```

and the single statement in ‡29 must be replaced by the two statements:

```
Get_Line(S, Last);
Car := Cars'Value(S(1..Last));
```

2.4 Attributes for string conversion

To convert from strings to values and back, *attributes* are used. Given a scalar type T (integer, real, or enumeration type), the attribute `T'Value` ‡29 is a function that converts a string to a value of the type §3.5(52–55). Conversely, the attribute `T'Image` ‡30–31 converts a value of the type to a string §3.5(35–37).

Language Comparison

The attribute `Image` is similar to the Java function `toString` with the following differences: (a) `Image` is defined only for scalar types; (b) `Image` cannot be overridden; (c) `Image` must be explicitly called to convert a value to a string, unlike in Java where the evaluation of the expression `"The answer="+N` would automatically invoke the method `toString` for the type of `N`.

2.5 Statements

Ada has the usual simple and compound executable statements §5.1: assignment §5.2, **if** §5.3, **case** §5.4, **loop** (both **for** and **while**) §5.5, and even a **goto** statement §5.8. There is also a **null** statement which does nothing §5.1(13).

A **loop** need not have a termination condition using **for** or **while**; this is particularly useful when writing servers that are not intended to terminate. The **exit** statement §5.7 may be used to leave a loop at any point within its execution. There is a special syntax **exit when** that makes the termination condition particularly readable. For example, we could add the dummy value `Quit` to the types `Cars` and `Countries` and then use an exit statement to leave the loop, instead of terminating the program with the exception `End_Error`:

```
exit when Car = Quit;
```

If you want to leave a nested loop, you can use a loop identifier §5.5(2), §5.7(2).

For-loops are used when you can compute the number of iterations in advance. The following statement will print the country of origin of all the cars declared as values of type `Cars`:

```
for C in Cars loop
  Put_Line(Cars'Image(C) & " is made in " &
    Countries'Image(Car_to_Country(C)));
end loop;
```

The loop parameter `C` is a constant §3.3(19) that is implicitly declared §5.5(6). Its scope is restricted to the loop statement §8.1(4), so if the value is needed later, an additional variable must be used:

```
Found_At: Integer := -1;          -- -1 if not found

for I in A'Range loop
  if A(I) = Key then
    Found_At := I;
    exit;
  end if
end loop;
```

A **return** statement ‡18–23 §6.5 must be used to return a value from a function. A procedure is normally left by "falling off" the final statement, but a **return** statement may be used to return at any point within the sequence of statements.

There is a rich syntax for **case** statements §5.4, as demonstrated (somewhat artificially) in the case study ‡16–24. The basic rule is that each possible value of the expression must be *covered* by exactly one of the alternatives. An **others** alternative is allowed if you do not want to explicitly list an action for all alternatives. For example, suppose that we wanted to associate a continent with a car and that we anticipate that most cars would be from Europe; then it might be reasonable to use **others**:

```
type Continents is (North_America, Asia, Europe);

case C is
  when Ford .. Dodge   => return North_America;
  when Honda..Hyundai => return Asia;
  when others          => return Europe;
end case;
```

If possible, the use of **others** should be avoided so that if a value is added to an enumeration type, a compile-time error will result if you forget to add an alternative for the value. Similarly, subranges should be avoided if there is no natural ordering of subsequences of values.

Language Comparison

Ada does not have a **do–while** construct for a termination condition at the end of a loop. However, **exit when** can be used to place a termination condition at any point in a loop, including just before the **end loop**.

Language Comparison

Case alternatives are not terminated by **break** statements, as in C and Java. When the statements of an alternative are completed, execution proceeds with the statement after the case statement. This prevents the serious errors caused by accidently falling through from one alternative to another.

Language Comparison

In C and Java, there is no rule requiring that all values of the expression type be covered; instead, the execution of a **switch** statement is silently skipped if the value of the expression is not covered. Again, the Ada rule causes a serious run-time error to become a simple compile-time error.

2.6 Exceptions

§11

> 1 This section defines the facilities for dealing with errors or other exceptional situations that arise during program execution. An *exception* represents a kind of exceptional situation; an occurrence of such a situation (at run-time) is called an *exception occurrence*. To *raise* an exception is to abandon normal program execution so as to draw attention to the fact that the corresponding situation has arisen. Performing some actions in response to the arising of an exception is called *handling* the exception.

The main subprogram in the case study has two exception handlers ‡34–35. The predefined exception `Constraint_Error` §11.1 will be raised if you enter a string that is not the name of a car declared in the type declaration. If this occurs, the normal execution will be abandoned and the sequence of statements in the exception handler will be executed instead. Here, it is the single statement that calls `Put_Line`; then, the execution of the subprogram enclosing the exception handler will terminate. The exception `End_Error` is defined in the input–output library §A.13(12) and will be raised if an attempt is made to read beyond the end of a file (or `ctrl-z` or `ctrl-d` is entered interactively).

There are four predefined exceptions §A.1(46):

- `Constraint_Error`, which you will encounter frequently, because any run-time violation of the type system will raise this exception;
- `Program_Error`, which is raised in unusual situations, such as "falling off" the end of a function without executing a return statement;
- `Storage_Error`, which is raised if the program runs out of memory;
- `Tasking_Error`, which is raised for errors in the multitasking constructs (Chapter 18).

> **Language Comparison**
>
> In Java and C++, exception handlers are written within a **`try–catch`** construct that is explicitly written to enclosed a sequence of statements where an exception might occur. In Ada, exception handlers are associated with a *body*, generally of a subprogram. The "try" implicitly covers all the statements in the body. It is possible to achieve the effect of a **`try–catch`** construct within a sequence of statements by using a block statement §5.6 (Section 3.5).

2.7 Types

Types are the heart and soul of Ada. The executable statements of the language are almost indistinguishable from those of other languages, but the type system is rich and, yes, complex.

2.7.1 *Why types?*

Why are types so important? Experience has shown that the key to good software design is not in the algorithms but in the data. You can write small programs to manipulate raw data in memory such as numbers and bytes, but any large program is necessarily modeling some complex applications area such as banking, medicine or transportation. The only way to write software that can be understood, validated and maintained is to model the application within the program.

Types are not merely descriptive. The Ada language provides for *type checking*. Since each type is modeling a different kind of real-world data, you cannot assign a value of one type to a variable of another type, or call a subprogram if the types of the actual parameters do not match the types of the formal parameters. If `Apple_Count` contains a value of type `Apples` and `Orange_Count` contains a value of type `Oranges`, the statement:

```
Apple_Count := Apple_Count + Orange_Count;
```

contains an error if the operator "+" is defined for two values of type `Apple` and two values of type `Orange`, but not for mixed fruit. An Ada compiler is required to reject such statements.

The advantage of type checking is a significant reduction in the number of logic and run-time errors in the software. Errors form a hierarchy defined by the severity of the effects of the error and the difficulty of discovering and fixing it:

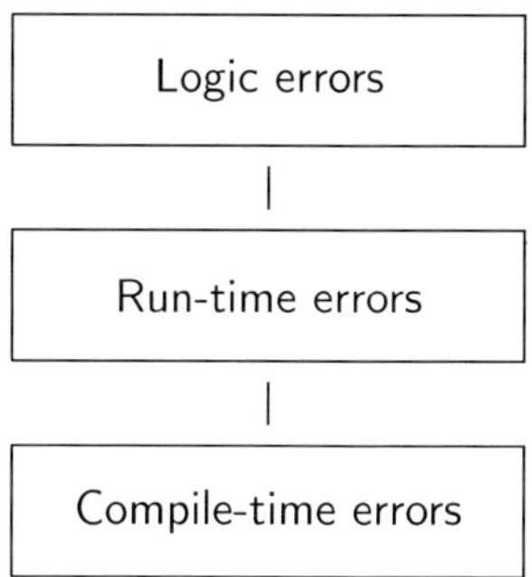

Compile-time errors These are the errors that are the easiest to find and correct. Some compile-time errors like missing punctuation are trivial; others, like visibility errors caused by misplaced declarations, are more difficult to find.

Run-time errors These are errors that cause the program to stop running and to display an error message. (Of course, run-time errors are extremely problematical in embedded systems that cannot "print an error.") Examples are trying to index an array beyond its bounds and trying to dereference a null pointer. In a language that supports run-time checking, these errors are relatively easy to diagnose, because you know where the program stopped and why. If the error is not caught when it occurs, it can cause memory assigned to unrelated variables to be "smeared." Such errors are exceedingly difficult to diagnose because the error is only discovered when the smeared variables are read, and that code is likely to be correct.

Logic errors This is the term used for errors that manifest themselves as incorrect functioning of a running program. For example, you might compute a thermostat setting that has no physical meaning even though the value is within the range of an integer variable. These errors are often found only after the system is delivered and installed.

The philosophy of Ada is to push errors *down* the hierarchy: to turn logic errors into run-time errors and if possible into compile-time errors. For critical software systems, logic errors are not merely embarrassing and expensive, they can be truly dangerous. Because it helps prevent logic errors, the Ada type system is an excellent technological tool for constructing reliable software.

Effective use of the Ada type system requires an investment of effort on your part:

- During the design of the software system, you must select types that best model the data in the system and that are appropriate for the algorithms to be used. If you write a program in which every variable is declared as `Integer`, `Float` or `Character`, you are not taking advantage of the capabilities of Ada.
- Occasionally, the rules for type checking are too strict and workarounds must be found. For example, a sequence of raw bytes received from a communications line will need to be interpreted as a structured message. There is an Ada construct for bypassing type checking (Section 5.4.4), as well as safer methods of solving some of these problems (Section 11.5).
- Certain language rules are checked at run-time, and the overhead of the checks must be taken into account, although optimizing compilers can reduce this overhead to a minimum. If needed, run-time checks can be suppressed (Section 10.7); usually, it will be sufficient to suppress checks in a small number of "hot spots" in the program.

An investment of the time needed to learn and effectively use the Ada type system will repay itself many times over in lower rates of logic and run-time errors in your programs.

2.7.2 *Definition of types*

§3.2

> 1 A *type* is characterized by a set of values, and a set of *primitive operations* which implement the fundamental aspects of its semantics. ...

Some types like the type `Integer` are predefined by the language. The set of values of `Integer` is implementation-defined, and the primitive operations include assignment (which is defined for all types except for limited types; see Chapter 6), and the arithmetical and relational operators §4.5. (The concept of primitive operation will be fully explained in Chapter 7.)

2.7.3 *Enumeration types*

Type `Cars` ‡3–10 is an *enumeration type* §3.5.1. The names listed in the type declaration are the *enumeration literals*, which are the values of the type. The predefined operations on enumeration types include assignment and the relational operators such as "=" and "<".

§3.5.1

> 7 Each enumeration literal corresponds to a distinct value of the enumeration type, and to a distinct position number. The position number of the value of the first listed enumeration literal is zero; the position number of the value of each subsequent enumeration literal is one more than that of its predecessor in the list.
>
> 8 The predefined order relations between values of the enumeration type follow the order of corresponding position numbers.

There are predefined values and functions called *attributes* §4.1.4 associated with each type; a list of all attributes is given in §K. Some attributes that are defined for enumeration and integer types are given in the following table, where `T` is a type, `V` is a value of the type, `N` is an integer and `S` is a string:

`T'First`	First value of `T`
`T'Last`	Last value of `T`
`T'Pred(V)*`	Previous value before `V`
`T'Succ(V)*`	Next value after `V`
`T'Pos(V)`	Position of `V`
`T'Val(N)*`	Value whose position is `N`
`T'Min(V1,V2)`	Minimum of `V1,V2`
`T'Max(V1,V2)`	Maximum of `V1,V2`
`T'Image(V)`	String denoting the value `V`
`T'Value(S)*`	Value denoted by `S`
`T'Width`	Maximum length of `T'Image`

Attributes marked with an asterisk may raise `Constraint_Error`, and in certain circumstances, `Pos` may raise `Program_Error` §3.5.5(8).

In the case study we used the attributes `Cars'Value` and `Cars'Image` for input–output, as described above. For extensive input–output of values of an enumeration type, it is better to instantiate the generic package `Enumeration_IO` (Chapter 9) for the type.

The fundamental principle of type checking is that a value of one type may not be assigned to a variable (or parameter) of another type §5.2(4), §6.4.1(3). This violation of type checking results in a compile-time error. Thus we cannot write:

```
Car := France;
```

because we are attempting to assign a value of type `Countries` to a variable of type `Cars`. Similarly, we cannot write the following function call:

```
Car_to_Country(63);
```

because the assignment of an actual parameter of type `Integer` to a formal parameter of type `Cars` is not legal.

*2.7.4 Name equivalence**

Given the declarations:

```
type Countries is (Greenland, Grenada, Guadeloupe, Guam);
type Islands   is (Greenland, Grenada, Guadeloupe, Guam);

C: Countries;
I: Islands;
```

we cannot assign `C` to `I` or vice versa. Each type declaration defines a separate type. The *name* of the type, rather than its structure, determines type equivalence.

This example demonstrates *overloading*.

§3.5.1

> 9 If the same defining_identifier or defining_character_literal is specified in more than one enumeration_type_definition, the corresponding enumeration literals are said to be *overloaded*. At any place where an overloaded enumeration literal occurs in the text of a program, the type of the enumeration literal has to be determinable from the context (see 8.6).

The following assignment is legal:

```
C := Greenland;
```

The *expected type* of an expression on the right-hand side of an assignment statement is the same type as that of the variable that is target of the assignment §5.2(4); this rule can be used to disambiguate the type of the expression `Greenland`.

2.8 Objects

§3.2

> 1 ... An *object* of a given type is a run-time entity that contains (has) a value of the type.

§3.3

> 13 An object is either a *constant* object or a *variable* object. The value of a constant object cannot be changed between its initialization and its finalization, whereas the value of a variable object can be changed....

All objects must be declared and explicitly given a type. An initial value is optional for a variable, but is required for a constant §3.3.1(5-6):

```
Current_Car:           Cars := Opel;
Wanted_Car:  constant Cars := Rolls_Royce;
```

> **Language Comparison**
>
> The term *object* is used in Ada as a single term to encompass both *constant* and *variable*. As such, it has no relation to the concept of "objects" in *object-oriented programming (OOP)*. Ada supports OOP through the constructs of tagged types and type extension (Chapter 6), but the term "objects" is not used in this context in the *ARM*.

2.9 Expressions

The syntax and semantics of expressions are similar to those of other programming languages §4.4. The operators are defined in §4.5 and include arithmetic operators (+, -, *, **, /, **rem**, **mod**, **abs**), logical operators (**and**, **or**, **xor**), relational operators (=, <, <=, >, >=), and the concatenation operator (&) that can be used with any one-dimensional array type, not just with strings (Section 4.5). Closely related to operators are the membership tests described in Section 2.10.2.

There is no required order for the evaluation of the operands of the operators §4.5(14). For the logical operators **and** and **or** this can be inconvenient, so the *short-circuit control forms* **and then** and **or else** §4.5.1(7) can be used when the order is important:

```
if Pointer /= null and then Pointer.Value < Key then ...

if Size = 0 or else Length / Size > Max then ...
```

Membership tests and the short-circuit control forms are not considered to be operators so they cannot be overloaded.

2.9.1 *Elaboration**

§3.1

> 11 The process by which a construct achieves its run-time effect is called *execution*. This process is also called *elaboration* for declarations and *evaluation* for expressions. …

While we don't normally think of a declaration as being executed, it is clear that it may have a run-time effect. For example, array bounds and initial values can be expressions, and the evaluation of the expressions can raise exceptions:

```
Default: Float := Get_Initial_Value_From_User;

A: array(1..Get_Bound_From_Property_File) of Float := (others => Default);
```

The exceptions are raised when the variable declarations are *elaborated*, and there are rules governing the handling of such exception occurrences (Section 10.3.2).

Declarations are elaborated in the order of their appearance (*linear elaboration*):

§3.11

> 7 The elaboration of a declarative_part consists of the elaboration of the declarative_items, if any, in the order in which they are given in the declarative_part.

This explains why the variable `Default` can be used in the declaration of the array `A` above.

There is one syntactical problem that must be resolved. Since it is possible to declare more than one object in a single declaration, the question arises whether the initial value is evaluated once for all objects, or once for each object:

```
F1, F2, F3: Float := Get_Initial_Value_From_User;
```

§3.3.1

> 7 Any declaration that includes a defining_identifier_list with more than one defining_identifier is equivalent to a series of declarations each containing one defining_identifier from the list, with the rest of the text of the declaration copied for each declaration in the series, in the same order as the list. …

In the example, the user would be prompted three times for initial values, because the declaration is equivalent to:

```
F1: Float := Get_Initial_Value_From_User;
F2: Float := Get_Initial_Value_From_User;
F3: Float := Get_Initial_Value_From_User;
```

2.10 Subtypes

Pascal was the first language whose design was based on programmer-defined types and compile-time type checking. However, the rules of (the initial version of) Pascal were too restrictive; consider a procedure to sort an array:

```
type Array_Type = array[1..100] of Real;
procedure Sort(var A: Array_Type);
```

The procedure is restricted to sorting arrays of type `Array_Type` with exactly the bounds `1..100` given for the index. Clearly, an algorithm for sorting arrays is exactly the same whatever the actual bounds, so some way is needed the separate "inflexible" information about the type (it is one-dimensional, its indices are integers and its components are real numbers) from "flexible" information like the bounds. In Ada this is achieved in a generalized way by distinguishing between a *type* and a *subtype*.

§3.2

> 8 A *subtype* of a given type is a combination of a type, a constraint on the values of the type, and certain attributes specific to the subtype. The given type is called the *type of the subtype*. Similarly, the associated constraint is called the *constraint of the subtype*. The set of values of a subtype consists of the values of its type that satisfy its constraint and any exclusion of the null value. Such values *belong* to the subtype.

A constraint that puts a restriction on the values of the type is checked at run-time. In the next chapter, we will see that the bounds of an array are considered to be a constraint, so a single procedure `Sort` can be called with arrays of different sizes. In this section, we will look at subtypes in the context of enumeration types.

First, some terminology: when declaring an object, we supply a subtype_indication.[1]

§3.3.1

> 2 object_declaration ::=
> defining_identifier_list : [**constant**] subtype_indication [:= expression];

[1] The syntax has been simplified.

§3.2.2

> 3 subtype_indication ::= subtype_mark [constraint]
> 4 subtype_mark ::= *subtype*_name

When creating an object, we can append a constraint to a subtype name and thus restrict the values that can be contained in the object. For an enumeration type, the appropriate constraint is a *range constraint* §3.5:

```
Car:        Cars;
French_Car: Cars range Peugeot..Citroen;
German_Car: Cars range BMW..Opel;
```

When executing an assignment statement, constraints are checked.

§5.2

> 11 The value of the expression is converted to the subtype of the target. The conversion might raise an exception (see 4.6).

```
French_Car := Car;           -- Might raise Constraint_Error
French_Car := German_Car;    -- Will raise Constraint_Error
```

Appending a constraint does not affect the *type* of an object. The second statement above is not a compile-time error, nor is `French_Car := BMW`, because the compiler checks only that the types are the same; in this case, the two variables and the value `BMW` are of type `Cars`. It is left to the executable code to check that the constraints are satisfied.

An Ada compiler is allowed to diagnose source code that necessarily raises an exception, and to emit machine code that simply raises the exception without doing the check. A friendly compiler will *warn* you of the inevitable exception, but a compilation error will not be reported.

2.10.1 Declaration of a named subtype

If you are planning to declare many objects with the same subtype indication, you can declare a *subtype* and then use its name, called a *subtype mark* §3.2.2(2,4). The following program shows an alternate way of implementing the function associating countries with cars.

country2

```
 1 function Car_to_Country(C: Cars) return Countries is
 2   subtype US_Car       is Cars range Ford..Dodge;
 3   subtype UK_Car       is Cars range Rover..Rolls_Royce;
 4   subtype French_Car   is Cars range Peugeot..Citroen;
 5   subtype German_Car   is Cars range BMW..Opel;
 6   subtype Japanese_Car is Cars range Honda..Toyota;
 7   subtype Korean_Car   is Cars range Daewoo..Hyundai;
 8 begin
 9     case C is
10       when US_Car       => return US;
11       when UK_Car       => return UK;
12       when French_Car   => return France;
13       when German_Car   => return Germany;
14       when Japanese_Car => return Japan;
15       when Korean_Car   => return Korea;
16     end case;
17 end Car_to_Country;
```

Lines ‡2–7 contain declarations of subtypes for each country by constraining the range of values of the type. A choice of a case statement can be a subtype mark; see §5.4(3), §3.8.1(4–5), §3.6.1(3).

A formal parameter must be a subtype mark and not a subtype indication §6.1(15):

```
function Korean_Car_to_Country(C: Korean_Cars)
  return Countries is ...          -- OK, subtype mark
function Korean_Car_to_Country(C: Cars range Daewoo..Hyundai)
  return Countries is ...          -- Error, subtype indication
```

2.10.2 *Membership tests*

A membership test can be used to check if an expression is in a subtype §4.5.2:

```
if C in French_Car then ...
```

If you want to check membership in a range, a subtype mark need not be given, and there is a convenient syntax for negations:

```
if C in Peugeot..Citroen then ...
if not (C in French_Car) then ...
if C not in French_Car   then ...       -- Nicer syntax
```

2.10.3 *First subtype**

We noted that paragraph §6.1(15) requires that formal parameters be *subtype* marks. What about *type* marks? That is, what is the name of a *type*? In order to simplify the presentation of the language, the phrase "type or subtype" is avoided, essentially by identifying a type with its *first subtype*.

§3.2.1

> 1 A type_declaration declares a type and its first subtype.
> 6 The defining_identifier of a type_declaration denotes the *first subtype* of the type. ...
> 7 A type defined by a type_declaration is a named type; such a type has one or more nameable subtypes. ... For a named type whose first subtype is T, this International Standard sometimes refers to the type of T as simply "the type T".

A named type has no name, although it has named subtypes. In normal usage, no confusion will result if we talk about the type `Cars`; in fact, such usage is sanctioned as noted above.

2.11 Lexical elements

We conclude this chapter with an overview of the lexical elements of an Ada program §2.

An Ada program is written in free-format:

§2.2

> 1 The text of a program consists of the texts of one or more compilations. The text of each compilation is a sequence of separate *lexical elements*. ... The meaning of a program depends only on the particular sequence of lexical elements that form its compilations, excluding comments.

Reserved words such as **`begin`** cannot be used for any other purpose §2.9. Certain identifiers such as `Integer` and `String` are predefined in package `Standard` §A.1; they can be redefined, but normally you wouldn't do that.

Comments are denoted by two minus signs and extend to the end of the line §2.7.

String §2.6 and character §2.5 literals, as well as comments, can use the character set defined by ISO/IEC 10646:2003 Universal Multiple-Octet Coded Character Set §2.1.

Identifiers are *case insensitive* §2.3(5.2) so that `Current_Value` and `current_VALUE` denote the same identifier. Similarly, reserved words §2.9(2) are case insensitive. The *ARM* recommends that reserved words be written in lower case and that identifiers be written in mixed case with underscores separating parts of identifiers.

Numeric literals §2.4 can use the underscore character _ ; this can prevent errors when large numbers appear in a program. Integer literals can have an exponent, and both integer and real literals can be written in any base from 2 to 16. Each of the following columns shows three equivalent numeric literals:

1000000	15	3.75
1_000_000	2#1111#	0.375E1
1E6	16#F#	2#11.11#

Language Comparison

There are no *block comments* in Ada similar to the `/* ... */` notation of languages descended from C.

Language Comparison

Ada is case insensitive, unlike languages descended from C. The convention is to use title case with underscores separating words. Thus, an identifier like `setCaretPositionInBuffer` in Java would be written `Set_Caret_Position_In_Buffer` in Ada.

Projects

1. Expand the car-to-country case study so that it takes into account that cars are assembled in countries other than the countries where the companies have their head offices. For example, although Nissan is a Japanese company, it assembles cars in the UK.
2. Using the facilities in `Ada.Text_IO`, write a program that prints out a formatted table of all the cars, their home countries, and the countries where they are manufactured.
3. Write a program that demonstrates that multiple objects in a single declaration are elaborated as if there were multiple declarations (Section 2.9.1).

Quizzes

Quiz 1:

```
subtype Letters is Character range 'A'..'Z';

Put(Letters'Val(42));
Put(Positive'Val(0));
```

Quiz 2:

```
X, Y, Z: Boolean;
B1: Boolean := X and Y and Z;
B2: Boolean := X and Y or Z;
```

Quiz 3:

```
Put( 16#a#e2 );
Put( 16#A#E2 );
Put( 16#E#EA );
```

Chapter 3
Subprograms

The concept of encapsulating local data and a sequence of statements in a subprogram is ubiquitous in all programming languages; nevertheless, there are differences between languages—especially in the area of parameter passing—that must be carefully studied. There is no separate case study for this chapter because subprograms appear in all programs in this book.

§6

> 1 A subprogram is a program unit or intrinsic operation whose execution is invoked by a subprogram call. There are two forms of subprogram: procedures and functions. A procedure call is a statement; a function call is an expression and returns a value. The definition of a subprogram can be given in two parts: a subprogram declaration defining its interface, and a subprogram_body defining its execution. Operators and enumeration literals are functions.

The subprogram declaration and body are written separately when the declaration is part of the declaration of a package specification, while the body is encapsulated in the package body (Section 6). Another use for separate declarations is to define mutually recursive subprograms. In the absence of a separate declaration, the subprogram_body by itself can also serve as the declaration of the subprogram §6.3(4).

The syntax of subprograms holds few surprises §6.1(2–16), §6.3(2). Here are several subprogram declarations from the input–output library:

```
function  Is_Open(File:  in  File_Type) return Boolean;
procedure Put(Item:      in  String);
procedure Put_Line(Item: in  String);
procedure Get(Item:      out String);
function  Get_Line return String;
procedure Get_Line(Item: out String; Last: out Natural);
```

The reserved words **in** and **out** (as well as their combination **in out**) are the parameter modes discussed in Section 3.1. The function Get_Line and the procedure Get_Line have the same name; this is an example of overloading (Section 3.2).

A subprogram *declaration* is a subprogram_specification terminated with a semicolon §6.1(2); a subprogram *body* has the reserved word **is** between the subprogram_specification and the local declarations and statements of the subprogram §6.3(2):

```
function Car_to_Country(C: Cars) return Countries is
  -- declarative part
begin
  -- handled sequence of statements
end Car_to_Country;
```

The name of the subprogram can be written after the **end** that terminates the body; although this is not required, it is good practice to do so, because it makes the program easier to read and because it can enable the compiler to recover gracefully from missing syntactical tokens. In the *ARM*, the "name" of a subprogram is called a designator, because it can also include the name of the parent library unit §6.1(8) (Section 15.3) or an operator like "+" (Section 3.4).

The return statement is familiar and was discussed briefly in Section 2.5. There is an extended return statement used primarily with limited types; see Section 6.10.

Language Comparison

The separator between formal parameters is a semicolon, not a comma as in Java.

3.1 Parameter modes

Most programming languages define parameter-passing *mechanisms* such as call-by-value and call-by-reference. In call-by-value, the value of the actual parameter is copied into the variable denoted by the formal parameter, whereas in call-by-reference, the formal parameter contains a pointer to the actual parameter. In Ada, each parameter has a *mode* associated with it that defines the permitted uses of the parameter and the direction of the information flow between the formal and actual parameters, rather than the mechanism used for passing parameters.

There are three modes:

in The formal parameter is considered to be a *constant* §3.3(17); the actual parameter must be an *expression* §6.4.1(4), which is used to initialize the constant when the subprogram is called. This is the default mode if no mode is specified. Functions may only have **in** parameters §6.1(18).

out The formal parameter is an uninitialized *variable* §6.4.1(15) and the actual parameter must also be a *variable*. When a subprogram is left, the value of variable in the formal parameter becomes the value of the variable in the actual parameter. An **out** parameter is used to pass data from the subprogram to the calling program.

in out This is like an **out** parameter, except that the initial value of the variable in the formal parameter is the value of the variable in the actual parameter.

As a matter of style, we explicitly write the reserved word **in** for parameters of mode **in** of procedure declarations, even though it is the default mode. This helps document the data flow to and from the procedure. Some people prefer to write **in** for the parameters of functions; since a function can only have **in** parameters, we prefer not to do so. Although functions can only have **in** parameters, these parameters can be access types (Section 5.4) or access parameters (Section 12.6), and the objects designated by these values can be modified.

3.1.1 *Implementation of parameter modes**

The three parameter modes, **in**, **out** and **in out**, are defined in terms of how parameters are used rather than how they are implemented. Parameter modes of Ada facilitate a clear specification the desired semantics of the program, regardless of the parameter passing mechanism selected by the compiler. For example, an array may be passed by reference, but if it is an **in** parameter, a reader of the program knows that the array will not be modified by the call. Nevertheless, the *ARM* does specify most aspects of the implementation, and you will occasionally need to be aware of these details.

There are two mechanisms for passing parameters:

§6.2

> 2 A parameter is passed either *by copy* or *by reference*. When a parameter is passed by copy, the formal parameter denotes a separate object from the actual parameter, and any information transfer between the two occurs only before and after executing the subprogram. When a parameter is passed by reference, the formal parameter denotes (a view of) the object denoted by the actual parameter; reads and updates of the formal parameter directly reference the actual parameter object.

An implementation is not always free to choose which method to use:

§6.2

> 3 A type is a *by-copy type* if it is an elementary type, ... A parameter of a by-copy type is passed by copy.
> 4 A type is a *by-reference type* if it is ...
> 10 A parameter of a by-reference type is passed by reference. ...
> 11 For parameters of other types, it is unspecified whether the parameter is passed by copy or by reference.

Thus *elementary types* (real and integer types, enumeration types and access types) are passed by copy. We have not yet studied types that are passed by reference, but these are types like task types that contain "invisible" data structures that must not be copied.

The language does not specify if arrays and records are passed by copy or by reference. This decision is left to the implementation. By aliasing two parameters, or a parameter and a global variable, it is not difficult to create a procedure whose effect depends on whether the implementation passes those parameters by copy or by reference. To ensure that programs are portable, never write a program whose effect depends on the implementation of parameter passing for arrays and records.

Language Comparison

In Java, parameters of primitive types (`int`, `double`, etc.) are passed by copy like **in** parameters of elementary types in Ada, but there is no equivalent to **out** and **in out** parameters for copying values back to the calling program. At most, a single value can be returned as a function result. For non-primitive types, the same rule applies, but what is being copied is an implicit reference to the object given as the actual parameter, so the object can be modified. This is similar to passing access types (and access parameters) in Ada, except that the fact that the parameter is a reference is explicitly written in Ada.

3.2 Overloading

§8.3

6 Two or more declarations are *overloaded* if they all have the same defining name and there is a place where they are all directly visible.

Consider:

```
with Ada.Text_IO;           use Ada.Text_IO;
with Ada.Integer_Text_IO;   use Ada.Integer_Text_IO;
procedure Main is
begin
  Put("The value is ");
  Put(42);
end Main;
```

A use_clause—the reserved word **use** followed by a list of package names—makes the visible declarations in the packages directly visible. Here there two subprograms with the name

Put: one subprogram from Ada.Text_IO performs output of strings, while the other from Ada.Integer_Text_IO performs output of integer values. The declarations are overloaded.

To give another example, almost every input–output subprogram has one declaration with an explicit parameter for the file and another that reads or writes to the *standard* files (usually connected by default to an interactive device):

```
procedure Put_Line(File: in File_Type; Item: in String);
procedure Put_Line(Item: in String);
```

When an overloaded name is used, the context determines which declaration is intended.

§8.6

> 30 For a complete context, if there is exactly one overall acceptable interpretation ... then that one overall acceptable interpretation is chosen. Otherwise, the complete context is *ambiguous*.
>
> 31 A complete context ... shall not be ambiguous.

The algorithm used to decide which subprogram to call is called *overload resolution* and is described in detail in clause §8.6; this clause is quite complex but the details are of interest primarily to compiler writers. When writing a program, it is always possible to disambiguate a call even if you are not sure why it is ambiguous; for example, the possible interpretations can be restricted to those in a specific package by explicitly writing the package name:

```
Ada.Integer_Text_IO.Put(...);
```

Qualification (Section 5.4.5) can be used to disambiguate overloaded calls.

*3.2.1 Overloading on the function result**

Two functions with the same name overload each other if they return different result types, even if the parameter profiles are identical. The following two functions overload each other:

```
function Func return Integer is
begin
  return 1;
end Func;

function Func return Boolean is
begin
  return True;
end Func;
```

and can be disambiguated from the context:

```
if Func then            -- Boolean type expected
I: Integer := Func;     -- Integer type expected
```

Recall (Section 2.7.4) that enumeration literals can also be overloaded; this is because they are considered to be parameterless functions §3.5.1(6).

> **Language Comparison**
>
> In Java, the result type of a function is not taken into account when determining if a function overloads another, so `int func()` cannot be declared in the same region as `float func()`.

3.3 Parameter associations and default expressions

Most programming languages use positional association for matching parameters; that is, the first actual parameter is matched with the first formal parameter and so on:

```
procedure Put_Line(F: in File_Type; Item: in String);

Put_Line(Error_File, "Execution error has occurred");
```

Commands of operating systems often use named association, where parameters are introduced by keywords:

```
java -classpath c:\project\lib\ioLib.jar Main
```

Named associations are particularly useful when there are a large number of parameters and the formal parameters have default values. The call will be easy to read if only a few parameters need be given and they can be written in an arbitrary order.

Ada supports both positional and named association for all subprogram calls, as well as in other contexts such as aggregates (Section 5.2).

§6.4

> 5 parameter_association ::=
> [*formal_parameter*_selector_name =>] explicit_actual_parameter
>
> 7 A parameter_association is *named* or *positional* according to whether or not the *formal_parameter*_selector_name is specified. Any positional associations shall precede any named associations. ...
>
> 9 A subprogram call shall contain at most one association for each formal parameter. Each formal parameter without an association shall have a default_expression ...

Default parameters are extensively used in libraries where you want to supply many options, but default values are sufficient for most purposes. For example, `Ada.Integer_Text_IO.Put` is declared §A.10.8(11) as:

```
procedure Put(
  Item:  in Num;
  Width: in Field       := Default_Width;
  Base:  in Number_Base := Default_Base);
```

Normally, you would print an integer with the default field width and the default base (decimal), but either or both can easily be changed:

```
Put(N, Base => 16);     -- Print in hexadecimal
```

In one style of writing Ada, parameter names are chosen so that they facilitate named association; for example:

```
procedure Put(Item: in Integer; Into:  Queue);

Put(Item => Test_Data(N), Into => Q);
```

The advantage of this style is improved readability; a disadvantage is that the source code can become too "wordy."

Default parameters can cause difficulties with overloading resolution. Given the following two procedure declarations:

```
procedure Proc(M: in Integer);
procedure Proc(N: in Integer; K: in Integer := 10);
```

the call `Proc(5)` is ambiguous, because it is impossible for the compiler to decide if the call is to the first procedure or to the second procedure with a default association.

3.4 Operators

While operators such as "+", "and" and "<=" are normally used with specific classes of types such as numeric or boolean types, they can be defined to apply to any type:

```
function "+"  (Left: Vector; Right: Vector) return Vector;
function "and"(Left: Vector; Right: Vector) return Vector;
```

A list of operators is given in §4.5(2–7). Only the types of the operands can be redefined, not the precedence or associativity of the operator (as in Prolog). There are no special restrictions on the bodies of functions that overload operators, but—just as you would choose good identifiers for subprogram names—so you should use operators intuitively: the function "+" above should add two vectors, not multiply them.

Examples of the definition of operators can be found in Sections 4.2.3, 7.2, and 6.8.2.

3.5 Block statement*

A block is like a parameterless procedure written within a sequence of statements.

§5.6

```
2 block_statement ::=
    [block_statement_identifier:]
      [declare
        declarative_part]
      begin
        handled_sequence_of_statements
      end [block_identifier];
```

Blocks are used to localize aspects of a computation. For example, if only a small portion of a large procedure makes use of some variable, it is preferable to encapsulate that portion of the code in a block, and to declare the variable local to that block. More importantly, blocks can have exception handlers so they are often used for computations that may fail and must be retried until they succeed. Both of these uses are shown in the following example:

country3

```
with Ada.Text_IO; use Ada.Text_IO;
procedure Country3 is
  type Cars is ...
  type Countries is ...
  function Car_to_Country(C: Cars) return Countries is ...
  Car: Cars;
begin
  loop                            -- Loop begins here
    Put("Enter the make of the car: ");
    declare                       -- Block begins here
      S: String := Get_Line;      -- Declaration local to the block
    begin
      Car := Cars'Value(S);
      Put_Line(...);
    exception
      when Constraint_Error => Put_Line(...);
      when End_Error        => exit;
    end;                          -- Block ends here
  end loop;                       -- Loop ends here
end Country3;
```

The declaration of the string S within the block allows it to be allocated a different amount of memory upon each execution of the block in the loop. The length of S will be the same as the length of the string returned by the function Get_Line. The computation of the make of the car is within the sequence of statements of the block, so that if Constraint_Error is raised, it is handled by the exception handler of the block. A computation that successfully completes the execution of the statements in the exception handler is considered to have successfully completed the block statement, so the loop can be executed again.

3.6 Implicit dereferencing*

In later chapters we discuss in depth the implicit dereferencing of pointers, called access values in Ada (Sections 5.4.3). In particular, this can be done for values of access-to-subprogram type (Section 12.2). We give here a few examples to round out the discussion of subprograms.

The following declaration declares an access-to-subprogram type whose designated type is a function with two parameters of type Float and with return type Boolean:

```
type Compare_Float_Access is
  access function(Left, Right: Float) return Boolean;
```

Suppose now that we define such a function:

```
function Almost_Equal(Left, Right: Float) return Boolean is
begin
  return abs (Left-Right) < 1.0e-10;
end Almost_Equal;
```

A reference to this function can be assigned to a variable of the access type:

```
F: Compare_Float_Access := Almost_Equal'Access;
```

The variable can now be used in a context where a function call with this profile is allowed:

```
if F(10.0, 10.1) then ...
```

The access value F is *implicitly deferenced* to obtain a function; since the function takes two parameters of type Float and returns a value of type Boolean, it is legal in that context.

If the subprogram has no parameters, an *explicit dereference* using the reserved word **all** must be given:

```
type No_Parameter_Access is access function return Boolean;
function Initial_Value return Boolean is ...
F: No_Parameter_Access := Initial_Value'Access;

if F.all then ...
```

See the case study in Section 12.2 for a larger example.

Projects

1. Write a procedure for some command with lots of default parameters. Write a main program to experiment with positional and named association.
2. Write a program that gives a different result depending on the method of passing arrays and records is by copy or by reference.
3. Write operators for floating point arithmetic in the range $0..2\pi$.

Quizzes

Quiz 1:

```
procedure Proc(N1: in Integer; N2: in Integer := N1) is ...
```

Quiz 2:

```
function "/="(Left, Right: Integer) return Boolean is
  B: Boolean := Left = Right - 1;
begin
  return B;
end "/=";

Put_Line(Boolean'Image(4 /= 3));
```

Quiz 3:

```
type My_Boolean is new Boolean;
function "="(Left, Right: Integer) return My_Boolean is
  B: Boolean := Left = Right + 1;
begin
  return My_Boolean(B);
end "=";
function "/="(Left, Right: Integer) return My_Boolean is
  B: Boolean := Left = Right - 1;
begin
  return My_Boolean(B);
end "/=";
M1: My_Boolean := 4 = 3;
M2: My_Boolean := 3 /= 4;

Put_Line(My_Boolean'Image(M1));
Put_Line(My_Boolean'Image(M2));
```

Chapter 4
Arrays

In this chapter and the next, we present the basic concepts of composite types (arrays and records) and access types (pointers). A comprehensive explanation of all the constructs relating to these types is deferred to Chapters 11 and 12, and numeric types are discussed in Chapter 13. The intervening chapters present constructs for structuring large programs and for extending types to support object-oriented programming. The chapter begins with a large case study, followed by a detailed presentation of the language constructs related to arrays.

4.1 Case study: fill and justify text

The case study is to implement a core algorithm used in word-processors:

> Read a text file and write it with the text filled (as many words as possible on a line) and justified (set flush with both margins). A word is a maximal sequence of non-space characters.

The following example shows four lines of input data, the two lines of text after filling, and the text after justification:

```
The␣␣␣quick␣␣brown
␣␣fox
jumped␣␣␣␣over
␣␣␣the␣␣lazy␣dog

The␣quick␣brown␣fox
jumped␣over␣the␣lazy␣dog

The␣␣␣quick␣␣␣brown␣␣␣fox
jumped␣over␣the␣lazy␣␣dog
```

The program begins with declarations of subtypes, constants and a file object `Input`. For simplicity, the file name, the output line length and the margin size are declared as constants:

justify

```
with Ada.Text_IO; use Ada.Text_IO;
procedure Justify is
  subtype Lines is String(1..80);
  subtype Index is Integer range 0..Lines'Last;

  Margin:     constant String(1..10) := (others => ' ');
  Width:      constant Index := Lines'Length - 2*Margin'Length;

  File_Name: constant String := "example.tex";
  Input:      File_Type;
```

Subtype `Lines` is a constrained array type that will be used to hold the characters of the output line. When writing algorithms on arrays, it frequently happens that index variables need an extra value, one less than the index of the first element or one more than the index of the last element. The subtype `Index` is defined for this purpose. The variable `Margin` is a fixed-length string initialized to blanks; from its length, we can statically compute the `Width` of the text itself.

`Get_Word` reads the next word from the input file. See the `Ada.Text_IO` library §A.10 for the specification of subprograms called. The parameter `Word` is used to return the word, and its length is returned in `Index`:

```
  procedure Get_Word(
      Word: out Lines; Length: out Index; EOF: out Boolean) is
    C: Character;
```

The first loop skips over ends of line and blanks:

```
  begin
    Length := 0;
    EOF := False;
    loop
      if End_Of_File(Input) then
        EOF := True;
        return;
      elsif End_Of_Line(Input) then
        Skip_Line(Input);
      else
        Get(Input, C);
        exit when C /= ' ';
      end if;
    end loop;
```

The second loop in the procedure reads the characters of the word until a blank is found:

```
28       loop
29         Length := Length + 1;
30         Word(Length) := C;
31         if Length > Width then
32           Skip_Line(Input);
33           Length := Width;
34           return;
35         end if;
36         exit when End_Of_Line(Input);
37         Get(Input, C);
38         exit when C = ' ';
39       end loop;
40     end Get_Word;
```

In the unlikely case that a single word is longer than a complete line, it is truncated ‡31–35.

The most difficult part of the program is the function `Insert_Spaces`, which performs justification. The function receives the output buffer `Line`, the `Length` of the valid data in the buffer and a count of the number of `Words` in the line; it returns a string containing the justified line:

```
41     function Insert_Spaces(
42           Line: Lines; Length: Index; Words: Index)
43         return Lines is
```

The new line is built in the variable `Buffer`. The indices `K1`, `K2` are used for copying characters and `L` holds the length of a word:

```
44       Buffer: Lines := (others => ' ');
45       K1, K2: Index := 1;
46       L:      Index;
```

The algorithm is implemented by creating an array `S` of the spaces to be inserted *after* each word. This array is initialized to the minimum one space, plus the number of extra spaces that can be evenly distributed among the words:

```
47       Spaces: Natural := Width - Length;
48       S:      array(1..Words) of Natural :=
49                 (others => (Spaces / (Words-1)) + 1);
```

The first loop in the subprogram distributes the remaining spaces by incrementing elements of the array `S`. The spaces are placed on the left or the right of alternate lines to avoid excessive space on one side of the page:

```
50  begin
51    for N in 1 .. Spaces mod (Words-1) loop
52      if Ada.Text_IO.Line mod 2 = 1 then
53        S(Words-N) := S(Words-N) + 1;
54      else
55        S(N) := S(N) + 1;
56      end if;
57    end loop;
58    S(Words) := 0;     --  Zero spaces after last word
```

We now construct the justified line in `Buffer`, using a loop over the number of words. A search for the end of a word is carried out ‡61–63 and then the word is moved to `Buffer` and concatenated (&) with the number of extra spaces ‡64:

```
59    for W in 1..Words loop
60      L := 1;
61      while Line(K1+L) /= ' ' loop
62        L := L + 1;
63      end loop;
64      Buffer(K2 .. K2+L + S(W)) := Line(K1 .. K1+L) & (1 .. S(W) => ' ');
65      K1 := K1 + L + 1;
66      K2 := K2 + L + S(W);
67    end loop;
68    return Buffer;
69  end Insert_Spaces;
```

The slice construct (Section 4.2.4) is used to assign consecutive elements of one array to matching elements of another without the use of an explicit loop.

Procedure `Put_Word` implements the fill operation by inserting a `Word` of length `Word_Length` into the output buffer `Line` at index `Position`. The number of `Words` in the buffer and the `Position` to insert are updated and returned:

```
70  procedure Put_Word(
71    Word:         in Lines;
72    Word_Length:  in Index;
73    Words:        in out Index;
74    Line:         in out Lines;
75    Position:     in out Index) is
```

If there is no room for the new word, `Insert_Spaces` is called to justify the line, which is then printed and the buffer reset:

```
  begin
    if Position - 1 + Word_Length > Width then
      if Words >= 2 then
        Line := Insert_Spaces(Line, Position-2, Words);
      end if;
      Put_Line(Margin & Line(1 .. Width));
      Line := (others => ' ');
      Position := 1;
      Words := 0;
    end if;
```

When there is room in the buffer, the new word can be placed there:

```
  Line(Position .. Position+Word_Length) := Word(1 .. Word_Length) & ' ';
  Position := Position + Word_Length + 1;
  Words := Words + 1;
end Put_Word;
```

The main loop of the program is written as a separate procedure `Main_Loop` so that its variables can be encapsulated in a local scope. The variables are just those needed to call `Get_Word` and `Put_Word` as described above:

```
procedure Main_Loop is
  Word:        Lines;
  Word_Length: Index;
  EOF:         Boolean;
  Buffer:      Lines := (others => ' ');
  Position:    Index := 1;
  Word_Count:  Index := 0;
```

The main loop is very simple and consists of sequential calls to `Get_Word` and `Put_Word`. When `EOF` is returned from `Get_Word`, the buffer is flushed before returning from the procedure:

```
begin
  loop
    Get_Word(Word, Word_Length, EOF);
    exit when EOF;
    Put_Word(Word, Word_Length, Word_Count, Buffer, Position);
  end loop;
  Put_Line(Margin & Buffer(1 .. Position-1));
end Main_Loop;
```

The main subprogram opens the input file, calls the main loop and then closes the input file:

```
begin
   Open(Input, In_File, File_Name);
   Main_Loop;
   Close(Input);
end Justify;
```

We now discuss the array constructs used in the program.

4.2 Array types

4.2.1 Unconstrained arrays

An array is defined by giving the number of dimensions, their types and bounds of the indices, and the subtype of the component. All these characteristics, except the bounds of the indices, are declared in an *unconstrained array definition*:

§3.6

3 unconstrained_array_definition ::=
  array(index_subtype_definition {, index_subtype_definition}) **of**
    component_definition
4 index_subtype_definition ::= subtype_mark **range** <>
7 component_definition ::= [**aliased**] subtype_indication | [**aliased**] access_definition

In all the examples in this chapter, the component_definition will be a subtype_indication (Section 2.10); aliased objects and access definitions are discussed in Chapter 12.

§3.6

15 An unconstrained_array_definition defines an array type with an unconstrained first subtype. Each index_subtype_definition defines the corresponding index subtype to be the subtype denoted by the subtype_mark. The compound delimiter <> (called a *box*) of an index_subtype_definition stands for an undefined range (different objects of the type need not have the same bounds).

The unconstrained array subtype `String` is predefined §A.1(37) as follows:

```
type String (Positive range <>) of Character;
```

Type `String` is a one-dimensional array type whose index type is `Integer` constrained to positive values by the subtype `Positive` §3.4.5(13); the component type is `Character`. The bounds of any particular string are *not* part of its type, as indicated by the syntax **range** <>.

The declaration of the predefined procedure `Put` for strings §A.10.1(48) is:

```
procedure Put(Item : in String);
```

Since the type of the parameter is an unconstrained array type, the procedure can be called with any string as its actual parameter, regardless of its bounds.

To create an object (variable or constant) of type `String`, an *index constraint* §3.6.1 must be given to specify the bounds. There are three ways to supply an index constraint:

- An explicit index constraint can be given as part of the subtype indication in an object declaration:

  ```
  S: String(1..80);
  ```

  The *range* §3.5(3) `1..80` explicitly gives the lower and upper bounds of the object.
- A constrained subtype can be declared and then used as the subtype of an object declaration:

  ```
  subtype Lines is String(1..80);
  Buffer: Lines := (others => ' ');
  ```

  The lower and upper bounds of the object `Buffer` are determined by the subtype `Lines`, so they need not be explicitly given in the initial value.
- If an initial value is given for an array, the compiler can determine the index constraint §3.3.1(9) from the number of components in the initial value:

  ```
  File_Name:          constant String := "example.tex";
  Current_File_Name:           String := File_Name;
  ```

  The bounds of both objects are `1..11`.

The expression in an object declaration need not be a static constant. An input file name can obtained at run-time by calling a function that returns an argument from the command line:

```
Input_Name:  constant String := Ada.Command_Line.Argument(1);
```

Then, an output file name can be obtained by modifying the input file name:

```
Output_Name: constant String := "output-" & Input_Name;
```

This example emphasizes that the order of the elaboration of declarations is *linear* §3.11(7). The elaboration of `Input_Name` results in the creation of the string object and the assignment of an initial value; this object can be used in computing the initial value of `Output_Name`.

4.2.2 *Operations on arrays*

Assignment and the equality operators are defined for array types: you can assign an array object to another one, or compare two objects for equality, provided that they are of the same type.

An *indexed component* §4.1.1 is obtained by appending a parenthesized expression (or sequence of expressions for multi-dimensional arrays) to the name of an array object.

For any array *object* `A` the following attributes are defined §3.6.2:

`A'First`	The lower bound of the index of `A`
`A'Last`	The upper bound of the index of `A`
`A'Range`	The range `A'First..A'Last`
`A'Length`	The number of components in `A`

Note that `A'First` and `A'Last` are indices, not components:

```
A( (A'First + A'Last) / 2 );       -- Middle element of the array
( A(A'First) + A(A'Last) ) / 2;    -- Average of first and last elements
```

There are versions of the attributes for multi-dimensional arrays §3.6.2(4,6,8,10).

The array attributes are also defined for constrained array *subtypes* like `Lines` (‡3 of the case study justify), but not, of course, for unconstrained subtypes like `String`.

It is impossible to over-emphasize the importance of using attributes. Once a constrained array subtype or an array object has been declared, subsequent declarations and statements should use the attributes, so that changes in the array bounds are automatically reflected in the source code. For example, given the following declarations ‡7,8,15:

```
subtype Lines is String(1..80);
subtype Index is Integer range 0..Lines'Last;
Width:  constant Index  := Lines'Length - 2*Margin'Length;
```

changing 80 to 120 does not require any additional change to the source code.

Alternatively, you can declare constants for bounds:

```
Line_Width:           constant Integer := 80;
subtype Line_Index is Integer range 1..Line_Width;
subtype Lines      is String(Line_Index);
```

In this case, `Line_Width` and `Lines'Last` are two names for the same value.

Language Comparison

Ada, unlike most other languages, uses rounded parentheses rather than square brackets to denote an indexed component. An array is properly seen as a mapping (that is to say, a *function*) from an index value to a component value, rather than simply as a contiguous piece of storage. Since the syntax of indexed components is the same as that of function calls, reading a component of an array `A(I)` can be replaced by a function call, and conversely, without otherwise modifying the program. See the case study country4 below.

> **Language Comparison**
>
> In Ada, an entire array can be assigned to a variable of the same array subtype provided that they are of the same length (see the explanation of *sliding* in Section 4.2.4). In C, the name of an array is a synonym for a pointer to the first element of the array, so `a1 = a2` assigns a pointer, not an element. Similarly, in Java, `a1 = a2` assigns the reference to an array object in a2 to the variable `a1`, and the elements are not copied.

4.2.3 *Aggregates*

Recall that a type consists of a set of values and a set of operations on those values. Strangely, most programming languages have no way of denoting a *value* of an array type! You are required to work explicitly in terms of components:

```
type    Vector (Integer range <>) of Float;
subtype Samples is Vector(0..255);

procedure Set_To_Zero(Sample: in out Samples) is
begin
  for S in Sample'Range loop
    Sample(S) := 0.0;
  end loop;
end Set_To_Zero;
```

In Ada, values can be dynamically constructed for all composite types.

§4.3

> 1 An *aggregate* combines component values into a composite value of an array type, record type, or record extension.

Array aggregates have a very rich syntax §4.3.3. The simplest form is to use **others** to give every component the same value:

```
Margin: constant String(1..10) := (others => ' ');
```

The procedure `Set_To_Zero`, above, can be replaced by a simple assignment of an aggregate:

```
Sample: Samples := (others => 0.0);
```

Named array aggregates §4.3.3(4–5,18) can be used to associate index values with components:

country4

```
Car_to_Country: constant array(Cars) of Countries :=
  (  Ford..Dodge                    => US,
     Rover..Rolls_Royce             => UK,
     Honda..Toyota                  => Japan,
     Peugeot | Renault | Citroen => France,
     BMW | Volkswagen | Opel       => Germany,
     Daewoo..Hyundai                => Korea);
```

The *function* `Car_to_Country` in the case study country1 has been replaced by an *array* without otherwise modifying the program!

When named aggregates are used, the order in which the component associations are written is not significant; **others** is allowed as a final component association to cover index values not explicitly named:

```
Step: Samples := (32..63 => 0.5, 0..31 => 1.0, others => 0.0);
```

Positional array aggregates §4.3.3(3) list the values of the components in increasing order of indices. An **others** choice is allowed as the final component in a positional aggregate §4.3.3(3):

```
Initial_Sample: Samples := (0.1, 0.2, 0.3, 0.4, others => 0.0);
```

Array aggregates cannot mix positional and named notation §4.3.3(2).

Aggregates are *expressions* §4.4(7) and can be used in any context where an expression is allowed, such as in an assignment statement, a return statement or as an actual parameter. Furthermore, the components of the aggregate are also expressions, and can be dynamically computed. In the following function, the sequence of statements is a single return statement whose expression is a positional array aggregate, all of whose components are dynamic expressions that depend on the formal parameters:

```
subtype Vector3 is Vector(1..3);

function "+"(Left, Right: Vector3) return Vector3 is
begin
  return ( Left(1)+Right(1), Left(2)+Right(2), Left(3)+Right(3) );
end "+";
```

When **others** is used, the indices of the aggregate are taken from the subtype indication:

```
V1: Vector(1..20) := (others => 1.0);      -- OK
V2: Vector3       := (others => 1.0);      -- OK
V3: Vector        := (others => 1.0);      -- Error
```

See Section 4.6 for more detail.

Aggregates for n-dimensional arrays are constructed from *subaggregates* of $n-1$-dimensional arrays §4.3.3(6):

```
type Matrix (Integer range <>, Integer range <>) of Float;

M: Matrix(1..3, 0..2) :=
  ((1.0, 2.0, 1.0), (2=>1.0, 1=>0.5, 0=>0.0), (others => 0.0));
```

Aggregates are always to be preferred over explicit loops because of the check that the number of components of the aggregate matches the context in which it is used.

Language Comparison

Java supports composite values when *initializing* an array, but not in other contexts like expressions in assignment statements and actual parameters.

4.2.4 *Slices and sliding*

Slices reduce the need for explicit loops when manipulating arrays.

§4.1.2

2 slice ::= prefix(discrete_range)

5 A slice denotes a one-dimensional array formed by the sequence of consecutive components of the array denoted by the prefix, corresponding to the range of values of the index given by the discrete_range.

Line ‡64 from the case study justify is repeated here:

```
Buffer(K2 .. K2 + L + S(W)) := Line(K1 .. K1 + L) & (1 .. S(W) => ' ');
```

A slice can be a variable, as shown on the left-hand side of the assignment statement, where a subsequence of the components of Buffer is assigned to. A slice can also be an expression, as shown by the slice of Line, which is concatenated to the aggregate of blanks. Without slices, the above statement would have to be written as two loops or as a loop with an inner if-statement. Note that the bounds of the range defining the slice are dynamically computed at run-time.

The following program shows a function that creates a palindrome from the string supplied as the actual parameter:

palin

```
with Ada.Text_IO; use Ada.Text_IO;
procedure Palin is
  function Palindrome(S: in String) return String is
    T: String(1..2*S'Length);
```

The parameter S is copied twice to the target string T. The first copy in the original order of the source string can be done using a slice, while the second copy in the reverse order requires an explicit loop:

```
   begin
      T(1..S'Length) := S;
      for N in S'Range loop
         T(T'Length - (N-S'First)) := S(N);
      end loop;
      return T;
   end Palindrome;
```

The main program calls the function:

```
   S1: String                          := "Hello world";
   S2: String(100..100+2*S1'Length-1) := Palindrome(S1);
   S3: String(1..2*S2'Length)          := Palindrome(S2);
begin
   Put_Line(S1);
   Put_Line(S2);
   Put_Line(S3);
end Palin;
```

The formal parameter of the function Palindrome is of type String, which is an *unconstrained* array subtype. The rules of parameter passing §6.4.1 specify that the actual parameter is *converted* to the formal parameter. For arrays, this means:

§4.6

> 38 If the target subtype is an unconstrained array subtype, then the bounds of the result are obtained by converting each bound of the value of the operand to the corresponding index type of the target type. For each nonnull index range, a check is made that the bounds of the range belong to the corresponding index subtype.

Therefore, within the function, the indices of the formal parameter are used: from 1 to S'Length.

Recall that a slice can be used either as a variable or as an expression. Consider the following program for swapping the halves of an even-length array:

swap

```
with Ada.Text_IO; use Ada.Text_IO;
procedure Swap is
   S:    String := "HelloWorld";
   Temp: String := S(1..S'Length/2);
```

The variable Temp is initialized with the first half of the string S.

The second half of S is assigned to the first half, and, finally, the string in Temp is assigned to the second half of S:

```
5 begin
6    S(1..S'Length/2) := S(S'Length/2+1..S'Length);
7    S(S'Length/2+1..S'Length) := Temp;
8    Put_Line(S);
9 end Swap;
```

In ‡6, one slice is the source expression of the assignment statement, while the other is the target variable. The subtype of the target is `String(1..5)`, which is not the same as the subtype `String(6..10)` of the source. Assignment is permitted if the *types* are the same, while the *subtypes* need only be *convertible*.

§5.2

> 3 The execution of an assignment_statement includes the evaluation of the expression and the *assignment* of the value of the expression into the *target*. ...
>
> 11 The value of the expression is converted to the subtype of the target. The conversion might raise an exception (see 4.6).

In the palindrome case study, the formal parameter was unconstrained and took its bounds from the expression in the actual parameter. For *constrained arrays*, the actual array will automatically be converted to the subtype of the formal array, and this will succeed if the number of components is the same in both the source and the target. The operation is called *sliding*, because we can think of sliding the indices of the source to match the indices of the target.

§4.6

> 37 If the target subtype is a constrained array subtype, then a check is made that the length of each dimension of the value of the operand equals the length of the corresponding dimension of the target subtype. The bounds of the result are those of the target subtype.

4.2.5 *Names and prefixes**

Much of the syntax of programming languages consists of giving *names* to entities; in a language as rich as Ada, the list of named entities is quite long:

§4.1

> 1 Names can denote declared entities, whether declared explicitly or implicitly (see 3.1). Names can also denote objects or subprograms designated by access values; the results of type_conversions or function_calls; subcomponents and slices of objects and values; protected subprograms, single entries, entry families, and entries in families of entries. Finally, names can denote attributes of any of the foregoing.

The *ARM* frequently uses the syntactic category prefix §4.1(4) as a general term that includes both names and *implicit deferences* as explained in Section 5.4.3.

4.3 Constrained array subtypes and objects*

Unconstrained arrays are flexible because you can declare a subprogram with formal parameters of the unconstrained subtype, and then call the subprogram with actual parameters that are of any subtype obtained by constraining the type. Very often, however, the nature of the problem is such that the bounds will be identical for all arrays of the type. In this case, you can reduce the number of names in the program and simplify the implementation of parameter passing by declaring a *constrained array subtype* §3.6(5,16):

```
type Spatial_Transform (1..3, 1..3) of Float;

type Telephone_Key is (
  One, Two, Three, Four, Five, Six, Seven, Eight, Nine, Star, Zero, Hash);
type Key_State (Telephone_Key) of Boolean;

Pressed:    Key_State := (others => False);
```

Of course, objects and formal parameters of type Key_State or Spatial_Transform are necessarily constrained and cannot have further constraints applied to them §3.6.1(5):

```
First_Row: Key_State(One..Three);          -- Error
```

Even if an array subtype is constrained, you should always use attributes so that expressions need not be modified if the bounds are changed.

The following statements show four ways of specifying the range of a loop that traverses the array Pressed; from top to bottom, they are progressively more robust to possible changes in the definition of Pressed:

```
for K in One .. Hash      loop Pressed(K) := ...; end loop;
for K in Telephone_Key    loop Pressed(K) := ...; end loop;
for K in Key_State'Range loop Pressed(K) := ...; end loop;
for K in Pressed'Range    loop Pressed(K) := ...; end loop;
```

A further shortcut is possible if you want to declare an *array object*, that is, a single array. This is one of four cases in Ada where an object can be declared without giving an explicit type name §3.3.1(2). (The other cases are tasks, protected objects, and objects of an anonymous access type.) Since the type is *anonymous* §3.2.1(7), the array cannot be used as an actual parameter because all formal parameters have named types; however, a type conversion can be used. Array objects are primarily used for objects that bear no relation to any other object, such as a global table of constants:

```
Sine_Table: constant array (0..90) of Float := (0.0, ..., 1.0);
```

4.4 Type conversion for arrays*

In Ada, type conversion is allowed only in carefully defined situations that will not break the type system §4.6. One permissible case is that arrays that "look" the same are *convertible* §4.6(9–12); that is, they can be converted to each other §4.6(36–39). Consider, for example, a program built from a subsystem that samples data from a sensor and then calls a subprogram from a generalized library:

```
type Samples is array(Integer range <>) of Float;
Data: Samples(0..1023) := Read_Sensor;

type Vector is array(Integer range <>) of Float;
procedure Transform(V: in out Vector);

Transform(Vector(Data));
```

The conversion succeeds because the types are both one-dimensional arrays with the same index type and the same component type.

4.5 Operations on one-dimensional arrays*

Most languages support binary operations that concatenate two strings or a string and a character. Since a string is nothing more than a one-dimensional array of characters (with a special syntax for literals), Ada generalizes this operation to all one-dimensional arrays:

§4.5.3

3 The concatenation operators & are predefined for every nonlimited, one-dimensional array type *T* with component type *C*. They have the following specifications:

4
```
function "&"(Left : T; Right : T) return T
function "&"(Left : T; Right : C) return T
function "&"(Left : C; Right : T) return T
function "&"(Left : C; Right : C) return T
```

Lexicographic order between two one-dimensional arrays whose component is of a *discrete* type may be tested using the relational operators §4.5.2(26). The restriction to discrete components is required because a predefined relational operator on the components is assumed.

The logical operators may be used on one-dimensional arrays whose component type is a boolean type §4.5.1. This is not intended for bitwise operations on numbers for which modular types §3.5.4 (Section 13.4) should be used.

4.6 The context of array aggregates*

Consider the following sequence of declarations:

```
S1: String(1..5) := (1..5 => '*');      -- OK
S2: String(1..5) := (2..6 => '*');      -- OK
S3: String       := (1..5 => '*');      -- OK
S4: String       := (2..6 => '*');      -- OK
S5: String       := (0..4 => '*');      -- Raises Constraint_Error
```

The index constraints in `S1` and `S2` match the discrete range defined by the named component of the aggregate (sliding if necessary). The index constraints of `S3` and `S4` can be determined from the ranges of the aggregate. `S5` is legal—it will compile correctly—but `Constraint_Error` will be raised because zero is not within the range of the index subtype `Positive` of `String` §4.3.3(28).

Consider now declarations with aggregates that have an **others** choice:

```
S6: String(1..5) := (others => '*');   -- OK
S7: String       := (others => '*');   -- Error
```

The meaning of **others** in the aggregate for `S6` can be determined from the index constraint of the variable. The declaration of `S7` is illegal because it is not possible to determine the bounds of the aggregate.

§4.3.3

> 10 An **others** choice is allowed for an array_aggregate only if an *applicable index constraint* applies to the array_aggregate. An applicable index constraint is a constraint provided by certain contexts where an array_aggregate is permitted that can be used to determine the bounds of the array value specified by the aggregate.
> ...

Paragraphs §4.3.3(11–15) go on to specify the contexts where an **others** choice is permitted, and §4.3.3(24–27) specifies the method for determining the bounds of an array aggregate.

The basic problem is this: for a named aggregate without **others** such as `(1..5 => '*')`, the index bounds of the aggregate are obvious. But for a positional aggregate `(10.0,6.2,1.4)`, or for any aggregate with **others**, the index bounds cannot be deduced from the aggregate itself. Instead, they are determined from the index constraint of the object to which the aggregate is assigned. It is not essential to learn the rules in detail; if the compiler refuses to accept an aggregate, you can easily specify the bounds in more detail, either in the index constraint (as for `S6`) or in the aggregate (as for `S3`). Specifying both, as in `S1`, should usually be avoided so that if the bounds change, you only have to change one or the other. If there is a problem, qualification (see Section 5.4.5) can sometimes help.

Projects

The following projects ask you to implement algorithms for image processing, where we assume that the data consists of square matrices of values in the range `0..255`:

1. Write a function to return the histogram of an image: an array whose index is `0..255` and whose components are the number of times that each value appears in the image.
2. Write a procedure to return a transformation of an image by replacing each value above the median of the histogram to `255` and each value below or equal to the median to `0`.
3. Write a procedure to smooth the image by replacing each non-edge element by the average of its four neighbors. Repeat for the eight neighbors, including the diagonal ones.

Quizzes

Quiz 1:

```
type Rec is
  record
    One, Two, Three, Four, Five: Integer;
  end record;
R: Rec := (1, 2, Four=>4, Five=>5, Three=>3);
type Vector is array(1..5) of Integer;
V: Vector := (1, 2, 3=>3, 4=>4, 5=>5);
```

Quiz 2:

```
type Name is array(Integer range <>, Integer range <>) of Character;
Names: constant Name(1..4, 1..6) :=
  ("Kirk  ", "Spock ", "McCoy ", "Scotty");

Put(Names(4,1));
```

Quiz 3:

```
X: String := "abcd";
procedure P(S: String) is
begin
  for I in S'Range loop
    Put_Line(S(I) & '*');
  end loop;
end P;
P(X(1..0));
```

Quiz 4:

```
type Vector is array(Integer range <>) of Integer;
V1: Vector(1..5) := (6..10 => 0);
V2: Vector(1..5) := (6 => 1, others => 0);
```

Quiz 5:

```
N: Integer;
procedure P(T: String) is
begin
  Put(T'Last);
end P;

Get(N);
P((1..N => 'X'));
P((1..10 => 'X', 11..N => 'Y'));
```

Chapter 5
Elementary Data Structures

This chapter is an introduction to the construction of data structures in Ada using arrays, records and access types. Here we discuss the language support for implementing data structures; their encapsulation into abstract data types will be presented in the next chapter.

The case study is the implementation of a *priority queue*, first using arrays and then using pointers. A priority queue is a data structure that stores items so that retrieval of the item of the highest priority can be done efficiently, although insertion of new items may be less efficient. In the case study, we assume that the items are simply integers and that higher-priority items have lower values. This is a common situation: customers in a store take numbered tickets and the lowest outstanding number is served first.

5.1 Case study: array priority queue

The elements of the priority queue are stored in an array whose lower bound is 0 (the lower bound of the subtype `Natural`) and whose upper bound is determined when the array is allocated. The queue itself is a record with three fields: (a) an array field `Data`, (b) `Size`, which contains the size of the array, and (c) `Free`, which holds an index to the first free position in the array:

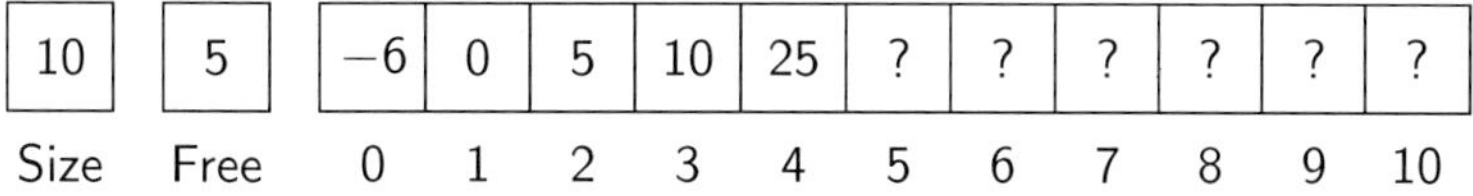

The elements of the queue are stored in increasing order as shown in the diagram. The element with the highest priority (the smallest value) is stored in the first position and can be retrieved in constant time. Inserting a new element is necessarily less efficient, because a search must be made for the correct place to insert the element and existing elements must be moved to free up the space.

The data structure is declared as a *record* with three components. The component `Size` is a *discriminant*, which is used to specify the index constraint of the component `Data`. Discriminants are discussed in detail in Section 11.4; for now, it is sufficient to know that a discriminant is a read-only component of a record whose value is supplied by a constraint when a record object is declared ‡41.

progpqa

```
with Ada.Text_IO; use Ada.Text_IO;
with Ada.Integer_Text_IO; use Ada.Integer_Text_IO;
procedure ProgPQA is
  type Vector is array(Natural range <>) of Integer;
  type Queue(Size: Positive) is
    record
      Data: Vector(0..Size);
      Free: Natural := 0;
    end record;

  Overflow, Underflow: exception;
```

The component `Free` has a *default expression*, which is the initial value given to a component whenever a record object is declared §3.8(6), §3.3.1(18). Two exceptions have been declared: `Underflow` will be raised when attempting to get an element from an empty queue and `Overflow` will be raised when attempting to put an element to a full queue.

The operations supported by the queue are: `Get` the lowest number, `Put` a new number in the queue, and check if the queue is `Empty`. The function `Empty` is trivial:

```
  function Empty(Q: in Queue) return Boolean is
  begin
    return Q.Free = 0;
  end Empty;
```

Since the `Queue` is modified by the `Put` operation, its parameter mode must be **`in out`**:

```
  procedure Put(I: in Integer; Q: in out Queue) is
```

The procedure `Put` first checks if there is room in the queue for more elements; if not, it executes the **`raise`** statement for the exception `Overflow`. The exception is *propagated* to the main procedure and handled, as discussed below.

```
    Index: Integer range Q.Data'Range := 0;
  begin
    if Q.Free = Q.Size then
      raise Overflow;
    end if;
```

The existing items in the queue are stored in `Q.Data(0..Q.Free-1)`. A *sentinel search* is performed to find the place to put the new element. `Data`, the array component of the queue, has `Size+1` elements, so there is always a place to store the sentinel. The new element `I` is placed in `Q.Data(Q.Free)` prior to beginning the search for an item greater than or equal to `I`. The sentinel ensures that even if `I` is greater than all existing items, the loop will terminate.

```
    Q.Data(Q.Free) := I;
    while Q.Data(Index) < I loop
      Index := Index+1;
    end loop;
```

When the correct place has been found, the subsequent elements are moved to the right to free up a position for the new element. Slices and sliding are used.

```
    if Index < Q.Free then
      Q.Data(Index+1..Q.Free) := Q.Data(Index..Q.Free-1);
      Q.Data(Index) := I;
    end if;
    Q.Free := Q.Free+1;
  end Put;
```

The element with the highest priority is always in the first position of the array. To remove it, simply copy the last element and move the other elements one place to the left:

```
  procedure Get(I: out Integer; Q: in out Queue) is
  begin
    if Q.Free = 0 then
      raise Underflow;
    end if;
    I := Q.Data(0);
    Q.Free := Q.Free-1;
    Q.Data(0..Q.Free-1) := Q.Data(1..Q.Free);
  end Get;
```

`Get` is implemented as a procedure rather than as a function, because a function is allowed to have only **in** parameters. An alternate solution is to use access parameters (Section 12.6).

To test the program, we declare a queue with ten elements and an array with test data ordered arbitrarily:

```
  Q: Queue(Size => 10);
  I: Integer;
  Test_Data: array(Positive range <>) of Integer :=
    (10, 5, 0, 25, 15, 30, 15, 20, -6, 40);
```

These ten elements are inserted into the queue and then removed:

```
45 begin
46   for N in Test_Data'Range loop
47     Put(Test_Data(N), Width => 5);
48     Put(Test_Data(N), Q);
49   end loop;
50   New_Line;
51   -- Put(17, Q);           -- Test overflow
52
53   while not Empty(Q) loop
54     Get(I, Q);
55     Put(I, Width => 5);
56   end loop;
57   New_Line;
58   Get(I,Q);              -- Test underflow
59 exception
60   when Underflow => Put_Line("Underflow from queue");
61   when Overflow  => Put_Line("Overflow  from queue");
62 end ProgPQA;
```

The program is correct if the elements are removed in increasing order.

The exception handlers at the end of the procedure print messages and terminate. To test for overflow, remove the comment from ‡51 and recompile.

5.2 Records

§3.8

> 1 A record object is a composite object consisting of named components. The value of a record object is a composite value consisting of the values of the components.

The difference between an array and a record is that a record can have components of different types, whereas all the components of an array are of the same type. Arrays enable dynamic access to an element through indexing, but a record component can be accessed only by selecting a component by name. Selection of a record component is done using the familiar dotted notation §4.1.3(2). The *selected component* is itself an object or value, and further indexing or selection operations can be applied as appropriate for the type of the component. In the case study, `Q` is of type `Queue`, `Q.Data` is of type `Vector`, and `Q.Data(Index)` is of type `Integer`.

Aggregates, both positional and named, can be used to create values of a record type §4.3.1. **others** is also permitted, but it is not as useful as it is for array aggregates, because record components are normally of different types. In an aggregate, components for the discriminants must also be given.

The following examples show some legal aggregates for values of the type Queue; note that either a subaggregate or an array value may be given for the component Data:

```
V1: Vector(0..10) := (0,-1,-2,-3,-4,-5,-6,-7,-8,-9,-10);

Q1: Queue := (10, (1,2,3,4,5,6,7,8,9,10,11), 0);
Q2: Queue := (10, (1..4 => 7, others => 1), 0);
Q3: Queue := (Data => V1, others => 10);
Q4: Queue := (Size => 10, Data => (others => 1), Free => 0);
Q5: Queue := (Free => V1'First, Data=> V1, Size => V1'Length-1);
```

An aggregate need not supply an explicit value for a component; instead, a box can be used to indicate that the value of this component of the aggregate should be the default value §4.3.1(4,19) that is specified in the declaration of the record type (or the default value for the subtype if there is no explicit default). Thus Q4 could also be written as:

```
Q4: Queue := (Size => 10, Data => (others => 1), Free => <>);
```

The box notation is important for limited types; see Section 6.6.1.

Ada 95

Ada 95 does not have the box notation for default values, so explicit expressions have to be given for all components in a record aggregate.

Language Comparison

An Ada record is the same as a record in Pascal or a **struct** in C. In Java there is no separate construct for creating compound data types from components. An Ada record would be equivalent to a Java class that contains declarations of fields but not of methods.

5.3 Case study: tree priority queue

Data structures like lists and trees are created using pointers to memory that is dynamically allocated. (Pointers to objects declared as variables or constants and to subprograms can also be created; see Section 12.2.) The second implementation of a priority queue uses an (unbalanced) binary tree, where the value of the data at a node is greater than all the values in its left subtree, and less than or equal to all the values in its right subtree:

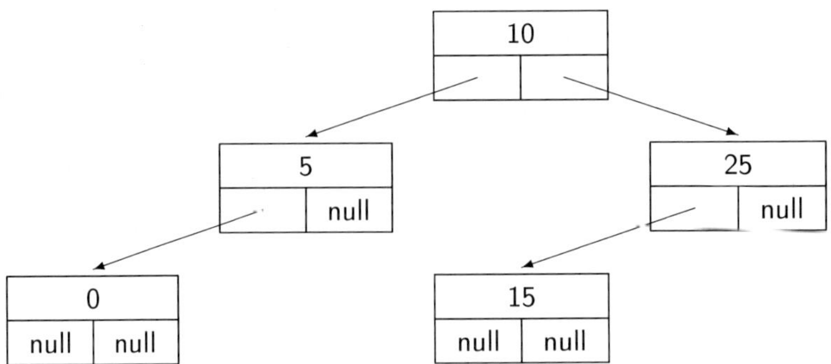

A `Node` is implemented as a record containing one component of type `Integer` and two components, `Left` and `Right`, of the access type `Link`:

progpqt

```
with Ada.Text_IO; use Ada.Text_IO;
with Ada.Integer_Text_IO; use Ada.Integer_Text_IO;
procedure ProgPQT is
  type Node;
  type Link is access Node;
  type Node is
    record
      Data: Integer;
      Left, Right: Link;
    end record;
```

The types are recursive since `Node` contains a component of type `Link`, which is itself defined as an access to `Node`. In general, a declaration is not visible until it is complete; however, it is possible to give an *incomplete type declaration* ‡4 §3.10.1 that just names the type and then to complete it later. Once the type `Node` has been declared, the access type `Link` can be declared and then used within the *completion* ‡6–10 §3.1.10(3) of `Node`. (See Section 6.7 for restrictions on where the completion must occur.)

The queue itself is declared as a separate type even though it is implemented as a record with just one component of type `Link`:

```
  type Queue is
    record
      Root: Link;
    end record;

  Overflow, Underflow: exception;
```

The exceptions `Overflow` and `Underflow` are declared as before to maintain the same interface to the data structure, although the check for `Overflow` will not implemented.

An empty tree is simply a tree with a null root:

```
17 function Empty(Q: in Queue) return Boolean is
18 begin
19   return Q.Root = null;
20 end Empty;
```

A recursive algorithm is used to put elements into the queue. Since the recursion is on the nodes, not on the queue, the recursive procedure ‡21–30 will overload the interface procedure ‡32–35 and be called from it ‡34 to start the recursion. To insert an element, the tree is traversed recursively, going left if the new element is less than the value stored in a node, and going right if it is greater than or equal to the value in the node. When a node is reached whose link is null, a new node is created for the item and linked into the tree:

```
21 procedure Put(I: in Integer; Node_Ptr: in out Link) is
22 begin
23   if Node_Ptr = null then
24     Node_Ptr := new Node'(I, null, null);
25   elsif I < Node_Ptr.Data then
26     Put(I, Node_Ptr.Left);
27   else
28     Put(I, Node_Ptr.Right);
29   end if;
30 end Put;
31
32 procedure Put(I: in Integer; Q: in out Queue) is
33 begin
34   Put(I, Q.Root);
35 end Put;
```

The procedure Get retrieves the smallest element in a tree by recursively traversing the leftmost path until a leaf is reached; the leaf is then removed and the pointer of its parent updated:

```
36 procedure Get(I: out Integer; Node_Ptr: in out Link) is
37 begin
38   if Node_Ptr.Left = null then
39     I := Node_Ptr.Data;
40     Node_Ptr := Node_Ptr.Right;
41   else
42     Get(I, Node_Ptr.Left);
43   end if;
44 end Get;
```

```
   procedure Get(I: out Integer; Q: in out Queue) is
   begin
     if Q.Root = null then
       raise Underflow;
     end if;
     Get(I, Q.Root);
   end Get;
```

The node becomes garbage and can be deallocated (see Section 5.4).

The main procedure is the same as the one for the array implementation except that the record for the queue has no discriminant:

```
   Q: Queue;
   I: Integer;
   Test_Data: array(Positive range <>) of Integer :=
     (10, 5, 0, 25, 15, 30, 15, 20, -6, 40);
begin
   -- As before
end ProgPQT;
```

Since overflow is not implemented, it needed not be tested for in the main program.

5.4 Access types

In this section, we discuss *named access types*; anonymous access types, access parameters and access discriminants are discussed in Chapter 12.

§3.10

> 1 A value of an access type (an access value) provides indirect access to the object or subprogram it *designates*.

The type of the object that is designated is called the *designated subtype* §3.10(10). In the following declarations, `Link` is an access type and `Node` is its designated subtype. The variables `L1` and `L2` are access objects that can hold values designating objects of type `Node` only:

```
type Link is access Node;
L1, L2: Link;
```

As with all (nonlimited) types, pointers can be assigned and compared for equality.

Language Comparison

The access types described here are similar to pointers in Pascal, while pointers in C are more flexible because they can point to any object. Chapter 12 discusses general and anonymous access types in Ada that expand the capabilities of access types without allowing the dangerous constructs of C. Java does not have explicit pointers. Instead, every non-primitive type is implemented with an implicit pointer called a reference.

5.4.1 *Null values*

§3.10

13 For each access type, there is a null access value designating no entity at all, which can be obtained by (implicitly) converting the literal **null** to the access type. The null value of an access type is the default initial value of the type. ...

Objects of an access type have a default initial value of null rather than whatever "garbage" happens to be in memory, so that an attempt to dereference the object will either return a valid value or raise an exception when the null value is dereferenced.

The type of **null** is *universal_access*. The concept of universal types is explained in Section 13.1.1, but in this context it simply means that the literal **null** can be implicitly converted to any access type §3.10(13). Variables of access types that have no explicit initial value have an implicit initial value of null §3.3.1(11).

5.4.2 *Allocators*

§4.8

1 The evaluation of an allocator creates an object and yields an access value that designates the object.

2 allocator ::=
new subtype_indication | **new** qualified_expression

4 An *initialized* allocator is an allocator with a qualified_expression. An *uninitialized* allocator is one with a subtype_indication. ...

The allocation of a designated object can be combined with setting its initial value by using an initialized allocator as shown in ‡24 of the case study:

```
Node_Ptr := new Node'(I, null, null);
```

This ensures that all components of the designated object are properly initialized.

> **Language Comparison**
>
> An initialized allocator is similar to a constructor in Java that assigns the values of its parameters to the instance variables. In Ada, you don't need to write code to achieve this effect.

5.4.3 *Dereference*

Dereferencing a value of an access type returns a value of the designated type.

§4.1

> 13 The evaluation of a dereference consists of the evaluation of the name and the determination of the object or subprogram that is designated by the value of the name. A check is made that the value of the name is not the null access value. Constraint_Error is raised if this check fails. The dereference denotes the object or subprogram designated by the value of the name.

Since most designated types are records, the dereference is usually followed immediately by the selection of a component; to simplify the notation, the dereference operation is implicit in Ada. Thus `Node_Ptr.Left` denotes an implicit dereference of the access object `Node_Ptr`, followed by a selection of the component `Left` from the designated record.

Occasionally, it is necessary to explicitly write the dereference operation, for example, to assign the entire contents of one designated object to another. Explicit deference is indicated by an artificial component named **all**. Consider the declarations and the statement:

```
Ptr1: Link := new Node'(1, null, null);
Ptr2: Link := new Node'(2, null, null);

Ptr1 := Ptr2;
```

After executing this statement, both variables point to the same designated object—the one whose component `Data` has the value 2—and the other object is now garbage. On the other hand, if we had written:

```
Ptr1.all := Ptr2.all;
```

the two variables still point to two designated objects, but both of them have 2 for the value of the component `Data`.

If the designated type is elementary, an explicit dereference must be used, because there are no components to select:

```
type Integer_Pointer is access Integer;
IP: Integer_Pointer := new Integer'(4);

Put(IP.all);
```

Language Comparison

Pascal and C both require explicit dereference: `Node_Ptr^.Left` and `(*Node_Ptr).Left`, respectively. C has an alternative syntax for dereferencing followed by selection: `Node_Ptr->Left`. In Java, of course, all dereferencing is implicit.

5.4.4 *Unchecked deallocation**

Explicit deallocation can lead to dangling pointers, which can cause serious run-time errors:

```
Ptr1: Link := new Node'(1, null, null);
Ptr2: Link := new Node'(2, null, null);

Ptr1 := Ptr2;
Deallocate(Ptr2);
   Lots of statements
Ptr1.Data := 3;              -- Where does the 3 go to?!
```

Designated objects that are no longer accessible become *garbage*. An Ada implementation is allowed to—but not required to—support *garbage collection* §13.11.3(6,8); in practice no implementation does so.

Explicit deallocation of storage allocated by an allocator is permitted, but the process is somewhat difficult. There is a generic procedure `Ada.Unchecked_Deallocation` §13.11.2(3):

```
generic
  type Object(<>) is limited private;
  type Name access Object;
procedure Ada.Unchecked_Deallocation(X: in out Name);
```

`Object` is the designated subtype and `Name` is the access subtype. The use of the word `Unchecked` is intended to inform the reader of your program that the type system is potentially broken. The procedure must be instantiated with the appropriate types; for our case study, the instantiation would be:

```
procedure Free is new Ada.Unchecked_Deallocation(Node, Link);
```

We could then call the procedure Free with a parameter of type Link such as Node_Ptr. The storage pointed to by Node_Ptr would be freed and Node_Ptr set to null §13.11.2(7).

An implementation is *advised* to actually reclaim storage when the subprogram is called, though it is not required to do so §13.11.2(17). In practice, all implementations reclaim storage.

5.4.5 *Qualification**

Syntactically, an initialized allocator is a qualified aggregate:

```
Node_Ptr := new Node'(I, null, null);
```

§4.7

> 1 A qualified_expression is used to state explicitly the type, and to verify the subtype, of an operand that is either an expression or an aggregate.
>
> 2 qualified_expression ::=
> subtype_mark'(expression) | subtype_mark'aggregate
>
> 4 The evaluation of a qualified_expression evaluates the operand (and if of a universal type, converts it to the type determined by the subtype_mark) and checks that its value belongs to the subtype denoted by the subtype_mark. The exception Constraint_Error is raised if this check fails.

Qualification is used to resolve ambiguity in contexts such as overloaded subprograms. For example, suppose that the following two overloaded procedures have been defined:

```
procedure Display(Item: Integer);
procedure Display(Item: Long_Integer);
```

Then the call Display(28) is ambiguous, because 28 is a literal convertible to both Integer type and Long_Integer type. Qualification can be used to specify which procedure to call:

```
Display(Long_Integer'(28));
```

A similar situation can occur with overloaded enumeration literals:

```
type RGB    is (Red, Green, Blue);
type Signal is (Red, Yellow, Green);

procedure Print(C: RGB);
procedure Print(C: Signal);

Print(RGB'(Green));
```

Be careful not to confuse qualification with type conversion, which performs a conversion of a value from one type to another. Qualification is used purely to identify the type or verify the subtype of an expression or aggregate. For example, if `N` is a variable of type `Integer`, then `Float(2*(N+1))` is a legal type conversion, because it is always legal to convert from one numeric type to another, but `Float'(2*(N+1))` is illegal because `2*(N+1)` is not of type `Float`.

Projects

1. Implement a priority queue as a sorted linked list.
2. Implement a priority queue as a binary heap.
3. Add deallocation of nodes to the tree implementation of the priority queue.
4. Rather than deallocate nodes, cache them in a linked list; when a new node is needed, it is taken from the cache, if possible, and only if the cache is empty is a new node allocated.

Quizzes

Quiz 1:

```
type Rec is
  record
    V: String;
  end record;
```

Quiz 2:

```
type T1 is null record;
X, Y: T1 := (null record);

Put(Boolean'Image( X = Y ));
```

Quiz 3:

```
S: String := "Hello world";

S(2..5) := S(1..4);
Put(S);
```

Quiz 4:

```
procedure Proc(Stop: Character) is
  Start:  constant Character := 'A';
  type R(C: Character) is
    record
      case C is
        when Start .. Character'Succ(Start) => I: Integer;
        when Stop   => B: Boolean;
        when others => F: Float;
      end case;
    end record;
begin
  null;
end Proc;
```

Chapter 6
Packages and Abstract Data Types

6.1 Modularization

Since a large software system must be decomposed into modules, the structures in a programming language for creating modules and for describing their interconnections determine the language's suitability for the development of complex systems. It is important to distinguish among three uses of modules:

- A module as a *unit of design and management*. Even before a single executable statement is written, the software will be designed as a system of modules. The project manager will then assign the responsibility for the development of each module to a software engineer or team of engineers.
- A module as a *unit of abstraction*. To abstract is to hide details of a resource so that it can be used without knowledge of its internal structure.
- A module as a *physical unit of source code*. Configuration management of a large software system requires a system for storing source code modules and for building versions of the software.

In Ada, the *package* is the unit of design. A package is divided into a *specification* and a *body*, which are separate physical units of source code. The specification and the body also serve to encapsulate abstractions by separating the interface from the implementation. Abstract data types in Ada are built by combining packages with *private types* that allow a client of an interface to use the type according to its public properties, while the details of its implementation remain hidden.

The development of very large programs is facilitated by *child units*, which provide a hierarchial structure for groups of related packages (Section 7.9). *Subunits* (Section 15.3) enable portions of a package to exist as independent physical units, while retaining their semantic status as part of the package; they have little use since child packages were introduced in Ada 95.

We will now develop a progression of six packages for priority queues that encapsulate the array and tree implementations given in the previous chapter. Each version will motivate and highlight a specific way of programming with packages.

Language Comparison

Most object-oriented languages like Java and C++ have a construct called the **class** that is used to declare a single type. The class also serves as the only unit of design (Java also has interfaces). In Ada, the package construct provides a rich way of combining related types, because the declaration of types (including tagged types used for type extension (Chapter 7)) is independent of the software design expressed in terms of packages. Zero, one or more than one type can be declared in a single package.

Language Comparison

The class is also the only unit of source code in most OO languages. (C++ has include files, but these simply insert text.) The source code separation of interface (the package specification) from implementation (the package body) contributes to the readability, maintainability and reliability of software written in Ada.

Language Comparison

Java uses the term **package** for a construct that facilitates controlling the namespace of large programs; it is not at all related to the package construct in Ada. (The **namespace** construct of C++ is similar.) By using **import** statements, it is possible to invoke a method like `setTitle` directly. But no control over encapsulation is provided, because you can always access any entity by writing a full name like `javax.swing.border.TitledBorder.setTitle`. Java **import** statements are similar to Ada's **use** clauses.

6.2 Case study: priority queue package—version 1

We start with a package that encapsulates a priority queue implemented with an array. The package specification §7.1 contains the declarations of three subprograms and two exceptions:

pqav1

```
package Priority_Queue is
  function  Empty return Boolean;
  procedure Put(I: in Integer);
  procedure Get(I: out Integer);

  Overflow, Underflow: exception;
end Priority_Queue;
```

The declarations in a specification specify the interface to the package; that is, the entities declared in the specification are *exported* from the package. The declarations must be basic_declarative_items §3.11(4); in particular, the specification cannot contain *bodies* of subprograms, packages, etc. §3.1(3).

The package body *must* contain the bodies of all the subprograms (like `Empty`) that are declared in the specification; the body may optionally contain other declarations. The body can be considered to be the implementation of resources promised in the specification, together with arbitrary encapsulated resources that are needed in the implementation.

§7.1

> 10 If a declaration occurs immediately within the specification of a package, and the declaration has a corresponding completion that is a body, then that body has to occur immediately within the body of the package. [See also §3.11.1]

Here is the body of the package `Priority_Queue`:

```
package body Priority_Queue is
  type Vector is array(Natural range <>) of Integer;
  type Queue(Size: Positive) is
    record
      Data: Vector(0..Size);
      Free: Natural := 0;
    end record;
  Q: Queue(Size => 100);

  function  Empty return Boolean is ... end Empty;
  procedure Put(I: in Integer)   is ... end Put;
  procedure Get(I: out Integer)  is ... end Get;
end Priority_Queue;
```

The package body starts with the declarations for the queue type and the declaration of a variable that holds the queue. This is followed by the bodies of the subprograms declared in the specification. The source code for the bodies is exactly the same as that shown in Section 5.1.

The *context clause* of the client unit (the main subprogram or another package) must contain a with_clause for the package §10.1.2:

```
with Priority_Queue;
with Ada.Text_IO;         use Ada.Text_IO;
with Ada.Integer_Text_IO; use Ada.Integer_Text_IO;
procedure PQAV1 is
```

The rest of the main program is unchanged, except that within the client an entity declared in the package *specification* is accessed by giving its *expanded name*—the package name followed by the entity name, as shown in ‡31, 35, 36, 40, 42, 43:

```
   I: Integer;
   Test_Data: array(Positive range <>) of Integer :=
     (10, 5, 0, 25, 15, 30, 15, 20, -6, 40);
begin
   for N in Test_Data'Range loop
     Put(Test_Data(N), Width => 5);
     Priority_Queue.Put(Test_Data(N));
   end loop;
   New_Line;

   while not Priority_Queue.Empty loop
     Priority_Queue.Get(I);
     Put(I, Width => 5);
   end loop;
   New_Line;
   Priority_Queue.Get(I);    --  Test underflow
exception
   when Priority_Queue.Underflow => Put_Line("Underflow from queue");
   when Priority_Queue.Overflow  => Put_Line("Overflow  from queue");
end PQAV1;
```

The client is said to *import* these entities from the package.

The client does not have access to declarations within the package body. A clever programmer might wish to quickly empty the queue by writing:

```
Q.Free := 0;
```

but this will be reported as a compilation error, because neither the variable `Q` nor the completion of the type `Queue` are visible outside of the body where they are declared.

6.2.1 Compilation

The Ada standard specifies that a compiler shall include an *environment*, whose structure is implementation-defined §10.1.4(3):

§10.1.4

> 1 Each compilation unit submitted to the compiler is compiled in the context of an *environment* declarative_part (or simply, an *environment*), ...
>
> 2 The declarative_items of the environment are library_items ...

library_items are the specifications and bodies of packages and subprograms that are declared directly within the environment, and that are not nested within another unit.

The environment is used, among other things, to ensure that both the package body and the clients are always consistent with respect to the same specification. The rules for consistency can be understood in terms of the order of compilation, although this is not necessarily the order in which the files are read by the compiler and is not related to how the machine code is generated. These implementation-dependent issues are discussed in more detail in Section 15.2.

A package specification must be compiled before the compilation of its body and before the compilation of any client. However, there is no prescribed order of compilation between the body and a client. This is shown in the following diagram:

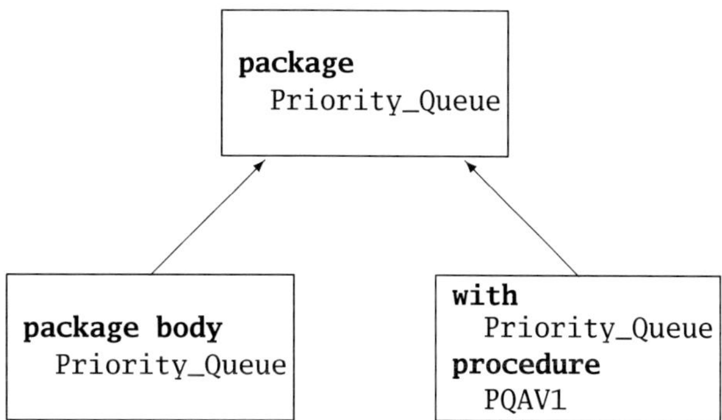

The arrows indicate *semantic dependences*:

§10.1.1

> 26 ... A library_unit_body depends semantically upon the corresponding library_unit_declaration, if any....
> A compilation unit depends semantically upon each library_item mentioned in a with_clause of the compilation unit. ...

§10.1.4

> 5 When a compilation unit is compiled, all compilation units upon which it depends semantically shall already exist in the environment; the set of these compilation units shall be *consistent* in the sense that the new compilation unit shall not semantically depend (directly or indirectly) on two different versions of the same compilation unit, nor on an earlier version of itself.

Clients can be written even before the package body has been written. This is extremely useful in the management of software development by project teams, because you can use packages as units of work:

- The designer writes and compiles the package specification.

- An engineer is assigned to develop the body.
- Engineers who program clients refer to the package specification; they may create simplified bodies to test their modules before the final package body is completed.

The fact that all programming is done relative to consistent specifications means that integration of all the packages in a system is immediate. There will be few, if any, last-minute surprises caused by misunderstandings or inconsistencies in the declarations.

The encapsulation of the implementation in the package body means that the package specification presents to the user an abstract concept of a priority queue, making available only its logical characteristics. As long as the semantics of the priority queue are maintained, the implementation in the body can be repeatedly modified with no effect on the clients. In fact, they need not even be recompiled!

We can demonstrate this by replacing the package body with one that implements the priority queue using a binary tree (the subprogram bodies are the same as in Section 5.3):

pqtv1

```
1 package body Priority_Queue is
2   type Node;
3   type Link is access Node;
4   type Queue(Size: Positive) is   --  Size is ignored!
5     record
6       Root: Link;
7     end record;
8   type Node is
9     record
10      Data: Integer;
11      Left, Right: Link;
12    end record;
13  Q: Queue(Size => 100);
14
15  function  Empty return Boolean is ... end Empty;
16  procedure Put(I: in Integer;  Node_Ptr: in out Link) is ... end Put;
17  procedure Put(I: in Integer)   is ... end Put;
18  procedure Get(I: out Integer; Node_Ptr: in out Link) is ... end Get;
19  procedure Get(I: out Integer)  is ... end Get;
20 end Priority_Queue;
```

(The discriminant Size is obviously not needed in the tree implementation, but it is retained for compatibility with subsequent versions of the package that we will develop.)

The package body contains the encapsulated recursive subprograms Put ‡16 and Get ‡18 that are needed to implement the exported subprograms Put ‡17 and Get ‡19 that were promised in the specification. Check that you can compile this package body in place of the previous one and proceed immediately to linking and running the program.

Is this package an adequate implementation of a priority queue in terms of abstraction and usability? Analyze this program yourself before continuing!

6.3 Case study: priority queue package—version 2

The programs in the previous section are adequate implementations of an *abstract data object*. The package declares a single queue, so that if we need several queues, we would have to write a separate package for each one. *Abstract data types* make it possible to declare multiple objects of the type, as well as to declare parameters and components of the type.

Before proceeding, we note that abstract data objects are more common than one would imagine from the emphasis on data types in OOP. Consider, for example, a air-traffic control system: while we would need a *type* `Airplanes` so that multiple airplane objects could be tracked, we might only need one data *object* to store the database of all the airplane objects. This database can be encapsulated within a package body as we did for the queue, and only operations such as `Get_Track`, `Update_Track` and `Delete_Track` would be exported.

Let us modify the package so that the declaration of the type `Queue` is placed in the package specification where it is visible to client packages. For the array implementation this is:

pqav2

```
package Priority_Queue is
  type Vector is array(Natural range <>) of Integer;
  type Queue(Size: Positive) is
    record
      Data: Vector(0..Size);
      Free: Natural := 0;
    end record;

  function  Empty(Q:  Queue) return Boolean;
  procedure Put(I: in Integer;  Q: in out Queue);
  procedure Get(I: out Integer; Q: in out Queue);

  Overflow, Underflow: exception;
end Priority_Queue;
```

We discuss below the changes in the specifications of the subprograms.

The package body contains the bodies of these subprograms:

```
package body Priority_Queue is
  function  Empty(Q: Queue) return Boolean       is ... end Empty;
  procedure Put(I: in  Integer; Q: in out Queue) is ... end Put;
  procedure Get(I: out Integer; Q: in out Queue) is ... end Get;
end Priority_Queue;
```

The package in the previous section that implemented a single data *object* contained the declaration of a variable Q of type Queue. In other words, the package has a *state* which includes the data maintained within the package, and this state can be modified by calls to the subprograms of the package. Since the state is associated with the package itself, the exported subprograms do not need a parameter for the queue:

```
function Empty return Boolean;
procedure Put(I: in Integer);
procedure Get(I: out Integer);
```

A package declaring a type usually does not have a state, because the subprograms of the package are used to process many different objects that are instances of the type. Therefore, the subprograms must include a parameter specifying which object the subprogram is to process:

```
function  Empty(Q: Queue) return Boolean;
procedure Put(I: in Integer;  Q: in out Queue);
procedure Get(I: out Integer; Q: in out Queue);
```

In the main program, a variable Q of type Queue is declared, and the imported operations are called with this object as an actual parameter ‡37, 41, 42, 46:

```
26 with Priority_Queue;
27 with Ada.Text_IO; use Ada.Text_IO;
28 with Ada.Integer_Text_IO; use Ada.Integer_Text_IO;
29 procedure PQAV2 is
30   Q: Priority_Queue.Queue(10);
31   I: Integer;
32   Test_Data: array(Positive range <>) of Integer :=
33     (10, 5, 0, 25, 15, 30, 15, 20, -6, 40);
34 begin
35   for N in Test_Data'Range loop
36     Put(Test_Data(N), Width => 5);
37     Priority_Queue.Put(Test_Data(N), Q);
38   end loop;
39   New_Line;
40
41   while not Priority_Queue.Empty(Q) loop
42     Priority_Queue.Get(I, Q);
43     Put(I, Width => 5);
44   end loop;
45   New_Line;
46   Priority_Queue.Get(I,Q);  --  Test underflow
47 exception
48   when Priority_Queue.Underflow => Put_Line("Underflow from queue");
49   when Priority_Queue.Overflow  => Put_Line("Overflow  from queue");
50 end PQAV2;
```

> **Language Comparison**
>
> In Java, a field in a class that is declared **static** is shared by all objects that are instances of the class. No special construct is needed in Ada to implement a variable shared by all instances of a type; simply declare the variable in the package body.

Analyze this program yourself before continuing!

6.4 Case study: priority queue package—version 3

The package declared a data *type*, but the type is not an *abstract* type because it is declared in the package specification, and, therefore, any modification of the specification potentially invalidates all the clients. If the implementation of the type in the package specification is changed from an array to a tree, all uses of resources of the package by clients must be checked to see if they need to be modified. Furthermore, since the implementation of the type is not hidden, unintended manipulation of objects of the type (such as `Q.Free := 0`) can be done. This creates unnecessary coupling between the data type and its clients.

We have a dilemma: if the type is declared in the package specification, it is not abstract, but if it is declared in the package body, clients cannot declare objects. Let us try the solution used for subprograms: declare the "specification" of the type in the specification of the package:

pqav3

```
package Priority_Queue is
  type Queue(Size: Positive);        -- Type "specification"

  function  Empty(Q:  in Queue) return Boolean;
  procedure Put(I: in Integer;  Q: in out Queue);
  procedure Get(I: out Integer; Q: in out Queue);

  Overflow, Underflow: exception;
end Priority_Queue;
```

and place the "implementation" of the type in the body of the package:

```
package body Priority_Queue is
  type Vector is array(Natural range <>) of Integer;
  type Queue(Size: Positive) is       -- Type "implementation"
    record
      Data: Vector(0..Size);
      Free: Natural := 0;
    end record;

  function  Empty(Q:  in Queue) return Boolean   is ... end Empty;
  procedure Put(I: in Integer;  Q: in out Queue) is ... end Put;
  procedure Get(I: out Integer; Q: in out Queue) is ... end Get;
end Priority_Queue;
```

Clearly, this will achieve the abstraction we desire, because we can replace the package body with a different implementation of the type without recompiling the clients.

Analyze this program yourself before continuing!

6.5 Case study: priority queue package—version 4

The package in the previous section is just what we need: the clients see the specification of the type, while its implementation is hidden in the package body. However, if the construct were legal, it would be impossible to write a compiler to implement it, if the compiler had access only to the package specification and not to the body (which may not even be written yet). Consider what must be done when compiling the following declaration:

```
Q1, Q2: Priority_Queue(100);
```

The compiler must allocate memory for the variables `Q1` and `Q2`. From the specification alone, the compiler cannot know how much memory to allocate for the variables. If the type is implemented as an array, memory must be allocated for `Size+3` integer values, while if the implementation is changed to the tree implementation, memory for one integer value and one address is sufficient. Furthermore, compiling an assignment statement such as `Q1 := Q2` requires that the size of these variables be known, because assignment is usually implemented by copying a fixed number of bytes from one location to another.

To summarize, the compiler needs information about the *representation* of a type that is not needed by the software engineer, who only needs to know the type name (and its discriminants, if any (Section 11.4)) in order to declare variables and to pass them as parameters to subprograms. Since the high level of abstraction in this version leads to a program that cannot be compiled without seriously compromising the separation between interface and implementation, we must weaken the abstraction.

> **Language Comparison**
>
> In a language like Java, this problem does not arise because *reference semantics* is used. All variables of non-primitive types are allocated the same amount of memory (whatever is needed to store a reference), and a parameter of a non-primitive type is always passed by copying the reference. In Ada, *value semantics* is used, so issues of memory allocation and parameter passing must be confronted. The equivalent of reference semantics can be obtained by declaring a type to be an access type, in which case, the representation of the designated type can be deferred to the package body as shown in Section 6.6.1.

6.5.1 *Private types*

A package specification is divided into two parts: a *visible part* and a *private part*. Declarations in the visible part of a specification are visible to clients, while those in the private part are not:

§7.1

> 6 The first list of declarative_items of a basic_package_specification of a package_specification of a package ... is called the *visible part* of the package. The optional list of basic_declarative_items after the reserved word **private** (of any package_specification) is called the *private part* of the package. ...
>
> 7 An entity declared in the private part of a package is visible only within the declarative region of the package itself .... In contrast, expanded names denoting entities declared in the visible part can be used even outside the package; furthermore, direct visibility of such entities can be achieved by means of use_clauses (see 4.1.3 and 8.4).

Within the visible part, you can declare a *private type*. The *completion* of a private type by a *full type declaration* must be given in the private part of the same package. The predefined operations on a private type are assignment, equality and inequality; other operations must be explicitly declared. Of course within the package body, all the operations permitted by the full type declaration are available.

The following specification shows the declaration of Queue as a private type in the visible part ‡2, and its completion as a record in the private part ‡11–15:

pqav4

```
package Priority_Queue is
  type Queue(Size: Positive) is private;

  function  Empty(Q:  in Queue) return Boolean;
  procedure Put(I: in Integer;  Q: in out Queue);
  procedure Get(I: out Integer; Q: in out Queue);

  Overflow, Underflow: exception;
private
  type Vector is array(Natural range <>) of Integer;
  type Queue(Size: Positive) is
    record
      Data: Vector(0..Size);
      Free: Natural := 0;
    end record;
end Priority_Queue;
```

The visibility of private types is defined in terms of *views*:

§7.3

> 4 A private_type_declaration ... declares a *partial view* of the type; such a declaration is allowed only as a declarative_item of the visible part of a package, and it requires a completion, which shall be a full_type_declaration that occurs as a declarative_item of the private part of the package. The view of the type declared by the full_type_declaration is called the *full view*. ...
>
> 15 A declaration of a partial view and the corresponding full_type_declaration define two views of a single type. The declaration of a partial view together with the visible part define the operations that are available to outside program units; the declaration of the full view together with the private part define other operations whose direct use is possible only within the declarative region of the package itself. ...

If the programmer of a client writes `Q.Free := 0`, a compilation error would result, because the source code of the client can only access the partial view in the visible part of the package, and from the partial view it is not known that `Queue` is a record, much less that it contains a component `Free`.

The designer of an Ada package can place a declaration in three places. The implications of each choice are as follows (where by "modification" we mean a change of implementation that is semantically equivalent to the original one):

Visible part of specification The declaration is accessible to clients. A modification potentially affects all clients, which must be recompiled and checked.

Private part of specification The declaration is not accessible to any client, but the object code of a client depends on the declaration. A modification never affects the correctness of a client;[1] however, all clients must be recompiled.

Body The declaration cannot be accessed outside the body, so the clients do not depend on the declaration. If the body is modified, clients need only be relinked, not recompiled.

To demonstrate that a modification of a full type declaration need not affect a client, we change the package specification to implement the queue using a binary tree. Since the visible part is not modified, the client need only be recompiled, not modified or checked. Since the partial view of the type must remain unchanged, the private type of the tree implementation retains the discriminant `Size` although it is not used:

pqtv4

```
package Priority_Queue is
  type Queue(Size: Positive) is private;

  function  Empty(Q:  in Queue) return Boolean;
  procedure Put(I: in Integer; Q: in out Queue);
  procedure Get(I: out Integer; Q: in out Queue);

  Overflow, Underflow: exception;
private
  type Node;
  type Link is access Node;
  type Node is
    record
      Data: Integer;
      Left, Right: Link;
    end record;
  type Queue(Size: Positive) is   --  Size ignored!
    record
      Root: Link;
    end record;
end Priority_Queue;
```

[1] Well, hardly ever! See Section 6.6.

Language Comparison

Private types are similar to Java classes whose fields are declared with the modifier **`private`**. (We ignore here the complication of visibility within Java packages.) The name of the class is visible, just as the name of an Ada private type is visible. Methods declared with the modifier **`public`** correspond to subprograms declared in the package specification, while methods declared with the modifier **`private`** correspond to subprograms declared in the package body. However, in Ada, only the declarations of the subprograms appear in the package specification, whereas Java puts *all* the source code of a class into a single file. Changing the implementation of a subprogram body that appears in a package body in Ada does not require recompilation of clients, while changing the implementation of a method in Java does.

6.6 Case study: priority queue package—version 5

Suppose that we declare two priority queues and assign one to the other:

```
Q1, Q2: Priority_Queue.Queue(10);

Q1 := Q2;
```

The assignment operation copies the block of memory allocated to `Q2` to the block of memory (of the same size) allocated to `Q1`. If the array implementation is used, the assignment correctly makes a copy of the queue:

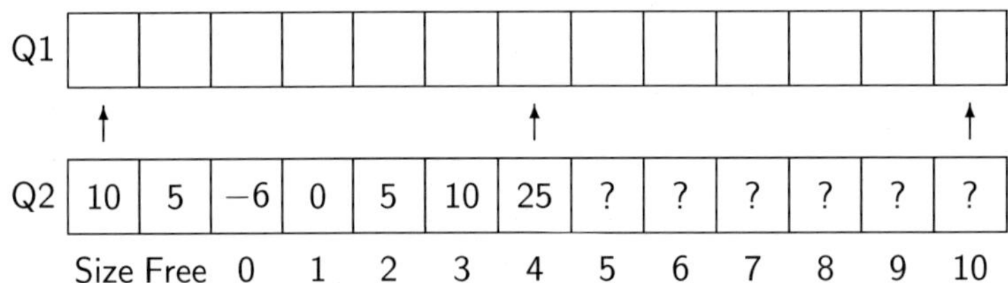

However, if the tree implementation is used, the assignment merely copies the access values so the two variables point to the same queue:

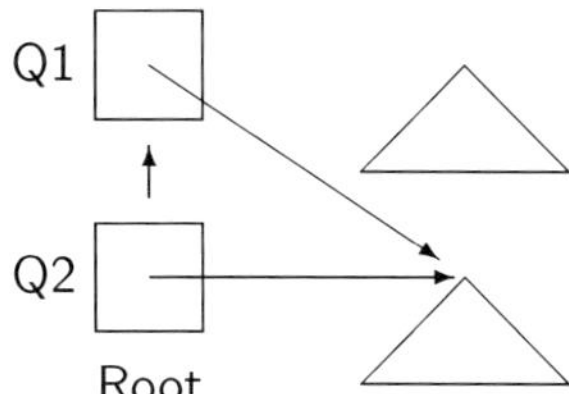

We promised that a semantically equivalent modification to the private part cannot affect the correctness of a client, yet here the meaning of a statement in the client changes when the implementation is changed. Furthermore, predefined equality, which is defined for all private types, is not meaningful for *either* implementation of a priority queue (why?).

6.6.1 *Limited types*

One solution to this problem is to use a *limited type* declaration:

§7.5

> 1 A limited type is (a view of) a type for which copying (such as for an assignment_statement) is not allowed. A nonlimited type is a (view of a) type for which copying is allowed.
>
> 8 There are no predefined equality operators for a limited type.

For a data structure such as a queue, the meaningful operations are those that are explicitly declared. Since there is no real need for assignment and equality, they can be made illegal by declaring the type limited:

pqtv5

```
package Priority_Queue is
  type Queue(Size: Positive) limited private;

  function  Empty(Q:  in Queue) return Boolean;
  procedure Put(I: in Integer; Q: in out Queue);
  procedure Get(I: out Integer; Q: in out Queue);
  ...
end Priority_Queue;
```

As with any operator, equality can be overloaded for any type, and this is particularly useful for limited types that have no predefined equality. However, the assignment symbol is not an operator in Ada and cannot be overloaded, though you can declare a normal procedure that implements assignment:

```
type Queue(Size: Positive) is limited private;
function "="(Left, Right: Queue) return Boolean;
procedure Assign(Target: out Queue; Source: in Queue);
```

The semantics of assignment can also be changed by using controlled types (Section 12.9).

6.7 Case study: priority queue package—version 6

Consider the package specification:

pqt

```
package Priority_Queue is
  type Queue(Size: Positive) is limited private;

  function  Empty(Q:  in Queue) return Boolean;
  procedure Put(I: in Integer; Q: in out Queue);
  procedure Get(I: out Integer; Q: in out Queue);

  Overflow, Underflow: exception;
private
  type Node;
  type Link is access Node;
  type Queue(Size: Positive) is limited
    record
      Root: Link;
    end record;
end Priority_Queue;
```

This differs from the previous specification in that a completion for the incomplete type declaration for Node has been omitted. Nevertheless, this specification is legal: type Queue contains one component of the access type Link and the compiler can determine the amount of memory to allocate for an object of access type without knowing the type of the designated object. Therefore, the complete type declaration can appear in the package body:

```
package body Priority_Queue is
  type Node is           --  Completion of the type declaration
    record
      Data: Integer;
      Left, Right: Link;
    end record;
  ...
end Priority_Queue;
```

§3.10.1

> 3 If the incomplete_type_declaration occurs immediately within the private part of a given package_specification, then the full_type_declaration shall occur later and immediately within either the private part itself, or the declarative_part of the corresponding package_body.

We can freely change the representation of `Node` in the package body without even recompiling the clients, since all the client can do is allocate a queue that is a single access value and pass the value as a parameter.

6.8 Nonlimited private types*

Private types are used not just for complex data structures, but also for simple information hiding of the components of a record where there is no reason to forbid predefined assignment and equality. The standard example of a nonlimited private type is the complex numbers. They have two natural representations (cartesian or polar) and you might want to declare a package that supplies the type while encapsulating the representation in the private part. Since complex numbers are predefined in §G.1 of the Numerics Annex,[2] we choose to give as an example a generalization of complex numbers called *quaternions*.

6.8.1 *Case study: quaternions*

Complex numbers are written $x + iy$, where x and y are real numbers and $i^2 = -1$. Quaternions are written $x + iy + jz + kw$, where x, y, z, w are real numbers and $i^2 = j^2 = k^2 = ijk = -1$. Multiplication of quaternions is not commutative:

$$ij = k,\quad ji = -k,\quad jk = i,\quad kj = -i,\quad ki = j,\quad ik = -j.$$

Quaternions have an important theoretical place in algebra, but they are also important in practice for the computation of three-dimensional rotations in airplane control systems and graphics software. A 3D rotation can be described by giving its *Euler angles*: *pitch* (the airplane rotates up and down along the axis defined by its wings), *roll* (the airplane rotates along the axis of its body), *yaw* (the airplane rotates left and right). However, computations using Euler angles are problematic because they are numerically unstable, and because the breakdown of a rotation into three separate components can cause difficulties in the physical implementation. These computations are efficient and stable when performed with quaternions. The transfor-

[2] The type `Complex` is not defined there as a private.

mations from Euler angles to quaternions and back is not difficult, but an explanation is beyond the scope of this book.

Quaternions were discovered by William R. Hamilton in 1843. For detailed information on quaternions, see:

- `http://mathworld.wolfram.com/Quaternion.html`,
- `http://www.euclideanspace.com/index.htm`,
- `http://www.j3d.org/matrix_faq/matrfaq_latest.html`.

Here we will just implement addition and multiplication for a private type `Quaternion` represented in two different forms.

6.8.2 *Quaternions as four-tuples of real numbers*

Package `QuaternionsR` defines the private type `Quaternion` together with four operations and four deferred constants:

quat

```
package QuaternionsR is
  type Quaternion is private;
  function  Construct(X, Y, Z, W: Float) return Quaternion;
  function  "+"(Q1, Q2: Quaternion) return Quaternion;
  function  "*"(Q1, Q2: Quaternion) return Quaternion;
  procedure Print(Q: in Quaternion);

  One: constant Quaternion;
  I:   constant Quaternion;
  J:   constant Quaternion;
  K:   constant Quaternion;
```

When a private type is declared, it is often useful to compare values of the type to a constant of the type, but since the type is private we cannot give the initial value that is required when a constant is declared §3.3.1(6). The solution is to use *deferred constants*:

§7.4

> 2 A *deferred constant declaration* is an object_declaration with the reserved word **constant** but no initialization expression. The constant declared by a deferred constant declaration is called a *deferred constant*. A deferred constant declaration requires a completion, which shall be a full constant declaration (called the *full declaration* of the deferred constant), ...
>
> 3 A deferred constant declaration that is completed by a full constant declaration shall occur immediately within the visible part of a package_specification. For this case, the following additional rules apply to the corresponding full declaration:
>
> 4 The full declaration shall occur immediately within the private part of the same package;

The first representation of type `Quaternion` is as a record with four components of type `Float`:

```
private
  type Quaternion is
    record
      X, Y, Z, W: Float := 0.0;
    end record;
  One: constant Quaternion := (1.0, 0.0, 0.0, 0.0);
  I:   constant Quaternion := (0.0, 1.0, 0.0, 0.0);
  J:   constant Quaternion := (0.0, 0.0, 1.0, 0.0);
  K:   constant Quaternion := (0.0, 0.0, 0.0, 1.0);
end QuaternionsR;
```

The package body implements the operations: the functions `Construct` and "+" are straighforward, as is the procedure `Print` (omitted, see the software archive):

```
with Ada.Text_IO, Ada.Float_Text_IO;
package body QuaternionsR is
  function Construct(X, Y, Z, W: Float) return Quaternion is
  begin
    return (X, Y, Z, W);
  end Construct;

  function "+"(Q1, Q2: Quaternion) return Quaternion is
  begin
    return (Q1.X+Q2.X, Q1.Y+Q2.Y, Q1.Z+Q2.Z, Q1.W+Q2.W);
  end "+";
```

The formula for multiplication is obtained by multiplying the formal expression

$$(x_1 + iy_1 + jz_1 + kw_1) * (x_2 + iy_2 + jz_2 + kw_2)$$

and collecting terms using the definitions given above. The function is written as an extended return statement §6.5(2.1, 5.8) (Section 6.10):

```
33    function "*"(Q1, Q2: Quaternion) return Quaternion is
34    begin
35      return Q: Quaternion do
36        Q.X := Q1.X*Q2.X - Q1.Y*Q2.Y - Q1.Z*Q2.Z - Q1.W*Q2.W;
37        Q.Y := Q1.X*Q2.Y + Q1.Y*Q2.X + Q1.Z*Q2.W - Q1.W*Q2.Z;
38        Q.Z := Q1.X*Q2.Z - Q1.Y*Q2.W + Q1.Z*Q2.X + Q1.W*Q2.Y;
39        Q.W := Q1.X*Q2.W + Q1.Y*Q2.Z - Q1.Z*Q2.Y + Q1.W*Q2.X;
40      end return;
41    end "*";
42  end QuaternionsR;
```

It could also have been written as an aggregate.

We create a library unit that consists only of a package *renaming* §8.5.3 (Section 15.6). This will enable us to use different packages for quaternions just by modifying these two lines:

```
43  with QuaternionsR;
44  package Quaternions renames QuaternionsR;
```

The following program tests the declaration and use of quaternions.

```
45  with Quaternions;
46  use type Quaternions.Quaternion;
47  procedure Test_Quaternion is
48    Q: Quaternions.Quaternion :=
49         Quaternions.Construct(0.8224, -0.3604, -0.4397, -0.0223);
50  begin
51    Quaternions.Print(Q);
52    Quaternions.Print(Q + Quaternions.K);
53    Quaternions.Print(Q * Quaternions.One);
54    Quaternions.Print(Q + Q);
55    Quaternions.Print(Q * Q);
56  end Test_Quaternion;
```

If you use quaternions extensively, you might want to include a use_clause for the package. In any case, it is essential to include a use_type_clause ‡46 §8.4(4,8) to make the operators visible (Section 15.7).

6.8.3 Quaternions as pairs of complex numbers

An alternate representation of quaternions is as a pair of complex numbers. The package `QuaternionsC` has the same interface as `QuaternionsR`, but a different implementation:

```
private with Ada.Numerics.Complex_Types;
package QuaternionsC is
  -- As before
private
  type Quaternion is
    record
      Z, W: Ada.Numerics.Complex_Types.Complex;
    end record;
  One: constant Quaternion := ((1.0, 0.0), (0.0, 0.0));
  I:   constant Quaternion := ((0.0, 1.0), (0.0, 0.0));
  J:   constant Quaternion := ((0.0, 0.0), (1.0, 0.0));
  K:   constant Quaternion := ((0.0, 0.0), (0.0, 1.0));
end QuaternionsC;
```

We wish to take advantage of the existing implementation of complex numbers in the Ada library, so a with_clause for `Ada.Numerics.Complex_Types` is needed. Like `Text_IO`, `Numerics` is a child package (Section 7.9) of the package `Ada`, and `Complex_Types` is a child of `Numerics`. For now, look upon `Ada.Numerics.Complex_Types` as simply the name of a package. Since the package is needed only in the private part and the body, a private with_clause has been used:

§10.1.2

> 12 A name denoting a library item that is visible only due to being mentioned in one or more with_clauses that include the reserved word **private** shall appear only within:
>
> 13 • a private part;
>
> 14 • a body, ...

When implementing the bodies of the subprogram in the body of the package, the numeric operations from `Ada.Numerics.Complex_Types` are freely used:

```
with Ada.Text_IO, Ada.Complex_Text_IO;
package body QuaternionsC is
  use Ada.Numerics.Complex_Types;

  function Construct(X, Y, Z, W: Float) return Quaternion is ...
  function "+"(Q1, Q2: Quaternion) return Quaternion is ...
  procedure Print(Q: in Quaternion) is ...
```

```
function "*"(Q1, Q2: Quaternion) return Quaternion is
  begin
    return Q: Quaternion do
      Q.Z := Q1.Z*Q2.Z + Q1.W*Conjugate(-Q2.W);
      Q.W := Q1.Z*Q2.W + Q1.W*Conjugate(Q2.Z);
    end return;
  end "*";
end QuaternionsC;
```

To use the new implementation we only need replace the renaming package declaration by:

```
with QuaternionsC;
package Quaternions renames QuaternionsC;
```

Ada 95

Private with_clauses are not supported in Ada 95, so ordinary with_clauses must be used. Do not use declarations from `Ada.Numerics.Complex` in the public part of the package specification so that the dependence of the quaternion package on the complex number package will not be exported to clients.

Nested aggregates must be used instead of the extended return statement.

6.9 Limited types that are not private*

Limited types appear most often as limited private types used to create abstract data types. However, the concept is more general; for example, tasks, synchronized and protected types (Chapter 18) are considered to be limited types for which assignment and equality are not available §7.5(4). In addition, *explicitly limited record types* §3.8(13.1) can be declared. An explicit declaration of a non-private limited type is useful when you want to hide part of an abstraction, but not all of it. For example, in a symbol table, we might want to hide the implementation of the map between symbols and their values, but not the other components of the table:

```
type Symbol_Map   is private;
type Symbol_Table is limited
  record
    Name:     String(1..20);
    Capacity: Positive;
    Mutable:  Boolean;
    Map:      Symbol_Map;
  end record;
```

It is reasonable not to define equality and assignment for a symbol table, so it is declared to be limited, but we choose to hide only the representation of the component Map and not of the entire table.

If a component type is limited, so is the type itself §7.5(6), as is a type derived from a limited type §7.5(6.1). Thus, a limited array type can be declared by giving it a limited component:

```
type Table_Array is array(Integer range <>) of Symbol_Table;
```

6.10 Initialization of limited types*

Assignment is not allowed for limited types; nevertheless, initialization of limited types is permitted by using an aggregate §7.5(2.1–2.2):

```
type Symbol is
  limited record
    Name:     String(1..20);
    Level:    Positive;
    Reserved: Boolean;
  end record;

S: Symbol := (Name => (others => ' '), Level => 1, Reserved => False);
```

The reason that this is permitted is that no copying need actually be done. It is not necessary to construct the aggregate and then copy it to the variable; instead, the aggregate value can be constructed *in place*. See §7.5(2.1–2.9) for the list of constructs in which expressions of limited types are permitted.

An object of limited type can be initialized by a function result, provided that no copying is done:

```
  function Init return Symbol is
  begin
    return (Name => (others => '*'), Level => 2, Reserved => True);
  end Init;
```

Suppose, however, that the construction of the aggregate is not simply a matter of assigning components; for example, an empty doubly-linked list needs several statements to allocate the sentinels and make them point to each other. Still, it should be possible to construct the aggregate in place so no copying is needed. The extended-return statement enables a function to compute in place on the object to which the returned value is "assigned":

§6.5

```
2.1 extended_return_statement ::=
      return defining_identifier : [aliased] return_subtype_indication [:= expression] [do
         handled_sequence_of_statements
      end return];
```

The identifier represents an object that can be used within the sequence of statements as a variable:

```
function Initial return Symbol is
begin
  return S: Symbol := (N => (others => ' '), C => 10, M => False) do
    for I in 1..S.N'Length loop
      S.N(I) := ...           -- Get the characters of the string
    end loop;
  end return;
end Initial;

S: Symbol := Initial;
```

Ada 95

The constructs in this section are new to Ada 2005 and initialization of an object of a limited type is not permitted. The only workaround is to initialize the components one-by-one (in the package body if the type is also private):

```
S: Symbol;

S.Name     := (others => ' ');
S.Capacity := 10;
S.Mutable  := False;
```

Projects

1. Implement all the arithmetical operations on quaternions, as well as subprograms to transform Euler angles to and from the equivalent quaternions.
2. Implement a third representation of quaternions as a scalar and a vector with three elements. You will have to implement arithmetic operations such as the inner product and the cross product on vectors.
3. Implement a symbol table as outlined in Sections 6.9–6.10.

Quizzes

Quiz 1:

```
package P is
  type T1 is private;
  C: constant T1;
  V: T1;
private
  type T1 is new Integer;
  C: constant T1 := 0;
end P;
```

Quiz 2:

```
package P is
  type Node;
  type Ptr is access Node;
end P;

package body P is
  type Node is
    record
      Key: Integer;
      Next: Ptr;
    end record;
end P;
```

Quiz 3:

```
package P is
  type T is limited private;
  type Array_Type is array(0..10) of T;
  procedure Proc;
private
  type T is
    record
      X: Integer := 0;
    end record;
end P;

package body P is
  A1, A2: Array_Type;
  procedure Proc is
  begin
    A1 := A2;
  end Proc;
end P;

with P;
procedure Main is
  A1, A2: P.Array_Type;
begin
  A1 := A2;
end Main;
```

Chapter 7
Type Extension and Inheritance

Object-oriented programming (OOP) is a widely used approach for software development. In the terminology of languages like Java and C++, the unit of design in OOP is the *class*, which defines a type consisting of data *fields* and operations called *methods*. A class is a template from which *objects* or *instances* can be created. Values can be assigned to the fields of an object and the methods can be invoked on it. Classes can organized into a hierarchy by inheritance: one class is derived from another *parent* class, inheriting the parent's fields and methods, possibly adding fields and methods, and possibly overriding the parent's methods.

The constructs we studied in the previous chapter—packages and private types—support OOP, but without type deriviation and inheritance. This chapter and the next one describe the Ada constructs that support these concepts. The chapter will introduce a case study for the *discrete event simulation* of a rocket; this case study will be used extensively in the rest of the book. While the details of the case study are artificial, its structure and the use of the language constructs are realistic. The size of the case study will require quite a few forward references to concepts discussed later in the chapter and in other chapters, but we prefer to show the constructs in context, rather than discussing them one-by-one.

Language Comparison

If you are an experienced OOP programmer learning Ada, please note that although the concepts are the same, the constructs and the terminology are quite different from those in Java or C++. In particular, Ada does not have a **class** construct that both defines a type and serves as a module. Types in Ada are defined by type declarations, while packages implement modules. OOP is a style of using these constructs, not something required (or even strongly encouraged) by the language definition. Finally, the **package** construct in Java serves only to organize the namespace of the program, not to specify what resources are imported like the Ada with_clause.

7.1 Case study: discrete event simulation

Simulations are invariably used during the design of large embedded systems. You cannot test or debug the design of a rocket by launching rocket after rocket. Extensive simulation is the only way to develop enough confidence in the design in order to build and launch one with a reasonable chance of success.

The case study in this chapter is a framework for a simulation of a rocket; we will omit all the physical calculations that would require domain-specific knowledge. The method used is discrete event simulation. Events are generated and placed on a queue, and each event is time-stamped with the time at which it is to "occur":

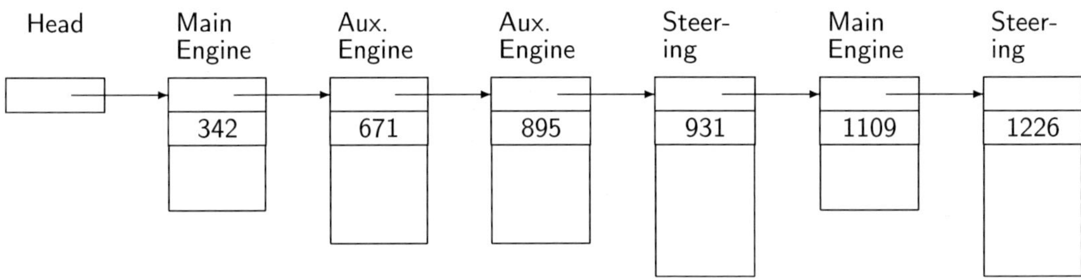

The program does not attempt to maintain a physical clock. Instead, the events are ordered by the time-stamps, and the program simply removes the event whose occurrence is "soonest" in the future and performs the simulation of the event. This is easily done by maintaining a priority queue, where higher priority is given to earlier events. Conveniently, we have already implemented a priority queue in the previous case studies, and we will adapt it for use here.

We simplify the program by generating all the events and placing them on the queue before the simulation begins:

```
for All_Events loop
  Put(Create_Event, Q);
end loop;

while Queue_Not_Empty loop
  Simulate(Get(Q));
end loop;
```

A multitasking simulation that generates and simulates events simultaneously will be developed in Section 19.9.

How should the events be represented in the program? If all the events were identical, a simple record would suffice. But, as shown in the diagram above, the event types are *heterogeneous*, because different events will have different components associated with them. Some components are, of course, identical for all event types: the link and the simulation time. However, most of the data for the simulation depends on the specific event type. For example, an engine event will need the fuel flow rate, while a steering event will need the deflection angles of the nozzles.

The simplest solution is to include all possible components in the record, but this is impractical because the records will be too large and confusing. Alternatively, variant records (Section 11.5) can be used. Each record will contain only the components required by the specific event type; however, the code that accesses event-dependent components will have to use a case-statement and this can make maintenance difficult.

Heterogeneous data types can be constructed using *derivation*. A root event type with the common components will be defined as a *parent type*, and additional, event-specific types will be *derived* from it for each new kind of event. The derived types for the specific events will inherit the common fields from the parent type and *extend* it with event-specific components.

7.2 Tagged types

We start by declaring package `Root_Event` with a record type `Event` containing a single component `Time`. `Event` is declared as a private type with its completion in the private part:

rocket

```
package Root_Event is
  type Event is abstract tagged private;

  -- Primitive operations
  function  Create return Event is abstract;
  procedure Simulate(E: in Event) is abstract;

  -- Class-wide operation
  function "<"(Left, Right: Event'Class) return Boolean;
private
  subtype Simulation_Time is Integer range 0..10_000;
  type Event is abstract tagged
    record
      Time: Simulation_Time;    --  Common component of all events
    end record;
end Root_Event;
```

The type is declared to be **`abstract`**; this is a technical term and can be ignored for now (Section 8.4). Do not confuse the declaration of an abstract type with the general concept of an abstract data type that encapsulates the implementation of the type and its operation.

The reserved word **`tagged`** indicates that the type `Event` can be *extended*. The choice of the word *tagged* will be explained in Section 7.7.

Two kinds of operations have been declared: `Create` and `Simulate`, which are *primitive* operations (Section 7.3), and "<", which is a *class-wide* operation (Section 7.6).

We now *extend* the type `Event` for each event type that is needed in the simulation. Package `Root_Event.Steering` declares a new type `Steering_Event` which is an extension of `Event`:

```
package Root_Event.Steering is
   type Steering_Event is new Event with private;

   --  Override primitive operations of Event.
   function Create return Steering_Event;
   procedure Simulate(E: in Steering_Event);
private
   type Commands is (Roll, Pitch, Yaw);
   subtype Degrees is Integer range -90 .. 90;
   type Steering_Event is new Event with
     record
       Command: Commands;
       Degree: Degrees;
     end record;
end Root_Event.Steering;
```

The extended name `Root_Event.Steering` declares that the package is a *child package* of the package `Root_Event`; this concept is explained in Section 7.9.

The extension is a *private extension*:

§7.3

> 3 private_extension_declaration ::=
> **type** defining_identifier [discriminant_part] **is**
> [**abstract**] [**limited** | **synchronized**] **new** *ancestor*_subtype_indication
> [**and** interface_list] **with private**;

(Interfaces and synchronized types are the subject of Chapter 17.)

The derived type itself is encapsulated in the private part by declaring that `Steering_Event` is a **new** `Event`, together **with** the components that appear in the record definition:

§3.4

> 2 derived_type_definition ::=
> [**abstract**] [**limited**] **new** *parent*_subtype_indication
> [**and** interface_list] [record_extension_part]

§3.9.1

> 2 record_extension_part ::= **with** record_definition

The two primitive operations Create and Simulate have been overridden (Section 7.4).

Package Root_Event.Telemetry declares the type Telemetry_Event, which is also derived from Event:

```
package Root_Event.Telemetry is
   type Telemetry_Event is new Event with private;
   function Create return Telemetry_Event;
   procedure Simulate(E: in Telemetry_Event);
private
   type Subsystems is (Engines, Guidance, Communications);
   type States is (OK, Failed);
   type Telemetry_Event is new Event with
     record
       ID:     Subsystems;
       Status: States;
     end record;
end Root_Event.Telemetry;
```

More than one derived type can be declared in the same package specification. Package Root_Event.Engine declares three types: Engine_Event, which is derived directly from Event, and Main_Engine_Event and Aux_Engine_Event, which are in turn derived from Engine_Event. The visible part of the package is:

```
package Root_Event.Engine is
   type Engine_Event is new Event with private;
   function Create return Engine_Event;
   procedure Simulate(E: in Engine_Event);

   type Main_Engine_Event is new Engine_Event with private;
   function Create return Main_Engine_Event;

   type Aux_Engine_Event is new Engine_Event with private;
   function Create return Aux_Engine_Event;
   procedure Simulate(E: in Aux_Engine_Event);
```

There is no declaration Simulate with a parameter of type Main_Engine_Event. This means that the subprogram will be *inherited* from the parent type Engine_Event (Section 7.3).

The private part declares the new components of the derived types:

```
private
  type Engine_Event is new Event with
    record
      Fuel, Oxygen: Natural;
    end record;

  type Main_Engine_Event is new Engine_Event with
    null record;

  type Aux_Engine_ID is (Left, Right);
  type Aux_Engine_Event is new Engine_Event with
    record
      Side: Aux_Engine_ID;
    end record;
end Root_Event.Engine;
```

The syntax **null record** is simply a shorthand for **record null; end record** §3.8(15), and means that the components of the derived type are the same as those of the parent type.

The types derived from Event can be displayed in a tree (Figure 7.1). The components of a derived type consist of the components *inherited* §3.4(12) from the parent type, together with

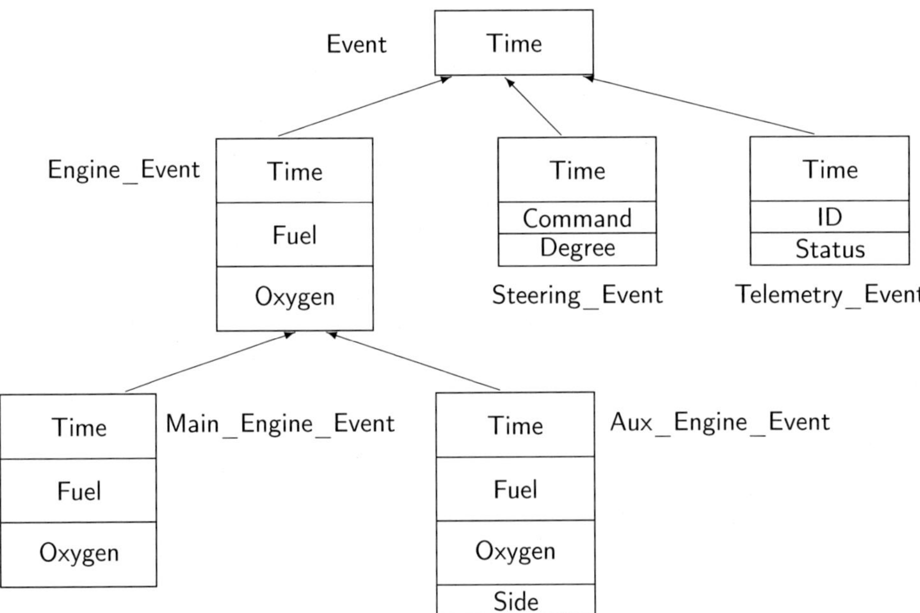

Fig. 7.1 Derivation class

the additional components, if any, that were added in the extension. Since there is no provision for removing components upon derivation, we can be sure that *every* component of a parent type is also contained in each descendant of the parent; for example, `Oxygen`, a component of the parent type `Engine_Event`, is also a component of the derived types `Main_Engine_Event` and `Aux_Engine_Event`.

A tree of derived types is called a *derivation class.*

§3.4.1

> 2 A derived type is *derived from* its parent type *directly*; it is derived *indirectly* from any type from which its parent type is derived. ... The derivation class of types for a type *T* (also called the class *rooted* at *T*) is the set consisting of *T* (the *root type* of the class) and all types derived from *T* (directly or indirectly) plus any associated universal or class-wide types (defined below).

Derivation creates a relation of descendant and ancestor between types:

§3.4.1

> 10 A specific type *T2* is defined to be a *descendant* of a type *T1* if *T2* is the same as *T1*, or if *T2* is derived (directly or indirectly) from *T1*. A class-wide type *T2*'Class is defined to be a descendant of type *T1* if *T2* is a descendant of *T1*. ... If a type *T2* is a descendant of a type *T1*, then *T1* is called an *ancestor of T2*. An *ultimate ancestor* of a type is an ancestor of that type that is not itself a descendant of any other type. ...

7.3 Primitive operations

The primitive operations of a type are operations that are so closely associated with the type that they are "carried along" with it. The following section of the *ARM* that defines primitive operations is extremely important; we quote it in full for future reference, though you may not understand all the concepts just yet:

§3.2.3

> 1 An operation *operates on a type T* if it yields a value of type *T*, if it has an operand whose expected type (see 8.6) is *T*, or if it has an access parameter or access result type (see 6.1) designating *T*. A predefined operator, or other language-defined operation such as assignment or a membership test, that operates on a type, is called a *predefined operation* of the type. The *primitive operations* of a type are the predefined operations of the type, plus any user-defined primitive subprograms.

§3.2.3

> 2 The *primitive subprograms* of a specific type are defined as follows:
> 3 • The predefined operators of the type (see 4.5);
> 4 • For a derived type, the inherited (see 3.4) user-defined subprograms;
> 5 • For an enumeration type, the enumeration literals (which are considered parameterless functions—see 3.5.1);
> 6 • For a specific type declared immediately within a package_specification, any subprograms (in addition to the enumeration literals) that are explicitly declared immediately within the same package_specification and that operate on the type;
> 7 • For a nonformal type, any subprograms not covered above that are explicitly declared immediately within the same declarative region as the type and that override (see 8.3) other implicitly declared primitive subprograms of the type.
> 8 A primitive subprogram whose designator is an operator_symbol is called a *primitive operator*.

Predefined operators are always primitive; for example, "+" is a primitive operation of the type `Integer`, and "=" is a primitive operation of the type `Event`. You can declare additional primitive operations, which are subprograms that are declared *immediately within the same package specification* as the type §3.2.3(6) and that have a parameter or result of the type §3.2.3(1). A primitive operation may also be declared in the private part, but it will not be accessible outside the package body and the children of the package.

The restriction to the package specification is crucial. It means that once a tagged type—with its components and primitive operations—is defined in a package specification, all clients of the package see exactly the same set of entities. Subprograms with a parameter of the type can be declared elsewhere, such as in clients or in the package body, but they are not primitive.

Primitive operations are *inherited* §3.4(17) by derived types, just like record components. Thus, the subprogram `Simulate` ‡48, which is a primitive operation of `Engine_Event`, is inherited by `Main_Engine_Event`. It is as if the declaration:

```
procedure Simulate(E: in Main_Engine_Event);
```

were written just after the declaration of the type `Main_Engine_Event` ‡50. A call to `Simulate` with a value of type `Main_Engine_Event` is a call to the inherited (primitive) subprogram:

```
M: Main_Engine_Event;

Simulate(M);              -- Calls Simulate of Engine_Event
```

7.4 Overriding an operation

The primitive operations of a parent type are inherited by the derived type, but they can also be *overridden* §8.3(10). An operation is overridden by declaring an operation with the same name, *replacing* the parameters of the parent type with parameters of the derived type. The new operation is used when called with actual parameters of the derived type, while the original operation is retained for calls with actual parameters of the parent type.

In the case study, the declaration of Aux_Engine_Event ‡53 is followed by declarations of Create and Simulate that override the inherited subprograms. A call to Simulate with a parameter type Aux_Engine_Event calls the overridden, not the inherited, subprogram:

```
M: Main_Engine_Event;
A: Aux_Engine_Event;

Simulate(M);          -- Calls inherited Simulate from Engine_Event
Simulate(A);          -- Calls overridden Simulate in Aux_Engine_Event
```

Overriding subprograms are themselves primitive operations §3.2.3(7) and can be overridden upon subsequent derivation. As with components, an operation cannot be removed, so that given an object of any type descended from Event, the subprogram Simulate is defined on the object: either it was overridden when the type was declared, or the deepest declaration of Simulate in the chain of ancestors is inherited.

7.5 The package bodies of the case study

The package body for Root_Event is very simple:

```
package body Root_Event is
  function "<"(Left, Right: Event'Class) return Boolean is
  begin
    return Left.Time < Right.Time;
  end "<";
end Root_Event;
```

Create and Simulate, the primitive operations of the type Event, are abstract; since abstract operations cannot be called, they cannot have bodies. The operator "<" is not abstract and a body must be given: it is implemented by calling "<" on the component Time. The operator is not primitive, because its operands are of class-wide type (Section 7.6), not of the tagged type.

The bodies of the packages containing the derived types are artificial. Create simply constructs an aggregate with random components and Simulate prints the data contained in the event record. (The bodies of the Simulate procedures have been omitted and can be found in the software archive.) The body for the engine types is:

```
86 with Ada.Text_IO; use Ada.Text_IO;
87 with Root_Event.Random_Time;
88 package body Root_Event.Engine is
89   G: Random_Time.Generator;
90
91   function Create return Engine_Event is
92   begin
93     return (Time   => Random_Time.Random(G),
94             Fuel   => Random_Time.Random(G) mod 100,
95             Oxygen => Random_Time.Random(G) mod 500);
96   end Create;
97
98   function Create return Main_Engine_Event is
99   begin
100    return Main_Engine_Event'(Engine_Event'(Create) with null record);
101  end Create;
102
103  function Create return Aux_Engine_Event is
104  begin
105    return (Engine_Event'(Create)
106      with Aux_Engine_ID'Val(Random_Time.Random(G) mod 2));
107  end Create;
108
109  procedure Simulate(E: in Engine_Event)     is ... end Simulate;
110  procedure Simulate(E: in Aux_Engine_Event) is ... end Simulate;
111 begin
112  Random_Time.Reset(G);
113 end Root_Event.Engine;
```

Values of types Main_Engine_Event and Aux_Engine_Event are constructed using *extension aggrgates* (Section 8.3). The package Root_Event.Random_Time is discussed below. The procedure Reset that initializes the random number generator G is put in the sequence of statements of the package body ‡112, which is executed when the package is elaborated:

§7.2

```
2 package_body ::=
    defining_program_unit_name is
      declarative_part
    [begin
      handled_sequence_of_statements]
    end [[parent_unit_name.]identifier];
```

6 For the elaboration of a nongeneric package_body, its declarative_part is first elaborated, and its handled_sequence_of_statements is then executed.

The bodies for `Root_Event.Steering` and `Root_Event.Telemetry` are similar and can be found in the software archive.

7.5.1 *The random number generator*

We instantiate the generic package `Ada.Numerics.Discrete_Random` §A.5.2 with the subtype `Simulation_Time` to obtain a random number generator type:

```
with Ada.Numerics.Discrete_Random;
private package Root_Event.Random_Time is
  new Ada.Numerics.Discrete_Random(Simulation_Time);
```

Once the package `Random_Time` has been declared, we can declare a variable `G` of type `Generator` ‡89 and call the function `Random` ‡93–95 to return a random value of type `Simulation_Time`. For simplicity, we use only a single generator and convert the returned random number to other numeric types.

7.6 Class-wide types

We now return to the problem of constructing a heterogeneous queue. We cannot create a heterogenous data structure containing items of arbitrary type; this would not be compatible with the strong type checking of Ada. Instead, the design of Ada chooses a flexible intermediate approach: objects of the *class* of all types *derived from* a parent type can be stored in a data structure. The specific type of an object is checked, if necessary, when it is used at run-time.

§3.4.1

> 4 Class-wide types
>
> Class-wide types are defined for (and belong to) each derivation class rooted at a tagged type (see 3.9). Given a subtype S of a tagged type *T*, S'Class is the subtype_mark for a corresponding subtype of the tagged class-wide type *T*'Class. Such types are called "class-wide" because when a formal parameter is defined to be of a class-wide type *T*'Class, an actual parameter of any type in the derivation class rooted at *T* is acceptable (see 8.6).

Given the derivation class of types shown in Figure 7.1, the values of the type `Event'Class` are the union of the values of all the derived types in the class. As noted in the last sentence of §3.4.1(4) above, if a formal parameter is of class-wide type, the actual parameter can be of any type in the class. For example, the function "<" ‡9 in package `Root_Event` takes two parameters of the class-wide type `Event'Class`, so it can be called with actual parameters of any event type. Of course, the body of the function ‡83 can only reference components that are common to all types in the class, here the single component `Time`.

An uninitialized object of a class-wide type cannot be declared:

```
EC: Event'Class;            -- Error!
```

The situation is analogous to that with unconstrained array types such as `String`. It is not possible to declare an uninitialized variable or an unconstained record component of the type:

```
S1: String;                 -- Error!

type String_Record is
  record
    S: String;              -- Error!
  end record;
```

An object can be of an unconstrained type provided that it is supplied with a constraint upon elaboration, either from an initial value or from an actual parameter:

```
S2: String := "Hello world";

function Palindrome(S: String) return String;
```

An access type whose designed type is an unconstrained array can be declared, because the compiler can determine the amount of memory needed to store an access value without knowing what it points to:

```
type String_Pointer is access String;
```

```
type String_Record is
  record
    S: String_Pointer;
  end record;
```

Of course, when an object is allocated, a constraint or an initial value must be given §4.8(4):

```
P: String_Pointer := new String(1..80);
```

Class-wide types are very similar to unconstrained array types; their common properties are defined by the term *indefinite type*:

§3.3

> 23 ... A subtype is an indefinite subtype if it is an unconstrained array subtype, or if it has unknown discriminants or unconstrained discriminants without defaults (see 3.7); otherwise the subtype is a *definite* subtype (all elementary subtypes are definite subtypes). A class-wide subtype is defined to have unknown discriminants, and is therefore an indefinite subtype. An indefinite subtype does not by itself provide enough information to create an object; an additional constraint or explicit initialization expression is necessary (see 3.3.1). A component cannot have an indefinite nominal subtype.

(Discriminants are discussed in Section 11.4.)

In the implementation of a heterogeneous priority queue, the Put procedure is declared with a parameter of class-wide type so that an event of any type in the class can be inserted into the queue. The Get function returns a result of class-wide type so that an event of any type can be removed from the queue:

```
with Root_Event; use Root_Event;
package Event_Queue is
  type Queue is limited private;
  type Queue_Ptr is access Queue;

  function  Empty(Q: in Queue) return Boolean;
  procedure Put(E: in Event'Class; Q: in out Queue);
  function  Get(Q: Queue_Ptr) return Event'Class;
private
  type Node;
  type Link is access Node;
  type Queue is
    record
      Root: Link;
    end record;
end Event_Queue;
```

A node of the queue cannot directly contain an item of class-wide type; instead, Node contains a pointer to the event:

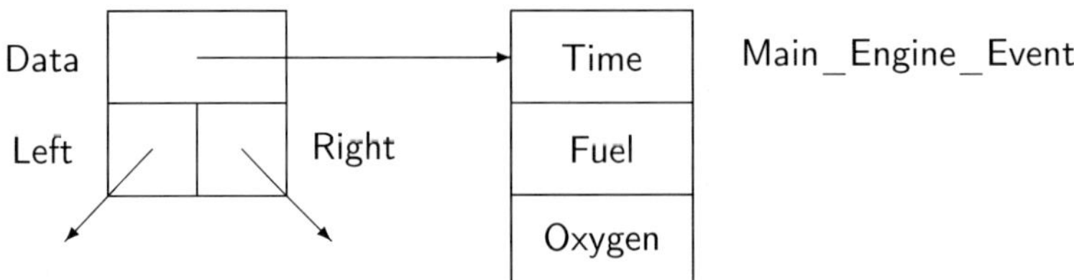

This data structure is encapsulated in the body of the package:

```
package body Event_Queue is
  type Event_Class_Ptr is access Event'Class;
  type Node is
    record
      Data: Event_Class_Ptr;
      Left, Right: Link;
    end record;
```

The allocation of a new node includes a nested allocation for the event itself:

```
  procedure Put(E: in Event'Class; Node_Ptr: in out Link) is
  begin
    if Node_Ptr = null then
      Node_Ptr := new Node'(new Event'Class'(E), null, null);
    elsif E < Node_Ptr.Data.all then
      Put(E, Node_Ptr.Left);
    else
      Put(E, Node_Ptr.Right);
    end if;
  end Put;
```

The other subprograms are implemented as before, except that the function Get dereferences the designated event object before returning it:

```
  procedure Put(E: in Event'Class; Q: in out Queue) is ... end Put;
  function Empty(Q: in Queue) return Boolean         is ... end Empty;
  procedure Get(Node_Ptr: in out Link; Found: out Link) is ... end Get;
  function Get(Q: Queue_Ptr) return Event'Class is
    Found: Link;
  begin
    Get(Q.Root, Found);
    return Found.Data.all;
  end Get;
end Event_Queue;
```

7.7 Dynamic dispatching

We are now ready to put the pieces together. The main subprogram follows the outline given at the beginning of the chapter. First, a queue object is allocated and the access value is assigned to the variable Q:

```
with Event_Queue;
with Root_Event.Engine, Root_Event.Telemetry, Root_Event.Steering;
use Root_Event;
procedure Rocket is
  Q: Event_Queue.Queue_Ptr := new Event_Queue.Queue;
```

Then Create is called fifteen times for each event type and the events put on the queue:

```
begin
  for I in 1..15 loop
    Event_Queue.Put(Engine.Main_Engine_Event'(Engine.Create), Q.all);
    Event_Queue.Put(Engine.Aux_Engine_Event' (Engine.Create), Q.all);
    Event_Queue.Put(Telemetry.Create,                         Q.all);
    Event_Queue.Put(Steering.Create,                          Q.all);
  end loop;
```

Finally, the events are removed one-by-one from the queue and Simulate is called for each one:

```
  while not Event_Queue.Empty(Q.all) loop
    Root_Event.Simulate(Event_Queue.Get(Q));
  end loop;
end Rocket;
```

There is a technical reason for the dynamic allocation of the queue. Get must be a function rather than a procedure so that it can return an indefinite type (see below), but Get modifies the queue data structure and a function cannot have **in out** parameters. Instead, an access value is passed to Get as a parameter of mode **in** as required by the function; it is permissible to modify the object designated by constant such as an **in** parameter. (A better solution is to use access parameters; see Section 12.6.)

Let us follow the processing of an event from creation to simulation, paying particular attention to the types of the objects and the parameters. We call a function such as Telemetry.Create and then pass the returned event to the procedure Event_Queue.Put:

```
Event_Queue.Put(Telemetry.Create, Q.all);
```

What is the type of the object that is returned by the function, and what type is expected for the first formal parameter of the procedure? From the declaration of the function Create ‡34 in package Root_Event.Telemetry, we see that the function returns an object of type Telemetry_Event. The first formal parameter of Put ‡141 in package Event_Queue is of type

Event'Class. By §3.4.1(4) (quoted in the previous section), a class-wide formal parameter matches an actual parameter of *any* specific type *in its class*. Therefore, the call is legal because the actual parameter (the object returned by Telemetry.Create) is of type Telemetry_Event, which is in the class rooted at Event. Similarly, the calls to the other Create functions all return objects of types within the class rooted at Event, so they match.

Consider now the removal of events from the queue and the call to the procedure Simulate:

```
Root_Event.Simulate(Event_Queue.Get(Q));
```

Again, let us examine what type is returned from the function Event_Queue.Get, and what type is expected by Simulate. The function Get ‡142 returns an object of type Event'Class:

```
function Get(Q: Queue_Ptr) return Event'Class;
```

Since the queue is heterogeneous, before calling Get we cannot know what the *specific* type of the returned event will be (the priority queue orders the events according to the Time component and these were assigned random numbers). But we do know that it is one of the types within the class.

The value returned by Get is the actual parameter of the call to the procedure Simulate. Although the call is written Root_Event.Simulate, the abstract procedure Simulate declared Root_Event has no body and cannot be called. Instead, we want to call one of the four overriding procedures declared for the various event types:

```
procedure Simulate(E: in Engine_Event);
  -- Also for Main_Engine_Event, by inheritance
procedure Simulate(E: in Aux_Engine_Event);
procedure Simulate(E: in Steering_Event);
procedure Simulate(E: in Telemetry_Event);
```

How can the compiler decide which subprogram to call?

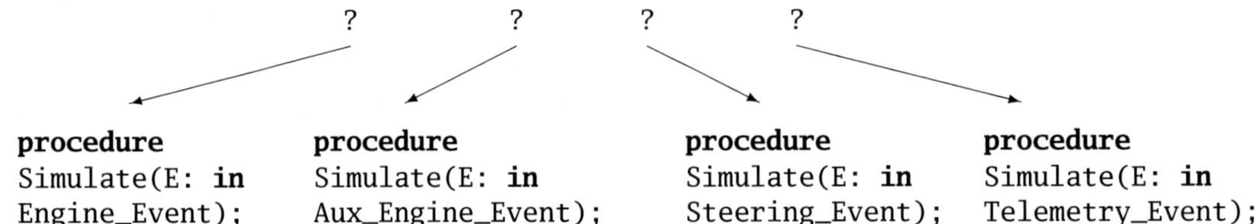

The answer is that the compiler doesn't decide! Instead, at run-time, the call checks the specific type of the actual parameter and jumps to the appropriate procedure for that object. This is called *dynamic dispatching* or simply *dispatching*. Although the actual parameter is of class-wide type (as returned by Get), the type of the *object* itself is one of the specific types in the class, and the call is dispatched to the procedure Simulate that is a primitive operation of the specific type. For an object of type Main_Engine_Event, this is the procedure inherited from

Engine_Event, while for the other event types, it is the overriding procedure declared just after the type.

The advantage of dynamic dispatching is that the simulation loop is written once and never needs to be changed (or even recompiled), regardless of how many additional event types are added to the system.

7.7.1 Tags

For dispatching to work, an object must carry with it a *run-time* indication of its specific type called a *tag*. If a primitive subprogram is called with an actual parameter of a specific type (the parameter is *statically tagged*), then the compiler can decide which subprogram to bind to the call. In the following declarations and statements, the types of the variable declarations provide a context for the *compiler* to decided which function Create to call and the same types are used to decide which subprogram Simulate to call:

```
use Root_Event.Engine;
E: Engine_Event     := Create;
A: Aux_Engine_Event := Create;

Simulate(E);
Simulate(A);
```

This is called *early* or *static* binding. However, if the actual parameter is *dynamically tagged*, that is, if it is of class-wide type, the compiler cannot bind the call and the binding is done dynamically at run-time. This is called *late* or *dynamic binding*

§3.9.2

> 1 The primitive subprograms of a tagged type ... are called *dispatching operations*. A dispatching operation can be called using a statically determined *controlling* tag, in which case the body to be executed is determined at compile time. Alternatively, the controlling tag can be dynamically determined, in which case the call *dispatches* to a body that is determined at run time; such a call is termed a *dispatching call*. ...
>
> 4 • The name or expression is *statically tagged* if it is of a specific tagged type ....
>
> 5 • The name or expression is *dynamically tagged* if it is of a class-wide type, ...

Note carefully that dispatching is only done on *primitive* subprograms. These subprograms have formal parameters of the tagged type called *controlling formal parameters*; the corresponding actual parameters are called *controlling operands*.

§3.9.2

> 2 A *call on a dispatching operation* is a call whose name or prefix denotes the declaration of a dispatching operation. A *controlling operand* in a call on a dispatching operation of a tagged type *T* is one whose corresponding formal parameter is of type *T* ...; the corresponding formal parameter is called a *controlling formal parameter*. ...
>
> 20 For the execution of a call on a dispatching operation, the action performed is determined by the properties of the corresponding dispatching operation of the specific type identified by the controlling tag value. ...

We wrote the dispatching call `Root_Event.Simulate` as an *expanded name* §4.1.3(4) to emphasize that to dispatch with a controlling operand of a class-wide type `Root_Event.Event'Class`, you (syntactically) call the primitive operation of the corresponding tagged type `Root_Event.Event`.

The function:

```
function "<"(Left, Right: Event'Class) return Boolean;
```

is *not* dispatching because the formal parameter is of class-wide type and the actual parameter may be of any type within the class. The function is not primitive, so overriding and dispatching are not relevant.

Summary

Let us summarize the rules that govern static vs. dynamic binding of calls:[1]

- The primitive operations of a tagged type are subprograms that are declared immediately within the same package specification and that have a parameter of the tagged type; inherited operations are also primitive.
- Primitive operations are dispatching.
- Formal parameters of the tagged type are controlling formal parameters; the actual parameters of the tagged type are controlling operands.
- Names or expressions of a tagged type are:
  - Statically tagged if they are of a specific type.
  - Dynamically tagged if they are of a class-wide type.
- The call is determined by the controlling tag:
  - If the controlling operands (actual parameters) are statically tagged, the call is bound at compile-time.
  - If the controlling operands (actual parameters) are dynamically tagged, the call is dispatched at run-time to the subprogram whose controlling formal parameters match the tags of the operand.

[1] The rules are more complicated when there are functions which return a tagged type (Section 8.10).

The rules for dispatching are displayed in the following table:

	actual specific	actual class-wide
formal specific	static	dynamic
formal class-wide	static	static

The terminology of these rules is more complex than the actual concept itself. Think always of the diagram on page 114: if you have an *actual parameter of class-wide type*, you cannot know what the tag (specific type) of the value is, so dispatching at run-time must be done. Any other combination is statically bound.

7.8 Types and packages

There are no particular encapsulation requirements for tagged types, except that primitive operations need to be declared in the same package specification as the type. The following specification, with all the types in a single package specification and with all the declarations in the visible part of the package, is correct:

rocketc

```
package Event_Package is
  subtype Simulation_Time is Integer range 0..10_000;
  type Event is abstract tagged ...
  function  Create return Event is abstract;
  procedure Simulate(E: in Event) is abstract;
  function "<"(Left, Right: Event'Class) return Boolean;

  type Engine_Event is new Event with ...
  function Create return Engine_Event;
  procedure Simulate(E: in Engine_Event);

  type Main_Engine_Event is new Engine_Event with ...
  function Create return Main_Engine_Event;

  type Aux_Engine_Event is new Engine_Event with ...
  function Create return Aux_Engine_Event;
  procedure Simulate(E: in Aux_Engine_Event);
```

```
   type Steering_Event is new Event with ...
   function Create return Steering_Event;
   procedure Simulate(E: in Steering_Event);

   type Telemetry_Event is new Event with ...
   function Create return Telemetry_Event;
   procedure Simulate(E: in Telemetry_Event);
end Event_Package;
```

The main program needs only minor modifications due to the change in the package name:

```
with Event_Queue;
with Event_Package; use Event_Package;
procedure RocketC is
   Q: Event_Queue.Queue_Ptr := new Event_Queue.Queue;
begin
   for I in 1..15 loop
      Event_Queue.Put(Main_Engine_Event'(Create), Q.all);
      Event_Queue.Put(Aux_Engine_Event'(Create),  Q.all);
      Event_Queue.Put(Telemetry_Event'(Create),   Q.all);
      Event_Queue.Put(Steering_Event'(Create),    Q.all);
   end loop;

   while not Event_Queue.Empty(Q.all) loop
      Simulate(Event_Queue.Get(Q));
   end loop;
end RocketC;
```

The type of the actual parameter in the call to Simulate is `Event'Class`, so the call is dispatched to the appropriate version of `Simulate` in the derivation class *for the type* `Event`.

7.9 Encapsulation and child packages

The limitation that a client can only see the visible part of a package is too inflexible for some applications. Consider the declaration of `Root_Event.Event`:

```
package Root_Event is
  type Event is abstract tagged private;
private
  type Event is abstract tagged
    record
      Time: Simulation_Time;    --  Common component of all events
    end record;
end Root_Event;
```

On the one hand, we wish to restrict the accessibility of the implementation of the type (the component `Time`), but, on the other hand, derived types should be able to access this component, because computations within `Simulate` may be time-dependent.

The solution is to use *child packages* to form a *subsystem* of packages §10.1(3), consisting of a root library package and all its children, their children and so on. (Subprograms may also be children of packages §6.1(4,7).) Packages within the subsystem share abstractions by granting child packages visibility of the *private* parts of their specifications. Child packages are denoted syntactically by concatenating the child's name to the parent's name using dotted notation. The hierarchy of descendants may be carried to any depth.

The visibility rules can be understood by pretending that a child package is declared *after* the parent's specification but *before* its body:

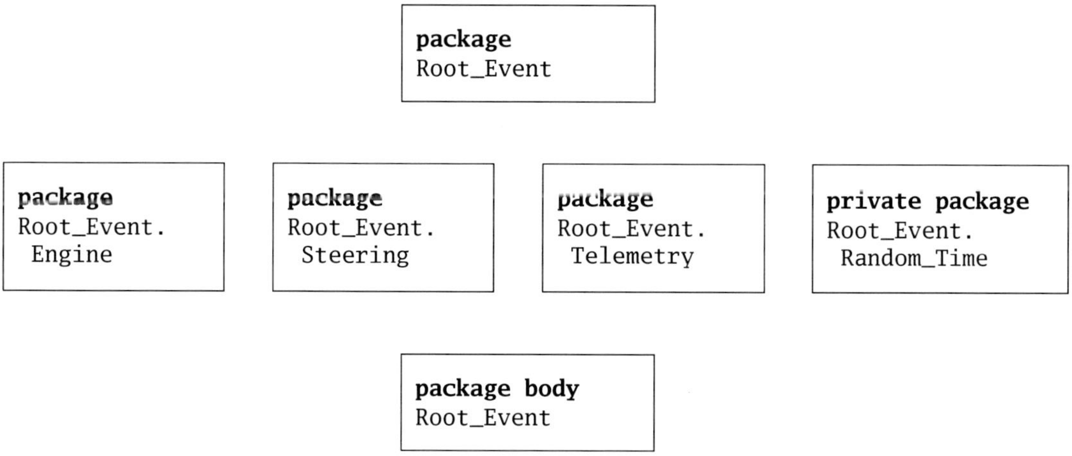

```
package
Root_Event
```

```
package              package              package              private package
Root_Event.          Root_Event.          Root_Event.          Root_Event.
 Engine               Steering             Telemetry            Random_Time
```

```
package body
Root_Event
```

The diagram is intended to show that the children can see the private part but not the body.

§8.1

> 7 The declarative region includes the text of the construct together with additional text determined (recursively), as follows:
>
> 9 If the declaration of a library unit ... is included, so are the declarations of any child units .... The child declarations occur after the declaration.

A package can have a with_clause for any package even if it is a child package. For example, the case study in Section 6.8.3 had a with_clause for `Ada.Numerics.Complex_Types`, which is in an entirely separate hierarchy of packages. In the simulation case study, `Root_Event.Steering` has a with_clause for its sibling `Root_Event.Random_Time`. The parent body has no special privileges and must also contain a with_clause for a child if it needs to access it.

Writing a with_clause for a package is the same as writing with_clauses for the package and for all its parents §10.1.2(6). In the main subprogram of the simulation, there are with_clauses for the child packages:

```
with Root_Event.Engine, Root_Event.Telemetry, Root_Event.Steering;
use Root_Event;
```

These clauses enable the use of resources in the parent clause `Root_Event`. The context clause also contains a use_clause for `Root_Event`, so we can directly refer to the child package (for example, `Telemetry.Create`):

§8.1

> 16 The children of a parent library unit are inside the parent's declarative region, even though they do not occur inside the parent's declaration or body. This implies that one can use (for example) "P.Q" to refer to a child of P whose defining name is Q, and that after "**use** P;" Q can refer (directly) to that child.

The private part of a child package can see the private part of the parent package, although we did not make use of this in the case study. However, we must prevent exporting of declarations from the private part:

```
package Root_Event.Telemetry_Event is
  subtype Telemetry_Time is Simulation_Time;    --  Error!
private
  ...
end Root_Event.Telemetry_Event;
```

because that would negate the purpose of private parts. There is a special rule that excludes the visible part of a child package specification from seeing the private part of its parent:

§8.2

> 4 • The immediate scope of a declaration in the private part of a library unit does not include the visible part of any public descendant of that library unit.

Consider, however, the random number generator package `Root_Event.Random_Time`. The package is declared as a generic instantiation of a package from the standard libraries, but in the context of our simulation program, an equivalent specification is as follows:

```
package Root_Event.Random_Time is
  type Generator is private;
  function Random(Gen: Generator) return Simulation_Time;
  procedure Reset(Gen: in Generator);
private
  ...
end Root_Event.Random_Time;
```

The function Random in the visible part returns a value of type Simulation_Time that is declared in the private part of its parent, in effect exporting the type. However, this will not be a problem in our case study, provided that we promise to restrict the use of Simulation_Time to children of Root_Event that *already* have visibility of its private part.

Ada defines two types of child packages: *public* and *private*. The rule in §8.2(4) that prevents visibility of the private part of a package in the visible part of a child holds only for public children. The visible part of a *private* child *is* allowed access to the private part of a parent. However, to prevent exporting the private declarations, a unit that has a with_clause for a private child must be within the family that already has access to the private part:

§10.1.2

> 8 If a with_clause of a given compilation_unit mentions a private child of some library unit, then the given compilation_unit shall be one of:
> 9 • the declaration, body, or subunit of a private descendant of that library unit;
> 10 • the body or subunit of a public descendant of that library unit, ...

In the simulation, Root_Event.Random_Time is declared to be a private child:

```
private package Root_Event.Random_Time is
  function Random(Gen: Generator) return Simulation_Time;
end Root_Event.Random_Time;
```

so the use of Simulation_Time is legal. However, a with_clause for Root_Event.Random_Time is only allowed for child packages rooted at Root_Event.

Library packages are children of the predefined package Standard §10.1.1(1). This explains the visibility of predefined entities like the type Integer.

Projects

1. Implement separate random number generators for each component of the events.
2. Use the array implementation of the priority queue instead of the tree implementation.
3. Implement the function

   ```
   function Get(Q: Queue_Ptr) return Event'Class;
   ```

   using an extended return statement.

Quizzes

Quiz 1:

```
package P is
  type T1 is tagged
    record I: Integer := 0; end record;
  type T2 is new T1 with
    record N: Integer := 0; end record;
end P;

with P; use P;
procedure Main is
  A: T2'Class := (I => 2, N => 4);
begin
  null;
end Main;
```

Quiz 2:

```
package P is
  type T1 is tagged
    record I: Integer := 0; end record;
  function "="(Left, Right: T1) return Boolean;
  type T2 is new T1 with
    record N: Integer := 0; end record;
end P;

package body P is
  function "="(Left, Right: T1) return Boolean is
  begin
    return abs(Left.I-Right.I) < 2;
  end "=";
end P;

with P; use P;
procedure Main is
  A: T2 := (I => 2, N => 4);    B: T2 := (I => 3, N => 4);
  C: T2 := (I => 3, N => 4);    D: T2 := (I => 3, N => 5);
begin
  Put_Line(Boolean'Image(A = B));
  Put_Line(Boolean'Image(C = D));
end Main;
```

Quiz 3:

```
type T is new Integer;
function "="(Left, Right: T) return Boolean is
begin
  return Integer(Left) /= Integer(Right);
end "=";

type Vector is array(1..2) of T;
A: Vector := (1, 2);
B: Vector := (3, 4);

Put_Line(Boolean'Image(A(1) = B(1)));
Put_Line(Boolean'Image(A = B));
```

Quiz 4:

```
package P is
  type T is private;
private
  type Ptr is access T'Class;
  type T is tagged
    record
      Next: Ptr;
    end record;
end P;
```

Chapter 8
Type Extension and Inheritance (Continued)

8.1 Designated receiver syntax

In most languages that support object-oriented programming, the syntax for invoking methods (subprograms) is designed so that there is a *designated receiver*, that is, an *object* that is the "receiver" of the method:

```
event.simulate();
```

Within the method, the designated receiver is an implicit parameter that is known by a special name (usually, **this**). Distinguished receiver syntax is also supported in Ada:

rocketp

```
with Event_Queue;
procedure Rocket is
  Q: Event_Queue.Queue_Ptr := new Event_Queue.Queue;
  procedure Create(Q: in Event_Queue.Queue_Ptr) is separate;
begin
  Create(Q);
  while not Event_Queue.Empty(Q.all) loop
    Event_Queue.Get(Q).Simulate;
  end loop;
end Rocket;
```

`Event_Queue.Get(Q).Simulate` denotes a *prefixed view* §4.1.3(9.1–9.2). The prefix must be of a specific or class-wide tagged type; in this case, `Event_Queue.Get(Q)` is of type `Event'Class`. The selector must denote a primitive or class-wide operation for the tagged type whose *first* parameter is of this type; here, `Simulate` is a primitive operation of the tagged type `Event` whose first parameter is of this type. The value returned by the call to `Event_Queue.Get(Q)` becomes the implicit first (and only) parameter in the (dispatching) call to `Simulate` §6.4(10.1).

Within the subprogram, there is no need for a special name for the implicit parameter, because it has an explicit declaration with the formal parameter name E:

```
procedure Simulate(E: in Event) is abstract;
```

The distinguished receiver syntax is not just syntactic sugar; recall that the other syntax required a with_clause for Root_Event:

```
Root_Event.Simulate(Event_Queue.Get(Q));
```

This is no longer required. The main subprogram has been modified to move the creation of the events to a subunit ‡4 (Section 15.3), so we can remove the context clauses that mentioned them. The source code of the main subprogram is no longer dependent on the precise nature of the events, and can be re-used without modification as a framework for simulation of events of a totally different nature.

Ada 95

The designated receiver syntax does not exist in Ada 95.

> **Language Comparison**
>
> The designated receiver syntax is the only syntax for invoking methods in Java and many other languages for OOP. The advantage has just been discussed. One advantage of the normal subprogram call in Ada is that you can supply your own (meaningful) name for the formal parameter. Another advantage is that multiple controlling operands (Section 8.9) can be used to dispatch to binary operators. In Java this cannot be done, while in C++ the **friend** construct must be used.

8.2 Type conversion

A value of a type in a derivation class can be converted to a value of another type in the class subject to the following rule:

§4.6

> 21 If there is a type that is an ancestor of both the target type and the operand type, or both types are class-wide types, then at least one of the following rules shall apply:
> 22 • The operand type shall be covered by or descended from the target type; or
> 23 • The operand type shall be a class-wide type that covers the target type; or

Cover is defined as follows:

§3.4.1

> 9 A class-wide or universal type is said to *cover* all of the types in its class. A specific type covers only itself.

A value of type Aux_Engine_Event can be converted to a value of type Engine_Event or to a value of type Event, since Aux_Engine_Event is descended from those types §4.6(22). The effect is simply to ignore the extra components that were added during the type derivation. By the same clause, a value of type Aux_Engine_Event can be converted to Engine_Event'Class or Event'Class which cover Aux_Engine_Event, as explained in Section 8.8. However, we cannot convert a value of type Engine_Event to Aux_Engine_Event or to Aux_Engine_Event'Class, because it has no Side component that is part of every value of these types. This can be expressed by saying that it is permissible to convert *up*, but not *down*, the hierarchy of the derivation class, as shown in Figure 7.1.

Consider now converting a class-wide type to a specific type that it covers §4.6(23):

```
EV_CL: Event'Class  := ...;
Eng:   Engine_Event := Engine_Event(EV_CL);
```

EV_CL contains a value of some specific type within Event'Class. If we are "lucky" and the value of E_CL is in fact of type Engine_Event (or Main_Engine_Event or Aux_Engine_Event), the conversion will succeed; otherwise, the conversion will fail and raise Constraint_Error §4.6(42). Do not do such a conversion unless you know that the conversion will succeed; for example, a membership test §4.5.2(30) can be used to check the type before performing the conversion:

```
if EV_CL in Engine_Event'Class then
  Eng := Engine_Event(EV_CL);          -- OK
else
  -- Do something else
end if;
```

8.3 Extension aggregates

Though a value of a parent type cannot be converted to a value of a type derived from it, it is possible to create a value of the derived type by supplying the additional components that are "missing" from the parent type:

§4.3.2

> 1 An extension_aggregate specifies a value for a type that is a record extension by specifying a value or subtype for an ancestor of the type, followed by associations for any components not determined by the ancestor_part.
>
> 2 extension_aggregate ::=
> (ancestor_part **with** record_component_association_list)
> 3 ancestor_part ::= expression | subtype_mark
>
> 6 For the record_component_association_list of an extension_aggregate, the only components *needed* are those of the composite value defined by the aggregate that are not inherited from the type of the ancestor_part, ...

An extension aggregate was used to create a value of type `Aux_Engine_Event`:

```
return (Engine_Event'(Create)
   with Aux_Engine_ID'Val(Random_Time.Random(G) mod 2));
```

The ancestor_part of the aggregate is the expression `Engine_Event'(Create)` that returns a value of the ancestor type `Event_Event`; this is followed by an association that gives a value for the component `Side` that was added during the derivation.

A value of type `Main_Engine_Event` adds no components to the parent value; nevertheless, a null record association must be given §4.3.2(9):

```
return (Engine_Event'(Create) with null record);
```

An extension aggregate built from a subtype_mark is intended to be used when the ancestor type is abstract. For example, an extension aggregate for `Engine` can be written:

```
return (Event with
          Fuel   => Random_Time.Random(G) mod 100,
          Oxygen => Random_Time.Random(G) mod 500);
```

Since `Event` is abstract, a value of the type cannot be created; instead, the subtype_mark is used to indicate that the default values of the ancestor type should be used.

§4.3.2

> 7 ... if the ancestor_part is a subtype_mark, the components of the value of the aggregate not given by the record_component_association_list are initialized by default as for an object of the ancestor type.

In the case study, the declaration of `Event` should have contained a meaningful default value for the component `Simulation_Time`:

```
Time: Simulation_Time := 0;
```

8.4 Abstract types

We will now explain abstract types and subprograms in more detail. The specification of the package `Root_Event` is repeated here for convenience:

rocket

```
package Root_Event is
  type Event is abstract tagged private;

  function  Create return Event is abstract;
  procedure Simulate(E: in Event) is abstract;

  function "<"(Left, Right: Event'Class) return Boolean;
private
  subtype Simulation_Time is Integer range 0..10_000;
  type Event is abstract tagged
    record
      Time: Simulation_Time;   --  Common component of all events
    end record;
end Root_Event;
```

The abstract type `Event` serves as the ancestor of all the event types. Promoting one of the actual event types to be the parent of all the other types would be arbitrary and inappropriate, so we declare an abstract event type, even though objects of this type are meaningless. In the simulation program, the abstract type `Root_Event.Event` is a convenient place to declare the common component `Time`. Frequently, an abstract type is declared as a null record.

The abstract primitive subprograms serve as ancestors of the concrete primitive subprograms that will be declared upon derivation.

§3.9.3

> 1 An *abstract type* is a tagged type intended for use as an ancestor of other type, but which is not allowed to have objects of its own. An *abstract subprogram* is a subprogram that has no body, but is intended to be overridden at some point when inherited. Because objects of an abstract type cannot be created, a dispatching call to an abstract subprogram always dispatches to some overriding body.

The call to `Root_Event.Simulate` is an example of the last sentence of the above clause (which is more formally stated in §3.9.3(7)).

The property of being an abstract (primitive) subprogram can be inherited by other abstract types; however, once a non-abstract type is declared, a nonabstract subprogram must be declared §3.9.3(4–6). For example, it would have been a good idea to declare `Engine_Event` as abstract, because any concrete engine is either a main engine or an auxiliary engine:

```
type Engine_Event is abstract new Event with private;
function Create return Engine_Event;          -- Not abstract
-- Abstract procedure Simulate is inherited from abstract type Event
```

Now that Engine_Event is abstract, `Simulate` *requires overriding* §3.9.3(6) for the concrete types:

```
type Main_Engine_Event is new Engine_Event with private;
function Create return Main_Engine_Event;
procedure Simulate(E: in Main_Engine_Event);

type Aux_Engine_Event is new Engine_Event with private;
function Create return Aux_Engine_Event;
procedure Simulate(E: in Aux_Engine_Event);
```

An abstract type is like an indefinite type in that objects of the type cannot be declared; see §3.9.3(8) for the full list of restrictions on abstract types. However:

§3.9.3

> 13 A class-wide type is never abstract. Even if a class is rooted at an abstract type, the class-wide type for the class is not abstract, and an object of the class-wide type can be created; the tag of such an object will identify some nonabstract type in the class.

As shown in the examples in the following sections, there is no problem declaring a variable of type `Event'Class`, even though `Event` is an abstract type.

Interface types (Chapter 17) are also abstract types §3.9.3(1.2).

8.5 Null procedures

Whenever an abstract subprogram is declared for an abstract tagged type, it must be overridden in all nonabstract types that extend it §3.9.3(6). It may happen, however, that only a few of the derived types require that the subprogram actual perform a computation. To save writing empty subprograms, a *null procedure*—equivalent to a procedure whose only statement is **`null`**—can be used instead. The null procedure can be inherited without overriding, but if it is called nothing happens.

Let us add a null procedure `Start` as a primitive subprogram for type `Event`:

rocketp

```
type Event is abstract tagged private;
procedure Start(E: in out Event) is null;
```

and encapsulate the creation of events on the queue in a subunit (Section 8.1):

```
with Root_Event.Engine, Root_Event.Telemetry, Root_Event.Steering;
use Root_Event;
separate(Rocket)
procedure Create(Q: in Event_Queue.Queue_Ptr) is
  procedure Create_Event(E: in Event'Class) is
    Ev: Event'Class := E;
  begin
    Ev.Start;
    Event_Queue.Put(Ev, Q.all);
  end Create_Event;
begin
  for I in 1..15 loop
    Create_Event(Engine.Main_Engine_Event'(Engine.Create));
    Create_Event(Engine.Aux_Engine_Event'(Engine.Create));
    Create_Event(Telemetry.Create);
    Create_Event(Steering.Create);
  end loop;
end Create;
```

(The formal parameter of `Start` is of mode **in out**, so its actual parameter must be a variable—here, `Ev`—not a constant like the parameter `E` of mode **in**.)

The subprogram `Start` is invoked for every event before it is put on the event queue. It matters not at all whether the subprogram was ever overridden in any of the specific types derived from `Event`. In the full program in the software archive, the subprogram has, in fact, been implemented for `Engine_Event` and inherited by `Main_Engine_Event` and `Aux_Engine_Event`; for `Steering_Event` and `Telemetry_Event`, the null procedure is called.

Ada 95

Null procedures do not exist in Ada 95, so abstract subprograms must be explicitly overridden for concrete types.

Language Comparison

Java uses *adapter* classes for this purpose. For example, there are three listener interfaces that contain methods that are invoked when mouse events occur (`MouseListener`, `MouseWheelListener`, `MouseMotionListener`); together they define nine methods. The class `MouseAdapter` declares empty methods that implement the methods declared in these interfaces, so only those methods that need to be overridden must be written.

8.6 Overriding indicators

You have just returned from a heavy lunch and decide to extend the type:

```
type Engine_Event is new Event with private;
procedure Simulate(E: in Engine_Event);
```

but, by mistake, you write `Simulates` instead of `Simulate`:

```
type Center_Engine_Event is new Engine_Event with private;
procedure Simulates(E: in Center_Engine_Event);
```

What happens? The procedure `Simulates` is simply a *new* (primitive) subprogram for the derived type. Any dispatching call to `Simulate` with an object of type `Center_Engine_Event` will invoke the subprogram that was *inherited* from `Engine_Event`. Such a bug will be difficult to diagnose because you will look at `Simulates` and see what you want to see: `Simulate`.

Overriding indicators §8.3.1 can be used to make this a simple compile-time error. Add the reserved word **overriding** in front of a subprogram:

```
type Engine_Event is new Event with private;
overriding
procedure Simulate(E: in Engine_Event);

type Center_Engine_Event is new Engine_Event with private;
overriding
procedure Simulates(E: in Center_Engine_Event);
```

The above declaration of `Simulates` is now a compilation error, because the compiler can diagnose that `Simulates` does not actually override any primitive subprogram.

A similar situation can occur if the number or types of the parameters change:

```
procedure Simulate(E: in String);
```

This subprogram—a non-primitive one—will simply overload the inherited subprogram. There is an indicator **not overriding** for situations where overloading, rather than overriding of a primitive subprogram, is intended:

```
not overriding
procedure Simulate(E: in String);
```

If, by accident, you write `Center_Engine_Event` instead of `String` as the type of the formal parameter, a compilation error will result, because the subprogram *is* overriding.

Overriding indicators can also be used on the instantiation of a generic subprogram §12.3(2) (Section 9.4).

Ada 95

Overriding indicators do not exist in Ada 95.

8.7 Objects of class-wide type

Why didn't we use a procedure for Event_Queue.Get?

```
procedure Get(E: out Event'Class; Q: in Queue_Ptr);
```

The type of the first formal parameter is a class-wide type and all such types are indefinite; however, the actual parameter for an **out** parameter must be a variable and the variable will contain an object with some tag. Any attempt to assign to this variable a value with some other tag will raise the exception Constraint_Error:

```
EV_CL: Event'Class := Engine_Event'(100, 4102, 5335);

Get(EV_CL, Q);  -- Suppose a Telemetry_Event is removed from the queue
```

With a function there is no problem, because when a function returns an object it allocates storage for the object. This object can then be used in an expression, for example, as an actual parameter of a dispatching subprogram call.

As with any other indefinite type, one way to create a class-wide *object* that can have values of different types within the class is to make it a formal parameter of a subprogram. The formal parameter is elaborated anew in each call and the constraint is taken from the actual parameter:

```
procedure Do_Simulation(EV_CL: in Event'Class) is
begin
  Root_Event.Simulate(EV_CL);
  Write_Event_to_Log(EV_CL);
end Do_Simulation;

while not Event_Queue.Empty(Q.all) loop
  Do_Simulation(Event_Queue.Get(Q));
end loop;
```

Alternatively, you can use a block statement:

```
while not Event_Queue.Empty(Q.all) loop
  declare
    EV_CL: Event'Class := Event_Queue.Get(Q);
  begin
    Root_Event.Simulate(EV_CL);
    Write_Event_to_Log(EV_CL);
  end;
end loop;
```

In each iteration of the loop, EV_CL is allocated and initialized with the object returned from Event_Queue.Get(Q). This object is discarded when leaving the block, just as local variables are discarded when leaving a subprogram. See Section 8.10 for another example of this technique.

8.8 View conversion and redispatching*

Type conversion of tagged types is quite different from what you normally think of as type conversion. A new value is *not* created; instead, you get a new *view* of the original value which hides components that are not part of the target type.

§4.6

> 5 A type_conversion whose operand is the name of an object is called a *view conversion* if both its target type and operand type are tagged, or if it appears in a call as an actual parameter of mode **out** or **in out**; other type_conversions are called *value conversions*.
> 42 • The tag of the result is the tag of the operand. ...
> 55 • If the target type is tagged, then an assignment to the view assigns to the corresponding part of the object denoted by the operand; ...

Since neither the tag §4.6(42) nor the value of the operand is changed by the conversion, you can always recover the original value and type.

During an assignment, both the source and the target objects retain their tags, and only the relevant components are copied:

```
E: Engine_Event     := ...;    -- Tagged as Engine_Event
A: Aux_Engine_Event := ...;    -- Tagged as Aux_Engine_Event

E := Engine_Event(A);          -- Side component ignored
Engine_Event(A) := E;          -- Side component not assigned to
```

View conversions can be used for *redispatching*. Consider the following tagged type Parent, where the derived type Derived inherits the primitive procedure Proc1 but overrides Proc2:

```
type Parent is tagged ...;
procedure Proc1(V: in Parent);
procedure Proc2(V: in Parent);

type Derived is new Parent with ...;
procedure Proc2(V: in Derived);
```

Suppose that P_CL is a class-wide object containing a value of type Derived:

```
D:    Derived      := ...;
P_CL: Parent'Class := Parent'Class(D);
```

What happens when Proc1(P_CL) is called? The value P_CL of class-wide type will be converted to the specific type Parent of the formal parameter V §4.6(42). However, the conversion is only a view conversion and V remains tagged as Derived. Within Proc1, the following statement will redispatch to the procedure Proc2 that was overridden for type Derived:

```
Proc2(Parent'Class(V));
```

because the tag of the result is taken from the tag of the operand, namely `Derived`. Redispatching works because tagged types are passed by reference §6.2(5), so that within `Proc1` the tag of its actual parameter exists unchanged.

8.9 Multiple controlling operands*

A primitive operation is allowed to have more than one controlling formal parameter. This is particularly useful for dispatching on binary operators:

```
type T is tagged ...;
function "<"(Left: T; Right: T) return Boolean;
```

This operator is primitive since its parameters are of the specific tagged type `T`, unlike the operator "<" in the case study, which had parameters of the class-wide type `Event'Class`.

Suppose now that a class of types `T1`, `T2`, ..., has been derived from `T`. Given two values `X` and `Y` of some types within `T'Class`, what is the meaning of `X < Y`? Clearly, if both `X` and `Y` are of the same specific type:

```
X: T2 := ...;
Y: T2 := ...;
```

the compiler binds to the function declared for the type, either the inherited function or an overriding function. It is equally obvious that if `X` and `Y` are of different specific types:

```
X: T1 := ...;
Y: T3 := ...;
```

no appropriate function exists. However, what happens if either `X` or `Y`, or both, are of the class-wide type `T'Class`?

§3.9.2

> 16 ... If there is more than one dynamically tagged controlling operand, a check is made that they all have the same tag. If this check fails, Constraint_Error is raised ...

Given the declarations:

```
X:  T'Class := T3'(...);
Y:  T'Class := T3'(...);
Z:  T'Class := T4'(...);
```

`X < Y` dispatches to the operation for `T3`, while `X < Z` raises `Constraint_Error`. You can compare the tags of values of class-wide type §3.9(17–18) before calling the operation:

```
if X'Tag = Z'Tag then
  if X < Z then ...      -- OK, dispatch!
  else ...
  end if;
else ...                 -- Different types, do something else
end if;
```

Since we are only comparing tags for equality and not asking if a value of class-wide type has a specific tag, the statement need not be modified if additional derivations are done.

Suppose, now, that one operand is of a specific type and one is of class-wide type:

```
V:  T3      := T3'(...);
W:  T'Class := T3'(...);
```

The expression `V < W` is illegal:

§3.9.2

> 8 A call on a dispatching operation shall not have both dynamically tagged and statically tagged controlling operands.

There is a special rule concerning the inheritance of the equality operator; see Quiz 2.

8.10 Dispatching on the function result*

So far, we have used expanded names and qualified expressions to indicate to the compiler which version of `Create` to call; no dispatching is required:

```
Event_Queue.Put(Engine.Aux_Engine_Event'(Engine.Create), Q.all);
Event_Queue.Put(Telemetry.Create,                        Q.all);
```

However, a call to a primitive function can be a *controlling operand* of a dispatching call.

§3.9.2

> 2 ... If the call is to a (primitive) function with result type *T*, then the call has a *controlling result* — the context of the call can control the dispatching. ...

Such a function call is called *tag indeterminate* §3.9.2(3,6); a tag-indeterminate operand is legal only if there is sufficient *context* to determine which function to call. In a call `Simulate(Create)`, there is not enough context to dispatch `Create` because there are several procedures `Simulate` for the different types in the class.

To demonstrate dispatching on the function results, let us modify the rocket simulation so that whenever an event is removed from the queue, a *new* event of the *same* type is inserted into the queue. This can be done by dispatching `Create` using a technique that we now describe. We declare a primitive subprogram `Another` with two controlling parameters, `Original` and `Copy`:

rocketf

```
package Root_Event is
  type Event is abstract tagged private;

  function  Create return Event is abstract;
  procedure Simulate(E: in Event) is abstract;
  function Another(Original: Event; Copy: Event) return Event'Class;
  function "<"(Left, Right: Event'Class) return Boolean;
private
  ...
end Root_Event;
```

Next, we modify the main loop of the simulation to call the function Another with two parameters: First, which is dynamically tagged of class-wide type, and Root_Event.Create, which is a tag-indeterminate function call:

```
  loop
    declare
      First:  Event'Class := Event_Queue.Get(Q);
      Second: Event'Class := Another(First, Root_Event.Create);
    begin
      Event_Queue.Put(Second, Q.all);
      Root_Event.Simulate(First);
    end;
  end loop;
```

There is now sufficient context to disambiguate the call to Create: since all dynamically tagged controlling operands (including calls to functions with controlling results §3.9.2(5)) must have the same tag, Create is dynamically dispatched to the version appropriate for the specific type contained in First.

The function Another is just a framework for this dispatching. All it does is convert the second parameter to the class-wide type; the first parameter is not used:

```
  function Another(Original: Event; Copy: Event) return Event'Class is
  begin
    return Event'Class(Copy);
  end Another;
```

A tag indeterminate operand is statically bound if all other parameters are statically bound:

```
T: Telemetry_Event;
E: Event'Class := Another(T, Create); -- Bound to Telemetry.Create
```

Dispatching on a function call can also occur in the default expression for a controlling formal parameter §3.9.2(11), in an assignment statement §5.2(9), and in enclosing tag-indeterminate calls §3.9.2(6). A program in the software archive demonstrates these features.

8.11 Indirect derivation*

The full and partial views of extensions need not be derived from the same tagged type. The full view of a private extension can be *indirectly* derived from any ancestor of the type §7.3(8). In the following specification, the partial view of `Main_Engine_Event` is derived *directly* from `Event`, while the full view is derived directly from `Engine_Event` and only indirectly from `Event`:

```
package Root_Event.Engine is
  type Engine_Event      is new Event with private;
  type Main_Engine_Event is new Event with private;
private
  type Engine_Event      is new Event with ...
  type Main_Engine_Event is new Engine_Event with ...;
end Root_Event.Engine;
```

8.12 Freezing*

Can we rearrange the declarations in `Event_Package` so that all the type derivations are declared before the primitive operations?

```
package Event_Package is
  type Event             is abstract tagged ...
  type Engine_Event      is new Event with ...
  type Main_Engine_Event is new Engine_Event with ...
  type Steering_Event    is new Event with ...
  type Telemetry_Event   is new Event with ...
  procedure Simulate(E:  in Event) is abstract;
  procedure Simulate(E:  in Engine_Event);
  procedure Simulate(E:  in Aux_Engine_Event);
  procedure Simulate(E:  in Steering_Event);
  procedure Simulate(E:  in Telemetry_Event);
end Event_Package;
```

The answer is no. As discussed in the next section, the implemention of dispatching calls requires that the entire set of primitive operations for a type be known when the type is extended.

It follows that the declarations of primitive operations must be "close to" the declaration of the tagged type or extension. The rule is expressed in terms of a concept called *freezing* §13.14:

§13.14

> 7 The declaration of a record extension causes freezing of the parent subtype.
> 16 The explicit declaration of a primitive subprogram of a tagged type shall occur before the type is frozen (see 3.9.2).

See §13.14 for the complete set of constructs that cause freezing.

8.13 Implementation of dispatching*

This book presents the Ada language as seen by a programmer, not the implementation techniques used in the compiler and run-time system. Nevertheless, an outline of a possible implementation of dynamic dispatching will enable you to understand the run-time overhead that is incurred. The following diagram shows a data structure that can be used to implement dispatching:

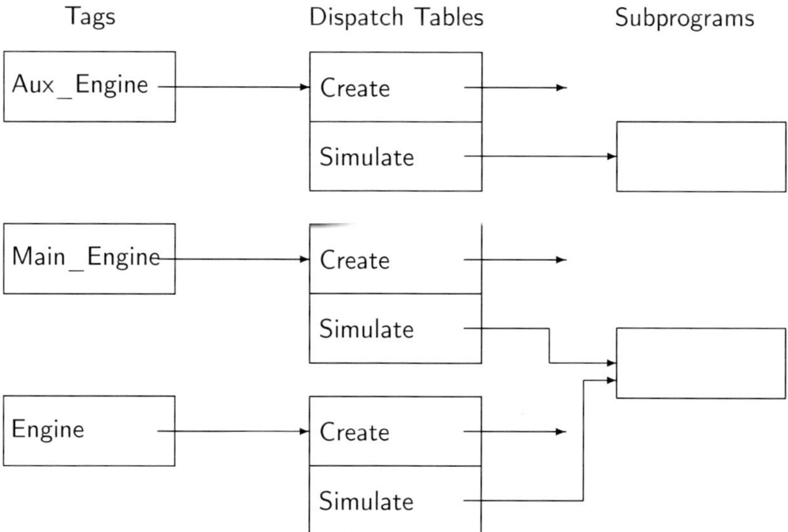

Dispatch tables for each specific type are created by the compiler and loaded at run-time. (To save space, some subprograms and the dispatch tables for `Telemetry` and `Steering` have been omitted.) Each object has a tag for its specific type; the tag is a pointer to the dispatch table for that type. When a dispatching call is made, the pointer is used to obtain the address of the dispatch table corresponding to the specific type of the controlling operands. The table contains a pointer to each primitive subprogram, and an indirect call on this pointer calls the subprogram. Since `Main_Engine_Event` inherits `Simulate` from `Engine_Event`, a new procedure is not created for the derived type; instead, the dispatch table pointer for `Main_Engine.Simulate` is directed to the procedure already declared for the parent type `Engine_Event`.

The implementation outlined in the diagram shows that the run-time overhead of dispatching is *small* and, more importantly, *fixed*. A few machine instructions will suffice for doing the indirect call to the subprogram, and for any processor and compiler the overhead can be computed or measured. *All* dispatching calls will have exactly this overhead, so there is no uncertainty that would prevent the use of dispatching in a real-time system.

Once a tagged type or extension is declared, additional derived descendants can be declared without recompiling the package specification that declares the ancestor. Each additional derivation will add a new dispatch table, and the code for any primitive subprograms overridden or added upon derivation. Existing tags and dispatch tables are not affected.

This explains why primitive subprograms must be declared in the package specification. A basic design principle of Ada is that clients of a package can be developed once the specification is written; the source code of clients is to be independent of the package body (unless there are generics or inlined subprograms). By forbidding the declaration of primitive subprograms outside the specification containing the tagged type definition, the dispatch table can be created during the compilation of the specification.

An additional requirement is that a derivation can only add primitive operations, not remove them, and that any operation that is not overridden is inherited. If a primitive operation `Proc` is defined for a tagged type `T`, then `Proc` will also be defined for any type in the derivation class; therefore, no run-time check is needed for a dispatching call of `Proc` with an operand of type `T'Class`.

Projects

1. Add overriding indicators to the rocket simulation.
2. Implement the rocket simulation with `Write_Event_to_Log` as outlined in Section 8.7.
3. Restructure the rocket simulation so that `Telemetry_Event` is derived from `Root_Event` and all other events are derived from `Telemetry_Event`. There will be a primitive subprogram `Format_Event` of type `Telemetry_Event` that will be overridden by each of the other event types to construct a string for each call of `Create` and `Simulate`; these strings will then be sent by the telemetry subsystem.

Quizzes

Quiz 1:

```
package P is
  type T1 is tagged null record;
  procedure Proc1(X: in out T1);
  type T2 is new T1 with null record;
  procedure Proc1(X: in out T2);
  procedure Proc2(X: in out T1);
end P;
```

Quiz 2:

```
package P is
  type Parent is tagged record N: Integer; end record;
  type Derived is new Parent with record M: Integer;
end record;
end P;

with P; use P;
with Ada.Integer_Text_IO; use Ada.Integer_Text_IO;
procedure Main is
  P: Parent := (N=>1);
  D: Derived := (N=>2, M=>3);
begin
  Parent(D) := P;
  Put(D.N);
  Put(D.M);
end Main;
```

Quiz 3:

```
package P is
  type T1 is tagged
    record I: Integer; end record;
  function F return T1;
  type T2 is new T1 with
    record N: Integer; end record;
end P;
```

Quiz 4:

```
package P is
  type T1 is tagged
    record
      N: Integer;
    end record;
  procedure Proc2(X: T1 := (N=>1));
end P;
```

Quiz 5:

```
package P is
  type T1 is tagged
    record
      N: Integer;
    end record;
  procedure Proc1(X: T1);
  Empty: constant T1;
  procedure Proc2(X: T1);
private
  Empty: constant T1 := (N => 1);
end P;
```

Chapter 9
Generics

In Chapter 5 we developed a priority queue abstract data type and showed how to change the implementation of the queue from an array to a tree without changing the client interface supplied by the package specification. However, that data structure was specialized for elements of type `Integer`, so when a priority queue was needed in Chapter 7 for elements of type `Event`, a new package was written.

Generic units enable the parameterization of data structures and algorithms by parameterizing packages and subprograms. A generic unit is a *template* from which *instances* can be created at *compile-time* by supplying actual parameters, which can be types, subprograms or even other generic units. The creation of an instance—called *instantiation*—is done at compile time. The compiler enforces type checking on the generic unit, and verifies that the actual parameters used in the instantiation match the formal parameters of the generic unit.

Generics are an alternative to heterogenous types that were discussed in the previous chapter. There are two drawbacks to heterogenous types: (a) additional overhead is required because indirect allocation must be used, and (b) a potentially dangerous type conversion must be done on all elements retrieved from the data structure.

This chapter presents generic units in Ada except for generic tagged and interface types, which are discussed separately in Chapter 17 on multiple inheritance.

Language Comparison

C++ supports *templates*, which are similar to Ada generics, although explicit instantiation is not supported, so every occurrence of a type must be written in the form `Priority_Queue<Event>`; this makes it difficult to read the source code. There is no contract model in C++, so the entire instance must be checked for legality. In Ada, most error messages will result from the actual parameters supplied in the instantiation not matching the formal parameters. In C++, error messages will refer the source code of the template, making it difficult to treat the template as an abstraction.

> **Language Comparison**
>
> Java supports heterogenous data structures, based upon defining every type to be an extension of a root type `Object`. Starting with Java 5, generics are supported in a manner similar to that of C++, but the generic parameters in Java can only be classes, not primitive types, arrays or other constructs, as in Ada.

9.1 Generic declaration and instantiation

A generic declaration declares a generic package or subprogram. Syntactically, a generic specification is a specification preceded by a *generic formal part*:

§12.1

> 4 generic_package_declaration ::= generic_formal_part package_specification;
> 5 generic_formal_part ::= **generic** {generic_formal_parameter_declaration | use_clause}

use_clauses can be helpful when there are many formal parameters that depend on the context clause or on a previous generic formal package parameter (Section 9.8).

9.1.1 Case study: generic priority queue

Here is a generic version of the specification of the package `Priority_Queue`:

pqgen

```
generic
   type Item is private;
   with function "<"(Left, Right: Item) return Boolean is <>;
package Priority_Queue is
   type Queue(Size: Positive) is limited private;
   function  Empty(Q:  in Queue) return Boolean;
   procedure Put(I: in Item; Q: in out Queue);
   procedure Get(I: out Item; Q: in out Queue);
   Overflow, Underflow: exception;
private
   -- as before except for the substitution of Item for Integer
end Priority_Queue;
```

The generic formal part is explained below. The package specification is unchanged except for the substitution of the generic formal parameter `Item` for `Integer`, and similarly for the generic body:

```
package body Priority_Queue is
  -- as before except for the subsitution of Item for Integer
end Priority_Queue;
```

§12.2

> 1 The body of a generic unit (a *generic body*) is a template for the instance bodies. The syntax of a generic body is identical to that of a nongeneric body.

The generic package can be compiled although this simply checks the legality of the code.

§12.3

> 12 A generic_instantiation declares an instance; it is equivalent to the instance declaration (a package_declaration or subprogram_declaration) immediately followed by the instance body, both at the place of the instantiation.
>
> 13 The instance is a copy of the text of the template. Each use of a formal parameter becomes (in the copy) a use of the actual, as explained below. An instance of a generic package is a package, that of a generic procedure is a procedure, and that of a generic function is a function.

Here is the outline of the main program (the complete program is in the software archive):

```
with Priority_Queue;
...
procedure PQGEN is
  package Integer_Queue is new Priority_Queue(Item => Integer);
  package Float_Queue   is new Priority_Queue(Item => Float);
  QI: Integer_Queue.Queue(10);
  QF: Float_Queue.Queue(10);
begin
    Integer_Queue.Put(Integer_Test_Data(N), QI);
    Float_Queue.Put(Float_Test_Data(N), QF);
    Integer_Queue.Get(I, QI);
    Float_Queue.Get(F, QF);
exception
  when Integer_Queue.Underflow | Float_Queue.Underflow =>  ...
end PQGEN;
```

The program instantiates `Priority_Queue` twice, once with `Integer` and once with `Float`. (The syntax of instantiations in given in §12.3(2–5).) As for any other library unit, a with_clause must be given for the generic package. The instances are normal packages and the entities declared in the visible part of the package can be accessed by using expanded names or use_clauses and direct names.

9.2 The contract model

Suppose that we try to instantiate the generic package Priority_Queue with the record:

```
type Point is
  record
    X: Float;
    Y: Float;
  end record;
```

as the generic actual parameter:

```
package Point_Queue is new Priority_Queue(Item => Point);
```

Since the package body of the instantiation Point_Queue is a copy of the text of the template with Point is substituted for Item, the body effectively includes the subprogram:

```
procedure Put(I: in Point; Node_Ptr: in out Link) is
begin
  if Node_Ptr = null then
    Node_Ptr := new Node'(I, null, null);
  elsif I < Node_Ptr.Data then
    Put(I, Node_Ptr.Left);
  else
    Put(I, Node_Ptr.Right);
  end if;
end Put;
```

Unfortunately, the program is now illegal: the expression I < Node_Ptr.Data is illegal since the operator "<" is not defined on the type Point.

It would be preferable if this error were discovered *before* compilation of the *body* in the instantiation. The whole point of separating the package specification from the body is to ensure that errors in the use of the package by clients are diagnosed from the declarations in the specification. The *contract model* in Ada has been designed to eliminate the problem with generic units. The idea is that the generic formal parameters contain sufficient information so that:[1]

- The generic unit can be compiled, that is, checked for legality.

---

[1] This explanation of the contract model is only approximate (see Section 9.10).

- The compilation of the instantiation may fail if the generic actual parameters do not match the generic formal parameters, but no other errors will occur in the instantiation. In particular, the body of the instance is semantically legal if the generic unit is legal and the generic contract is obeyed by the actuals.

Generic formal parameters form a contract between the programmer writing the generic unit and the programmers using the unit. The contract model is illustrated in the following diagram:

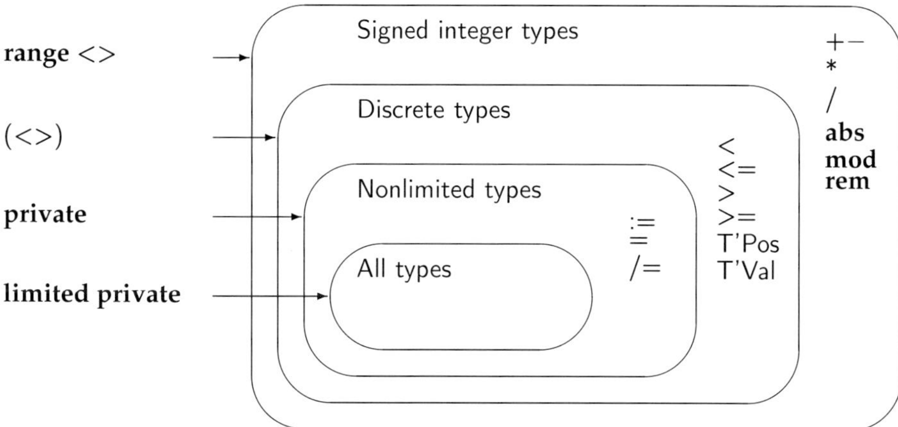

A generic *formal* parameter declaration (left side of the figure) specifies a *category of types*. The generic unit is allowed to use *at most* the operations common to all types in the category. The generic *actual* parameter must be a type which supplies *at least* those operations.

For example, if the generic formal parameter is declared **private**, the generic unit is allowed to create objects of the type, to perform assignments and to use the equality and inequality operators. In an instantiation, the generic actual parameter can be any nonlimited type. The actual parameter may, of course, be the type `Integer`, which also supplies operations like addition, but the generic unit is not allowed to use such operations, only those operations that are common to *all* types in the category of nonlimited types.

Similarly, if the formal parameter `Item` is in the category denoted by `(<>)`—the category of all discrete types—the generic unit could contain the statement:

```
for N in Item'Range loop
```

because any discrete type can be used as the type of a loop parameter. We could instantiate the unit with `Character` or `Cars` or even `Integer`, but not with `Point`.

Categories of types do not always form a simple inclusion hierarchy as implied by diagram; for example, floating point operations are neither a superset nor a subset of integer operations, so they have distinct formal parameter declarations, and a generic floating point formal parameter cannot be associated with an actual parameter of type `Integer`.

The generic formal parameters for scalar types are as follows:

§12.5.2

> 1 A *formal scalar type* is one defined by any of the formal_type_definitions in this subclause. The category determined for a formal scalar type is the category of all discrete, signed integer, modular, floating point, ordinary fixed point, or decimal types.
>
> 2 formal_discrete_type_definition ::= (<>)
> 3 formal_signed_integer_type_definition ::= **range** <>
> 4 formal_modular_type_definition ::= **mod** <>
> 5 formal_floating_point_definition ::= **digits** <>
> 6 formal_ordinary_fixed_point_definition ::= **delta** <>
> 7 formal_decimal_fixed_point_definition ::= **delta** <> **digits** <>

Do not try to read too much into the syntax of generic formal parameters like `(<>)`. Familiar reserved words and symbols are reused in a manner that hints at the semantics, but you must learn the exact meaning of each construct.

Let us return to the problem of the priority queue. One possibility would be to declare the generic formal parameter `Item` to be of the category discrete:

```
generic
   type Item is (<>);
```

This would allow us to instantiate the package for any discrete type such as `Character` or `Integer`. The package would compile correctly, because "<" is predefined for every discrete type. However, it would not allow us to create a priority queue of floating point values; although "<" is predefined for floating point types, they are not in the category of discrete types. Nor would it allow us to create a priority queue of objects of type `Point` or `Event`, even assuming that "<" were defined (though not predefined) for the type. What is needed is a way of supplying a generic actual function that will be substituted for "<", and this can be done using generic subprogram parameters.

9.3 Generic formal subprogram parameters

A *generic formal subprogram parameter* declares a subprogram that can be invoked within the generic unit. An instantiation must supply as an actual parameter a matching subprogram that will be called by the instance. A generalized generic priority queue package can obtained by declaring the type `Item` as **`private`** so that a queue can be instantiated for any nonlimited type, together with a *generic formal function* for the less-than operator:

```
generic
  type Item is private;
  with function "<"(Left, Right: Item) return Boolean is <>;
package Priority_Queue is ...
```

The reserved word **with** is reused here as a syntactic marker to indicate that the subprogram specification is that of a formal parameter, not of a generic subprogram.

§12.6

> 2.1 formal_concrete_subprogram_declaration ::=
>   **with** subprogram_specification [**is** subprogram_default];
>
> 3 subprogram_default ::= default_name | <> | **null**

The contract requires that the instantiation supply as an actual parameter a subprogram that is mode-conformant with the formal parameter §12.6(8). (See the Glossary for the definition of mode-conformant.)

Let us declare a function that compares two values of type Point:

```
function Less_Than(Left, Right: Point) return Boolean is
begin
  return Left.X < Right.X or (Left.X = Right.X and Left.Y < Right.Y);
end Less_Than;
```

Now the generic priority queue package can be instantiated for type Point:

```
package Point_Queue is new Priority_Queue(Item => Point, "<" => Less_Than);
```

The declaration of the formal subprogram for "<" used a box <> as the default.

§12.6

> 10 If a generic unit has a subprogram_default specified by a box, and the corresponding actual parameter is omitted, then it is equivalent to an explicit actual parameter that is a usage name identical to the defining name of the formal.

This means that if there is a visible conforming function, it will be used by default; for example, "<" for type Float is always visible, so it is sufficient to give a generic actual parameter for Item:

```
package Float_Queue is new Priority_Queue(Float);
```

If the function Less_Than for type Point is declared by overloading the "<" operator, and if this declaration is visible, we do not have to give it explicitly as an actual parameter:

```
type Point is ...
function "<"(Left, Right: Point) return Boolean is ...

package Point_Queue is new Priority_Queue(Item => Point);
```

If the subprogram_default is **null**, there is no need to provide an actual parameter §12.6(10.1); a null procedure (Section 8.5) is provided automatically.

A generic formal subprogram can be declared to be abstract, in which case it must have a parameter of a controlling type and the generic actual parameter must be dispatching on this type; see Section 14.4 for an example.

Ada 95

Ada 95 does not have null or abstract formal subprogram parameters.

9.4 Generic formal array types

The generic formal function "<" has parameters which are of the formal type `Item` that was declared previously in the same generic_formal_part. Dependence of one generic formal parameter on another is common, in particular, when the parameter is of an array type §12.5.3 or an access type §12.5.4. This can be seen in the declaration of the generic procedure for sorting `Ada.Containers.Generic_Array_Sort` §A.18.16(3) from the container library (Chapter 16):

```
generic
  type Index_Type is (<>);
  type Element_Type is private;
  type Array_Type is array (Index_Type range <>) of Element_Type;
  with function "<" (Left, Right : Element_Type) return Boolean is <>;
procedure Ada.Containers.Generic_Array_Sort(Container : in out Array_Type);
```

The generic formal array type `Array_Type` depends on previous formal parameters for both its `Index_Type` and its component type `Element_Type`. The procedure can be instantiated with any discrete type `D` for the index type (as indicated by `(<>)`) and with any nonlimited type `P` for the component type (as indicated by **private**); the actual parameter matching `Array_Type` must be an array whose index type is `D` and whose component type is `P`.

If `Index_Type` had been declared to be a (signed) integer type **range** <>, the implementation of the sort procedure could be as it appears in textbooks:

```
  for I in Container'First .. Container'Last - 1 loop
```

But this cannot be done here, since the generic actual type given for `Index_Type` can be any discrete type, including enumeration types such as `Character` or `Cars`, for which arithmetic operations are not defined. Instead, it is necessary to use the attributes `Pred` and `Succ` that are defined for every discrete type (Section 2.7.3). If you have to do more complicated arithmetic—such as computing the midpoint of a range for Quicksort—you will have to convert the indices to positions and back using the attributes `Pos` and `Val`.

§12.5.3 gives the rules for matching actual array types with formal array types; in particular, both types must be either unconstrained (as in the example) or constrained. If the formal is unconstrained then any object of the type declared in the generic must have *explicit* constraints, so actual must also be unconstrained; the converse applies if the formal is constrained. For this reason, there is a separate generic procedure §A.18.16(7):

```
Ada.Containers.Generic_Constrained_Array_Sort
```

for sorting when the index type is constrained.

9.4.1 *Case study: sorting*

Here is an example of instantiating the sort subprogram from the container library. First the component type and the unconstrained array type are declared:

sort

```
with Ada.Containers.Generic_Array_Sort;
procedure Sort is
  type Point is
    record
      X, Y: Float;
    end record;
  type  Point_Vector is array(Character range <>) of Point;
```

Then, a function for comparing components is declared:

```
  function "<"(Left, Right: Point) return Boolean is
  begin
    return Left.X < Right.X or
      (Left.X = Right.X and Left.Y < Right.Y);
  end "<";
```

Now, the generic subprogram can be instantiated:

```
  procedure Point_Sort is
    new Ada.Containers.Generic_Array_Sort(Character, Point, Point_Vector);
```

and called:

```
  A: Point_Vector := ((10.0,1.0), (4.0,2.0), (5.0,3.4), (10.0,0.5));
begin
  Point_Sort(A);
  -- Print the array A
end Sort;
```

9.5 General access types*

Named and anonymous access types can be given as general formal parameters; the types can be access-to-object or access-to-subprogram. Null exclusions can also be given on generic access types §12.5.4(4).

9.5.1 *Case study: sorting with access types*

We show how to write a generic procedure to sort an array of accesses to objects.

sortacc

```
generic
  type Index  is (<>);
  type Node   is private;
  type Item   is access Node;
  type Vector is array(Index range <>) of Item;
  with function "<"(Left, Right: Item) return Boolean is <>;
procedure SelectionSort(A: in out Vector);
```

The procedure body is written just as it would be for a sort subprogram that does not use access types, because automatic dereferencing is done when a component of an array is read or written. The changes to the main program are shown here:

```
with SelectionSort;
procedure SortAcc is
  type Point        is ...
  type Point_Link   is access Point;
  type Point_Vector is array(Character range <>) of Point_Link;

  function "<"(Left, Right: Point_Link) return Boolean is ...

  procedure Point_Sort is
    new SelectionSort(Character, Point, Point_Link, Point_Vector);

  A: Point_Vector :=
    (new Point'(10.0,1.0),  new Point'(4.0,2.0),
     new Point'(5.0,3.4),   new Point'(10.0,0.5));
begin
  Point_Sort(A);
  -- Print the array A
end SortAcc;
```

9.6 Generic formal objects*

Objects, both constants and variables, can be generic parameters.

§12.4

1 A generic formal object can be used to pass a value or variable to a generic unit.

2 formal_object_declaration ::=
defining_identifier_list : mode [null_exclusion] subtype_mark [:= default_expression];
defining_identifier_list : mode access_definition [:= default_expression];

7 For a generic formal object of mode **in**, the actual shall be an expression. For a generic formal object of mode **in out**, the actual shall be a name that denotes a variable for which renaming is allowed (see 8.5.1).

10 In an instance, a formal_object_declaration of mode **in** is a *full constant declaration* and declares a new stand-alone constant object whose initialization expression is the actual, whereas a formal_object_declaration of mode **in out** declares a view whose properties are identical to those of the actual.

A generic formal object of mode **in** can be used to pass configuration data to a generic unit, while a formal object of mode **in out** might be used to give the unit access to a variable in the unit enclosing the instantiation:

```
generic
  Size:     in     Integer := 100;
  Current:  in out Integer;
package P is
  subtype Name is String(1..Size);
  procedure Increment_State;
end P;

package body P is
  procedure Increment_State is
  begin
    Current := Current + 1;
  end Increment_State;
end P;
```

Note the difference between the use of `Size` as a generic formal object and the use of `Size` as a discriminant of the type `Priority_Queue` in the case study in Section 9.1.1. All objects of type `Name` from a single instantiation of package `P` will have the same `Size`, while we can declare queues of different sizes from a single instantiation of `Priority_Queue`.

9.7 Indefinite type parameters*

Can we instantiate the priority queue package with type Event'Class?

```
package Event_Queue is new Priority_Queue(Event'Class);
```

The answer is no, because the instantiation would declare a record type with components of an indefinite type (here, a class-wide type) and this is illegal:

```
type Node is
   record
     Data: Item;             -- Illegal if Item is Event'Class
     Left, Right: Link;
   end record;
```

To preserve the contract model, it is illegal to use an indefinite type as the actual parameter for a definite generic formal private parameter §12.5.1(6).

A generic priority queue package that will accept items of type Event'Class can be written by changing the body to use indirect allocation as we did in Chapter 7, and then declaring the formal parameter to have unknown discriminants:

rocketq

```
generic
   type Item(<>) is private;
   with function "<"(Left, Right: Item) return Boolean is <>;
package Heterogeneous_Priority_Queue is
   type Item_Ptr is access Item;     -- OK if Item is Event'Class
   type Node is
     record
       Data: Item_Ptr;
       Left, Right: Link;
     end record;
   ...
end Heterogeneous_Priority_Queue;
```

The contract is now valid: objects of type Item are subject to the rules for indefinite types within the generic package, so there is no reason to forbid instantiation with indefinite types §12.5.1(15).

9.8 Formal package parameters*

Composing abstractions is an important programming technique. With generic package parameters, you can supply one abstraction with a second abstraction, without listing all the types and operations of the second abstraction as separate parameters.

§12.7

> 1 Formal packages can be used to pass packages to a generic unit. The formal_package_declaration declares that the formal package is an instance of a given generic package. Upon instantiation, the actual package has to be an instance of that generic package.
>
> 2 formal_package_declaration ::=
> **with package** defining_identifier **is**
> **new** *generic_package*_name formal_package_actual_part;
>
> 3 formal_package_actual_part ::=
> ([**others** =>] <>)
> | [generic_actual_part]
> | (formal_package_association , formal_package_association [, **others** => <>])
>
> 4 The *generic_package*_name shall denote a generic package (the *template* for the formal package); the formal package is an instance of the template.
>
> 5 The actual shall be an instance of the template. ...

The syntax for the actual part is complex; in the following case study, we use only the simplest alternative: `(<>)`, while the other possibilities are discussed in Sections 9.8.2, 9.8.3.

Section 13.11 contains an example of the direct composition of generics. The following case study demonstrates the use of an empty generic package to specify an abstraction needed by another generic unit.

> **Language Comparison**
>
> A generic package parameter is similar to a class parameter in a C++ or Java template.

9.8.1 *Case study: generic simulation*

We generalize the rocket simulation by declaring a generic simulation package that can be instantiated for *any* event type and *any* implementation of a priority queue. We start by declaring a `Root_Event` package:

rocket1

```
package Root_Event is
   type Event is abstract tagged private;
   function  Create return Event is abstract;
   procedure Simulate(E: in Event) is null;
   function "<"(Left, Right: Event'Class) return Boolean;
private
   -- as before
end Root_Event;
```

The procedure `Simulate` is declared to be a null procedure (Section 8.5), but a primitive funtion like `Create` must return a value so it cannot be null. This is discussed in more detail in Section 8.4.

The next stage is to declare an empty generic package (often called a *signature*) for a generic event priority queue. The meaning of the signature is that an event priority queue is *any* package that supplies the type and subprograms declared as generic formal parameters.

```
with Root_Event; use Root_Event;
generic
   type Queue(Size: Positive) is limited private;
   with function  Empty(Q: access Queue) return Boolean     is <>;
   with procedure Put(E: in Event'Class; Q: access Queue)   is <>;
   with function  Get(Q: access Queue)   return Event'Class is <>;
package Generic_Event_Priority_Queue is
end;
```

The signature is used as a generic formal package parameter for the `Generic_Simulator`:

```
with Root_Event;
with Generic_Event_Priority_Queue;
generic
   with package Event_Queue is new Generic_Event_Priority_Queue(<>);
package Generic_Simulator is
   procedure Add_Event(E: in Root_Event.Event'Class);
   procedure Run;
end Generic_Simulator;
```

The meaning of `(<>)` as the formal_package_actual_part is that the package used as the actual parameter in the instantiation can be *any* instantiation of `Generic_Event_Priority_Queue`.

The body of `Generic_Simulator` uses the subprograms `Empty`, `Put` and `Get` promised by the signature:

```
package body Generic_Simulator is
  Q: aliased Event_Queue.Queue(100);
  procedure Add_Event(E: in Root_Event.Event'Class) is
  begin
    Event_Queue.Put(E, Q'Access);
  end Add_Event;
  procedure Run is
  begin
    while not Event_Queue.Empty(Q'Access) loop
      Root_Event.Simulate(Event_Queue.Get(Q'Access));
    end loop;
  end Run;
end Generic_Simulator;
```

In terms of the contract model, the formal package parameter specifies the types and subprograms that the package will supply for use within the generic unit; the actual parameter must be a package that provides *at least* those types and subprograms.

`Generic_Simulator` is instantiated in three stages.

First, we need a package that supplies the resources declared in the formal part of the signature `Generic_Event_Priority_Queue`. It is convenient to obtain that package by instantiating the generic package described above in Section 9.7:

```
generic
  type Item(<>) is private;
  with function "<"(Left, Right: Item) return Boolean is <>;
package Tree_HPQ is
  ...
end Tree_HPQ;
```

This generic package is instantiated for the type `Event'Class`:

```
with Tree_HPQ;
with Root_Event; use Root_Event;
package Event_Tree_Queue is new Tree_HPQ(Event'Class);
```

This package is now used to instantiate the signature `Generic_Event_Priority_Queue` to obtain `Event_Queue_1`:

```
with Event_Tree_Queue; use Event_Tree_Queue;
with Generic_Event_Priority_Queue;
package Event_Queue_1 is new Generic_Event_Priority_Queue(Queue);
```

The use_clause for `Event_Tree_Queue` makes the subprograms visible so they are used by default as the actual subprogram parameters in the instantiation.

Third, we instantiate the generic simulator package with Event_Queue_1:

```
with Generic_Simulator;
with Event_Queue_1;
package Simulator_1 is new Generic_Simulator(Event_Queue_1);
```

As required by §12.7(4–5), the actual package parameters are themselves instantiations of the generic formal package parameters.

So far we have not said anything about the rocket! The hierarchy of events for the rocket simulation is defined in a child of Root_Event. Except for the package names, the source code for the rest of the rocket packages is unchanged and is omitted here.

```
package Root_Event.Rocket_Event is
  type Event is abstract new Root_Event.Event with null record;
  ...
end Root_Event.Rocket_Event;
```

Let us define another priority queue, Event_Queue_2, by instantiating the signature with Event_Array_Queue, obtained by instantiating a generic package Array_HPQ with the type Root_Event.Event'Class. The tree and the array implementations have the same visible part and they both match the signature package Generic_Event_Priority_Queue. A second simulator package, Simulator_2, is obtained by instantiating Generic_Simulator with Event_Queue_2. The main subprogram can use both simulators:

```
with Simulator_1; with Simulator_2;
with Root_Event.Rocket_Event.Engine;
with Root_Event.Rocket_Event.Telemetry;
with Root_Event.Rocket_Event.Steering;
procedure Rocket1 is
  use Root_Event.Rocket_Event;
begin
  for I in 1..15 loop
    Simulator_1.Add_Event(Engine.Main_Engine_Event'(Engine.Create));
    ...
  end loop;
  for I in 1..15 loop
    Simulator_2.Add_Event(Engine.Main_Engine_Event'(Engine.Create));
    ...
  end loop;

  Simulator_1.Run;
  Simulator_2.Run;
end Rocket1;
```

Although the sequence of instantiations may seem complex, it is quite straightforward. Formal package parameters facilitate the composition of abstractions.

9.8.2 Parameterization of package parameters

In the above examples, the box notation (<>) was used as the formal_package_actual_part in the declaration of the formal package parameters. The meaning is that *any* instantiation of the formal package is acceptable as an actual parameter when the generic unit is instantiated. Here we present the two other alternatives in §12.7(3) that are used to create a dependence among generic parameters.

The case study in Section 13.10.1 contains a generic unit `Generic_Complex_Vectors` with two generic package parameters: `Complex_Types` for the type for the complex numbers themselves and `Complex_Functions` for the elementary functions on the complex numbers:

```
with Ada.Numerics.Generic_Complex_Types;
with Ada.Numerics.Generic_Complex_Elementary_Functions;
generic
  use Ada.Numerics;
  with package Complex_Types is new Generic_Complex_Types (<>);
  with package Complex_Functions is
    new Generic_Complex_Elementary_Functions(Complex_Types);
package Generic_Complex_Vectors is
```

The actual parameter matching the formal parameter `Complex_Types` must be obtained by instantiating `Ada.Numerics.Generic_Complex_Types` §G.1.1(2), which takes a parameter of any floating point type §3.5.7. The actual parameter matching `Complex_Functions` must be obtained by instantiating `Ada.Numerics.Generic_Elementary_Functions` §G.1.2(2), which itself takes a formal package parameter that is any instantiation of the complex number package:

```
with package Complex_Types is new Ada.Numerics.Generic_Complex_Types (<>);
```

We would not use one precision for the operations of `Complex_Types` used directly in the vector package and another precision for the operations of `Complex_Types` used indirectly through the instantiation of the elementary functions package. Therefore, the formal package parameter for the complex functions uses a generic_actual_part for the formal_package_actual_part (the second alternative of §12.7(3)):

```
  with package Complex_Functions is
    new Generic_Complex_Elementary_Functions(Complex_Types);
```

The effect is to limit instantiations of `Generic_Complex_Vectors` to those where the elementary functions package is an instantiation obtained using the same generic actual parameter as that used for the formal `Complex_Types`.

It is also possible to specify restrictions on *some* of the actual parameters used in the instantiation of an actual package parameter, as we show in the following case study.

9.8.3 Case study: generic simulation with signatures

We start with a signature for a generic event:

rocket2

```
1 generic
2    type Event(<>) is tagged private;
3    with function  Create return Event is abstract <>;
4    with procedure Simulate(E: in Event) is abstract <>;
5    with function "<"(Left, Right: Event'Class) return Boolean is <>;
6 package Generic_Root_Event is end;
```

and a signature for a generic priority queue for events:

```
7 generic
8    type Event(<>) is tagged private;
9    type Queue(Size: Positive) is limited private;
10   with function  Empty(Q: access Queue) return Boolean is <>;
11   with procedure Put(E: in Event'Class; Q: access Queue) is <>;
12   with function Get(Q: access Queue) return Event'Class is <>;
13 package Generic_Event_Priority_Queue is end;
```

Then we declare a generic simulator that has these signatures as formal package parameters:

```
14 with Generic_Root_Event;
15 with Generic_Event_Priority_Queue;
16 generic
17   with package Root_Event  is new Generic_Root_Event(<>);
18   with package Event_Queue is
19     new Generic_Event_Priority_Queue(
20       Event => Root_Event.Event, others => <>);
21 package Generic_Simulator is
22   procedure Add_Event(E: in Root_Event.Event'Class);
23   procedure Run;
24 end Generic_Simulator;
```

Line ‡20 uses a formal_package_association (the third alternative of §12.7(3)) to require that the type used as the actual parameter for the formal parameter `Event` ‡2 in the instantiation of the actual package parameter for `Generic_Root_Event` be the *same* as that used as the actual parameter for the formal parameter Event †8 in the instantiation of the actual package parameter for Generic_Event_Priority_Queue. In this context, the difference between a generic_actual_part and a formal_package_association is that the latter can use the box notation to specify that an actual parameter is not restricted.

The simulation program is obtained by a sequence of instantiations. We start by instantiating the signature for Generic_Root_Event with an event package; for simplicity, we use the one with all event types in a single package (Section 7.8):

```
25 package Rocket_Event is
26   subtype Simulation_Time is Integer range 0..10_000;
27   type Event is tagged ...
28   function  Create return Event;
29   procedure Simulate(E: in Event) is null;
30   function "<"(Left, Right: Event'Class) return Boolean;
31   ...
32 end Rocket_Event;
33
34 with Generic_Root_Event;
35 with Rocket_Event; use Rocket_Event;
36 package Rocket_Root_Event is new Generic_Root_Event(Rocket_Event.Event);
```

Next we instantiate the signature for Generic_Event_Priority_Queue with a package that is itself an instantiation of the generic package introduced in the previous case study:

```
37 with Tree_HPQ;
38 with Rocket_Event; use Rocket_Event;
39 package Rocket_Tree_Queue is new Tree_HPQ(Event'Class);
40
41 with Rocket_Event;
42 with Rocket_Tree_Queue; use Rocket_Tree_Queue;
43 with Generic_Event_Priority_Queue;
44 package Rocket_Event_Queue is
45   new Generic_Event_Priority_Queue(Rocket_Event.Event, Queue);
```

Finally, we obtain a simulator by instantiating Generic_Simulator:

```
46 with Rocket_Root_Event;
47 with Rocket_Event_Queue;
48 with Generic_Simulator;
49 package Rocket_Simulator is
50   new Generic_Simulator(Rocket_Root_Event, Rocket_Event_Queue);
```

You can trace back through the instantiations to verify that the actual parameters matching the formal parameters Event in both Rocket_Root_Event and Rocket_Event_Queue are the same.

The complete source code for this case study can be found in the source code archive.

9.9 Generic children*

A non-generic package may have generic children §10.1.1(13); for example, `Ada.Numerics` is not generic but its children are. However, the child of a generic unit must itself be generic §10.1.1(17). If the child package were not generic, the child would have to be compiled for every instantiation of the parent, whether it is needed or not. By requiring that the child be generic, instances are created only when explicitly requested.

The following example demonstrates generic children (a realistic application will be given in Section 13.11). A generic child of a generic parent package is declared:

genchild

```
generic
   type T is private;
package Parent is
   V1: T;
end Parent;

generic
package Parent.Child is
   V2: T;
end Parent.Child;
```

Then an instance of the parent is declared:

```
with Parent;
package Parent_Instance is new Parent(Integer);
```

followed by an instance of the child:

```
with Parent.Child;
with Parent_Instance;
package Child_Instance is new Parent_Instance.Child;
```

The instantiation of the generic child package requires two with_clauses. The first is the usual with_clause for `Parent.Child`, the generic package being instantiated. However, what is actually being instantiated is the generic child of the *instance* of the parent, which is implicitly present in each instance of the parent §10.1.1(19), so there must also be a with_clause for `Parent_Instance`. This enables the instance to access the generic actual parameter of the instance, so that the compiler can know that the variable `Child_Instance.V2` is of type `Integer`.

9.10 The fine print in the contract model*

The explanation of the contract model in Section 9.2 was only approximate. Occasionally, you will have to understand the precise details of the model as discussed in this section.

Consider the following rule on type derivations:

§3.9.1

> 3 ... If the parent type or any progenitor type is nonlimited, then each of the components of the record_extension_part shall be nonlimited. ...

This rule makes sense. If a type is declared to be nonlimited:

```
type Parent is tagged
  record
    Time: Integer;
  end record;
```

the reason is that equality and copying are assumed to be meaningful operations on objects of the type. If we add a limited component:

```
type Stack is limited
  record
    ...
  end record;

type Derived is new Parent with
  record
    S: Stack;
  end record;
```

then it is impossible to decide the legality of the following construct at compile time:

```
procedure P(A: in Parent'Class) is
  B: Parent'Class := A;
```

because some calls are with an actual parameter of type `Parent` for which copying is legal, while others have a parameter of type `Derived` for which it is not. Nor does it make sense to implement the check at run-time, because limitedness is a compile-time concept with no effect on the execution of a program.

Now, does §3.9.1(3) apply to the declaration of `T1` in the following generic package?

legal

```
generic
  type Parent         is tagged limited private;
  type Component_Type is limited private;
package P is
  type T1 is new Parent with
    record
      X: Component_Type;
    end record;
  procedure Proc(A: T1);
end P;
```

The formal type `Parent` *is* limited, so the component `X` in the extension can be of the formal limited type `Component_Type`. This generic package specification compiles successfully. The technical term is "assume-the-best": since the formal parameters are declared to be limited, the compiler assumes that the actual parameters will also be limited. The compiler will also verify that the generic body does not contain illegal operations on such types.

Consider, however, an instantiation of the package `P` where the actual parameter associated with `Parent` is *nonlimited* and the actual parameter associated with `Component_Type` is *limited*:

```
with P;
package Legal is
  type Non_Lim is tagged null record;
  type Lim     is tagged limited null record;
  package Instance is new P(Parent => Non_Lim, Component_Type => Lim);
end Legal;
```

The type `Instance.T1` is an extension of the nonlimited type `Non_Lim` with a limited component of type `Lim`—clearly, a violation of the Legality Rule §3.9.1(3).

§12.3

> 11 In a generic unit Legality Rules are enforced at compile-time of the generic_declaration and generic body, given the properties of the formals. In the visible part and formal part of an instance, Legality Rules are enforced at compile-time of the generic_instantiation, given the properties of the actuals. ...

According to the second sentence of this rule, legality rules such as §3.9.1(3) are enforced during the compilation of the instantiation; therefore, the declaration of `T1` in the *instance* is a compile-time error. This is somewhat surprising, since there is nothing wrong with the instantiation in terms of matching the generic formal part with the actual parameters in the instantiation, and, furthermore, the generic specification itself compiles correctly.

The contract model is between the author of the generic and the author of the instance: if the right parameters are provided, a semantically correct instance will be constructed. In most cases the contract is enforced by checking the actuals, but in some cases it requires checking the specification of the instance, including the private part §7.3(8). Furthermore, in some cases there is a preemptive check that forbids some constructs in the generic body,

An instantiation will never cause the generic body to become illegal; conversely, a modification of the body cannot make an instantiation illegal. Almost all violations of the contract will be caught as conflicts between the generic actual parameters and the generic formal parameters, but occasionally—as shown here—the conflict may be with the specification.

Suppose that a similar record T2 were declared in the private part of the package:

```
generic
   type Parent         is tagged limited private;
   type Component_Type is limited private;
package P is
   ...
private
   type T2 is new Parent with
      record
         X: Component_Type;
      end record;
end P;
```

In general, Legality rules are not enforced in the private part of a generic package; however, the final sentence of the above rule reads as follows:

§12.3

> 11 ... In other parts of an instance, Legality Rules are not enforced; this rule does not apply when a given rule explicitly specifies otherwise.

Therefore, the declaration of T2 would not be rejected, except for the fact that it is *explicitly specified* that this Legality rule be checked:

§3.9.1

> 3 ... In addition to the places where Legality Rules normally apply (see 12.3), these rules apply also in the private part of an instance of a generic unit.

A list of the legality rules that apply in the private part of a generic instance can be found in the index of the *ARM* under the entry *generic contract issues*.

Finally, what happens if the extension T3 is declared in the body of package P? It appears that the instantiation will cause the body to be illegal—precisely the situation that the contract model was intended to avoid. The solution is simply to forbid this construct so that the compilation of the generic *body* is already illegal, regardless of the actual parameters supplied during the instantiation.

§3.9.1

> 4 A type extension shall not be declared in a generic body if the parent type is declared outside that body.

This is known as "assume-the-worst." Though it is unlikely that an extension of a formal type in the body will cause a problem, it is in fact possible, so all such extensions are forbidden. The workaround in this case is to move the extension to the private part of the specification.

To summarize, the generic contract specifies the rules that make an instantiation legal. Most of these rules are enforced when matching the actual parameters of the instantiation with the formal parameters of the generic part. Some of the rules require that the specification of the instance itself be checked, and, in some cases, the private part of the instance as well.

Projects

1. Implement your own generic procedure for sorting an array using the generic formal part shown in Section 9.4.
2. Develop a rocket simulation where engine events are declared in a generic child package so that many types of such events can be implemented by instantiation.
3. Write a generic package that uses a generic formal object for maintaining the state of a computation, as outlined in Section 9.6.

Quizzes

Quiz 1:

```
generic
  type Item is private;
  type Vector is array(1..10) of Item;
procedure Proc;
```

Quiz 2:

```
package P is
  Local_Max: Integer := 100;
  generic
    Max: Integer := Local_Max;
  package GP is
    procedure Proc;
  end GP;
end P;
```

```
package body P is
  package body GP is
    procedure Proc is
    begin
      Put(Max);
    end Proc;
  end GP;
end P;

with P;
procedure Main is
  package First_GP is new P.GP;
  function Init return Integer is
  begin
    P.Local_Max := 200;
    return 1;
  end Init;
  N: Integer := Init;
  package Second_GP is new P.GP;
begin
  First_GP.Proc;
  Second_GP.Proc;
end Main;
```

Quiz 3:

```
generic
  type T(A: Integer) is private;
procedure Proc;
procedure Proc is
begin
  null;
end Proc;

type Base(D: Integer) is null record;
type R(Disc: Integer) is new Base(D => Disc);
type S is new Base(D => 10);

procedure Proc1 is new Proc(T => R);
procedure Proc2 is new Proc(T => S);
```

Quiz 4:

```
generic
  type T is range <>;
  with function Formal(Left, Right: T) return T;
package GP is
  function Func(Left, Right: T) return T;
end GP;

package body GP is
  function Func(Left, Right: T) return T is
  begin
    return 2*(Left+Right);
  end Func;
end GP;

with GP;
generic
  with package GFP is new GP(<>);
--  with package GFP is new GP(Integer, "+");
procedure Proc;

procedure Proc is
  package GIO is new Ada.Text_IO.Integer_IO(GFP.T);
begin
  GIO.Put(GFP.Func(1,2));
  GIO.Put(GFP.Formal(1,2));
end Proc;

with GP; with Proc;
procedure Main is
  function Actual(Left, Right: Long_Integer) return Long_Integer is
  begin
    return 4*(Left+Right);
  end Actual;
  package GP_Instance is new GP(Long_Integer, Actual);
  procedure Proc_Instance is new Proc(GP_Instance);
begin
  Proc_Instance;
end Main;
```

What happens if the generic formal package parameter were changed to the commented line?

Quiz 5:

```
package Q is
  type Parent is null record;
  procedure Proc(A: in Parent);
  type Actual is new Parent;
  procedure Proc(A: in Actual);
end Q;

package body Q is
  procedure Proc(A: in Parent) is
  begin Put_Line("Parent"); end Proc;
  procedure Proc(A: in Actual) is
  begin Put_Line("Actual"); end Proc;
end Q;

with Q;
generic
  type Formal is new Q.Parent;
package P is
  type Derived is new Formal;
  procedure Inside;
end P;

package body P is
  procedure Inside is
    D: Derived;
  begin
    Proc(D);
  end Inside;
end P;

with P; with Q;
procedure Main is
  package Instance is new P(Q.Actual);
  D: Instance.Derived;
begin
  Instance.Inside;
  Instance.Proc(D);
end Main;
```

Quiz 6:

```
package P is
  type T is array(0..5) of Natural;
end P;

with P;
generic
  with procedure Proc(Parm: in P.T);
package Gen is
  procedure ProcG;
end Gen;

package body Gen is
  type TG is array(0..10) of Natural;
  GG: TG := (0,1,2,3,4,5,6,7,8,9,10);
  procedure ProcG is
  begin
    Proc(P.T(GG));
  end ProcG;
end Gen;

with P, Gen, Ada.Text_IO;
procedure Main is
  procedure M(PP: in P.T) is
  begin
    for I in P.T'Range loop
      Ada.Text_IO.Put(Natural'Image(PP(I)));
    end loop;
  end M;
  package GM is new Gen(Proc => M);
begin
  GM.ProcG;
end Main;
```

Chapter 10
Exceptions and Run-Time Checks

Type checking in Ada is designed to discover and prevent compile-time errors. However, there are some errors that can occur only at run-time; for example, input that is not in the expected format or that exceeds the range of an input variable. Run-time errors cause *exceptions* to be *raised* during execution, and the exception occurrences can be *handled* in order to recover from the error or to display information that will help diagnose the error.

10.1 Declaring and raising exceptions

Exceptions are declared with an object-like syntax:

§11.1

> 1 An exception_declaration declares a name for an exception.
>
> 2 exception_declaration ::= defining_identifier_list : **exception**;

In the priority queue case study in Section 5.1, two exceptions were declared:

```
Overflow, Underflow: exception;
```

There are also predefined exceptions §11.1(4) (see Section 2.6) that are raised by the run-time system. Exceptions that are not predefined must be explicitly raised using a raise_statement:

§11.3

> 1 A raise_statement raises an exception.
>
> 2 raise_statement ::= **raise**;
> | **raise** exception_name [**with** string_expression];

A raise_statement without an exception_name is called a *re-raise* statement (Section 10.5.1). When the second form of the statement raises the named exception, the optional string following the **with** can be retrieved by Ada.Exceptions.Exception_Message (Section 10.4).

Raising an exception causes the computation to be *abandoned*:

§11.4

> 3 When an exception occurrence is raised by the execution of a given construct, the rest of the execution of that construct is *abandoned*; that is, any portions of the execution that have not yet taken place are not performed. . . .

In the priority queue case study, an attempt to Get an element from an empty queue should raise an exception:

```
if Q.Free = 0 then
  raise Underflow;
end if;
I := Q.Data(0);
Q.Free := Q.Free-1;
Q.Data(0..Q.Free-1) := Q.Data(1..Q.Free);
```

If Q.Free is zero, the exception Underflow is raised and the rest of the computation is abandoned; this prevents the execution of the last assignment statement which is meaningless when the queue is empty.

Here is another example from the country of origins case study (Section 2.1):

```
begin
  loop
    Put("Enter the make of the car: ");
    Car := Cars'Value(Get_Line);
    Put_Line(Cars'Image(Car) & " is made in " &
      Countries'Image(Car_to_Country(Car)));
  end loop;
exception
  when Constraint_Error =>
         Put_Line("Car make is not recognized");
   when End_Error =>
         null;
end Country1;
```

The function Get_Line will raise the exception Ada.Text_IO.End_Error §A.10.1(85) if an end-of-file indication (ctrl-z or ctrl-d) is encountered. Evaluation of the attribute Cars'Value will raise the predefined exception Constraint_Error if the input string does not match one of the values of the enumeration type Cars. In either case, the execution of the subprogram body is abandoned.

Ada 95

Associating a message with an exception (**with** string_expression) is not allowed. The procedure `Raise_Exception` §11.4.1(4) in package `Ada.Exceptions` can be used instead:

```
procedure Raise_Exception(E: in Exception_Id; Message: in String := "");
```

10.2 Handling exceptions

Exceptions enable the continuation of the computation in spite of the occurrence of an error. The executable statements of a subprogram (or a block) form a handled_sequence_of_statements, and *exception handlers* can be written to specify what is to be done when an exception is raised within the sequence:

§11

> 2 When an exception arises, control can be transferred to a user-provided exception_handler at the end of a handled_sequence_of_statements, or ...

A separate handler can be given for each exception or group of exceptions:

§11.2

> 3 exception_handler ::=
> **when** [choice_parameter_specification:] exception_choice | exception_choice =>
> sequence_of_statements

An exception is handled by executing the sequence of statements associated with the handler for the exception:

§11.4

> 5 • If the construct is the sequence_of_statements of a handled_sequence_of_statements that has a handler with a choice covering the exception, the occurrence is handled by that handler;
> 7 When an occurrence is *handled* by a given handler, ... the sequence_of_statements of the handler is executed; this execution replaces the abandoned portion of the execution of the sequence_of_statements.

The subprogram where the exception occurred is left after executing the statements of the handler. If you want to retry the computation, you can use a block statement within a loop as shown in Section 3.5.

10.3 Propagating exceptions

It is not required that there be an exception handler associated with every sequence of statements, nor is it required that the handlers *cover* every exception. If there is no handler covering an exception, the exception is *propagated* to the caller.

§11.4

> 6 Otherwise, the occurrence is *propagated* to the innermost dynamically enclosing execution, which means that the occurrence is raised again in that context.

For data structures like the priority queue, the conditions that raise the exceptions `Overflow` and `Underflow` depend on the implementation of the package, which is not known to the clients using the package. On the other hand, the package providing the queue should not decide how to handle the exceptions; that should be left to the clients to decide. For example, displaying an error message would be appropriate in an interactive application but not in a real-time application. Therefore, the exceptions `Overflow` and `Underflow` are not handled within the subprograms where they are raised, but instead are propagated to the caller, in this case the main subprogram (Section 6.3):

```
with Priority_Queue;
procedure PQAV2 is
begin
  -- Priority_Queue.Get and Priority_Queue.Put can propagate exceptions
exception
  when Priority_Queue.Underflow => Put_Line("Underflow from queue");
  when Priority_Queue.Overflow  => Put_Line("Overflow  from queue");
end PQAV2;
```

In general, exceptions are declared in the visible part of package specifications so that they can appear in exception_choices of exception handlers of clients of the packages.

Exceptions are propagated up the dynamic chain of calls, starting with the *innermost dynamically enclosing execution*:

§11.4

> 2 Within a given task, if the execution of construct *a* is defined by this International Standard to consist (in part) of the execution of construct *b*, then while *b* is executing, the execution of *a* is said to *dynamically enclose* the execution of *b*. The *innermost dynamically enclosing execution* of a given execution is the dynamically enclosing execution that started most recently.

10.3.1 *Case study: propagating exceptions*

Propagation of exceptions is demonstrated in the following program. The operations on the queue are not called directly from the main program, but from the procedure `Get_And_Process`, which is also responsible for handling the exceptions:

propagate1

```
with Array_Priority_Queue; use Array_Priority_Queue;
with Ada.Text_IO; use Ada.Text_IO;
procedure Propagate1 is
  Q: Queue(Size => 10);
  I: Integer;

  procedure Get_And_Process is
    procedure Get_The_Data is
    begin
      Get(I, Q);
    end Get_The_Data;

    procedure Process is
    begin
      Get_The_Data;
    exception
      when Underflow => Put("Underflow handled in Process");
    end Process;

  begin -- Get_And_Process;
    Process;
  exception
    when Underflow => Put("Underflow handled in Get_And_Process");
  end Get_And_Process;
begin
  Get_And_Process;
end Propagate1;
```

`Get_And_Process` contains two nested procedures: `Process` and `Get_The_Data` which is called from `Process`. The exception `Underflow` is raised within `Get` and propagated to the caller `Get_The_Data`. There is no handler within `Get_The_Data` either, so the exception is propagated again. We now ask: What execution encloses `Get_The_Data`? The procedure `Get_And_Process`, where `Get_The_Data` is declared, or the procedure `Process`, which calls `Get_The_Data`. By §11.4(2), the answer is the *dynamically enclosing execution*, namely, that of `Process`. Check that the program prints `Underflow handled in Process`.

10.3.2 Exceptions in the declarative part

An exception can be raised during the elaboration of the declarative part of subprogram. Suppose that the priority queue package contained a *function* Get:

```
function Get(Q: access Queue) return Integer is
  I: Integer;
begin
  Get(I, Q.all);
  return I;
end Get;
```

An access parameter (Section 12.6) has been used because the parameter Q is modified but a function cannot have a parameter of mode **in out**.

Consider, now, a call to this function in the declaration of a variable in Process:

propagate2

```
procedure Get_And_Process is
  procedure Process is
    I: Integer := Get(Q'Access);
  begin
    Put_Line(Integer'Image(I));
  exception
    when Underflow => Put("Underflow handled in Process");
  end Process;
begin -- Get_And_Process;
  Process;
exception
  when Underflow => Put("Underflow handled in Get_And_Process");
end Get_And_Process;
```

The exception is *not* handled in the exception handler for Process, but rather is propagated to the calling procedure Get_And_Process and handled there. By §11.4(5), handlers are associated with a handled_sequence_of_statements and these do not include the declarations of a subprogram or block. Since the exception handler can use the variables and constants declared in the subprogram, it is important to delay the transfer of responsibility for exception handling until all the declarations have been elaborated.

10.4 Package Exceptions*

Package Ada.Exceptions §11.4.1 declares two types: the private type Exception_Id and the limited private type Exception_Occurrence. There is a value of type Exception_Id for each distinct exception, both predefined and declared. The attribute `E'Identity` §11.4.1(9) returns the identity associated with exception `E`. Since an exception can be raised many times, each occurrence gives rise to a value of type `Exception_Occurrence`. The package `Ada.Exceptions` contains functions for converting between exceptions and their occurrences, and for obtaining information about them in the form of strings.

Within the handler, we can obtain information about the exception occurrence E. The function `Exception_Identity(X)` §11.4.1(5,11) returns the `Exception_Id` of E, and this we can convert to a string by calling `Exception_Name` §11.4.1(2,12,12.1). As a shortcut, `Exception_Name` is overloaded for a parameter of type `Exception_Occurrence` to return the string identifying the exception of the exception occurrence §11.4.1(5).

The function `Exception_Message` §11.4.1(4,10.1) returns the message associated with the exception occurrence; this is the string given after the **with** in a **raise** statement (or the second parameter of the procedure `Raise_Exception`). The function `Exception_Information` §11.4.1(5,13,19) returns more extensive (implementation-defined) information about an exception occurrence, which can be useful for debugging.

10.4.1 Case study: information about exceptions

The following program demonstrates the use of `Exception_Information`:

info

```
with Array_Priority_Queue; use Array_Priority_Queue;
with Ada.Text_IO; use Ada.Text_IO;
with Ada.Exceptions; use Ada.Exceptions;
procedure Info is
  Q: Queue(10);
  I: Integer;
  Queue_Error: exception;

  procedure Get_The_Data is
  begin
    Get(I, Q);
  exception
    when E: Overflow | Underflow =>
      Put(Exception_Information(E));
      raise Queue_Error;
  end Get_The_Data;
```

Although `Overflow` cannot occur when calling `Get`, let us assume that it can be, and let us further assume that we want both exceptions to be handled by the same handler. This is easy to do because a handler can be associated with more than one exception_choice §11.2(3). The handler prints the exception information and raises a new exception called `Queue_Error`, which is handled in the main program:

```
begin
   Get_The_Data;
exception
   when E: Queue_Error =>
      Put(Exception_Information(E));
end Info;
```

The handler for `Queue_Error` also prints the exception information; for the compiler that I used, the output is:

```
Exception name: ARRAY_PRIORITY_QUEUE.UNDERFLOW
Message: array_priority_queue.adb:29
Exception name: INFO.QUEUE_ERROR
Message: info.adb:15
```

An exception handler can have a *choice parameter* (`E` in the program above) that can be used as a parameter to the subprograms of package `Ada.Exceptions`:

§11.2

> 9 A choice_parameter_specification declares a choice parameter, which is a constant object of type Exception_Occurrence (see 11.4.1). During the handling of an exception occurrence, the choice parameter, if any, of the handler represents the exception occurrence that is being handled.

Exception occurrences can be written to streams §11.4.1(6.1,6.2,15.1); see Section 14.3.

10.5 Re-raising exceptions*

A raise statement that names an exception is permitted within an exception handler §11.3(3,4); it raises a *new* occurrence of the named exception. A statement consisting of the reserved word **raise** alone is called a *re-raise statement*; it raises the *same* occurrence of the exception. In both cases, the exception is propagated to the caller of the subprogram.

10.5.1 Case study: re-raising an exception

The following program demonstrates the difference between raising a new exception and re-raising the same exception:

reraise

```
with Array_Priority_Queue; use Array_Priority_Queue;
with Ada.Text_IO; use Ada.Text_IO;
procedure Reraise is
  Q: Queue(Size => 10);
  I: Integer;
  Queue_Error: exception;
```

To keep track of the exception *occurrences*, we will write a time-stamp with each one using the function `Time_Stamp` that can be found in the software archive. The **raise** statements call this function:

```
  procedure Get(I: out Integer; Q: in out Queue) is
  begin
    if Q.Free = 0 then
      raise Underflow with Time_Stamp;
    end if;
    ...
  end Get;
```

There are three versions of the procedure `Get_The_Data`. In the first one, the exception is handled within the procedure, and the main procedure will not know that an exception has occurred:

```
  procedure Get_The_Data0 is
  begin
    Get(I, Q);
  exception
    when E: Underflow =>
      Put_Line("Underflow from 0 at " & Exception_Message(E));
  end Get_The_Data0;
```

In the second version, the exception is re-raised and will be propagated:

```
  procedure Get_The_Data1 is
  begin
    Get(I, Q);
  exception
    when E: Underflow =>
      Put_Line("Underflow from 1 at " & Exception_Message(E));
      raise;
  end Get_The_Data1;
```

In the third version, a different exception, `Queue_Error`, is raised and propagated:

```
  procedure Get_The_Data2 is
  begin
    Get(I, Q);
  exception
    when E: Underflow =>
      Put_Line("Underflow from 2 at " & Exception_Message(E));
      raise Queue_Error with Time_Stamp;
  end Get_The_Data2;
```

Here is the main procedure:

```
begin
  begin
    Get_The_Data0;
  exception
    when E: Underflow   =>
      Put_Line("Underflow from main at " & Exception_Message(E));
  end;
  begin
    Get_The_Data1;
  exception
    when E: Underflow   =>
      Put_Line("Underflow from main at " & Exception_Message(E));
  end;
  begin
    Get_The_Data2;
  exception
    when E: Queue_Error =>
      Put_Line("Queue_Error from main at " & Exception_Message(E));
  end;
end Reraise;
```

Check that the output (except for the absolute values of the time-stamps) is:

```
Underflow from 0 at 2008-9-27-51380.088049397
Underflow from 1 at 2008-9-27-51380.107685971
Underflow from main at 2008-9-27-51380.107685971
Underflow from 2 at 2008-9-27-51380.109337857
Queue_Error from main at 2008-9-27-51380.109368028
```

The time stamps of the two lines for `Get_The_Data1` have the same time-stamp, showing that re-raise raises the same exception occurrence, whereas for `Get_The_Data2`, the time-stamps are different since the exception occurrences are different.

10.6 Saving exceptions*

Exception occurrences can be saved in data structures and then retrieved for later analysis or even in order to be re-raised. Since the type `Exception_Occurrence` is limited private, it cannot be copied using normal assignment statements.

§11.4.1

```
3  type Exception_Occurrence_Access is access all Exception_Occurrence;
6  procedure Save_Occurrence(
      Target : out Exception_Occurrence;
      Source : in Exception_Occurrence);
   function Save_Occurrence(Source : Exception_Occurrence)
      return Exception_Occurrence_Access;
```

15 The Save_Occurrence procedure copies the Source to the Target. The Save_Occurrence function uses an allocator of type Exception_Occurrence_Access to create a new object, copies the Source to this new object, and returns an access value designating this new object; the result may be deallocated using an instance of Unchecked_Deallocation.

10.6.1 Case study: saving exceptions

In the following program, three subprograms `P1`, `P2`, `P3` are called and all the exception occurrences are saved in a priority queue. We declare a record type `Exception_Record` that contains a numeric field representing the "priority" associated with an occurrence; the second field is an access to the exception occurrence:

save

```
with Priority_Queue;
with Ada.Text_IO; use Ada.Text_IO;
with Ada.Exceptions; use Ada.Exceptions;
procedure Save is
  type Exception_Record is
    record
      Priority:   Positive;
      Occurrence: Exception_Occurrence_Access;
    end record;
```

Function "<" compares values of the type by comparing the `Priority` components:

```
  function "<"(Left, Right: Exception_Record) return Boolean is
  begin
    return Left.Priority < Right.Priority;
  end "<";
```

The generic priority queue package from Section 9.1 is instantiated with `Exception_Record` and (as a default actual parameter) with this function:

```
  package Exception_Queue is new Priority_Queue(Exception_Record);
  use Exception_Queue;
```

Then a queue is declared as are three exceptions:

```
  Q: aliased Queue;
  Ex1, Ex2, Ex3: exception;
```

In the body of the main procedure, the exceptions are raised, and in their handlers, an aggregate of type `Exception_Record` is put on the queue. The function `Save_Occurrence` allocates an exception occurrence object and returns an access value that is stored in the record that is saved in the queue:

```
begin
  begin
    raise Ex1;
  exception
    when E: others => Put(Exception_Record'(13, Save_Occurrence(E)), Q);
  end;
  begin
    raise Ex2;
  exception
    when E: others => Put(Exception_Record'(6, Save_Occurrence(E)), Q);
  end;
  begin
    raise Ex3;
  exception
    when E: others => Put(Exception_Record'(8, Save_Occurrence(E)), Q);
  end;
```

The elements of type `Exception_Record` are removed from the queue in numerical order of their `Priority` components. The function `Exception_Information` is used to obtain a string containing information about the occurrence:

```
   while not Empty(Q) loop
     Put(Exception_Information(Get(Q'Access).Occurrence.all));
   end loop;
 end Save;
```

Check that the exception occurrences are printed in ascending order of `Priority`:

```
Exception name: SAVE.EX2
Message: save.adb:27
Exception name: SAVE.EX3
Message: save.adb:32
Exception name: SAVE.EX1
Message: save.adb:22
```

Alternatively, we could have re-raised the exception occurrences §11.4.1(4,10.2):

```
while not Empty(Q) loop
  begin
    Reraise_Occurrence(Get(Q'Access).Occurrence.all);
  exception
    when EE: others => Put(Exception_Information(EE));
  end;
end loop;
```

Note that the same *occurrences* are re-raised and they will contain the same information that they had when they were raised. To raise a *new* occurrence of the same *exception*, we call `Exception_Identity` to obtain the `Exception_Id` and then call `Raise_Exception` §11.4.1(4,10):

```
Raise_Exception(
  Exception_Identity(Get(Q'Access).Occurrence.all),
  Message => " from main procedure");
```

The software archive contains complete programs with these modifications.

Ada 95

In Ada 95:

- If the function `Exception_Message` is called for an exception occurrence raised by a **raise** statement, the string returned is implementation-defined because the **with** form is not allowed. The workaround is to call `Raise_Exception`.
- There are no procedures for writing exceptions to streams.
- There are no functions returning `Wide_String` or `Wide_Wide_String`. The workaround is to convert a value of type `String` to these types; however, `Raise_Exception` must always be called with a value of type `String`.

10.7 Suppressing checks*

A frequent complaint against languages like Ada is that programs are inefficient because they require run-time checks, such as checking if the indices of arrays are out of bounds. Consider a program that does image processing, where one way of improving an image is to replace every pixel by the average of its neighbors:

```
type Image is array(0..1023, 0..1023) of Byte;
A: Image;

Get_Image(A);
for I in Image'First(1)+1 .. Image'Last(1)-1 loop
  for J in Image'First(2)+1 .. Image'Last(2)-1 loop
    A(I,J) := (A(I-1,J) + A(I+1,J) + A(I,J-1) + A(I,J+1)) / 4;
  end loop;
end loop;
```

If a check is made that the indices of the array `A` are in bounds for each of the four reads and the single write, the program will be inefficient.

The inefficiency associated with type checking is highly exaggerated. First, a good optimizing compiler can remove many of the checks. In the above example, it is clear from the loop bounds that no index will be outside the array bounds. Second, efficiency problems almost invariably arise from "hot spots" in the program such as inner loops. In those cases where inefficiency has been *measured* and its cause identified, the language-defined checks can be *suppressed*. If you suppress checks, the program will become erroneous §1.1.5(9–10) if the error occurs §11.5(26).

§11.5

> 1 *Checking pragmas* give instructions to an implementation on handling language-defined checks. A pragma Suppress gives permission to an implementation to omit certain language-defined checks, while a pragma Unsuppress revokes the permission to omit checks.
>
> 2 A *language-defined check* (or simply, a "check") is one of the situations defined by this International Standard that requires a check to be made at run-time to determine whether some condition is true. A check *fails* when the condition being checked is false, causing an exception to be raised.

Paragraphs §11.5(9–25) define the checks; for example, `Index_Check` §11.5(14) checks the bounds of an array value against its index constraint. A failure of this check will cause `Constraint_Error` to be raised. There is also a check `All_Checks` §11.5(25) that can be used to suppress all of the specific checks.

A check is suppressed by using **pragma** `Suppress` with the name of the check; if a check has been suppressed, **pragma** `Unsuppress` can be used to restore the check:

§11.5

> 4 **pragma** Suppress(identifier);
>
> 4.1 **pragma** Unsuppress(identifier);
>
> 8 A pragma Suppress gives permission to an implementation to omit the named check (or every check in the case of All_Checks) for any entities to which it applies. If permission has been given to suppress a given check, the check is said to be *suppressed*.
>
> 8.1 A pragma Unsuppress revokes the permission to omit the named check (or every check in the case of All_Checks) given by any pragma Suppress that applies at the point of the pragma Unsuppress.

You should not make any semantic use of pragma Suppress, because an implementation is allowed to ignore it:

§11.5

> 29 There is no guarantee that a suppressed check is actually removed; hence a pragma Suppress should be used only for efficiency reasons.

Two checks that are often suppressed are `Overflow_Check` §11.5(16), because it is inefficient to implement without hardware support, and `Elaboration_Check` §11.5(20), since it is unlikely to occur once you have successfully built and tested a system (Section 15.5).

Transformations performed by the compiler for the purpose of optimization may subtly effect the semantics of a program, especially where exceptions are involved. For example, a compiler could "optimize away" the creation of the variable `H`, provided that `H` is not used elsewhere in the program:

```
subtype Hex is Character range 'A'..'F';

H: Hex := Char'Succ('F');
C: Character := H;
```

In doing so, the compiler has "optimized away" the exception that would be raised as a result of assigning `'G'`, the result of `Char'Succ('F')`, to the variable `H` of subtype `Hex`. Furthermore, optimization that involves moving code may cause an exception to occur in an unexpected location in the program. An implementation is permitted to perform such optimizations §11.6.

10.8 Assertions*

Assertions §11.4.2 are an alternative to explicit if-statements that raise exceptions if a boolean condition is false. In the array priority queue, we could replace the explicit checks for underflow and overflow by using **pragma** Assert:

assert

```
pragma Assert(Free < Q.Size);

pragma Assert(Q.Free > 0);
```

If the expression ever becomes false, the exception Ada.Assertions.Assert_Error is raised; the exception is defined in package Ada.Assertions §11.4.2(11–15), which also contains procedures for checking assertions.

Checking assertions is controlled by **pragma** Assertion_Policy §11.4.2(5–7,10):

```
pragma Assertion_Policy(Check);
pragma Assertion_Policy(Ignore);
```

The default policy is implementation-defined, so a program will be portable only if the policy is specified explicitly.

The advantage of assertions over if-statements is that they can be ignored at compilation time just by changing the policy pragma. In general, assertions should not be ignored; however, if you can *prove* that an assertion is always true, it is reasonable to ignore it. For example, the following Get statement will never cause the underflow assertion to be false:

```
while not Empty(Q) loop
  Get(I, Q);
  ...
end loop;
```

If all Get statements appear in such contexts, the assertion can safely be ignored.

Ada 95

Assertions were not included in the Ada 95 standard although some implementations supported them. The workaround is to use explicit if-statements and exceptions; the if-statement can check a global variable or constant to see if the expression should be checked:

```
if Configuration.Check_Assertions and then Q.Free = 0 then ...
```

Note the use of the short-circuit control form **and then** to avoid evaluating a possibly complex expression if assertions are not to be checked.

Projects

1. In the image-processing algorithms that you developed as projects in Chapter 4, try suppressing checks and see if the running time is reduced. Check both for optimized and unoptimized compilations.
2. Add assertions wherever relevant in the case study for filling and justifying text (Section 4.1).

Quizzes

Quiz 1:

```
package P is
  procedure Proc;
end P;

package body P is
  Inner: exception;
  procedure Proc is
  begin
    raise Inner;
  end Proc;
end P;

with P; use P;
procedure Main is
begin
  Proc;
exception
  when E: others => Put(Ada.Exceptions.Exception_Name(E));
end Main;
```

Chapter 11
Composite Types

11.1 Characters and strings

The support for character and string handling in Ada is extensive. In this section we discuss "ordinary" characters and strings, while in the next section we give an overview of multibyte characters and their strings; these are used in programs that process text in non-European natural languages and other notations. This is followed by a case study that demonstrates string handling as well as the container library.

`Ada.Characters.Latin_1` §A.3.3 supplies names for all the characters in the ISO 8859-1 set, except for the digits `'0'` through `'9'` and the upper case letters `'A'` through `'Z'`, which are assumed to be directly available on any keyboard.

`Ada.Characters.Handling` §A.3.2 contains functions like `Is_Upper` and `Is_Alphanumeric` for classifying characters, as well as conversion functions such as `To_Upper`. Note that the category *letters* includes international characters such as the French letter ç (named `LC_C_Cedilla` in `Ada.Characters.Latin_1`); the predefined upper/lower case conversion functions take account of these characters.

`Ada.Strings` §A.4.1 has child packages that provide operations for three string types:

Fixed

This is the predefined type `String`; the length of a string value is fixed when it is allocated, as for all array types.

H	e	l	l	o		W	o	r	l	d

Bounded

A bounded string object is declared with a *maximum* length; the *current* length is automatically maintained by the library subprograms. A bounded string object can vary in size during its lifetime, up to the declared maximum.

11		H	e	l	l	o		W	o	r	l	d		

Unbounded

An unbounded string has no fixed or maximum length; an operation that causes the length of the string to be changed will cause storage to be allocated. Typically, unbounded strings are implemented as controlled types (Section 12.9), and finalization takes care of reclaiming storage.

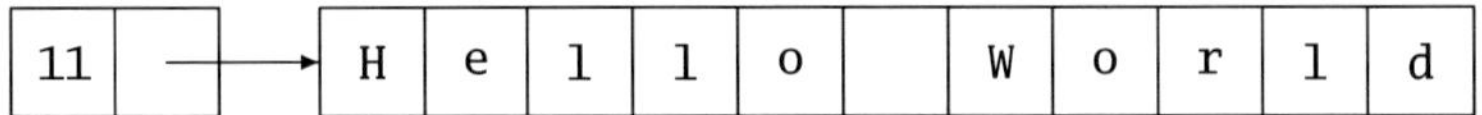

Ada supports null-terminated strings (see `Interfaces.C.Strings` §B.3.1) that are used to manipulate strings passed to or received from external subprograms written in C or in any language that uses that representation.

Obviously, the more flexible the string type, the more overhead is required. For bounded strings, the maximum length must be at least as large as the longest string of the type that will be used; this will waste memory if many of the strings are much shorter. For unbounded strings, allocation and deallocation of memory may be needed for each operation. The subprogram libraries for all three types are very similar, so it is easy to change the string type without extensive modifications to a program.

Package `Ada.Strings.Maps` §A.4.2 implements operations on type `Character_Set`, which will be familiar if you have used a string processing language like SNOBOL or Icon, or libraries for pattern matching in other languages. Character sets are used as patterns in search operations such as "find the first occurrence of any upper case character." The package also declares the type `Character_Mapping`, which can be used to translate one set of characters to another. The case study in Section 11.3 demonstrates the use of these packages.

11.2 Multibyte characters and strings*

Once upon a time, the 7-bit ASCII code sufficed for representing characters and strings. Today, there is a demand for software that can manipulate text in all natural languages, as well as other notations like that used for musical scores. Because writing systems have been developing for thousands of years, text processing is a complex subject that should be studied in detail before you undertake to write multilingual software. The Unicode website (`http://unicode.org`) is a good place to start.

In Ada 83, the only character and string types were the one-byte `Character` type, and the type `String`, which is a packed array of components of type `Character`. Ada 95 added the two-byte `Wide_Character` type and the associated type `Wide_String`, while Ada 2005 supports the four-byte `Wide_Wide_Character` type and the associated type `Wide_Wide_String`. The

Ada 2005 reference manual defines the types in terms of the ISO/IEC 10646 international standard, the *Universal Character Set (UCS)*. (UCS is similar to the Unicode standard.)

§3.5.2

> 2 The predefined type Character is a character type whose values correspond to the 256 code positions of Row 00 (also known as Latin-1) of the ISO/IEC 10646:2003 Basic Multilingual Plane (BMP). . . .
>
> 3 The predefined type Wide_Character is a character type whose values correspond to the 65536 code positions of the ISO/IEC 10646:2003 Basic Multilingual Plane (BMP). . . . The first 256 values of Wide_Character have the same character_literal or language-defined name as defined for Character. . . .
>
> 3.1 The predefined type Wide_Wide_Character is a character type whose values correspond to the 2147483648 code positions of the ISO/IEC 10646:2003 character set. . . . The first 65536 values of Wide_Wide_Character have the same character_literal or language-defined name as defined for Wide_Character.

The values of `Character` form an initial subsequence of the values of `Wide_Character`, which in turn form an initial subsequence of the values of `Wide_Wide_Character`. This means that it is straightforward to convert a value of type `Character` to `Wide_Character` and a "small" value of type `Wide_Character` to `Character`. Similar conversions can be done between `Character` or `Wide_Character` and `Wide_Wide_Character`.

Any of these characters can be used when writing a program §2.1(1). However, these standard character sets only define the *abstract* lexical units of an Ada program, not the actual encoding of the source files. An implementation is free to use any encoding such as UTF-8, the popular Unicode encoding. To faciliate the maintenance of programs in an international environment, it is recommended that wide and wide-wide characters not be used outside of strings and comments.

11.2.1 *Case study: currency symbols*

If you need only a few characters and strings belonging to a local writing system, it is possible to write a portable program that uses them. We will demonstrate this by showing how to display currency symbols. (These symbols can be used in the case study in Section 13.8.1.) The 256 values of type `Character` defined in the ISO 8859-1 encoding are given names in the package `Ada.Characters.Latin_1` §A.3.3. This set includes characters needed to write European languages (like French, German and the Scandinavian languages), as well as many useful symbols such as those for the British Pound and the Japanese Yen §A.3.3(21).

curr

```
1 with Ada.Wide_Text_IO; use Ada.Wide_Text_IO;
2 with Ada.Characters.Conversions, Ada.Characters.Latin_1;
3 procedure Curr is
4   Yen:    constant Character := Ada.Characters.Latin_1.Yen_Sign;
5   S:      String := "The symbol for the Yen is  " &  Yen;
```

The Euro symbol did not exist when the ISO 8859-1 encoding was created. (It does exist at position 164 in the ISO 8859-9 encoding, which your implementation may support.) The code for the symbol is 20AC (in hexadecimal), which can be stored in a constant of type `Wide_Character`. The attribute `Val` §3.5.5(5–7) can be used to convert the integer code to a value of type `Wide_Character`:

```
6   Euro1: constant Wide_Character := Wide_Character'Val(16#20AC#);
7   WS1:   Wide_String := "The symbol for the Euro is " & Euro1;
```

There is also a language-defined name (string) that uses hexadecimal numbers for all characters whose code is greater than 256 §3.5.2(3.2). This string can be converted by the attribute `Value` §3.5(40–43) to a value of type `Wide_Character`:

```
8   Euro2: constant Wide_Character := Wide_Character'Value("Hex_000020AC");
9   WS2:   Wide_String := "The symbol for the Euro is " & Euro2;
```

As mentioned above, an implementation may support any representation for the characters in a source file. For example, the GNAT implementation supports a convenient syntax for wide characters that is useful when strings rather than individual characters are needed:

```
10  Euro3: constant Wide_Character := '["20AC"]';
11  WS3: Wide_String := "The symbol for the Euro is " & Euro3;
12
13  Euro_Rupee_Yuan: Wide_String :=
14    "Euro is ["20AC"], Rupee is ["20A8"], Yuan is ["5143"]";
```

Values of type `Wide_String` can be printed out using the package `Ada.Wide_Text_IO`, which is similar to `Ada.Text_IO`. The variable `S` ‡5 is of type `String` so we first convert it to `Wide_Character` before calling `Put_Line`:

```
15 begin
16   Put_Line(Ada.Characters.Conversions.To_Wide_String(S));
17   Put_Line(WS1);
18   Put_Line(WS2);
19   Put_Line(WS3);
20   Put_Line(Euro_Rupee_Yuan);
21 end Curr;
```

These characters may not actually be displayed on your computer if they do not exist in the font you are using, but you are assured that they will be on an appropriately localized computer.

Do not try to mix output of type `String`, `Wide_String` and `Wide_Wide_String` in the same file; files can carry an indication of their encoding and an encoding appropriate for one type may not be appropriate for another.

Ada 95

The hexadecimal names "Hex_nnnnnnnn" are not in Ada 95, nor are `Wide_Wide_Character` and `Wide_Wide_String`. Check what encodings your implementation supports.

11.3 Case study: dot2dot

This case study demonstrates the use of the libraries for strings and containers. Chapter 16 is an overview of the container library that you may wish to read before this case study.

The program reads a file in the format of the DOT language for describing graphs, which is used by the GRAPHVIZ suite of tools. The `dot` program employs sophisticated algorithms to lay out graphs described in the DOT language, and to generate the output in a variety of graphics formats like PNG. Here is an example of a directed graph described in DOT:

```
digraph "third"  {
  graphs [ ranksep = .25 size = "16,12" ];
  nodes  [ fontsize = 14 height = 1.2 width = 1.6 ];
  edges  [ style = bold ];
  0 [ color = red label = "11. wantq = 1\n" ];
  1 [ color = red label = "12. !wantp\n" ];
     ...
  6 [ label = "6. wantp = 0\n" ];
  7 [ label = "6. wantp = 1" ];
  0 -> 1 [ color = red ];
  0 -> 4;
     ...
  6 -> 7;
  7 -> 1;
}
```

(This is a simplified form of the state graph of a concurrent program.)

The first line gives the name of the directed graph. This is followed by a sequence of one or more lines specifying global attributes of the graph, the nodes or the edges. Next is a list of the nodes in the graph; each node has a name (here, a number), and is optionally followed by a list of attributes local to the node. The edges are given by a pair of node names, separated by the token ->, and optionally followed by a list of attributes local to the edge.

The program in the case study reads a file in DOT format and writes a file with the elements sorted and formatted in a uniform manner. The program accepts a subset of the DOT language, and you may wish to extend it to accept the full language as described in the documentation on the GRAPHVIZ website (`http://graphviz.org`). In particular, we limit the attributes and their names to fixed-length strings, and use bounded strings with a maximum length for statements in the source file.

11.3.1 Defining the data structures

Subtype `Name` will be used for the attributes, and the fixed-length strings will be padded with spaces. The length of an input line is limited to `Line_Length`:

dot2dot

```
package Config is
  subtype Name is String(1..20);
  Line_Length: constant Positive := 120;
end Config;
```

Package `Lines`, an instantiation of `Ada.Strings.Bounded.Generic_Bounded_Length` §A.4.4, contains the type `Bounded_String`; its maximum length is `Config.Line_Length`:

```
with Config;
with Ada.Strings.Bounded;
package Lines is
  new Ada.Strings.Bounded.Generic_Bounded_Length(Config.Line_Length);
```

`Ada.Text_IO.Bounded_IO` §A.10.11 for input–output of bounded strings is instantiated:

```
with Lines; with Ada.Text_IO.Bounded_IO;
package Lines_IO is
  new Ada.Text_IO.Bounded_IO(Lines);
```

This generic package has a formal package parameter, which must be a generic package:

```
generic
  with package Bounded is
    new Ada.Strings.Bounded.Generic_Bounded_Length (<>);
```

The actual parameter must be an instantiation of the formal parameter (Section 9.8).

A list of attributes (associated either globally with all nodes or edges, or locally with a single node or edge) is stored in an *ordered map* (Section 16.4.2) that associates values called *elements* with *keys*. The generic package Ada.Containers.Ordered_Maps has the formal type parameters Key_Type and Element_Type. Here, the keys are the attribute names and the elements are the attribute values; for our simplified program, both are fixed strings of subtype Config.Name:

```
with Config;
with Ada.Containers.Ordered_Maps;
package Attribute_Maps is
  new Ada.Containers.Ordered_Maps(Config.Name, Config.Name);
```

The package declares the (tagged) private type Map and a large set of operations §A.18.4. An instantiation of Ada.Containers.Ordered_Maps requires an actual parameter that is a function "<" for comparing values of type Key_Type. Here, it is implicitly supplied (Section 9.3) as the function "<" for type String, which is declared in package Standard and always visible.

Our next task is to design a data structure for storing the elements of the graph—the nodes and edges; the same record type Element is used for both. It has three components: a node Source, a second node Target (which is blank for nodes), and a map of attributes, initialized to the empty map §A.18.6(6):

```
with Config; with Attribute_Maps;
package Elements is
  Blanks: constant Config.Name := (others => ' ');
  type Element is
    record
      Source:     Config.Name;
      Target:     Config.Name        := Blanks;
      Attributes: Attribute_Maps.Map := Attribute_Maps.Empty_Map;
    end record;
```

For the purpose of storing the elements in a data structure and sorting them, we define the operators "=" and "<".

```
   function "="(Left, Right: Element) return Boolean;
   function "<"(Left, Right: Element) return Boolean;
end Elements;
```

They are implemented in the package body by comparing the source and target nodes; the attribute map is ignored by these functions. (The source code is in the software archive.)

The data structure that we choose for graph elements is the *vector*, which is an array that expands automatically as needed (Section 16.2). This is implemented in the container library Ada.Container.Vectors §A.18.2, which is a generic package that takes three formal parameters: a discrete Index_Type, a private Element_Type and an equality function "=" for the elements. In the following instantiation, the actual parameter for the equality function is implicitly taken as the function that is made visible by the use_clause for the package Elements:

```
with Ada.Containers.Vectors;
with Elements; use Elements;
package Element_Vectors is
  new Ada.Containers.Vectors(Natural, Element);
```

The package defines the (tagged) private type `Vector` and a set of operations on the type.

We are finally ready to define the data structure that will hold the global attributes and the elements of the graph. The record type `Table` contains four components: the name of the graph, an array of three maps for the global attributes (of the graph, the nodes and the edges), a vector of elements for the nodes, and another vector for the edges:

```
with Ada.Text_IO;
with Element_Vectors, Attribute_Maps, Lines, Config;
package Dot_Tables is
  type Attribute is (Graphs, Nodes, Edges);

  type Attribute_Map_Arrays is array(Attribute) of Attribute_Maps.Map;

  type Table is
    record
      Graph_Name:          Config.Name;
      Attribute_Map_Array: Attribute_Map_Arrays;
      Nodes:               Element_Vectors.Vector;
      Edges:               Element_Vectors.Vector;
    end record;
```

In our simplified program, the only operations on a table are to sort it and to write the data to an output file:

```
  procedure Sort(T: in out Table);
  procedure Put(T:  in Table; Output: in Ada.Text_IO.File_Type);
end Dot_Tables;
```

11.3.2 Reading, sorting and writing the graph files

The generic package `Generic_Sorting` (declared locally within both `Ada.Containers.Vectors` §A.18.2(75–79) and `Ada.Containers.Doubly_Linked_List` §A.18.3(47–52)) is used to sort the node and edge vectors. It is instantiated with the "<" operator as the actual parameter:

```
with Ada.Text_IO, Ada.Characters.Handling, Ada.Strings.Fixed;
with Elements, Element_Vectors;
package body Dot_Tables is
  package Element_Sort is
    new Element_Vectors.Generic_Sorting(Elements."<");

  procedure Sort(T: in out Table) is
  begin
    Element_Sort.Sort(T.Nodes);
    Element_Sort.Sort(T.Edges);
  end Sort;
```

We will be using the function Ada.Strings.Fixed.Trim §A.4.3(31,89) frequently. The function is renamed as a local function for two reasons. First, it shortens the name of the function without employing a use_clause. Second, since the second parameter will always be the same, the renaming declaration can specify it as a default parameter §8.5.4(7):

```
  function Trim(
    Source: in String;
    Side:   in Ada.Strings.Trim_End := Ada.Strings.Right) return String
      renames Ada.Strings.Fixed.Trim;
```

To implement the function Put, we need to iterate over all the elements in each of the maps and vectors. Each container has a first and last element and, in addition, a (private) type Cursor is defined for references to the "current" Position in the container:

Given a position in a map, it is easy to obtain the values of the key and element at that position §A.18.4(31–34). These are used in Put_Attribute, which is to be called for the attribute at each position in each of the maps:

```
  procedure Put(T: in Table; Output: in Ada.Text_IO.File_Type) is
    use Ada.Text_IO;
    procedure Put_Attribute(Position: in Attribute_Maps.Cursor) is
    begin
      Put(Output,
          Trim(Attribute_Maps.Key(Position))     & " = " &
          Trim(Attribute_Maps.Element(Position)) & ' ');
    end Put_Attribute;
```

The procedure Put_Element is to be called for the element at each position in the two vectors Nodes and Edges of a table. First, the source node and the target node for an edge are printed:

```
   procedure Put_Element(Position: in Element_Vectors.Cursor) is
     E: Elements.Element renames Element_Vectors.Element(Position);
   begin
     Put(Output, Trim(E.Source));
     if E.Target /= Elements.Blanks then
       Put(Output, " -> " & Trim(E.Target));
     end if;
```

Next, E.Attributes, the map of attributes for the element must be printed. Printing of *all* the attributes in the map is accomplished automatically by calling the procedure Iterate §A.18.4(74–75) with a pointer to the procedure Put_Attribute that prints each attribute. The Access attribute returns the address of the subprogram:

```
     if not Attribute_Maps.Is_Empty(E.Attributes) then
       Put(Output, " [ ");
       Attribute_Maps.Iterate(E.Attributes, Put_Attribute'Access);
       Put(Output, "]");
     end if;
     Put_Line(Output, ";");
   end Put_Element;
```

The body of the procedure Put begins with calls to Iterate with Put_Attribute'Access for each list of global attributes:

```
 begin
   Put_Line(Output, "digraph " & Trim(T.Graph_Name) & "  {");
   for A in Attribute loop
     Put(Output, "  " &
         Ada.Characters.Handling.To_Lower(Attribute'Image(A)) & " [ ");
     Attribute_Maps.Iterate(
       T.Attribute_Map_Array(A), Put_Attribute'Access);
     Put_Line(Output, "]");
   end loop;
```

Iterate is called to execute Put_Element for each node and edge. This results in nested calls to Iterate for each element of the map contained in each element of the vector.

```
   Element_Vectors.Iterate(T.Nodes, Put_Element'Access);
   Element_Vectors.Iterate(T.Edges, Put_Element'Access);
   Put_Line(Output, "}");
 end Put;
end Dot_Tables;
```

The main procedure `Dot2Dot` contains four local subprograms:

- Function `Pad`, which calls the `Head` subprogram §A.4.3(97–98) to pad strings;
- Procedure `Get_Name`, which gets the next token from the input;
- Procedure `State_Machine`, which parses the input;
- Procedure `Main_Loop`, which calls `Get_Name` and `State_Machine` as long as there is input.

The full source code of the first three of these subprograms and the global declarations for the parser are omitted and can be found in the software archive.

```
with Ada.Text_IO, Ada.Exceptions, Ada.Command_Line;
with Ada.Strings.Fixed, Ada.Strings.Bounded;
with Config, Lines, Lines_IO, Dot_Tables;
procedure Dot2Dot is
  -- The declarations for the parser are omitted
  Syntax_Error: exception;
  Table:        Dot_Tables.Table;

  function  Pad(S: in String) return Config.Name is ...
  procedure State_Machine(N: in Config.Name) is separate;
  procedure Get_Name(
    L:      in out Lines.Bounded_String;
    Finish: in out Natural;
    N:      out Config.Name) is separate;
```

The bodies of the subprogram `Get_Name` and `State_Machine` are declared as *subunits* with **`separate`** §10.1.3, partly to reduce the size of the source file and partly to limit the number of **`with`** clauses needed on each unit (Section 15.3).

The main loop is straightforward:

```
  procedure Main_Loop(Input, Output: in Ada.Text_IO.File_Type) is
    S:      Lines.Bounded_String;
    N:      Config.Name;
    Finish: Natural := 0;
  begin
    loop
      S := Lines_IO.Get_Line(Input);
      loop
        Get_Name(S, Finish, N);
        exit when Finish = 0;
        State_Machine(N);
      end loop;
    end loop;
```

When a syntax error is encountered by the parser, an exception is raised and propagated to this procedure, where it is handled by printing an error message (see Section 10.4):

```
exception
  when E: Syntax_Error =>
    Ada.Text_IO.Put_Line(
      Ada.Exceptions.Exception_Message(E) & " expected");
    Lines_IO.Put_Line(S);
```

When the entire input has been parsed and the data from the file placed in `Table`, exception `End_Error` is raised and its exception handler calls subprograms to sort and print the data:

```
  when Ada.Text_IO.End_Error =>
    Dot_Tables.Sort(Table);
    Dot_Tables.Put(Table, Output);
end Main_Loop;
```

The body of the main subprogram `Dot2Dot` (omitted here) gets the file name from the command line (see `Ada.Command_Line` §A.15) and constructs a name for the output file using the functions `Index` §A.4.3(57) and `Insert` §A.4.3(77).

We present here an outline of the procedure `Get_Name` that is called when parsing the input. String maps (`Ada.Strings.Maps` §A.4.2) are used to identify classes of characters. We use three sets that are defined according to the syntax of DOT:

- `Space_Set`, which includes commas and tabs in addition to the space character;
- `Word_Set`, which includes underscores and the decimal point;
- `Punc_Set` for the punctuation characters.

```
with Ada.Characters.Latin_1, Ada.Characters.Handling;
with Ada.Strings.Maps.Constants;
separate (dot2dot)
procedure Get_Name(
  L: in out Lines.Bounded_String;
  Finish: in out Natural; N: out Config.Name) is
  use Lines, Ada.Strings.Maps;

  Space_Set: constant Character_Set :=
    To_Set(" ," & Ada.Characters.Latin_1.HT);
  Word_Set:  constant Character_Set :=
    Constants.Alphanumeric_Set or To_Set("._");
  Punc_Set:  constant Character_Set :=
    To_Set("{}[];=");
  First: Positive;    -- For call of Find_Token
```

The function `To_Set` §A.4.2(44-47) is used to transform a string into a set of characters.

Here is one case of `Get_Name` that demonstrates how to use the subprograms in the string library. Function `Is_In` §A.4.2(40–41) checks if the first `Element` §A.4.4(96–97) of the (rest of the) input string is within `Word_Set`. If so, it calls `Find_Token` §A.4.4(51,103), §A.4.3(67–68) to find the indices of the beginning and end of the longest consecutive sequence of characters that are `Inside` the set `Word_Set`.

```
   elsif Is_In(Element(L, 1), Word_Set) then
     Find_Token(L, Word_Set, Ada.Strings.Inside, First, Finish);
     if Finish = 0 then return; end if;
```

Once a token is found, it is extracted from the bounded string into a fixed string by calling `Slice` §A.4.4(100–101) and then `Move` §A.4.3(44-56):

```
   Ada.Strings.Fixed.Move(Slice(L, 1, Finish), N);
end Get_Name;
```

The procedure `State_Machine` is fairly long and we will limit ourselves to presenting two statements that insert values into the data structures: inserting a node into a vector and adding an attribute to the node. Recall that a line describing a node looks like:

```
1 [ color = red label = "12. !wantp\n" ];
```

When the string "1" is read into the variable `Current_Name`, a node with that name will be entered into the vector `Nodes` of the variable `Table` of type `Dot_Tables.Table`:

```
   Element_Vectors.Append(
     Table.Nodes,
     (Source => Current_Name, Target => <>, Attributes => <>));
```

The subprogram `Append` places the node at the end of the vector:

§A.18.2

172 **procedure** Append(Container : **in out** Vector; New_Item : **in** Vector);

173 Equivalent to Insert (Container, Last_Index (Container) + 1, New_Item).

Note that many operations like `Append` are defined in terms or other operations, in this case `Insert` and `Last_Index`.

Since there are default values for the components `Target` and `Attributes`, they can be initialized using the box symbol in the aggregate §4.3.1(19.1).

Following the name of the node is the list of the attributes, in this case, one for the color of the node and one for its label. The list appears in the same DOT statement as the name, so we know that the attributes are to be placed in the last element appended to the vector §A.18.2(205–206). The vector element is copied into a local variable:

```
E := Element_Vectors.Last_Element(Table.Nodes);
```

Then the attribute name and value are inserted into the attribute map component of the vector element §A.18.4(48–49).

```
Attribute_Maps.Insert(E.Attributes, Current_Name, N);
```

Finally, the vector element is replaced back into the vector §A.18.2(134–135).

```
Element_Vectors.Replace_Element(
  Table.Nodes, Element_Vectors.Last(Table.Nodes), E);
```

The function `Last` §A.18.2(61) returns the position of the last element in the vector.

Ada 95

Ada 95 does not have the box notation for aggregates; this is not a problem here since the default values are visible.

The Container library is new in Ada 2005, as is `Ada.Text_IO.Bounded_IO` §A.10.11.

11.4 Discriminants

Discriminants are used for parameterizing types. We have met *known discriminants* in the implementation of a queue by an array:

```
type Queue(Size: Positive) is
  record
    Data: Vector(0..Size);
    Free: Natural := 0;
  end record;
```

and *unknown discriminants* in generic formal parameters:

```
generic
  type Item is (<>);
package Priority_Queue is ...
```

§3.7

1 A composite type (other than an array type or interface type) can have discriminants, which parameterize the type. A known_discriminant_part specifies the discriminants of a composite type. A discriminant of an object is a component of the object, and is either of a discrete type or an access type. An unknown_discriminant_part in the declaration of a view of a type specifies that the discriminants of the type are unknown for the given view; all subtypes of such a view are indefinite subtypes.

3 unknown_discriminant_part ::= (<>)

4 known_discriminant_part ::=
    (discriminant_specification {; discriminant_specification})

5 discriminant_specification ::=
    defining_identifier_list: [null_exclusion] subtype_mark [:= default_expression]
  | defining_identifier_list: access_definition [:= default_expression]

Discriminants are primarily used to parameterize record types, but they can also parameterize tasks and protected objects (Sections 18.1, 19.9). A discriminant in a record type declaration declares a *constant* §3.3(18) component of the record §3.8(9). When an object of a discriminated type is created, a value must be given for each discriminant either by a discriminant constraint §3.7.1 as we did in the priority queue programs:

```
Q: Queue(Size => 4);
```

or by an initial value:

```
Q: Queue := (Size => 4, Data => (0, 1, 2, 3, 4), Free => <>);
```

As with unconstrained arrays, a formal parameter with a discriminant takes its constraint from an actual parameter, so we can call the procedure Put:

```
procedure Put(I: in Integer; Q: in out Queue);
```

with queues whose Size discriminant takes on different values.

Since discriminants are constants, it is illegal to assign a value to them. The reason is that discriminants are used to control which components exist in a record and changing the discriminant would break type-checking:

```
Q: Queue(Size => 10);

Q.Size      := 100;        -- Illegal, otherwise ...
Q.Data(62) := 35;          -- ... this would be legal
```

While it is not possible to change the discriminant alone, a discriminated record can be assigned to as a whole in an assignment statement or during the assignment of an actual parameter to a formal parameter. There is a check that the discriminants match to ensure that the two records have the same components:

```
Q1: Queue := (Size => 4, Data => (0, 1, 2, 3, 4), Free => <>);
Q2: Queue := (Size => 4, Data => (4, 3, 2, 1, 0), Free => <>);
Q3: Queue := (Size => 3, Data => (4, 3, 2, 1),    Free => <>);

Q2 := Q1;          -- OK
Q3 := Q1;          -- Error
```

Assignment statements (and parameter passing §6.4.1(10,11,14)) include a type conversion:

§5.2

> 11 The value of the expression is converted to the subtype of the target. The conversion might raise an exception (see 4.6).

and constraints are checked during type conversion:

§4.6

> 51 After conversion of the value to the target type, if the target subtype is constrained, a check is performed that the value satisfies this constraint. ...
> 57 ... Any other check associated with a conversion raises Constraint_Error if it fails.

Within a record declaration, a discriminant can be used in a default *expression* for another component, but if it is used to constrain a component it must appear directly and not as part of a larger expression §3.8(12):

```
type Queue(Size: Positive) is
  record
    Data: Vector(0..Size+1);       -- Error
    Free: Natural := 0;
  end record;
```

11.5 Variant records

Discriminants can be used to create variant records, where the existence of some of the record components *depends on* §3.7(20,22) the discriminants. An important use of variant records is in the conversion of unstructured data to a structured record. For example, a buffer of bytes from a communications link can be converted to any one of a set of structures depending upon a discriminant.

11.5.1 *Case study: message conversion*

The following program shows how to use variant records for structuring a sequence of bytes. The case study also demonstrates modular types (Section 13.4) and representation attributes (Section 20.2).

First we define a type `Byte` as one *storage unit* and an input–output package for the type:

message

```
with Ada.Text_IO; use Ada.Text_IO;
with Ada.Integer_Text_IO; use Ada.Integer_Text_IO;
with System; with Ada.Unchecked_Conversion;
procedure Message is
  type Byte is mod 2**System.Storage_Unit;
  for  Byte'Size use System.Storage_Unit;

  package Byte_IO is new Ada.Text_IO.Modular_IO(Byte);
  use Byte_IO;
```

Type `Structured_Message` is a variant record whose discriminant is the enumerated type `Codes`. The record has four common components: the discriminant `Code`, `Addressee`, `Sender` and `Sequence_Number`; the other components depend on the discriminant:

```
  type Codes is (M0, M1, M2, M3);
  for  Codes'Size use System.Storage_Unit;

  type Structured_Message(Code: Codes) is
    record
      Addressee:       Byte;
      Sender:          Byte;
      Sequence_Number: Byte;
      case Code is
        when M0 => null;
        when M1 => A: Integer;
        when M2 => B: Character;
        when M3 => C: Integer; D: Integer;
      end case;
    end record;
  pragma Pack(Structured_Message);
```

(See Section 20.2.1 for an explanation of **pragma** `Pack`.)

Type `Raw_Message` is an array of bytes of exactly the size needed to hold a value of type `Structured_Message`:

```
Max_Bytes: constant Integer :=
  Structured_Message'Size/System.Storage_Unit;
type Raw_Message is array(1..Max_Bytes) of Byte;
pragma Pack(Raw_Message);
```

Type conversion between Structured_Message and Raw_Message must be done by instantiating the generic function Ada.Unchecked_Conversion §13.9:

```
function To_Raw is new Ada.Unchecked_Conversion(
  Source => Structured_Message, Target => Raw_Message);

function To_Structured is new Ada.Unchecked_Conversion(
  Source => Raw_Message, Target => Structured_Message);
```

While the size of Raw_Message was computed from the size of Structured_Message, there is no assurance that the value of the byte for the message code corresponds to the value of the discriminant for the message structure.

To send a message over a communications line requires only that a structured message be converted to a raw message:

```
function Send_Message(S: Structured_Message) return Raw_Message is
begin
  return To_Raw(S);
end Send_Message;
```

The procedure Process_Message receives a raw message, converts it to a structured messages and "processes" it (prints the values of the components) using a case-statement that takes the variants into account:

```
procedure Process_Message(R: Raw_Message) is
  S: Structured_Message := To_Structured(R);
begin
  -- Put common components, then
  case S.Code is
    when M0 => null;
    when M1 => Put(S.A);
    when M2 => Put(S.B);
    when M3 => Put(S.C); Put(S.D);
  end case;
  New_Line;
end Process_Message;
```

To test the program, aggregates for messages are created, sent and then processed:

```
begin
   Process_Message(Send_Message((M1, 11, 32, 1, 54)));
   Process_Message(Send_Message((M2, 32, 11, 2, 'X')));
   Process_Message(Send_Message((M3, 32, 11, 3, 45, 68)));
end Message;
```

In an aggregate, the discriminant is just another component with the restriction that it must be static since it determines which components are needed §4.3.1(17). In order to verify that the remaining components have the proper type, we need to know statically what components are present, and thus the value of the discriminant must be static as well.

11.6 Unconstrained types

§3.7.2

> 1 If a discriminated type has default_expressions for its discriminants, then unconstrained variables of the type are permitted, and the discriminants of such a variable can be changed by assignment to the variable. ...

Such objects are often called *mutable records*.

The default expression serves two purposes: it gives the initial value of the discriminant so it won't have an undefined value, and it is a syntactic marker that unconstrained records of this type can be created.

Unconstrained records can be used to implement bounded strings:

```
subtype Index is Natural range 0..255;
type Bounded_String(Length: Index := 80) is
  record
    S: String(1..Length);
  end record;
```

Let us declare the constrained variables B1 and B2, and the *unconstrainted variable* B3:

```
B1: Bounded_String(90) := (90, (others => ' '));
B2: Bounded_String(50) := (50, (others => ' '));
B3: Bounded_String;
```

Assignment of B1 to B2 or conversely will raise Constraint_Error. The declaration of B3 is legal because its discriminant has a default expression (of 80). Either of the variables B1 or B2 can be assigned to B3. It is still illegal to assign to the discriminant alone, but by assigning to the entire record, we ensure the consistency of the discriminant with the components that depend upon it.

There is no difficulty in understanding how B2 with 50 characters can be assigned to B3, but how can we assign B1 with 90 characters to B3, which has only 80 characters? One possibility is to allocate and deallocate memory as needed, but this is inefficient. Instead, the *maximum* amount of memory needed to contain any value of the type can be allocated:

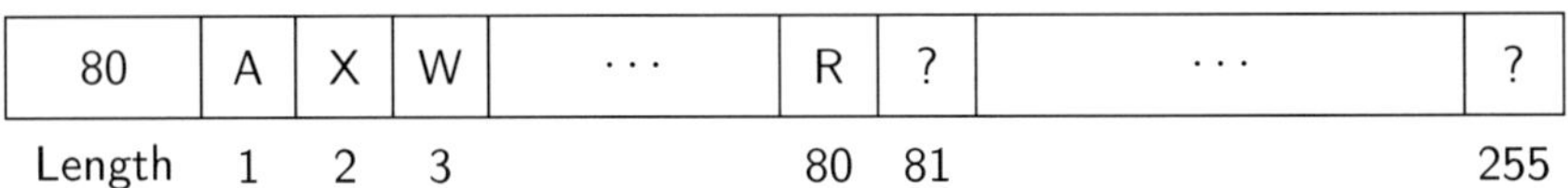

The discriminant exists solely for the purposes of type-checking that the value of Length is less than or equal to the size of the string.

Sharp-eyed readers will have noted that we defined the subtype of the discriminant to be Index, which is constrained to 256 values, rather than, say, Positive. If Positive were used, your implementation will probably try to allocate Positive'Last bytes to each unconstrained variable of this type, raising Storage_Error!

> **Language Comparison**
>
> Unconstrained variant records in Ada are similar to *union types* in C in that both enable an object of a type to hold differently structured values at different times during the execution of a program. One difference is that the discriminants in Ada are components that require memory. For interfacing with C, Ada 2005 supports *unchecked unions* (Section 20.3.4).

11.7 Discriminants of private types*

Discriminants are allowed for private types so that a private type can be parameterized even though the client does not know what use is made of the discriminant.

§7.3

> 9 If the declaration of a partial view includes a known_discriminant_part, then the full_type_declaration shall have a fully conforming (explicit) known_discriminant_part (see 6.3.1, "Conformance Rules"). . . .

This construct was used in the priority queue package, where the type Queue had the same discriminant, both in its partial view and its full type declaration:

```
    type Queue(Size: Positive) is private;
  private
    type Queue(Size: Positive) is ...
```

Consider now:

```
  type Queue is private;
private
  type Queue ???
```

If the partial view has no discriminant, the client can create an object of the type, so the full type declaration *must* be for a definite subtype:

§7.3

> 12 If a partial view has neither known nor unknown discriminants, then the full_type_declaration shall define a definite subtype.

A partial view may also have *unknown discriminants*:

§7.3

> 11 If a partial view has unknown discriminants, then the full_type_declaration may define a definite or an indefinite subtype, with or without discriminants.

Since the type is indefinite §3.3(23), the client cannot declare uninitialized objects of this type, and there need be no restrictions on the full type. You can use unknown discriminants to force the client to call an explicit initialization function:

```
package Priority_Queue is
  type Queue(<>) is private;
  function Init return Queue;
private
  type Queue is array(Natural range <>) of Integer;
end Priority_Queue;

  Q1: Priority_Queue.Queue;           -- Error, indefinite
  Q2: Priority_Queue.Queue := Init;   -- OK, constrained by initial value
```

11.8 Inheriting discriminants*

What happens if the parent type in a type extension has a discriminant:

```
type T(Size: Positive) is tagged
  record
    S: String(1..Size);
  end record;
```

Certainly, the following declaration is illegal:

```
type T1(Count: Positive) is new T with ...
```

because the parent type T must be constrained §3.7(13) so that the implementation can know how much memory to allocate its components. The discriminant of the parent type must be used in one of three ways.

§3.7

> 18 For a type defined by a derived_type_definition, each discriminant of the parent type is either inherited, constrained to equal some new discriminant of the derived type, or constrained to the value of an expression. ...

The three cases are demonstrated in the following modification of the simulation case study.

11.8.1 Case study: simulation with discriminants

Suppose that each object of type Event can represent multiple real events, where the number of events is given by the discriminant Number:

rocketd

```
package Event_Package is
  type Event(Number: Positive) is abstract tagged
    record
      Time: Simulation_Time;
      Code: String(1..Number);
    end record;
```

The discriminant is used to constrain a string of codes containing one character for each of the multiple events.

Engine_Event *replaces* the discriminant Number with new ones, and one of them is used to constrain the parent type:

```
  type Engine_Event(Count: Positive; Engines: Positive) is
     new Event(Number => Count) with ...
```

Steering_Event *inherits* the discriminant Number:

```
  type Steering_Event is new Event with ...
```

Telemetry_Event has no discriminants; instead it *constrains* the discriminant of the parent with an expression:

```
  type Telemetry_Event is new Event(Number => 4) with ...
```

11.9 Untagged derived types*

A new type can be derived from any type, not just from a tagged type. The concepts of primitive operation, inheritance and overriding are the same; however, untagged types cannot be extended, class-wide types cannot be declared, and there is no dynamic polymorphism.

Derived types are used among other things to define numeric types (Chapter 13). Derived types can also be used to declare a new type with the same structure as an existing type. Consider the definition of the type Queue in the tree implementation of a priority queue:

```
type Queue is
  record
    Root: Link;
  end record;
```

The purpose of the definition is to ensure that Queue and Link are different types, even though Queue is implemented as a single Link. This improves type checking and makes it possible to overload a subprogram name on both types. The same effect could be achieved by deriving Queue from Link:

```
type Queue is new Link;
```

although Queue would inherit the primitive subprograms defined for Link, which we do not want here.

11.9.1 Case study: representation conversion

A derived type can have a different representation §13.6 from the parent type, and type conversion between the two record types will convert between representations.

In the following program, the record Instruction has two fields:

rep

```
with Ada.Text_IO; use Ada.Text_IO;
procedure Rep is
  type Operators is (Op0, Op1, Op2, Op3, Op4, Op5, Op6, Op7);
  type Byte is mod 256;
  type Instruction is
    record
      Op_Code: Operators;
      Operand: Byte range 0..31;
    end record;
```

An implementation will typically store values of type Instruction in two words or bytes, but suppose that a packed representation is needed, where an 8-bit instruction stores Op_Code in three bits and Operand in five. This is implemented by deriving a new type, and then providing a *record representation clause* §13.5.1 to lay out the record and a *representation attribute* §13.3 for the size (Section 20.2):

```
   type Packed_Instruction is new Instruction;
   for Packed_Instruction use
     record
       Op_Code at 0 range 0..2;
       Operand at 0 range 3..7;
     end record;
   for Packed_Instruction'Size use 8;
```

Now values can be converted from one type to the other and their components can be accessed in either representation, although it is to be expected that accessing the packed components will be less efficient:

```
   PI: Packed_Instruction := (Op3, 26);
   I:  Instruction        := Instruction(PI);
begin
   Put(Operators'Image(PI.Op_Code));
   Put(Byte'Image(PI.Operand));
   Put(Operators'Image(I.Op_Code));
   Put(Byte'Image(I.Operand));
end Rep;
```

Language Comparison

Most programming languages do not allow records to be packed. When multiple bit fields within a byte or word are necessary, they must be accessed using shift and mask instructions, which are quite error-prone.

11.10 Untagged derived types and discriminants*

Since no components can be added upon derivation of an untagged type, any new discriminants must use the same memory that was reserved for the old discriminants:

§3.7

> 14 If the parent type is not a tagged type, then each discriminant of the derived type shall be used in the constraint defining the parent subtype;

Suppose that the types in the Event were untagged:

```
type Event(Number: Positive) is    -- Untagged
  record
    Time: Integer;
    Code: String(1..Number);
  end record;
```

The following declaration is an error:

```
type Engine_Event(Count: Positive; Engines: Positive) is
  new Event(Number => Count);
```

because there is nowhere to store the discriminant Engines. The following derivations are legal:

```
type Aux_Engine_Event(Count: Positive) is new Event(Number => Count);
type Steering_Event  is new Event;
type Telemetry_Event is new Event(Number => 4);
```

The derived type can have fewer discriminants than the parent type, as long as all are used to constrain the parent:

```
type Event(Number: Positive; Kind: Character) is
  record
    Code: String(1..Number);
    Symbol: Character := Kind;
  end record;

type Engine_Event(Count: Positive) is
  new Event(Number => Count, Kind => 'X');
```

Projects

1. Modify the `dot2dot` case study so that a discriminated record is used to store nodes with less memory than the edges.
2. Extend the `dot2dot` case study to recognize more of the `dot` graphics language.
3. Implement the tree priority queue using an untagged derived type as outlined in Section 11.9.
4. Find out how floating point numbers are stored on your computer and, using the techniques in Section 11.5, write a subprogram to construct a floating point value from a sign, an exponent and a mantissa. Write a subprogram to unpack these values from a floating point value. You many want to use unchecked unions (Section 20.3.4).
5. One way of implementing a text editor is to use an array, storing the characters in front of the cursor at the beginning of the array and the characters after the cursor at the end of the array. Define an appropriate data structure using a discriminated record and implement the relevant operations on the data structure.

Quizzes

Quiz 1:

```
type Rec(D: Positive := 100) is
  record
    V: String(1..D);
  end record;
R: Rec;
```

Quiz 2:

```
type Rec(D: Positive) is
  record
    V: String(1..D-1);
  end record;
```

Quiz 3:

```
subtype Index is Integer range 1..100;
type Rec(Disc: Index := 100) is
  record
    Data: String(1..Disc);
  end record;
R1: Rec(100);
C1: Character renames R1.Data(100);
R2: Rec;
C2: Character renames R2.Data(100);
```

Quiz 4:

```
subtype Sizes is Integer range 1..5000;
type Queue(Size: Sizes := 100) is tagged null record;
```

Quiz 5:

```
subtype S is Integer range 0..127;
type T(First: S := 0; Second: S) is
  record
    C1: S := First;
    C2: S := Second;
  end record;
```

Quiz 6:

```
type Parent(Number: Positive; Size: Positive) is
  record
    X: String(1..Number);
    Y: String(1..Size);
  end record;
type Derived(Count: Positive) is new Parent(Count, Count);
P: Parent  := (2, 3, "ab", "cde");
D: Derived := (3, "uvw", "xyz");

D := Derived(P);
Put_Line(D.X);   Put_Line(D.Y);
```

Quiz 7:

```
package Inst is
  type Operators is (Op0, Op1, Op2, Op3, Op4, Op5, Op6, Op7);
  type Byte is mod 256;
  type Instruction is          -- as in Section 11.9.1
  procedure Print_Instruction(I: Instruction);
end Inst;

with Inst;
procedure Main is
  type Packed_Instruction is new Inst.Instruction;
  for Packed_Instruction use   -- as in Section 11.9.1
begin
  null;
end Main;
```

Chapter 12
Access Types

12.1 General access types

The access types we have been using are called *pool-specific* access types, because every access value points to a designated object that is allocated in a *storage pool* on the heap.

§3.10

> 8 Access-to-object types are further subdivided into *pool-specific* access types, whose values can designate only the elements of their associated storage pool, and *general* access types, whose values can designate the elements of any storage pool, as well as aliased objects created by declarations rather than allocators, and aliased subcomponents of other objects.

General access types can be used just like pool-specific access types to hold pointers to allocated objects:

```
type Pointer is access all Integer;
P1:  Pointer := new Integer;
```

The reserved word **all** indicates that Pointer is a general *access-to-variable* type §3.10(10).
In addition, they can be used to create pointers to declared objects:

```
N:  aliased Integer;
P2: Pointer := N'Access;
```

P2 contains a pointer to a declared object N; it is created by applying the attribute Access §3.10.2(24) to the object. The attribute can only be used on objects that are *aliased* §3.10(9). This property is usually specified explicitly by including the reserved word **aliased** §3.3.1(2) in the declaration of an object. The explicit declaration is a warning to the programmer reading the code that there might be more than one way of accessing the variable (the variable name N and the dereference P2.**all**). It is also an indication to the compiler that optimization techniques such as storing the value of the variable in a register may not be appropriate.

The rules for determining if an object is aliased (and hence if the attribute Access can be applied) are contained in §3.10(9). The dereference of an access-to-object value is aliased, so if X is a parameter of an access type or an access parameter (Section 12.6), X.**all**'Access is legal.

A formal parameter of any tagged type is aliased.

A general access type can be an *access-to-constant* type §3.10(10). Access values of these types cannot be used to modify the designated object:

```
type Pointer is access constant Integer;
N:   aliased Integer := 4;
P3:  Pointer         := N'Access;

P3.all := 5;                           --  Error
```

Do not confuse an object of an access-to-constant type with a constant object that happens to be of an access type:

```
type Pointer1 is access Integer;
N:   aliased Integer   := 4;
P4:  Pointer1          := N'Access;
P5:  constant Pointer1 := N'Access;

P5     := P4;                          -- Error
P5.all := 5;                           -- OK
```

The object P5 is an ordinary constant object that cannot be assigned to, but it is of type access-to-variable so the designated object may be assigned to.

A value of a general or pool-specific access to a type T1 can be converted to a value of a general access to a type T2, provided certain rules are followed §4.6(24.11–24.27). The converse is not possible: you cannot convert a general access type to a pool-specific access type.

12.1.1 Case study: ragged arrays

General access types can be used to implement *ragged arrays*. A ragged array is an array whose components are of different sizes. Recall that you cannot create an array of strings, because the component of an array or record must be definite:

```
String_Array: constant array(Positive range <>) of String :=    -- Error
   ("Hello ", "World");
```

To create an array of strings of arbitrary length, an array of pointers to strings can be declared:

```
type String_Pointer is access String;
String_Array: constant array(Positive range <>) of String_Pointer :=
   (new String'("Hello "), new String'("World"));
```

But now every string might be stored twice: once as constant data (possibly in read-only memory (ROM)), and once on the heap when the aggregate is created. This is unacceptable in embedded systems for two reasons: first, there may not be enough memory to store every string twice; second, copying the strings from ROM to the heap may take too much time upon start or restart of the system. (Implementations are encouraged to be more efficient in this case (Section 12.8), so check if double allocation and copying are done in your implementation.)

By using values of access-to-constant type, the double allocation can be avoided:

ragged

```
with Ada.Text_IO;
procedure Ragged is
  OK_EN:      aliased constant String := "OK";
  Apply_EN:   aliased constant String := "Apply";
  Help_EN:    aliased constant String := "Help";
  Cancel_EN:  aliased constant String := "Cancel";

  type Label_Pointer is access constant String;

  Labels: constant array(Natural range <>) of Label_Pointer :=
    (OK_EN'Access, Apply_EN'Access, Help_EN'Access, Cancel_EN'Access);
begin
  for L in Labels'Range loop
    Ada.Text_IO.Put_Line(Labels(L).all);
  end loop;
end Ragged;
```

12.2 Access-to-subprogram types

An *access-to-subprogram type* is used to define pointers to subprograms:

§3.10

> 11 An access_to_subprogram_definition defines an access-to-subprogram type and its first subtype; the parameter_profile or parameter_and_result_profile defines the *designated profile* of the access type. ...

An object of this type can be assigned an access value obtained by applying the attribute Access to any subtype-conformant subprogram §3.10.2(32):

```
type Func_Pointer is access function(L, R: Float) return Boolean;
function Compare(Left, Right: Float) return Boolean is ...
F: Func_Pointer := Compare'Access;
```

Access-to-subprogram types can be used to implement downward closures (Section 16.1.5).

12.2.1 *Case study: callbacks*

The following case study demonstrates the use of access-to-subprogram types to implement *callbacks*. This is a programming technique used in event-driven software such as graphical user interfaces. A subprogram is associated with an object such as a "button," and when the button is activated by a mouse click the subprogram is called.

Let us start by declaring two enumeration types, one for buttons and one for mouse clicks:

callb

```
with Ada.Text_IO;
procedure CallB is
  type Buttons is (OK, Apply, Help, Cancel);
  package Buttons_IO is new Ada.Text_IO.Enumeration_IO(Buttons);

  type Clicks is (Left, Middle, Right);
  package Clicks_IO is new Ada.Text_IO.Enumeration_IO(Clicks);
```

Next, the callback procedures are declared. To simplify the program, all the procedures will just display the button labels and the mouse clicks, so a generic procedure can be used:

```
  generic
    B: in Buttons;
  procedure Proc(C: in Clicks);
  procedure Proc(C: in Clicks) is
  begin
    Ada.Text_IO.Put("Clicked ");
    Clicks_IO.Put(C);
    Ada.Text_IO.Put(" on ");
    Buttons_IO.Put(B);
    Ada.Text_IO.New_Line;
  end Proc;

  procedure Proc_OK     is new Proc(OK);
  procedure Proc_Apply  is new Proc(Apply);
  procedure Proc_Help   is new Proc(Help);
  procedure Proc_Cancel is new Proc(Cancel);
```

An access-to-subprogram type is now declared. The designated subprogram of a value of this type can be any procedure with exactly one parameter of type Clicks. A constant array of pointers to callback procedures is declared and initialized with accesses to the four procedures:

```
type Callback_Pointer is access procedure(C: in Clicks);

Callbacks: constant array(Buttons) of Callback_Pointer :=
  (Proc_OK'Access,   Proc_Apply'Access,
   Proc_Help'Access, Proc_Cancel'Access);
```

The main program simulates the event-driven software by asking the user for the name of a button and mouse click, and then calling the appropriate callback procedure:

```
begin
  loop
    declare
      B: Buttons;
      C: Clicks;
      use Ada.Text_IO;
    begin
      Put("Click mouse: ");
      Clicks_IO.Get(C);
      Put("on button:   ");
      Buttons_IO.Get(B);
      Skip_Line;
      Callbacks(B)(C);
    exception
      when Data_Error => Put_Line("Invalid button pressed");
      when End_Error  => exit;
    end;
  end loop;
end CallB;
```

In `Callbacks(B)(C)`, the access-to-subprogram value `Callbacks(B)` is implicitly dereferenced before the parameter is passed; to call a parameterless subprogram pointed to by an access value, explicit dereferencing with **`all`** must be used.

12.3 Null exclusions

One of the worst run-time errors is dereferencing a null pointer:

```
Pointer: Link := Init(...) ;    -- Suppose Init returns null

Pointer.Data  := 5;             -- Where is the value 5 stored???
```

The null value may be zero or some other value that does not designate any object. An attempt to store a value using this address can cause the computer to crash. Therefore, Ada requires that access values be checked for null before they are dereferenced; if the check fails, `Constraint_Error` is raised.

Null values are frequently used when building a data structure like a tree, but—just as frequently—the program is designed so that an access object cannot receive a null value. One example is a doubly-linked list that uses sentinel nodes which point to themselves to denote the ends of the list. Consider, also, what happens when an access object is passed as a parameter:

```
type Queue_Pointer is access all Queue;

procedure Put(I: in Item; Q: in Queue_Pointer);
```

It should be possible to prove that this procedure would never be called with a null value for `Q`. Furthermore, even if this is possible, the queue pointer is not "suddenly" going to become null; a single check at the point of call should be sufficient.

Access types and subtypes, as well as subtype indications and parameters of access type, can be given a *null exclusion*, denoted by the pair of reserved words **not null**, which specifies that values of the type or object cannot have the value null. `Constraint_Error` is raised if this restriction is violated. Given:

```
type Queue_Pointer is not null access all Queue;
```

values of this type cannot have the value null. This forbids:

```
Q: Queue_Pointer;
```

because the default value of an access object is null, so an initializing expression must be given, as for a constant:

```
The_Queue: aliased Queue;
Q:         Queue_Pointer := The_Queue'Access;
```

Alternatively, the parameter can be given a null exclusion:

```
type Queue_Pointer is access all Queue;

procedure Put(I: in Item; Q: in not null Queue_Pointer);
```

In this case:

```
Q: Queue_Pointer;
```

is legal, but we have to ensure that `Q` is given a non-null value before the procedure is called. Within the procedure, the compiler can omit all checks for null pointers when deferencing the parameter, although it must ensure, of course, that `Q` is not assigned the value null. Clearly, `Q := **null**` is an error, but what about `Q := Get_Queue`? If the function is declared:

```
function Get_Queue return not null Queue_Pointer;
```

all is well. If the null exclusion is not given, the value returned by the function has to be checked at run time.

Null exclusions should have been used in the previous case studies:

```
type Label_Pointer is not null access constant String;
```

for the ragged array case study, and:

```
type Callback_Pointer is not null access procedure(C: in Clicks);
```

for the callback case study.

Null exclusions can also be used with generic formal objects §12.4(8.3–8.5) and generic access types §12.5.4(4).

Ada 95

Null exclusions are new to Ada 2005.

12.4 Accessibility rules

Consider the following short program:

level

```
1 with Ada.Text_IO;
2 procedure Level is
3   type Pointer is access all Integer;
4   Global: aliased Integer := 6;
5
6   function F return Pointer is
7   begin
8     return Global'Access;
9   end F;
10
11   P: Pointer := F;
12 begin
13   Ada.Text_IO.Put_Line(Integer'Image(P.all));
14 end Level;
```

An access to the variable Global ‡4 is returned by the function F ‡8 and used to initialize the access object P ‡11. The program runs as expected and prints 6.

Consider now the following version of the program:

level

```
with Ada.Text_IO;
procedure Level is
  type Pointer is access all Integer;

  function F return Pointer is
    Local: aliased Integer := 7;
  begin
    return Local'Access;
  end F;

  P: Pointer := F;
begin
  Ada.Text_IO.Put_Line(Integer'Image(P.all));
end Level;
```

This program should not be legal: the pointer `P` is initialized with the access value returned by the function; it points to the variable `Local`, but the variable `Local` no longer exists. Local variables are allocated on the stack when a subprogram is called and deallocated upon return from the subprogram. An interrupt handler, for example, could have overwritten the stack memory between the return from `F` and the use of the value `P.all` in the put statement.

An access object whose value points to an address that is no longer a valid designated object is called a *dangling pointer*. Assigning a value to the object designated by a dangling pointer (`P.all` := 10) can cause a catastrophic failure of the software.

One way of creating a dangling pointer is to deallocate a designated object that is pointed to by a pool-specific type (Section 5.4.4):

```
Link1: Link := new Node'(...);
Link2: Link := Link1;

-- Deallocate object designated by Link1 using Ada.Unchecked_Deallocation
```

The node pointed to by `Link1` is deallocated and `Link1` set to null, but `Link2` retains an access to the node which no longer exists. The word *unchecked* in `Ada.Unchecked_Deallocation` emphasizes that this serious error is not checked for.

As shown above, for general access types, dangling pointers can be created by seemingly innocent constructs such as applying the attribute `Access` to an object. To prevent such errors, *accessibility rules* are used to forbid such constructs.

§3.10.2

> 3 The accessibility rules, which prevent dangling references, are written in terms of *accessibility* levels, which reflect the run-time nesting of *masters*. As explained in 7.6.1, a master is the execution of a certain construct, such as a subprogram_body. An accessibility level is *deeper than* another if it is more deeply nested at run-time. For example, an object declared local to a called subprogram has a deeper accessibility level than an object declared local to the calling subprogram. The accessibility rules for access types require that the accessibility level of an object designated by an access value be no deeper than that of the access type. This ensures that the object will live at least as long as the access type, which in turn ensures that the access value cannot later designate an object that no longer exists. The attribute `Unchecked_Access` may be used to circumvent the accessibility rules.

(`Unchecked_Access` is defined in §13.10.)

In the second version of the program, the accessibility level of the access type `Pointer` is one level deeper than that of the environment task that calls the main program `Level`. Since the run-time call to `F` is nested within `Level`, the accessibility level of `Local`, the object designated by the return value, is one level *deeper than* that of `Pointer`, the access type of the value returned by the function. Therefore, it is illegal apply the attribute `Access` to the local variable.

The rules for determining the accessibility level of each construct are given in §3.10.2. Violations of the accessibility rules can generally be determined at compile-time §3.10.2(4). In a few cases, the check is made at run-time and a violation will cause the exception `Program_Error` to be raised §3.10.2(29). Unfortunately, the rules in §3.10.2 are extremely complex. If you receive a compile-time or run-time error related to accessibility levels, try to move the designated object to a more global scope, even to the library level, if possible.

12.5 Anonymous access types*

In Section 6.7, we noted that the full type definition corresponding to an incomplete type definition in the private part of a package can be given in the package body §3.10.1(3). The incomplete definition can only be used as the designated type of an access type, because all pointers to values in a single storage pool have the same representation, so it really doesn't matter what they point to.

Given two general access types:

```
type Pointer1 is access all Integer;
type Pointer2 is access all Integer;
```

values of either type can be converted to the other one because all pointers are alike and, as long as the designated types are the same (or have convertible tags), no problems will arise:

```
P1: Pointer1 := new Integer'(1);
P2: Pointer2 := Pointer2(P1);
```

An access value cannot be converted to a pool-specific access type, because we do not know if it is in the same pool.

The next step is to remove the type declarations altogether and to use *anonymous access types*, in which case, no explicit type conversion is required:

```
P1: access Integer := new Integer'(1);
P2: access Integer := P1;
```

For example, in the ragged array case study, there is no reason to declare a named access type; an anonymous access type for the array component would simplify the program:

```
Labels: constant array(Natural range <>) of
           not null access constant String := ( ... );
```

A similar situation holds for the callback case study:

```
Callbacks: constant array(Buttons) of
             not null access procedure(C: in Clicks) := ( ... );
```

Anonymous access types can be used in place of incomplete views, for example, in the tree implementation of a priority queue (Section 5.3):

```
type Node is
  record
    Data: Integer;
    Left, Right: access Node;   -- Instead of Link
  end record;
```

But this raises a new problem: since the type is anonymous, it has no name that can be used as the subtype mark of a parameter:

```
procedure Put(I: in Integer; Node_Ptr: in out ????) is ...
```

The solution is to use access parameters as described in the next section.

Ada 95

The only anonymous types in Ada 95 are access parameters (Section 12.6) and access discriminants (Section 12.7). The workaround is to use named types and explicit type conversion.

12.6 Access parameters

Access parameters §6.1(24) allow a subprogram to be called with actual parameters of more than one access type, as well as with parameters of anonymous access types.

§6.4.1

> 6 The type of the actual parameter associated with an access parameter shall be convertible (see 4.6) to its anonymous access type.

The accessibility level is passed along with the access parameter and is dynamically checked.

§3.10.2

> 13 • The accessibility level of the anonymous access type of an access parameter specifying an access-to-object type is the same as that of the view designated by the actual.

Consider:

```
procedure Main is
  I: aliased Integer;
  A: access Integer;

  procedure Proc1(P: access Integer) is
  begin
    A := P;    -- Accessibility level of P is that of the actual  parameter
  end Proc1;

begin
  Proc1(I'Access);
end Main;
```

The program will run without error because the accessibility level of I is the same at that of A, and this level is passed to the procedure Proc1 in the access parameter. However, if Proc1 is called with an access value to an object at a deeper access level:

```
  procedure Proc2 is
    J: aliased Integer;
  begin
    Proc1(J'Access);
  end Proc2;
```

Constraint_Error will be raised at run-time.

For subprograms, the rule is different:

§3.10.2

> 13.1 • The accessibility level of the anonymous access type of an access parameter specifying an access-to-subprogram type is deeper than that of any master; all such anonymous access types have this same level.

In the following code:

```
A: access procedure;

procedure Proc1(AP: access procedure) is
begin
  A := AP;  -- Accessibility level of AP is always deeper than that of A
end Proc1;
```

the assignment of the access parameter AP to the variable A is a compile-time error, because the accessibility level of AP is deeper than *any* other level, including the level of the actual parameter, whatever it may be.

Dynamic dispatching can be done on an access parameter §6.1(24). In the following declarations, Proc1 is a primitive subprogram for the tagged type Parent:

```
type Parent tagged null record;
procedure Proc1(X: access Parent);
```

It can be overridden when deriving a type:

```
type Derived is new Parent with null record;
procedure Proc1(X: access Derived);
```

If the actual parameter is any access to a type in Parent'Class, dispatching will be done. Dispatching is not done if named access types are used for the formal parameter.

The software archive contains a version of the event simulation using an access parameter:

```
procedure Simulate(E: not null access Event) is abstract;
```

12.6.1 *Case study: priority queue with an anonymous access type*

The following program implements the tree priority queue of Section 5.3 using anonymous access types and access parameters.

An anonymous access type is used instead of the named type Link for the node:

pqtaccess

```
procedure PQTAccess is
  type Node is
    record
      Data: Integer;
      Left, Right: access Node;
    end record;
```

and for the root node of the queue:

```
type Queue is
  record
    Root: access Node;
  end record;
```

An access parameter is of mode **in** §6.1(24), so it is a constant §3.3(17) that cannot be used to return a value. This requires a redesign of the algorithm; instead of using **in out** parameters to modify the pointers, the access parameter is passed a pointer to the *parent* of a node:

```
procedure Put(I: in Integer; Node_Ptr: access Node) is
begin
  if I < Node_Ptr.Data then
    if Node_Ptr.Left = null then
      Node_Ptr.Left := new Node'(I, null, null);
    else
      Put(I, Node_Ptr.Left);
    end if;
  else
    if Node_Ptr.Right = null then
      Node_Ptr.Right := new Node'(I, null, null);
    else
      Put(I, Node_Ptr.Right);
    end if;
  end if;
end Put;

procedure Put(I: in Integer; Q: in out Queue) is
begin
  if Q.Root = null then
    Q.Root := new Node'(I, null, null);
  else
    Put(I, Q.Root);
  end if;
end Put;
```

The changes to the rest of the program are similar; see the full source code in the software archive. The archive also contains a version of the event simulation that uses access parameters.

Ada 95

In Ada 95, the actual parameter corresponding a formal access parameter cannot be null; in Ada 2005, an explicit null exclusion must be used if a null formal parameter is to be excluded.

12.7 Access discriminants*

Both named and anonymous access types can also be used as discriminants. In Section 19.10, we will demonstrate the use of access discriminants to pass configuration data to a task or synchronized object.

12.7.1 Case study: simulation with access discriminant

Access discriminants can be used to implement a self-referential data structure:

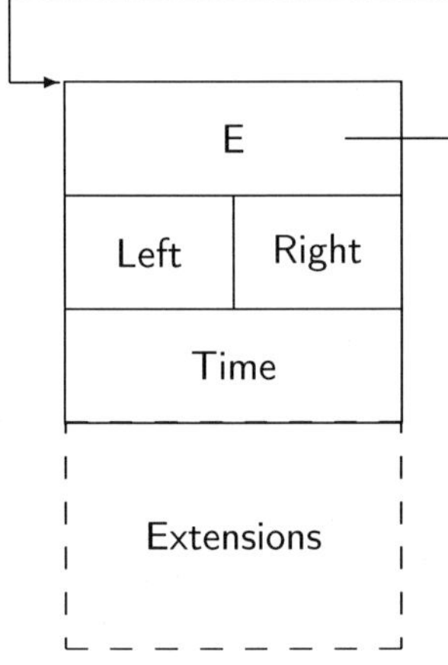

rocketad

```
package Root_Event is
  type Event is tagged;
  type Event_Ptr is access Event;

  type Node;
  type Link is access all Node;
  type Node(E: access Event'Class) is
    record
      Left, Right: Link;
    end record;
```

The type Node has an access discriminant E, which is an access to Event'Class.

The type Event has a component of type Node and the discriminant of this component is an access to the same type Event:

```
   subtype Simulation_Time is Integer range 0..10_000;
   type Event is abstract tagged limited
     record
       Inner: aliased Node(Event'Access);
       Time: Simulation_Time;
     end record;
   ...
end Root_Event;
```

The name Event in Event'Access refers to the *current instance* §8.6(17) of the type, not to the type itself. When an event object is allocated, the discriminant is set to point to the object itself as shown in the diagram above.

The queue package links the events by linking the *contained* nodes. Given a pointer to a node, the enclosing event is accessed by using the discriminant, as shown in the right operand of "<":

```
package body Event_Queue is
   procedure Put(E: access Event'Class; Node_Ptr: in out Link) is
   begin
     if Node_Ptr = null then
       Node_Ptr := E.Inner'Access;
     elsif E.all < Node_Ptr.E.all then
       Put(E, Node_Ptr.Left);
     else
       Put(E, Node_Ptr.Right);
     end if;
   end Put;
   ...
```

Similarly, when a search of the tree returns the smallest node, the discriminant is used to return the enclosing event Found.E.**all**:

```
   function Get(Q: access Queue) return access Event'Class is
     Found: Link;
   begin
     Get(Q.Root, Found);
     return Found.E.all;
   end Get;
end Event_Queue;
```

Ada 95

In Ada 95, an access discriminant can only be given for a limited type.

12.8 Storage pools*

Allocation of dynamic memory need not be done from a single heap.

§13.11

> 1 Each access-to-object type has an associated storage pool. The storage allocated by an allocator comes from the pool; instances of Unchecked_Deallocation return storage to the pool. Several access types can share the same pool.

A derived access type shares a single storage pool with its parent access type §3.10(7).

For each access type, the attribute `Storage_Size` §13.11(14) enables you to define the size of the pool for objects of the designated type. Package `System.Storage_Pools` §13.11(5–10) defines an abstract type `Root_Storage_Pool` that you can override to define your own storage allocation scheme. The attribute `Storage_Pool` §13.11(13) can then be used to assign different storage pools to different types.

12.9 Controlled types*

§7.6

> 1 Three kinds of actions are fundamental to the manipulation of objects: initialization, finalization, and assignment. Every object is initialized, either explicitly or by default, after being created (for example, by an object_declaration or allocator). Every object is finalized before being destroyed (for example, by leaving a subprogram_body containing an object_declaration, or by a call to an instance of Unchecked_Deallocation). An assignment operation is used as part of assignment_statements, explicit initialization, parameter passing, and other operations.

In other languages, these actions are performed by constructors, destructors and copy constructors. In Ada, user-defined actions for a type can be defined for controlled types.

§7.6

> 2 Default definitions for these three fundamental operations are provided by the language, but a *controlled* type gives the user additional control over parts of these operations. In particular, the user can define, for a controlled type, an Initialize procedure which is invoked immediately after the normal default initialization of a controlled object, a Finalize procedure which is invoked immediately before finalization of any of the components of a controlled object, and an Adjust procedure which is invoked as the last step of an assignment to a (nonlimited) controlled object.

These operations are primitive operations of the abstract tagged type `Controlled` defined in package `Ada.Finalization` §7.6(4–8). You can derive from this type and override one or more of these operations. There is also a type `Limited_Controlled` without the `Adjust` operation, since limited types cannot be assigned.

12.9.1 *Case study: priority queue with controlled type*

The following version of the priority queue package demonstrates the use of controlled types. Type `Node` is derived from `Controlled`:

pqtct

```
with Ada.Finalization;
package Priority_Queue is
  type Node is new Ada.Finalization.Controlled with private;
  function Create(I: Integer) return Node;
  function Value(N: Node) return Integer;

  type Queue(Size: Positive) is limited private;
  ...
private
  type Link is access Node;
  type Node is new Ada.Finalization.Controlled with
    record ... end record;
  procedure Initialize(Object: in out Node);
  procedure Adjust(Object:     in out Node);
  procedure Finalize(Object:   in out Node);

  type Queue(Size: Positive) is ...
end Priority_Queue;
```

Procedures to create a node from an integer value and return the value from a node are defined; these will simplify the explanations below:

```
with Ada.Text_IO; use Ada.Text_IO;
with Ada.Unchecked_Deallocation;
package body Priority_Queue is
  function Create(I: Integer) return Node is
  begin
    return (Ada.Finalization.Controlled with I, null, null);
  end Create;

  function Value(N: Node) return Integer is
  begin
    return N.Data;
  end Value;
```

Since Controlled is abstract §7.6(5), an extension aggregate with a *subtype mark* for the ancestor part §4.3.2(3) must be used to create a value of type Node.

The three procedures Initialize, Adjust and Finalize are overridden to print messages so that we can trace the execution:

```
  procedure Initialize(Object: in out Node) is
  begin
    Put_Line("Initialize " & Integer'Image(Object.Data));
  end Initialize;

  procedure Adjust(Object: in out Node) is
  begin
    Put_Line("Adjust " & Integer'Image(Object.Data));
  end Adjust;

  procedure Finalize(Object: in out Node) is
  begin
    Put_Line("Finalize " & Integer'Image(Object.Data));
  end Finalize;
```

The rest of the package body can be found in the software archive.

The main subprogram inserts elements in the queue and then retrieves them:

```
with Priority_Queue;
with Ada.Text_IO; use Ada.Text_IO;
procedure PQTCT is
  Q: Priority_Queue.Queue(10);
  Test_Data: array(Positive range <>) of Integer :=  (10, 5, 25, 15);
begin
  for I in Test_Data'Range loop
    Put_Line("Put " & Integer'Image(Test_Data(I)));
    Priority_Queue.Put(Priority_Queue.Create(Test_Data(I)), Q);
  end loop;

  declare
    N: Priority_Queue.Node;
  begin
    while not Priority_Queue.Empty(Q) loop
      Priority_Queue.Get(N, Q);
      Put_Line("Get " & Integer'Image(Priority_Queue.Value(N)));
    end loop;
  end;
end PQTCT;
```

Each call to `Put` shows that `Adjust` is called once and `Finalize` twice:

```
Put        10
Adjust     10
Finalize   10
Finalize   10
```

`Initialize` is *not* called because the allocator is explicitly initialized with an aggregate §7.6(10). However, the value returned by `Create` is used as an actual parameter when `Put` is called; this is an assignment operation so `Adjust` is called §7.6(13–15). `Finalize` is called twice: once when the aggregate object is finalized and once when the formal parameter is finalized.

When `N` is declared, `Initialize` is called:

```
Initialize 0
```

Then, for each call to `Get`, the following messages are printed:

```
Finalize   0
Adjust     5
Finalize   5
Get        5
```

`Finalize` is called to finalize the "old" value of `N`. Then the assignment to the **out** parameter of `Get` is made and `Adjust` is called. `Unchecked_Deallocation` is used to deallocate the node and `Finalize` is called when this happens.

12.10 Mutually dependent types*

The tree implementation of a priority queue (Section 5.3) uses the mutually dependent types `Node` and `Link`, where an incomplete view of the type `Node` is declared §3.10.1. The rule that makes this possible is that the completion must be declared in the same package §3.10.1(3).

Suppose, however, that two mutually dependent types represent different abstractions that should appear in two separate packages. This is possible using limited_with_clauses that enable one package to obtain a limited view of another §10.1.2(4.1,17).

§10.1.1

> 12.1 ... The limited view of a package contains:
> 12.3 For each type_declaration in the visible part, an incomplete view of the type; if the type_declaration is tagged, then the view is a tagged incomplete view.

12.10.1 *Case study: automata*

Mutually dependent types will be demonstrated using a case study for implementing *nondeterminisitic finite automata (NDFA)*. Here is a very simple NDFA:

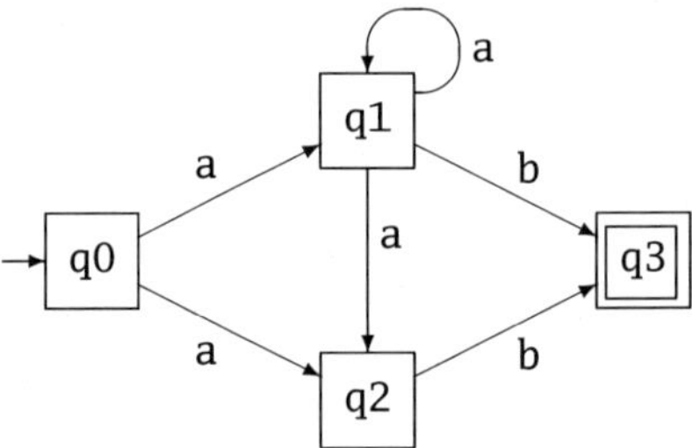

The automaton is nondeterministic because in states `q0` and `q1`, if the next input symbol is `a`, there are two choices for the transition to the next state.

An NDFA is defined by sets of states and transitions:

```
States:
  q0 (initial),  q1, q2, q3 (final)
Transitions:
  (q0, a, q1)  (q0, a, q2)  (q1, a, q1), (q1, a, q2)  (q1, b, q3)  (q2, b, q3)
```

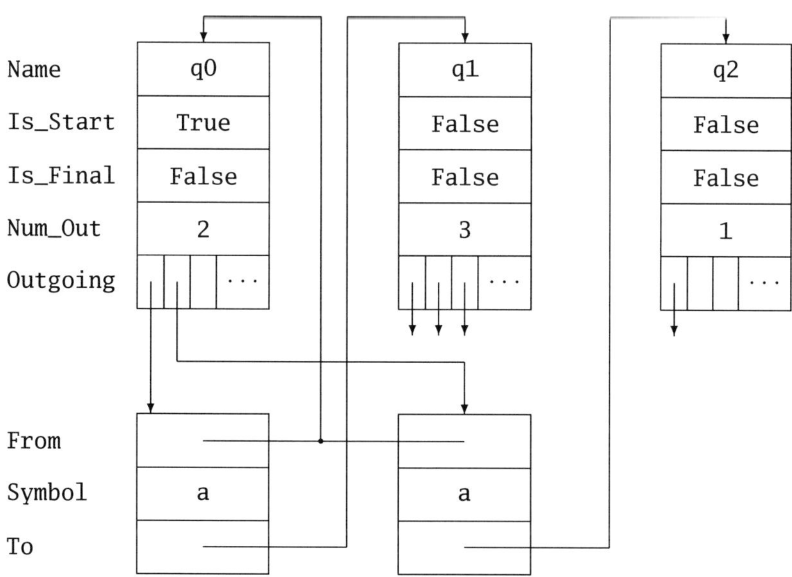

Fig. 12.1 Mutually references between data structures

Clearly, a transition is defined in terms of states (source and target). An efficient implementation will want to maintain a data structure that holds the set of outgoing transitions from each state (Figure 12.1). Therefore, states are defined in terms of transitions and the types are mutually dependent. Let us assume that associated with each state and transition are additional data, so that we wish to encapsulate the states and transitions in separate packages.

First, we define a state as a record containing the name, indications of whether it is a start or final state, and a set of pointers to the outgoing transitions from this state:

ndfa

```
limited with Transitions;
package States is
  subtype State_Name is String (1 .. 3);
  type Transition_Set is array(0..10) of access Transitions.Transition;
  type State is
    record
      Name:         State_Name;
      Is_Start:     Boolean := False;
      Is_Final:     Boolean := False;
      Num_Outgoing: Natural := 0;
      Outgoing:     Transition_Set;
    end record;
end States;
```

A limited_with_clause is used to obtain a partial view of the type Transition and this partial view is sufficent to declare an access to the type.

The components of the type Transition are the symbol labeling the transition and the pointers to the source and target states:

```
limited with States;
package Transitions is
  type Transition is
    record
      From:   access States.State;
      Symbol: Character;
      To:     access States.State;
    end record;
end Transitions;
```

Here, too, a limited_with_clause is used.

An NDFA is declared as a limited type because there is no reason to copy values of the type; it is a private type because operations on the type will be implemented in child packages:

```
with States; with Transitions;
package NDFAs is
  type NDFA is limited private;
```

The first two procedures insert states and transitions into the data structure, while the third uses the transitions to set the Outgoing component in a state:

```
  procedure Insert_State
    (A: access NDFA; N: in States.State_Name; S, F: in Boolean);
  procedure Insert_Transition
    (A: access NDFA; F : in Integer; S: in Character; T: in Integer);
  procedure Generate_Transitions_At_States(A: access NDFA);
```

The type NDFA is completed by a record containing arrays of states and transitions:

```
private
  type State_Array      is array(0..20) of aliased States.State;
  type Transition_Array is array(0..50) of aliased Transitions.Transition;
  type NDFA is
    record
      Num_States:      Natural := 0;
      States:          State_Array;
      Num_Transitions: Natural := 0;
      Transitions:     aliased Transition_Array;
    end record;
end NDFAs;
```

Procedure Insert_State and Insert_Transition are straightforward, except that the component Outgoing of a state is initialized with an array of **null**; the correct value of the component will be computed later:

```
package body NDFAs is
  procedure Insert_State
    (A: access NDFA; N: in States.State_Name; S, F: in Boolean) is
   begin
     A.States (A.Num_States) := (N, S, F, 0, (others => null));
     A.Num_States := A.Num_States + 1;
   end Insert_State;

  procedure Insert_Transition
    (A: access NDFA; F: in Integer; S: in Character; T: in Integer) is
   begin
     A.Transitions (A.Num_Transitions) :=
       (A.States (F)'Access, S, A.States(T)'Access);
     A.Num_Transitions := A.Num_Transitions + 1;
   end Insert_Transition;
```

Procedure Generate_Transitions is called for each state to compute the value of the component Outgoing. Each transition is examined to see if its source state is equal to this state; if so, a pointer is added to Outgoing:

```
  procedure Generate_Transitions
    (N: access States.State; T: access Transition_Array) is
  begin
    for I in  T'Range loop
      if (T(I).From = N) then
        N.Outgoing(N.Num_Outgoing) := T(I)'Access;
          N.Num_Outgoing := N.Num_Outgoing + 1;
      end if;
    end loop;
  end Generate_Transitions;

  procedure Generate_Transitions_At_States(A: access NDFA) is
  begin
    for I in  0 .. A.Num_States - 1 loop
      Generate_Transitions(A.States (I)'Access, A.Transitions'Access);
    end loop;
  end Generate_Transitions_At_States;
end NDFAs;
```

A subprogram to run the NDFA is given in a child package so that its body can have access to the private part of the package NDFAs:

```
package NDFAs.Run_NDFA is
   procedure Run(A : access NDFAs.NDFA; Input : in String);
end NDFAs.Run_NDFA;
```

The rest of the source code for this case study is in the software archive.

Ada 95

limited_with_clauses do not exist in Ada 95. To implement the NDFA program, the two mutually dependent types must be declared in the *same* package:

ndfa95

```
package States_Transitions is
    type Transition;
    type Transition_Ptr is access all Transition;

    type State is record ... end record;
    type State_Ptr is access all State;

    type Transition is record ... end record;
end States_Transitions;
```

Since there are no anonymous access types, named access types must be used.

The source code of this version is given in the software archive.

Projects

1. Combine the ragged-array and callbacks case studies so that each button has a string of arbitrary length as its name.
2. Extend the above project to support multiple languages for the buttons that can be changed at run-time.
3. Implement callbacks using a tagged type and dispatching.
4. Write a program to implement addition and multiplication of polynomials represented as linked lists. Be sure to simplify a polynomial before storing it; for example, $(x^3 + x + 1) + (x^3 - x + 1) = (2x^3 + 2)$, not $(2x^3 + 0x + 2)$.
5. Declare the polynomials as controlled types where simplification is performed as part of the Adjust operation.
6. Write a program for simulating a nondeterministic Turing Machine.

Quizzes

Quiz 1:

```
N1: Integer := 5;
type Pointer is access Integer;
N2: Pointer := new Integer'(5);
procedure Proc(K: out Integer; P: out Pointer) is
begin
  Put_Line(Integer'Image(K));
  Put_Line(Integer'Image(P.all));
end Proc;

Proc(N1, N2);
```

Quiz 2:

```
package P is
  type Pointer is access all Integer;
end P;

with P;
procedure Main is
  N: aliased Integer;
  Q: P.Pointer := N'Access;
begin
  null;
end Main;
```

Quiz 3:

```
package P is
  type Parent is tagged null record;
  type Parent_Pointer is access all Parent;
  procedure Proc1(X: Parent_Pointer);
  procedure Proc2(X: access Parent);
  type Derived is new Parent with null record;
  D: aliased Derived;
end P;

with P; use P;
procedure Main is
begin
  Proc1(D'Access);
  Proc2(D'Access);
end Main;
```

Quiz 4:

```
type String_Pointer is access String;
S: String_Pointer := new String'("Hello world");
type Integer_Pointer is access Integer;
I: Integer_Pointer := new Integer'(10);

Put_Line(S(1..5));
Put(I);
```

Quiz 5:

```
type Int_Pointer is access all Integer;
N: aliased Integer;
function Func return Int_Pointer is
begin
  return N'Access;
end Func;

Func.all := 5;
Put(N);
```

Quiz 6:

```
package P is
  protected type PT is
    entry E(X: access Integer);
  end PT;
  task type T is
    entry E(X: access Integer);
  end T;
end P;
```

Quiz 7:

```
package P is
  type Rec(D: access Integer) is limited null record;
  type Pointer is access Rec;
end P;

with P; use P;
procedure Main is
  N: aliased Integer;
  R: Pointer := new Rec(N'Access);
begin
  null;
end Main;
```

Quiz 8:

```
  type AV is access Integer;
  type AC is access constant Integer;
  P: AV := new Integer'(1);
  C: AC := new Integer'(2);

  C := AC(P);
  P := AV(C);
```

Chapter 13
Numeric Types

There are three approaches to defining the precision of numeric types:

- In C, the precision is not part of the type; for example, the type **int** might be implemented with 16 bits on one computer and 64 bits on another. Programs in C are, therefore, not portable, although clever use of macros can work around this problem.
- Java specifies the precision of each type. Values of type **int** are required to be 32-bit signed integers, so Java programs are portable. However, this may result in reduced performance, because a choice of precision might not be optimal for a particular computer. For example, if the values of a variable are bounded by 10,000, type **int** will be optimal for a 32-bit machine, while **short** will be optimal for a 16-bit controller. The program will be portable regardless of which type you choose, but the performance on one machine can be suboptimal.
- In Ada, you can declare the *required precision* of a numeric type. When the program is compiled, the implementation will choose a representation that is appropriate for the machine. For example, a type declared as an integer type with a range of 1 to 100,000 will be represented as a double word on a 16-bit machine and as a single word on a 32-bit machine. To port the program to another machine requires only recompilation.

Ada supports the definition of both integer and real types with a specified precision. Both floating point and fixed point real types are supported. Fixed point types are not found in most programming languages, but they are useful in applications where absolute, rather than relative, precision is required.

13.1 Basic concepts

13.1.1 Universal types

The numeric types in Ada form derivation hierarchies, similar to classes of tagged types (Figure 13.1). The classes are called *universal types* §3.4.1(6–7) and the specific types at the roots of

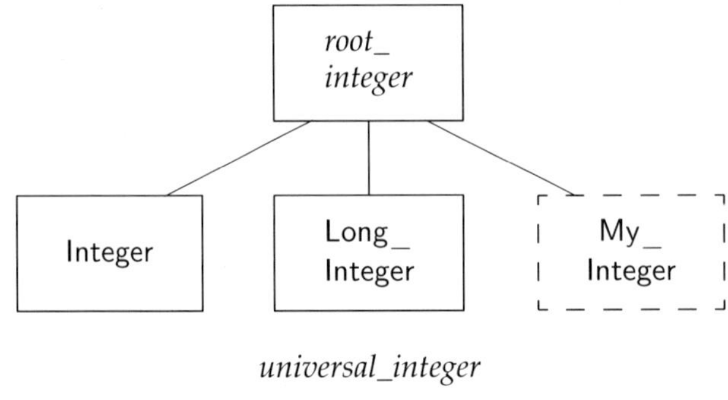

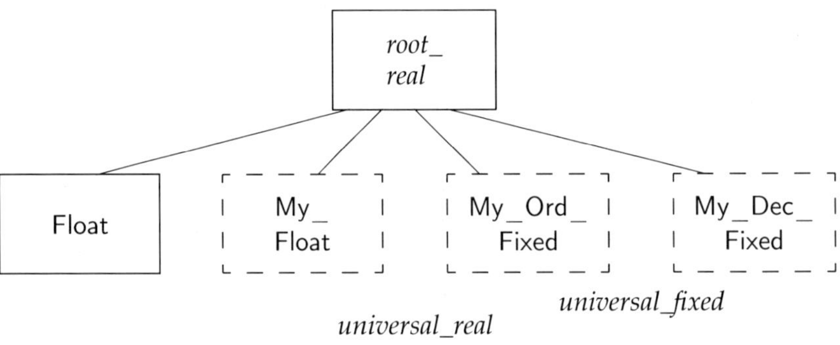

Fig. 13.1 Numeric types: universal and root types

the derivation trees are called *root types* §3.4.1(8). These types are conceptual; you cannot explicitly declare an object or parameter to be of type *root_integer* or *universal_integer*. The specific types `Integer` and `Float` are predefined, and an implementation can predefine other types such as `Short_Integer` and `Long_Integer`. You can declare new integer, float point, ordinary fixed point and decimal fixed point types as indicated by the dashed boxes in the Figure.

§3.4.1

6 Universal types are defined for (and belong to) the integer, real, fixed point, and access classes, and are referred to in this standard as respectively, *universal_integer*, *universal_real*, *universal_fixed*, and *universal_access*. These are analogous to class-wide types for these language-defined elementary classes. As with class-wide types, if a formal parameter is of a universal type, then an actual parameter of any type in the corresponding class is acceptable. In addition, a value of a universal type (including an integer or real numeric_literal, or the literal **`null`**) is "universal" in that it is acceptable where some particular type in the class is expected (see 8.6).

§4.2

> 8 An integer literal is of type *universal_integer*. A real literal is of type *universal_real*. The literal **null** is of type *universal_access*.

The expression `N+27` is legal for `N` of any integer type, because the literal `27` of type *universal_integer* is converted in its context as an operand of the operator to the type of `N`. Note that some attributes have parameters of universal type; for example, `Pos` returns a value of type *universal_integer* and `Val` takes a parameter of type *universal_integer* §3.5.5. `Character'Pos(C)` for a variable `C` is an example of an expression that is of universal type but not static.

13.1.2 Type conversion

Ada does not usually allow implicit conversion between numeric types. Not only would this defeat type checking, but the rules for implicit type conversion can be complex, especially in the presence of overloading. For example, given that `N` is of type `Integer`, is `Put(N)` a call to the procedure `Put` with a parameter of type `Integer`, or is it an implicit conversion of `N` to `Long_Integer`, followed by a call to the procedure `Put` with a parameter of type `Long_Integer`?

Explicit conversion between two numeric types is always allowed.

§4.6

> 2 type_conversion ::=
> subtype_mark(expression)
> | subtype_mark(name)
>
> 3 The *target subtype* of a type_conversion is the subtype denoted by the subtype_mark. The *operand* of a type_conversion is the expression or name within the parentheses; its type is the *operand type*.
>
> 24.1 • If the target type is a numeric type, then the operand type shall be a numeric type.

Type conversion is not restricted to conversion *within* a universal class, as the analogy with derivation classes of tagged types would imply. It is perfectly legal to convert an integer type to a real type, and conversely.

13.1.3 Named numbers

Constants of universal numeric types are called *named numbers*:

§3.3.2

> 1 A number_declaration declares a named number.
>
> 2 number_declaration ::=
> defining_identifier_list : **constant** := *static*_expression;
>
> 5 The named number denotes a value of type *universal_integer* if the type of the *static*_expression is an integer type. The named number denotes a value of type *universal_real* if the type of the *static*_expression is a real type.

The following declaration appears in `Ada.Numerics` §A.5(3):

```
Pi: constant :=
  3.14159_26535_89793_23846_26433_83279_50288_41971_69399_37511;
```

The value of a named number need not be a literal and can be any static expression:

```
Two_Pi: constant := 2.0 * Ada.Numerics.Pi;
```

Be careful not to confuse named numbers with constant objects:

```
Two_Pi:       constant       := 2.0 * Ada.Numerics.Pi;
Float_Two_Pi: constant Float := 2.0 * Ada.Numerics.Pi;
```

`Two_Pi` is of type *universal_real* and will be implicitly converted to a specific type in each context in which it appears. `Float_Two_Pi` is a constant object of type `Float`. Its initial value `2.0*Ada.Numerics.Pi` of type *root_real* is converted to type `Float`—losing precision—when the object is elaborated:

```
L1: Long_Float := Two_Pi;                    -- Maximal precision
L2: Long_Float := Long_Float(Float_Two_Pi);  -- Lower precision
```

Language Comparison

In C and Java, a numeric literal has a type. By default, an integer literal is of type **`int`** and a floating point literal is of type **`double`**. The notations `28L` and `2.8F` are used for literals of type **`long int`** and **`float`**, respectively. Ada uses the context where a literal appears to convert a literal of a universal type to a value of a specific type. If, for example, the type of a variable is changed, all the assignments of literals to the variable are automatically changed.

13.2 Signed integer types

Signed integer types are familiar from all programming languages. An implementation must support at least one predefined (sub)type called `Integer`.

§3.5.4

3 signed_integer_type_definition ::=
range *static*_simple_expression .. *static*_simple_expression

9 A signed_integer_type_definition defines an integer type whose base range includes at least the values of the simple_expressions and is symmetric about zero, excepting possibly an extra negative value. A signed_integer_type_definition also defines a constrained first subtype of the type, with a range whose bounds are given by the values of the simple_expressions, converted to the type being defined.

11 There is a predefined signed integer subtype named Integer, declared in the visible part of package Standard. It is constrained to the base range of its type.

12 Integer has two predefined subtypes, declared in the visible part of package Standard:

13
```
subtype Natural  is Integer range 0 .. Integer'Last;
subtype Positive is Integer range 1 .. Integer'Last;
```

Base range is discussed in Section 13.11 and can be ignored for now.

Given the following type and variable declarations:

```
type Altitude is range 0 .. 100_000;

A: Altitude;
```

the compiler can allocate a single word for `A` on a 32-bit machine and a double word on a 16-bit machine. There is no need to modify the source code when porting the program.

The range of predefined `Integer` and its subtypes `Natural` and `Positive` is implementation-defined, and programs using them are not strictly portable. It is reasonable to use `Integer` for array indices because their ranges almost invariably fall within the minimum range (16-bits) of `Integer` §3.5.4(21), but for integer computation you should define your own types. An implementation is permitted §3.5.4(25) to provide additional predefined integer types with names like `Long_Integer`, `Short_Integer` and `Long_Long_Integer`, though they need not be implemented with different precisions. Needless to say, such types are not portable.

13.3 Types versus subtypes

Recall that *types* are checked at compile-time, while *subtypes* are checked at run-time. The variable `A` of type `Altitude` defined above *cannot* be assigned to a variable `I` of type `Integer` because the types are different. The type conversions `I := Integer(A)` and `A := Altitude(I)` are, of course, legal, because they are conversions between numeric types (Section 13.1.2).

Computation (expressions, assignment, parameters) involving different *subtypes* is always legal at compile type, although Constraint_Error may be raised at run-time. Consider the following declarations:

```
type    Altitude      is range 0 .. 100_000;
subtype Low_Altitude  is
  Altitude range Altitude'First .. 35_000;
subtype High_Altitude is
  Altitude range Low_Altitude'Last+1 .. Altitude'Last;

Num:  Integer       := 1_000;
Low:  Low_Altitude  := 1_000;
High: High_Altitude := 50_000;
```

In the assignment statement:

```
High := High_Altitude(Num + Integer(Low));
```

the exception Constraint_Error will be raised when trying to convert 2000 of type Integer (the result of the addition) to the subtype High_Altitude, while in the following statement:

```
High := Altitude(Num + Integer(Low));
```

the type conversion to Altitude will succeed but the assignment will raise the exception.

13.4 Modular types

When an arithmetic operation on an integer type produces a value outside the range of the type, Constraint_Error will result when assigning the value to a variable of the type (see Section 13.11.3):

```
type Integer_Byte is range 0..255;
B: Integer_Byte := 255;

B := B + 1;                 -- Raises Constraint_Error
```

Computation on *modular types* is performed with "wrap-around" semantics:

```
type Byte is mod 2**8;
B1: Byte := 255;
B2: Byte := 200;

B1 := B1 + 1;               -- B1 is now 0
B2 := B2 + 100;             -- B2 is now 44
```

§3.5.4

1 ... A modular type is an integer type with all arithmetic modulo a specified positive *modulus*; such a type corresponds to an unsigned type with wrap-around semantics.

4 modular_type_definition ::= **mod** *static*_expression

10 A modular_type_definition defines a modular type whose base range is from zero to one less than the given modulus. ...

19 For a modular type, if the result of the execution of a predefined operator (see 4.5) is outside the base range of the type, the result is reduced modulo the modulus of the type to a value that is within the base range of the type.

The modulus need not be a power of two; a prime modulus can be used as the index of an array implementing a hash table.

`Constraint_Error` will never be raised when computing with a modular type, though it may be raised if you try to convert another type to the modular type.

The logical operators **and**, **or**, **xor** and **not** can be used on modular types §4.5.1(2); they perform bit-wise boolean operations.

13.4.1 *Case study: checksum*

The following program computes the checksum of an array of bytes. The type `Byte` is declared as a modular type with a range from 0 to 255:

check

```
1 with Ada.Text_IO; use Ada.Text_IO;
2 procedure Check is
3    type Byte        is mod 2**8;
4
5    type Byte_Array is array(Natural range <>) of Byte;
6    for  Byte_Array'Component_Size use 8;
7    pragma Pack(Byte_Array);
```

Line ‡5 is an *attribute definition clause* §13.3(68–70) that directs the implementation to choose a size of 8 bits for components of the array `Byte_Array`. **pragma** `Pack` requests the compiler to pack the bytes of the array into words.

Function `Checksum` computes the modular sum of the components of the array and returns the result:

```
   function Checksum(A: Byte_Array) return Byte is
     C: Byte := 0;
   begin
     for I in A'Range loop
       C := C + A(I);
     end loop;
     return C;
   end Checksum;
```

Check that the following call prints the value 160:

```
   Message: Byte_Array := (134, 56, 121, 38, 206, 117);
begin
   Put_Line(Byte'Image(Checksum(Message)));
end Check;
```

13.4.2 *Mixed signed and modular computation*

Sometimes there is a need to mix computation of signed integers and modular integers. For example, suppose that we have an array of 8-bit *signed* integers (range −128..127), and we want to consider them as unsigned bytes for computing a checksum:

check-signed

```
type Short       is range -(2**7)..2**7-1;

type Short_Array is array(Natural range <>) of Short;
for  Short_Array'Component_Size use 8;
pragma Pack(Short_Array);
```

To compute the checksum we have to convert each signed value to the modular value represented by the same sequence of bits; this is done using the attribute `S'Mod` §3.5.4(16.1–16.3):

```
function Checksum(A: Short_Array) return Byte is
  C: Byte := 0;
begin
  for I in A'Range loop
    C := C + Byte'Mod(A(I));
  end loop;
  return C;
end Checksum;
```

Ada 95

The attribute `S'Mod` is not available in Ada 95, so `Ada.Unchecked_Conversion` must be used.

13.5 Real types

Ada uses the term *real types* to including both floating point and fixed point types.

§3.5.6

> 1 Real types provide approximations to the real numbers, with relative bounds on errors for floating point types, and with absolute bounds for fixed point types.
>
> 2 real_type_definition ::=
>   floating_point_definition | fixed_point_definition
>
> 3 A type defined by a real_type_definition is implicitly derived from *root_real*, an anonymous predefined (specific) real type. Hence, all real types, whether floating point or fixed point, are in the derivation class rooted at *root_real*.
>
> 4 Real literals are all of the type *universal_real*, the universal type (see 3.4.1) for the class rooted at *root_real*, allowing their use with the operations of any real type. Certain multiplying operators have a result type of *universal_fixed* (see 4.5.5), the universal type for the class of fixed point types, allowing the result of the multiplication or division to be used where any specific fixed point type is expected.

The conceptual difference between floating point and fixed point types is whether the error bound is *relative* or *absolute*.

§3.5.7

> 1 For floating point types, the error bound is specified as a relative precision by giving the required minimum number of significant decimal digits.

§3.5.9

> 1 A fixed point type is either an ordinary fixed point type, or a decimal fixed point type. The error bound of a fixed point type is specified as an absolute value, called the *delta* of the fixed point type.

Suppose that the precision of a floating point type is six digits. An error of 1 in the least significant digit of 0.123456×10^{12} is an absolute error of $1,000,000$, while the same error in 0.123456×10^{7} is an absolute error of only 10. Though the absolute error varies widely, in both cases the error is a constant relative error of 0.0008%.

Consider now a six-digit fixed point type with a delta of 0.01 and a range of 0.00 to 9999.99. An error of one in the least significant digit causes an absolute error of 0.01, which is independent of the value of the number. The drawback of fixed point types is that the *range* of values for a given number of bits is limited.

Floating point types are usually used in scientific computation, where we may want to compute the thrust of a rocket to a relative accuracy of, say, 0.01%. Fixed point types are used in financial calculations, where the absolute error must be limited to 0.01 or 0.0001 of the currency unit. The range limitation is usually not a problem in financial applications.

Fixed point types are further divided into ordinary fixed point types whose delta is usually a power of two, and decimal fixed point types whose delta is a power of ten. The former are used for hardware interfacing and the latter for financial calculations. Fixed point types are also used for measuring time in Ada (Section 19.3).

13.6 Floating point types

§3.5.7

2 floating_point_definition ::=
    digits *static*_expression [real_range_specification]

3 real_range_specification ::=
    range *static*_simple_expression .. *static*_simple_expression

12 There is a predefined, unconstrained, floating point subtype named Float, declared in the visible part of package Standard.

A floating point type declaration declares a new type that is represented in the machine with *at least* the precision requested. The type is explicitly convertible to all other numeric types, including integer types. There is one predefined (sub)type `Float`, though the implementation may define others such as `Long_Float`. For serious computational tasks, you should avoid the non-portable predefined types and define your own.

13.6.1 Case study: Euler's method

The following program computes a solution to an elementary differential equation using Euler's method. It solves an equation:

$$\frac{dy}{dx} = f(y)$$

by dividing the range into steps, and then starting from an initial value, computing each successive point by extending the tangent of the previous one. The example used is $dy/dx = y$ on the interval 0.0 to 1.0; given an initial condition of 1.0, the answer is $y = e^x$.

The procedure Euler is generic in the floating point type, an array type for returning the results, and an access type for passing the function:

diff

```
1 generic
2    type Float_Type    is digits <>;
3    type Vector        is array(Integer range <>) of Float_Type;
4    type Function_Ptr is access function (X: Float_Type) return Float_Type;
5 procedure Euler(
6    F: in Function_Ptr; Init, H: in Float_Type; Result: out Vector);
```

The computation in the body of the generic procedure uses attributes to get the indices of formal parameter Result. F is implicitly dereferenced when it is called with a parameter ‡12:

```
7 procedure Euler(
8    F: in Function_Ptr; Init, H: in Float_Type; Result: out Vector) is
9 begin
10   Result(Result'First) := Init;
11   for N in Result'First+1..Result'Last loop
12     Result(N) := Result(N-1) + H * F(Result(N-1));
13   end loop;
14 end Euler;
```

The procedure is tested with a 6-digit floating point type Real, for which we also instantiate the package Float_IO:

```
15 with Ada.Text_IO; with Euler;
16 procedure Diff is
17   type Real is digits 6;
18   package Real_IO is new Ada.Text_IO.Float_IO(Real);
19   use Real_IO;
```

After declaring appropriate types for the array and the function access, the generic procedure is instantiated:

```
20   type Vector is array(Integer range <>) of Real;
21   type Ptr is access function (X: Real) return Real;
22
23   procedure Solve is new Euler(Real, Vector, Ptr);
```

The function Ident is the function that will be passed to the procedure Solve:

```
  function Ident(X: Real) return Real is
  begin
    return X;
  end Ident;
```

Check that it matches the profile of the access type.

Solve is called with an access to the function; the results will be returned in the array Answer:

```
  Answer: Vector(1..21);
begin
  Solve(Ident'Access, 1.0, 0.05, Answer);
  for N in Answer'Range loop
    Put(0.05 * Real(N-1), Exp => 0);
    Put(Answer(N), Exp => 0);
    Ada.Text_IO.New_Line;
  end loop;
end Diff;
```

13.6.2 Numerical libraries

Generic units with formal parameters of floating point type can be used to create numerical libraries. A library can be instantiated with types of different precisions, and the different instantiations used within the same program.

Elementary functions such as the trigonometric functions are predefined in the generic package `Ada.Numerics.Generic_Elementary_Functions` §A.5.1, which can be instantiated with any floating point type. `Ada.Numerics.Elementary_Functions` is a predefined instantiation for `Float`.

A package generating random numbers of type `Float` is defined in §A.5.2. There is also a generic package for random numbers that can be instantiated with a *discrete* type; we used this package in the rocket simulation. An unusual feature of these packages is the ability to save and reset the state of a random number generator §A.5.2(35–56).

Annex §G Numerics has three sections:

- §G.1 Complex Arithmetic defines packages for complex numbers, including elementary functions and input–output.
- §G.2 Numeric Performance Requirements gives a detailed model of computation with real types. The Annex is briefly discussed in Section 13.11.
- §G.3 Vector and Matrix Manipulation describes two generic packages:
  - §G.3.1 `Ada.Numerics.Generic_Real_Arrays`;
  - §G.3.2 `Ada.Numerics.Generic_Complex_Arrays`.

As well as the appropriate declarations of types and elementary objects, these packages include the basic operations of linear algebra, such as solving and inverting matrices, and computing determinants and eigenvalues.

13.7 Ordinary fixed point types

§3.5.9

3 ordinary_fixed_point_definition ::=
  delta *static*_expression real_range_specification

8 The set of values of a fixed point type comprise the integral multiples of a number called the *small* of the type. ... For a type defined by an ordinary_fixed_point_definition (an *ordinary* fixed point type), the *small* may be specified by an attribute_definition_clause (see 13.3); if so specified, it shall be no greater than the *delta* of the type. If not specified, the *small* of an ordinary fixed point type is an implementation-defined power of two less than or equal to the *delta*.

The *small* of an ordinary fixed point type is normally a power of two, so that values of the type can be exactly represented in binary. Ordinary fixed point types are extremely useful for programming embedded systems for two reasons: (a) computers for embedded systems may not have floating point hardware, and (b) external peripherals transfer binary numbers that represent physical quantities.

13.7.1 Case study: conversion to fixed point

The following program shows how a 16-bit word received from a sensor can be converted to an ordinary fixed point value:

temp

```
with Interfaces; with Ada.Unchecked_Conversion;
with Ada.Text_IO; use Ada.Text_IO;
procedure Temp is
   Sensor: Interfaces.Integer_16 := 2#0001_0001_0001_1100#;
```

Let us assume that the least significant bit represents 1/16 of a degree of temperature; then the value that initializes the variable Sensor represents:

$$256 + 16 + 1 + 1/2 + 1/4 = 273.75.$$

A fixed point type `Temperature` is declared, followed by representation attributes that request that 16 bits should be used for objects of the type and that specify that the least significant (binary) digit represents 1/16:

```
type Temperatures        is delta 2.0**(-4) range -2048.0..2047.0;
for  Temperatures'Size  use 16;
for  Temperatures'Small use 2.0**(-4);
```

`Ada.Unchecked_Conversion` is used to convert between the two representations:

```
function To_Temp is new Ada.Unchecked_Conversion(
  Source => Interfaces.Integer_16, Target => Temperatures);
```

and the result of the conversion is printed:

```
begin
   Put_Line(Temperatures'Image(To_Temp(Sensor)));
end Temp;
```

The definition of the multiplication and division operators for fixed point operations is discussed below in Section 13.9 in the context of decimal fixed point types, but the principles are the same for ordinary fixed point types.

13.8 Decimal fixed point types*

§3.5.9

> 4 decimal_fixed_point_definition ::=
> **delta** *static*_expression **digits** *static*_expression [real_range_specification]
>
> 8 The set of values of a fixed point type comprise the integral multiples of a number called the *small* of the type. ...
> 9 For a decimal fixed point type, the *small* equals the *delta*; the *delta* shall be a power of 10. ...

The values of the following type are in the range ±9,999,999,999.99:

```
type Money is delta 0.01 digits 12;
```

Multiplication and division are problematical for fixed point types. Suppose that `M1` and `M2` are two variables of type `Money` that both contain the value 0.25. What is the type of `M1*M2` which equals 0.0625? This answer is that the type must be given by the context; the rules are given in §4.5.5 and will be demonstrated in the case study in the next subsection. If the expression `M1*M2` were assigned to a variable of type `Money`, the value will be truncated to 0.06 §4.5.5(21).

Historically, there has been a large gap between the world of scientific and systems programming, and business programming. Of course, most of the requirements for a language for business programming are not different from those of other fields: reliability, efficiency, system interfaces and support for software engineering. The primary extension needed is in the area of decimal types. The decimal fixed point types in Ada provide this basic functionality, though an implementation need not support such types §3.5.9(21). Implementations conforming to Annex §F Information Systems are required to implement decimal fixed point types, as well as several packages: (a) `Ada.Decimal`, which contains named numbers specifying properties of the decimal types and a generic procedure for arbitrary decimal fixed point division; (b) `Ada.Text_IO.Editing` for formatted input–output, together with versions for wider strings and characters: `Ada.Wide_Text_IO.Editing` and `Ada.Wide_Wide_Text_IO.Editing`.

13.8.1 *Case study: currency conversion*

The program in this case study reads a currency and an amount, and writes the equivalent value in six other currencies (US Dollar, British Pound, Euro, Japanese Yen, Swiss Franc, Indian Rupee, Chinese Yuan Renminbi). `Currencies` is an enumeration type that declares the standard three-letter codes. `Ada.Text_IO.Enumeration_IO` §A.10.10 is instantiated to facilitate input–output of these codes:

convert

```
with Ada.Strings.Bounded;
with Ada.Characters.Latin_1;
with Ada.Text_IO.Editing;
use Ada.Text_IO;
procedure Convert is
  type Currencies     is (USD, GBP, EUR, JPY, CHF, INR, CNY);
  package Currency_IO is new Enumeration_IO(Currencies);
```

Currencies have a sign, such as the dollar sign $, that is used when displaying monetary amounts. `Signs` is an array of bounded strings for display of the currency symbols:

```
  package Sign_Strings is
    new Ada.Strings.Bounded.Generic_Bounded_Length(10);
  use Sign_Strings;
```

Package `Ada.Characters.Latin_1` §A.3.3 contains the names of the characters for the Dollar, the Pound and the Yen:

```
Signs: constant array(Currencies) of Bounded_String := (
  To_Bounded_String((1=>Ada.Characters.Latin_1.Dollar_Sign)),
  To_Bounded_String((1=>Ada.Characters.Latin_1.Pound_Sign)),
  To_Bounded_String("Euro"),
  To_Bounded_String((1=>Ada.Characters.Latin_1.Yen_Sign)),
  To_Bounded_String("SF"),
  To_Bounded_String("Rupee"),
  To_Bounded_String("Yuan"));
```

The signs for the Euro, Rupee and Yuan are not within the type Character; to display them you will have to use type Wide_Character as described in Section 11.2.

Amounts of money are stored in variables of type Money, and Ada.Text_IO.Decimal_IO §A.10.9 is instantiated to read and write these values:

```
type Money       is delta 0.01 digits 12;
package Money_IO is new Decimal_IO(Money);
```

A separate decimal fixed point type is used for the conversion rates, since they need to be represented with greater precision than amounts of money. Fortunately, the range of values is not very large. The rates in the table were obtained from a website and are certainly not up-to-date by the time you read this:

```
type Rates is delta 0.00000001 digits 11;

Conversion: constant array(Currencies, Currencies) of Rates :=
(( 1.0, 0.5059, 0.6775,  108.645, 1.1126,  5.4004,  7.2735),
 (1.9767,    1.0, 1.3392, 214.4697, 2.1993, 77.6415, 14.3775),
 (1.4760, 0.7467,    1.0, 160.2895, 1.6423, 58.0039, 10.7358),
 (0.0092043,  0.00466267,  0.0062387,
        1.0,   0.0101983,   0.361912, 0.066988),
 (0.8989, 0.4547, 0.6087,  98.0551,     1.0, 35.3045,  6.5374),
 (0.0255, 0.0129, 0.0172,   2.7631, 0.0283,     1.0,  0.1852),
 (0.1375, 0.0696, 0.0931,  14.9281, 0.1530,  5.4004,     1.0));
```

The editing package for values of decimal fixed point types is explained in Section 13.8.2:

```
package Edit is new Editing.Decimal_Output(Money);
Money_Picture: Editing.Picture :=
  Editing.To_Picture("#####*_***_***_**9.99");
```

The main subprogram performs the interactive dialog within a block so that if an exception is raised, a new transaction can be carried out. The user is prompted to enter a currency code and an amount of money in that currency:

```
36 begin
37   loop
38     declare
39       Source: Currencies;
40       Amount: Money;
41     begin
42       Put("Currency ( ");
43       for C in Currencies loop
44         Currency_IO.Put(C);
45         Put(" ");
46       end loop;
47       Put(") and amount: ");
48       Currency_IO.Get(Source);
49       Money_IO.Get(Amount);
50       Skip_Line;
```

The amount of money is displayed after formatting with the picture; then the conversions are performed for each other currency and similarly displayed. The expression in ‡55 is discussed in depth in Section 13.9:

```
51       Edit.Put(Amount, Money_Picture, To_String(Signs(Source)));
52       Put_Line(" is worth ");
53       for Target in Currencies loop
54         if Source /= Target then
55           Edit.Put(Conversion(Source, Target) * Amount,
56                    Money_Picture, To_String(Signs(Target)));
57           New_Line;
58         end if;
59       end loop;
```

Entering an invalid code for a currency will raise `Data_Error` §A.13(6). If the value is too large, either `Constraint_Error` will be raised during the computation, or `Picture_Error` §F.3.3(9) will be raised during formatting. To terminate the program, pressing a key (`ctrl-z` or `ctrl-d`) will cause End_Error §A.13(12) to be raised and the loop is exited:

```
60     exception
61       when Data_Error              => Skip_Line; Put_Line("Illegal input");
62       when Editing.Picture_Error => Put_Line("Formatting error");
63       when Constraint_Error      => Put_Line("Computation error");
64       when End_Error               => exit;
65     end;
66   end loop;
67 end Convert;
```

13.8.2 *Editing*

The display of amounts of money uses package `Ada.Text_IO.Editing.Decimal_Output` §F.3.3, which is instantiated with type `Money` ‡33. This package supplies a private type `Picture` that is used for format control. A value of type `Picture` is created by calling `To_Picture` with a string of format control characters ‡34–35. The syntax and semantics of formatting are specified in §F.3.1 and §F.3.2. The picture used is `"###*_***_**9.99"`, where the meaning of each character is as follows:

- `'9'` Decimal digit
- `'.'` Radix mark ("decimal point")
- `'_'` Separator character
- `'*'` Fill character
- `'#'` Currency string

The amount of 4156.34 Swiss Francs will be written as `␣SF***4,156.34`.

Fill characters are used instead of blanks to prevent forgery. The picture characters listed above are fixed in the language, but the characters that are actually displayed are parameters of the procedure `Put` and can be changed for localization. Alternatively, new default values can be specified when `Decimal_IO` is instantiated.

Language Comparison

Ada's picture construct was inspired by COLBOL, but localization features are not found in COBOL, and the language does not have the `'#'` currency string, which allows a fixed-width currency field (unlike `'$'`).

13.9 Fixed point multiplication and division*

Addition and subtraction pose no difficulties for fixed point types and are specified in Ada as for the other numeric types §4.5.3. The result of an addition like:

$$\$123.45 + \$67.89 = \$191.34$$

can, at worst, overflow the range, but that can happen with any arithmetic operation. Nor is it a problem to multiply or divide a fixed point type by an integer §4.5.5(13–14):

$$\$123.45 * 5 = \$617.25.$$

The difficult is with multiplication and division of one fixed point number by another. The problem is that the precision of the result is greater than that of either operand:

$$0.5059 * \$123.45 = £62.453355.$$

In Ada, these fixed point operations are performed by implicitly converting each operand to the type *universal_fixed*:

§4.5.5

> 18 Multiplication and division between any two fixed point types are provided by the following two predefined operators:
>
> 19
> ```
> function "*"(Left, Right : universal_fixed) return universal_fixed
> function "/"(Left, Right : universal_fixed) return universal_fixed
> ```

As explained in Section 13.1.1, you cannot declare an object or parameter of a universal type, so an expression of universal type must appear in a context where an implicit conversion is made to the appropriate type. For example:

```
Converted_Amount: Money := Conversion(Source, Target) * Amount;
```

The result of multiplying an expression of type `Rates` (the component type of `Conversion`) by one of type `Money` (the type of the variable `Amount`) is implicitly converted to a value of type `Money` and assigned to the variable. Similarly, since the procedure `Put` of package `Ada.Text_IO.Editing.Decimal_IO` §F.3.3(15) expects that its first parameter be of the generic fixed point type parameter (here `Money`), this also provides a context for the implicit conversion in ‡55.

Suppose, now, that a foreign exchange office has a special offer: on weekends, each conversion rate is multiplied by ten percent. For simplicity, we model this as a constant:

```
Special: constant Rates := 1.1;
```

that is used when the conversion is performed:

```
Conversion(Source, Target) * Special * Amount
```

Unfortunately, this statement is illegal because we have lost the context: whichever multiplication is done first, the result is used as an operand in a subsequent multiplication, rather than being copied into a variable or parameter. In the absence of a context that will allow implicit type conversion, an *explicit* type conversion must be done:

```
Rates(Conversion(Source, Target) * Special) * Amount
```

The situation becomes more difficult if you overload these operators (see Section 13.11).

13.10 Complex numbers*

Annex §G Numerics defines support for complex arithmetic including elementary functions and IO. Here is an outline of the generic package `Ada.Numerics.Generic_Complex_Types`:

§G.1.1

```
2  generic
      type Real is digits <>;
   package Ada.Numerics.Generic_Complex_Types is
3     type Complex is
         record
            Re, Im : Real'Base;
         end record;
4     type Imaginary is private;
5     i : constant Imaginary;
      j : constant Imaginary;
22 private
      type Imaginary is new Real'Base;
23    i : constant Imaginary := 1.0;
      j : constant Imaginary := 1.0;
24 end Ada.Numerics.Generic_Complex_Types;
```

The type `Complex` is visible so values can be constructed using ordinary aggregates such as `(5.0, 6.3)` or `(Re => 5.0, Im => 6.3)`. `Imaginary` is declared as a separate type in order to allow expressions of the form `R1 + I1*i`. Not shown are the arithmetical operators, which are overloaded for all combinations of parameters of types `Real'Base`, `Complex` and `Imaginary`.

§G.1.2 declares a generic package for complex elementary functions and §G.1.3 declares a generic package for IO. These packages have a single generic formal parameter, which is the package `Ada.Numerics.Generic_Complex_Types`; the actual parameter can be any instantiation of the package obtained by supplying a floating point type for the formal parameter `Real`.

`Ada.Numerics.Complex_Types` is a predefined instantiation of the generic package for type `Float` §G.1.1(25). Similarly, there exist predefined instantiations of the package for complex IO §G.1.3(9.1) and complex elementary functions §G.1.2(9).

Ada 95

A predefined instantiation of `Complex_IO` for type `Float` was not included in Ada 95.

13.10.1 Case study: complex vectors

Here is the outline of a package for complex vectors. There are two generic formal package parameters, one for the complex type and one for the elementary functions:

complex

```
with Ada.Numerics.Generic_Complex_Types;
with Ada.Numerics.Generic_Complex_Elementary_Functions;
generic
  use Ada.Numerics;
  with package Complex_Types is
    new Generic_Complex_Types (<>);
  with package Complex_Functions is
    new Generic_Complex_Elementary_Functions(Complex_Types);
```

The generic package exports the type Vector and two subprograms:

```
package Generic_Complex_Vectors is
  type Vector(<>) is private;
  function Initialize return Vector;
  function Distance(Left, Right: Vector) return Complex_Types.Real'Base;
private
  type Vector is array(Integer range <>) of Complex_Types.Complex;
end Generic_Complex_Vectors;
```

The generic package body uses the functions Compose_From_Cartesian and Sqrt that are defined in the generic package parameters:

```
package body Generic_Complex_Vectors is
  use Complex_Types;
  function Initialize return Vector is ... end Vector;
  function Distance(Left, Right: Vector) return Real is
    Sum: Complex := Compose_From_Cartesian(0.0);
  begin
    for N in Left'Range loop
      Sum := Sum + Left(N) * Right(N);
    end loop;
    return abs(Complex_Functions.Sqrt(Sum));
  end Distance;
end Generic_Complex_Vectors;
```

Let us define our own floating point type:

```
package Signals is
  type Real is digits 12;
end Signals;
```

Now, in sequence, we instantiate the generic package for complex types:

```
32 with Signals;
33 with Ada.Numerics.Generic_Complex_Types;
34 package Signals_Complex is
35   new Ada.Numerics.Generic_Complex_Types(Signals.Real);
```

then the generic package for complex elementary functions:

```
36 with Signals;
37 with Signals_Complex;
38 with Ada.Numerics.Generic_Complex_Elementary_Functions;
39 package Signals_Complex_EF is new
40   Ada.Numerics.Generic_Complex_Elementary_Functions(Signals_Complex);
```

and finally the generic package for complex vectors:

```
41 with Signals_Complex;
42 with Signals_Complex_EF;
43 with Generic_Complex_Vectors;
44 package Signals_Complex_Vectors is new
45   Generic_Complex_Vectors(
46     Signals_Complex, Signals_Complex_EF);
```

Once all the instantiations have been done, these packages can be used like any other:

```
47 with Signals, Signals_Complex, Signals_Complex_Vectors;
48 with Ada.Text_IO;
49 procedure Signal_Test is
50   V1: Signals_Complex_Vectors.Vector := Initialize;
51   V2: Signals_Complex_Vectors.Vector := Initialize;
52   R:  Signals.Real;
53 begin
54   R := Signals_Complex_Vectors.Distance(V1, V2);
55   Ada.Text_IO.Put_Line(Signals.Real'Image(R));
56 end Signal_Test;
```

In Section 9.9, we noted that a generic package can have a generic child. The following package extends the complex vector abstraction by creating an abstraction of a pair of vectors. Its implementation ‡62–65 is allowed to use the full view of the type `Vector` ‡14, because the private part of the parent is visible in the private part of a child package:

```
generic
package Generic_Complex_Vectors.Generic_Pair is
  type Pair is private;
private
  subtype Max is Integer range 0..100;
  type Pair(Size: Max := 10) is
    record
      First, Second: Vector(1..Size);
    end record;
end Generic_Complex_Vectors.Generic_Pair;
```

Signals_Complex_Vectors.Pair is created by instantiating the generic child Generic_Pair of the *instance* Signals_Complex_Vectors.

```
with Signals_Complex_Vectors;
with Generic_Complex_Vectors.Generic_Pair;
package Signals_Complex_Vectors.Pair is
  new Signals_Complex_Vectors.Generic_Pair;
```

13.11 Advanced concepts*

Ada is perhaps unique among programming languages in its support for portable numeric computation, in particular, portable computation with real numbers. This section presents some of the finer details of numeric computation in Ada. Most software engineers will not need to read this material.

13.11.1 Attributes

There are a large number of attributes associated with floating point (§3.5.8, §A.5.3) and fixed point types (§3.5.10, §A.5.4). The ones in the body of the *ARM* concern properties seen by the programmer; for example, a fixed point type S is declared with a **delta** and the attribute S'Delta §3.5.10(3) returns this value at run-time. The attributes in Annex §A are *representation-oriented*, relating to the implementation of the types; for example, S'Machine_Rounds and S'Machine_Overflows §A.5.3(11–12), §A.5.4(3–4) enable you to write a program that takes into account the computational properties of the machine executing the program.

13.11.2 *Rounding*

When converting from a real type to an integer type, the real type is rounded:

§4.6

> 33 If the target type is an integer type and the operand type is real, the result is rounded to the nearest integer (away from zero if exactly halfway between two integers).

Some machines have a built-in rounding operation that rounds toward zero instead of away from zero. You can take advantage of such a fast hardware instruction using the attribute `S'Machine_Rounding` §A.5.3(41.1), though that will make your application non-portable.

Ada 95

`S'Machine_Rounding` does not exist in Ada 95.

> **Language Comparison**
>
> Java specifies rounding *toward* zero. In Ada, 1.5 will be rounded to 2, whereas in Java, it will be rounded to 1.

13.11.3 *Base range*

Clearly, a computer will not support different hardware formats for each floating point type such as **digits** 6, **digits** 7, **digits** 8. The implementation will represent values of each type in a hardware format that can contain at least the values of the type, but possibly more. Similarly, an enumeration or integer type will be stored in a hardware format whose range of values may be significantly more than the minimum required.

§3.5

> 6 The *base range* of a scalar type is the range of finite values of the type that can be represented in every unconstrained object of the type; it is also the range supported at a minimum for intermediate values during the evaluation of expressions involving predefined operators of the type.
>
> 15 S'Base—S'Base denotes an unconstrained subtype of the type of S. This unconstrained subtype is called the *base subtype* of the type.

Of course the base range is implementation dependent, so `S'Base` should not normally be used in writing Ada programs.

Overflow checks are based on the base range and are typically checked by the CPU itself. Range checks, which are done for assignment statements, parameter passing, etc., are based on the subtype's range as defined by the programmer. Range checks never apply to an unconstrained subtype; consider:

```
type Altitude is range 0 .. 30_000;
A1:  Altitude := 25_000;
A2:  Altitude := 20_000;
A3:  Altitude := (A1 + A2) / 2;
```

Suppose that `Altitude'Base` has a 32-bit range because all computation is performed in 32-bit registers. If "+" were defined on parameters of type `Altitude`, the addition would be required to raise `Constraint_Error`. However, addition is defined on the base range, so no range check need be done until the assignment to `A3` and `Constraint_Error` will not be raised. You can declare variables of the unconstrained subtype to explicitly hold intermediate values:

```
Temp: Altitude'Base := A1 + A2;
A3:   Altitude      := Temp / 2;
```

The predefined subtype `Integer` is constrained §3.5.4(11) to its base range, while the predefined subtype `Float` is unconstrained §3.5.7(12). Predefined arithmetical operators are defined §A.1(15–18) for the unconstrained subtype `Integer'Base`, not for the constrained subtype `Integer`.

13.11.4 Preference for root types

What is the type of `N` in the following loop statement?

```
for N in 1..100 loop
```

Since the literals are of type *universal_integer*, the type should be ambiguous, because there is no context that can be used to convert the range to a specific type such as `Integer` or `Short_Integer`.

§8.6

> 29 There is a *preference* for the primitive operators (and ranges) of the root numeric types *root_integer* and *root_real*. In particular, if two acceptable interpretations of a constituent of a complete context differ only in that one is for a primitive operator (or range) of the type *root_integer* or *root_real*, and the other is not, the interpretation using the primitive operator (or range) of the root numeric type is *preferred*.

It follows from this rule that the range `1..100` is of type *root_integer*.

§3.6

> 18 If the type of the range resolves to *root_integer*, then the discrete_subtype_definition defines a subtype of the predefined type Integer with bounds given by a conversion to Integer of the bounds of the range;

Since `1..100` is of type *root_integer*, the discrete_subtype_definition §3.6(6) of the for-loop §5.5(4) is a subtype of type `Integer`.

13.11.5 *Case study: preference for root types*

In the following program, the variables `I` and `J` are declared to be of type `Integer`, so the function overriding predefined `"<"` is called. However, the literals `5` and `4` are of type *universal_integer* §3.4(6), so the predefined operator for *root_integer* §3.4(7) is *preferred* over the new one for `Integer`:

pref

```
with Ada.Text_IO; use Ada.Text_IO;
procedure Pref is
  function "<"(Left, Right: Integer) return Boolean is
  begin
    return Left >= Right;
  end "<";
  I: Integer := 5;
  J: Integer := 4;
begin
  if I < J then Put("Strange "); else Put("OK "); end if;
  if 5 < 4 then Put("Strange "); else Put("OK "); end if;
end Pref;
```

Check that the program prints `"Strange OK "`.

13.11.6 *Overloading fixed point operators*

Consider, again, the multiplication in the currency conversion case study discussed in Section 13.9. We modified the program so that the conversion rates were multiplied by a constant `Special`:

```
Rates(Conversion(Source, Target) * Special) * Amount
```

Suppose, now, that valued customers are to have the constant `Special` increased by an extra percent. To encapsulate this arrangement, the higher rate is computed by overloading the predefined multiplication operator:

```
function "*"(Left, Right: Rates) return Rates is ... end "*";
```

The expression:

```
Rates(Conversion(Source, Target) * Special) * Amount
```

is now illegal. To understand this, recall that multiplication of fixed-point types needs a context:

§4.5.5

18 Multiplication and division between any two fixed point types are provided by the following two predefined operators:

```
19 function "*"(Left, Right : universal_fixed) return universal_fixed
   function "/"(Left, Right : universal_fixed) return universal_fixed
```

19.1 The above two fixed-fixed multiplying operators shall not be used in a context where the expected type for the result is itself *universal_fixed*—the context has to identify some other numeric type to which the result is to be converted, either explicitly or implicitly. ...

The paragraph now continues:

§4.5.5

19.1 ... Unless the predefined universal operator is identified using an expanded name with prefix denoting the package Standard, an explicit conversion is required on the result when using the above fixed-fixed multiplication operator if either operand is of a type having a user-defined primitive multiplication operator such that:
19.2 • it is declared immediately within the same declaration list as the type; and
19.3 • both of its formal parameters are of a fixed-point type.
19.4 A corresponding requirement applies to the universal fixed-fixed division operator.

The first operand `Rates(...*...)` of the outer multiplication is of a type `Rates` having a user-defined primitive multiplication operator and the conditions §4.5.5(19.2–19.3) are satisfied. Therefore, the universal operator defined in §4.5.5(18) is no longer available without an explicit conversion, and it is this universal operator that we need to multiply the left operand of type `Rates` by the variable `Amount` of type `Money`.

Reading §4.5.5(19.1) carefully, we see that an *explicit conversion* of the result to the type `Money`:

```
Money(Rates(Conversion(Source, Target) * Special) * Amount)
```

will make the predefined operator available. But the same reasoning applies to the inner multiplication of two expressions of type `Rates`: because of the *explicit conversion* of the result, both the predefined operator and the overloaded one are available and the expression is ambiguous.

The problem can be solved as follows:

```
Money(Conversion(Source, Target) * Special * Amount)
```

For the two leftmost operands, there is the overloaded operator for "*"; furthermore, by the second sentence of §4.5.5(19.1) it is the only one available. Now the result of type Rates and the rightmost operand of type Money have to be multiplied, and the only possibility is the predefined one, which (again by the second sentence of §4.5.5(19.1)) we can use by supplying an explicit conversion (here to the type Money).

Another possibility is to use the expanded name for the operator:

```
Standard."*"(Conversion(Source, Target) * Special, Amount)
```

Before leaving this complicated subject, let us consider the implementation of the overloaded operator:

```
Extra: Boolean := True;

function "*"(Left, Right: Rates) return Rates is
begin
  if Extra then
    return Left * (Right+0.01);
  else
    return Left * Right;
  end if;
end "*";
```

The expressions in the return statements are ambiguous because two multiplication operators are visible: the predefined one and the operator just overloaded for Rates. Clearly, we don't want the latter, because that would lead to unbounded recursion, so we need to specify that the standard operator is to be used:

```
Standard."*"(Left, Right+0.01);
```

13.11.7 Model numbers

The definition of floating point computation is very difficult because even simple numbers like 0.2 do not have a finite representation on a binary computer. The value actually used depends on exactly how floating point numbers are represented, so floating point computation is necessarily machine-dependent:

§3.5.7

> 8 The set of values for a floating point type is the (infinite) set of rational numbers. The *machine numbers* of a floating point type are the values of the type that can be represented exactly in every unconstrained variable of the type. . . .

Nevertheless, it is possible to give a portable definition of the accuracy of floating point computation, and this is done in Annex §G using an idealization of machine numbers called *model numbers*. Some values of floating point type, such as $0.5_{10} = 0.1_2$, are equal to model numbers; others, such as $0.2_{10} = 0.00110011\ldots_2$, do not equal model numbers, and are represented by the *model interval* between the model numbers closest to the value. An arithmetical operation applied to two model intervals yields another model interval.

An implementation may find some accuracy requirements difficult to achieve efficiently. In addition to the required *strict mode* of computation that fully conforms with the standard, an implementation may offer a *relaxed mode* of computation §G.2(1–3).

Floating point computation is explained in detail in Annex §G of the *Rationale* for Ada 95.

Projects

1. In the simulation case study, change the type `Simulation_Type` from a subtype to an integer type.
2. Use modular types to implement the calculation of cyclic redundency checks.
3. Implement Euler's method using access-to-subprogram types.
4. Implement algorithms for inertial navigation. If you are not familiar with the concept, do the following one-dimensional computation. Given a position x_0, read a series of values of velocities $v_0, v_1, v_2, \ldots$ that are sampled at a fixed interval Δt. Compute $x_{i+1} = x_i + v_i \cdot \Delta t$. Do the computations in fixed point arithmetic and assume that the samples are 12 bits, where the first six bits represent numbers from -32 to 31 and the next six bits represent the fractions $\frac{0}{64}$ to $\frac{63}{64}$.
5. Certain currencies like the Japanese Yen do not have fractional parts; modify the currency conversion case study so that a different picture can be associated with each currency.

Quizzes

Quiz 1:

```
type T1 is range 5..10;
type T2 is new T1 range 50..100;
```

Quiz 2:

```
type My_Boolean is new Boolean;
I, J: Integer := 1;
M: My_Boolean := My_Boolean(I = J);

if M then Put("Equal"); else Put("Not equal"); end if;
```

Quiz 3:

```
type Int is range 0..10_000;
A: Int := 1_000;
B: Int := 20;
C: Int := (A * B) / 5;

Put_Line( Int'Image(C) );
```

Quiz 4:

```
Put( "+"(Left => 2, Right => 3) );
```

Quiz 5:

```
type M is mod 23;
X1: M := 21;
X2: M := 10;

Put_Line( M'Image( X1 xor X2 ) );
```

Quiz 6:

```
type Fixed is delta 0.5 range 0.0 .. 10.1;

Put_Line(Fixed'Image(10.1));
```

Quiz 7:

```
N1: aliased constant Integer := 1;
N2: aliased constant := 1;
```

Quiz 8:

```
I: Integer;

case Integer'Pos(I) is
  when Integer'First..Integer'Last => null;
end case;
```

Quiz 9:

```
package P is
  type T1 is range 1..100;
  procedure Proc(X: T1; Y: T1);
  type T2 is new T1 range 1..50;
end P;

package body P is
  procedure Proc(X: T1; Y: T1) is
  begin
    Put(Integer(X));
    Put(Integer(Y));
  end Proc;
end P;

with P; use P;
procedure Main is
  Z: T2 := 10;
begin
  Proc(Z, 99);
end Main;
```

Quiz 10:

```
package P is
  type T1 is range 1..100;
  subtype Sub is T1 range 1..50;
  procedure Proc(X: Sub; Y: Sub);
  type T2 is new T1 range 51..100;
end P;

package body P is
  procedure Proc(X: Sub; Y: Sub) is
  begin
    Put(Integer(X));
    Put(Integer(Y));
  end Proc;
end P;

with P; use P;
procedure Main is
  Z1: T2 := 88;
  Z2: T2 := 99;
begin
  Proc(Z1, Z2);
end Main;
```

Quiz 11: On page 272, we showed that the following expression is legal and unambiguous:

```
Money(Conversion(Source, Target) * Special * Amount)
```

What about:

```
Money(Conversion(Source, Target) * (Special * Amount))
```

Chapter 14
Input–Output

14.1 Libraries for input–output

Sections §A.6–§A.14 of Annex §A describe the input–output facilities of Ada. We have used Ada.Text_IO §A.10 extensively for input and output of characters and strings. There are packages of identical functionality for Wide_Character, Wide_String, Wide_Wide_Character, and Wide_Wide_String in §A.11:

- Ada.Wide_Text_IO
- Ada.Wide_Wide_Text_IO

Subprograms for IO of characters and strings are declared directly within Ada.Text_IO; for bounded and unbounded strings, generic subpackages must be instantiated §A.10.11, §A.10.12:

- Ada.Text_IO.Bounded_IO
- Ada.Text_IO.Unbounded_IO

The following generic subpackages of Ada.Text_IO can be instantiated for IO of scalar types:

- Ada.Text_IO.Integer_IO
- Ada.Text_IO.Modular_IO
- Ada.Text_IO.Float_IO
- Ada.Text_IO.Fixed_IO
- Ada.Text_IO.Decimal_IO
- Ada.Text_IO.Enumeration_IO

If you are going to use these packages frequently in your system, it is more efficient at compile-time if you instantiate them once, for example, as library packages:

```
package P is
  type Countries is (US, UK, France, Germany, Japan, Korea);
end P;
```

```
with P;
with Ada.Text_IO;
package Countries_IO is
  new Ada.Text_IO.Enumeration_IO(P.Countries);
```

For each predefined integer type §A.10.8(20–22) and floating point type §A.10.9(32–34), non-generic packages are predefined which are equivalent to instantiations with these types. For example, `Ada.Integer_Text_IO` is predefined for type `Integer`.

Here is an overview of `Ada.Text_IO`:

- Most subprograms are overloaded with one declaration containing a parameter of type `File_Type` §A.10.1(3) for IO to a file and another for IO to a default file. The default files are usually the keyboard and screen, but this can be changed using the subprograms described in §A.10.3.
- Text files are considered to be composed of logical *pages, lines* and *columns* §A.10(7–11). Subprograms that query and modify the logical structure of the file are described in §A.10.4 and §A.10.5. For example, function `End_Of_File` §A.10.5(24) checks if the end of an input file has been reached, and procedure `New_Page` §A.10.5(15) causes a *page terminator* (however that is implemented) to be written to an output file.
- Input–output may be done to internal strings as well as to external files §A.10(3).
- Ordinary parameters are used to specify format information. A simple subprogram call like `Put(N)` uses default values for format parameters. Named parameter association can be used to change just one of these values: `Put(N, Base=>16)`.
- There is no support for output of more than one value in a single subprogram call. A workaround is to construct a single string using the attribute `Image` for scalar types and functions for other types.

Binary input–output can be done using the generic packages `Ada.Sequential_IO` §A.8.1 and `Ada.Direct_IO` §A.8.4. The packages have a generic formal private type parameter that is used to specify the type of the file elements.

Other sections of Annex §A pertaining to input–output are:

- §A.7 defines the terminology used for files and §A.8.2 describes subprograms that perform file management such as opening and closing a file.
- Package `Ada.Storage_IO` §A.9 implements input–output to and from a memory buffer rather than an external file. It can be used to create your own input–output package, since it translates from an internal representation which includes dope vectors and tags to a flat buffer of storage elements.
- Exceptions that may be raised upon input–output are declared in `Ada.IO_Exceptions` §A.13. Other packages rename the exceptions so you don't need a with_clause for this package.
- §A.14 discusses what happens if an external file is associated with more than one internal file object.
- Stream input–output §A.12 is discussed in Section 14.3.

Ada 95

`Ada.Text_IO.Unbounded_IO`, `Ada.Text_IO.Bounded_IO`, and `Ada.Wide_Wide_Text_IO` are new for Ada 2005.

14.2 Interface with the operation system

There are three packages for interfacing with the operating system environment:

- `Ada.Command_Line` §A.15 enables reading the name of the command that invoked the program and the command-line arguments.
- `Ada.Directories` §A.16 contains a comprehensive set of types and subprograms such as `Current_Directory`, `Set_Directory`, and `Create_Directory` for working within an operating system's file system.
- `Ada.Environment_Variables` §A.17 provides constructs for using the system's *environment variables* that form a persistent store. Environment variables are stored associatively, that is, parameter values are accessed by providing the name of the parameter. The package includes the subprograms `Value`, `Exists`, `Set`, and `Clear`, as well as an iterator over all variables.

Clearly, there will be implementation dependences in these packages.

Ada 95

The packages `Ada.Directories` and `Ada.Environment_Variables` are new for Ada 2005. If you need this functionality, check if your implementation has non-standard packages for Ada 95.

> **Language Comparison**
>
> A source of difficulty in file processing is that the separator characters are implmentation dependent. The Java class `java.io.File` declares static fields such as `pathSeparator` to facilitate portability. While similar declarations do not exist in Ada, you can portably construct a full file name using the function `Ada.Directories.Compose` §A.16(81–82).

14.3 Streams*

`Ada.Sequential_IO` performs input–output on values of a single type. *Streams* are used for input–output of values of more than one type to a single file. Values of all types are written as a sequence of bytes that can be reconstructed into values of the same types when read. A stream file is much more portable than a binary file; while the encoding of elementary types is implementation dependent, there is a canonical order defined for encoding composite types §13.13.2(9). Streams are used not only to create files, but also to pass data between the partitions of a distributed system (Section 22.1).

Package `Ada.Streams` §13.13.1 declares type `Root_Stream_Type` as an abstract tagged type from which all streams are derived. A stream is composed of a sequence of values of the modular type `Stream_Element`. The following diagram shows how streams work:

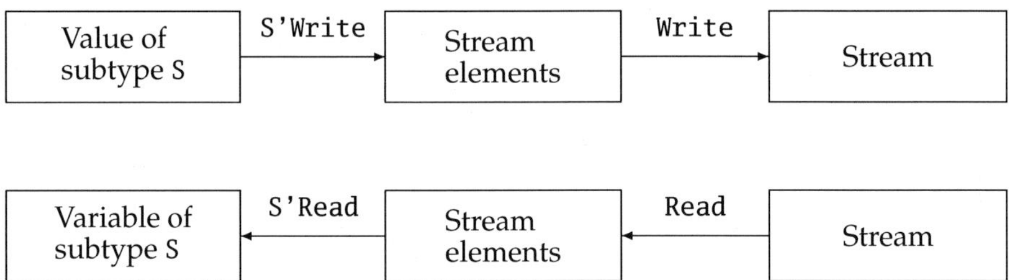

Two operations are involved in writing to a stream. The attribute `S'Write` transforms values of a subtype `S` into stream elements, which the subprogram `Write` writes to the stream. Reading does these steps in the opposite direction.

§13.13.2

3 S'Write S'Write denotes a procedure with the following specification:

4
```
procedure S'Write(
   Stream : not null access Ada.Streams.Root_Stream_Type'Class;
   Item : in T)
```

5 S'Write writes the value of *Item* to *Stream*.

6 S'Read S'Read denotes a procedure with the following specification:

7
```
procedure S'Read(
   Stream : not null access Ada.Streams.Root_Stream_Type'Class;
   Item : out T)
```

8 S'Read reads the value of *Item* from *Stream*.

The subprograms `Write` and `Read` are not explicitly called; instead, the attributes call them automatically §13.13.1(1). You can override the abstract subprograms `Write` and `Read` §13.13.1(5–6) when you define a stream for a new type, and you can supply an attribute definition clause to specify the attributes §13.13.2(38).

The following case study shows how you can use streams without a detailed knowledge of package `Ada.Streams`. To create a stream file, you do not need to explicitly declare a stream. Instead, you can declare a file of type `File_Type` from package `Ada.Streams.Stream_IO` §A.12.1.

This package declares a function that returns an access to the stream associated with the file, and this access is then used as the first actual parameter of the Read and Write attributes.

§A.12.1

```
 4 type Stream_Access is access all Root_Stream_Type'Class;
13 function Stream (File : in File_Type) return Stream_Access;
      -- Return stream access for use with T'Input and T'Output
```

§A.12.1

> 29 The Stream function returns a Stream_Access result from a File_Type object, thus allowing the stream-oriented attributes Read, Write, Input, and Output to be used on the same file for multiple types. Stream propagates Status_Error if File is not open.

Finally, package Ada.Text_IO.Text_Streams §A.12.2 enables you to obtain a stream associated with a text file, which can be used to include binary data within the file.

14.3.1 *Case study: simulation with streams*

This version of the discrete event simulation creates and writes events to a file. The file can then be repeatedly read to rerun the same simulation scenario. The attributes Input and Output are used instead of Read and Write for reasons explained below.

After the preliminary declarations:

rocketst

```
with Event_Queue;
with Root_Event.Engine, Root_Event.Telemetry, Root_Event.Steering;
use Root_Event;
with Ada.Streams.Stream_IO; use Ada.Streams.Stream_IO;
procedure RocketST is
   Q:          Event_Queue.Queue_Ptr := new Event_Queue.Queue;
   Event_File: File_Type;
   S:          Stream_Access;
begin
   Create(Event_File, Name=>"Event.Str");
```

the function Stream returns a value of type Stream_Access which is assigned to S:

```
   S := Stream(Event_File);
```

S is then used as a parameter of attribute `Event'Class'Output` to output events to the stream:

```
    for I in 1..15 loop
      Event'Class'Output(S,
        Event'Class(Engine.Main_Engine_Event'(Engine.Create)));
      Event'Class'Output(S,
        Event'Class(Engine.Aux_Engine_Event'(Engine.Create)));
      Event'Class'Output(S, Event'Class(Telemetry.Create));
      Event'Class'Output(S, Event'Class(Steering.Create));
    end loop;
    Close(Event_File);
```

The same stream variable is then used to read the events from the stream:

```
    Open(Event_File, In_File, Name=>"Event.Str");
    S := Stream(Event_File);
    for I in 1..45 loop
      Event_Queue.Put(Event'Class'Input(S), Q.all);
    end loop;
    Close(Event_File);

    while not Event_Queue.Empty(Q.all) loop
      Root_Event.Simulate(Event_Queue.Get(Q));
    end loop;
  end RocketST;
```

§13.13.2 describes how values are transformed to stream elements by `Write` and how stream elements are transformed to values by `Read`. Given:

```
subtype Line is String(1..120);
```

`Line'Write` will write 120 stream elements and `Line'Read` will read the same 120 stream elements.

Consider now the following procedure with the unconstrained formal parameter of type `String`:

```
procedure Write_String(S: in Stream_Access; Str: in String) is
begin
  String'Write(S, Str);
end Write_String;
```

Each call to the procedure will write just the stream elements that represent the current value of `Str`. To recover the string, you would need to *explicitly* write additional information on the stream (such as the length of the string) in order to read it correctly. This can be done automatically by using the attribute `S'Output` §13.13.2(19–21), which is the same as `S'Write` except that array bounds and discriminants, if any, are automatically written to the stream. Similarly,

S'Input §13.13.2(22–24) is like S'Read, except that it can use this information to determine how much data to read and how to arrange it in an object.

For class-wide types, the attributes S'Class'Write and S'Class'Read §13.13.2(10–16) dispatch to the attributes S'Write and S'Read according to the specific type of the actual parameter. S'Class'Output and S'Class'Input §13.13.2(28–34) are similar except that a representation of the tag is written to the stream and used upon input to reconstruct a value of the corresponding specific type. This is clearly what was required in the case study, so that the tag of each event will be written and then restored upon reading. Fortunately, S'Input and S'Class'Input are functions, rather than procedures, so we can use the result to give an initial value to an indefinite type, or as an actual parameter to a subprogram with a formal parameter of indefinite type ‡24.

Since streams are written in a canonical format, they are portable and a stream written by one implementation can be read by another. The only problem is with numerical and enumeration types, where the implementation is allowed to choose the representation. Suppose that we define Simulation_Time in the simulation case study as a new integer type, rather than as a subtype of Integer:

```
type Simulation_Time is range 0..10_000;
```

If values of the type are represented on one machine using 16 bits and on another using 32 bits, the streams will not be compatible. We can solve this problem by adding a representation attribute §13.13.2(1.1–1.5):

```
for Simulation_Time'Stream_Size use 16;
```

This ensures that values of the type will be represented using 16 bits in the stream; the implementation is responsible for converting the stream elements to and from its internal representation.

Ada 95

The attribute Stream_Size is not available in Ada 95 and there is no portable workaround.

14.4 Generic dispatching constructors*

The attributes S'Input and S'Output support I/O of different types of a class of types to a stream. Suppose, however, that we wish to construct a value of a type within a class as a function of arbitrary data. A good example is selecting an item from a list on a pulldown menu, where the menu listener returns the index of the selected item. The obvious way to do this is to write a case- or if-statement:

```
Value: access T'Class;

case Selection is
  when 0 => Value := new T0'Create(...);
  when 1 => Value := new T1'Create(...);
  ...
end case;
```

This technique is frowned upon in object-oriented programming where polymorphism is supposed to facilitate type derivation with minimal modification of existing code.

Generic dispatching constructors, also known as *factory functions*, take the tag of a type and optional additional parameters and dispatch to a constructor function:

§3.9

```
18.2  generic
         type T (<>) is abstract tagged limited private;
         type Parameters (<>) is limited private;
         with function Constructor (Params : not null access Parameters)
            return T is abstract;
      function Ada.Tags.Generic_Dispatching_Constructor
         (The_Tag : Tag; Params : not null access Parameters)
            return T'Class;
```

The generic function has three formal parameters. The first is the tagged type whose values are to be constructed, and the second is for additional data that can be a parameter of the constructor. The third parameter is the function that is to be called. The formal function is declared **abstract**, which means that the generic actual parameter has to be a dispatching operation of the controlling return type T §12.6(8.4–8.5).

Generic dispatching constructors can also be used to write your own stream functions (see Section 2.6 of the Ada 2005 Rationale).

Ada 95

Generic dispatching constructors are new to Ada 2005.

14.4.1 *Case study: simulation with a generic dispatching constructor*

Let us modify the simulation so that events can be created interactively. First, the constructor `Create` has to be modified so that its profile fits the formal function parameter `Constructor`. In this program, no additional data is needed, so the parameter is simply a null record:

rocketfac

```
package Root_Event is
  type Event is abstract tagged private;
  type Parameters is null record;
  function  Create(Params: not null access Parameters)
                return Event is abstract;
  procedure Simulate(E: in Event) is abstract;
end Root_Event;
```

In the main program, the generic dispatching constructor is instantiated:

```
-- with's as needed
use Root_Event;
procedure RocketFAC is
  Q: Event_Queue.Queue_Ptr := new Event_Queue.Queue;
  function Constructor is
    new Ada.Tags.Generic_Dispatching_Constructor(Event, Parameters, Create);
```

An array is used to map the index of an item selected from a menu into a tag:

```
  T: array(Natural range <>) of Ada.Tags.Tag :=
      (Engine.Main_Engine_Event'Tag, Engine.Aux_Engine_Event'Tag,
       Telemetry.Telemetry_Event'Tag, Steering.Steering_Event'Tag);
```

A dummy value is used for the additional parameters:

```
  Dummy: aliased Parameters := (null record);
```

The selection from a menu is represented by the input of the value of the index, which is used as an index into the array of tags:

```
begin
  for I in 1..5 loop
    Ada.Text_IO.Put("Click on event: ");
    Event_Queue.Put(
      Constructor(
        T(Integer'Value(Ada.Text_IO.Get_Line)), Dummy'Access), Q.all);
  end loop;
end RocketFAC;
```

If event types are added, the only change needed is to add the tag to the array.

Projects

1. Use the `Iterate` procedure of `Ada.Environment_Variables` to fetch and display all the environment variables on your system. Write an interactive program to update the variables.
2. Extend the case study in Section 14.4 so that the parameters of each event can be entered interactively and then passed to dispatching constructors.
3. Reimplement the stream case study in Section 14.3 by overriding the subprograms `Input` and `Output` so that the elements of the stream are written as strings.

Quizzes

Quiz 1:

```
File1, File2: File_Type;

File1 := File2;
```

Quiz 2:

```
File: File_Type;

procedure Get_Data(F: in File_Type) is
begin
  Open(F, In_File, "name.txt");
  Close(F);
end Get_Data;

Get_Data(File);
```

Quiz 3:

```
with Ada.Text_IO; use Ada.Text_IO;
with Ada.IO_Exceptions;
procedure Main is
  File: File_Type;
begin
  Open(File, In_File, "name.txt");
exception
  when Name_Error => Put_Line("File not found");
end Main;
```

Chapter 15
Program Structure

15.1 Compilation and execution

This section discusses topics from Section §10 Program Structure and Compilation Issues. The basic definitions are given in §10.1.

§10.1

> 1 A *program unit* is either a package, a task unit, a protected unit, a protected entry, a generic unit, or an explicitly declared subprogram other than an enumeration literal. Certain kinds of program units can be separately compiled. Alternatively, they can appear physically nested within other program units.
>
> 2 The text of a program can be submitted to the compiler in one or more compilations. Each compilation is a succession of compilation_units. A compilation_unit contains either the declaration, the body, or a renaming of a program unit. The representation for a compilation is implementation-defined.

A context clause is associated with a single compilation_unit §10.1.1(3), §10.1.2, so if several units that are semantically dependent the same package are contained in one compilation, each unit must have a with_clause for the package.

§10.1

> 3 A library unit is a separately compiled program unit, and is always a package, subprogram, or generic unit. Library units may have other (logically nested) library units as children, and may have other program units physically nested within them. A root library unit, together with its children and grandchildren and so on, form a *subsystem*.

A task is not a library unit.

§10.1

> 4 An implementation may impose implementation-defined restrictions on compilations that contain multiple compilation_units.

The GNAT compiler exploits the permission given in §10.1(4) and forbids multiple compilation units in a compilation; instead, a tool is provided for "chopping" a file containing several units into files with one unit apiece.

Semantic dependences §10.1.1(23–26) are used to determine both visibility and the compile-time dependence of one unit on another. Before a unit can be compiled, *consistent* versions of all units upon which the unit depends semantically must exist §10.1.4(5) and must be legal for the compilation to succeed.

Compiled units are stored an *environment* §10.1.4(1). The environment is usually the operating system's file system, but the rules are intentionally vague to allow any implementation that can satisfy the requirements of dependence and consistency.

15.1.1 *Inline subprograms*

pragma `Inline` §6.3.2 is a recommendation §6.3.2(6) to the compiler that the code for a subprogram be expanded inline at the points where it is called. This saves the overhead of a jump to and return from the subprogram, and can also facilitate optimization because the code of the subprogram is compiled within a larger context. Improved optimization can reduce both the time and the space of a program, although excessive inlining can significantly increase the amount of memory needed, so be sure to measure what happens when you specify inline.

Check also if your compiler can turn inlining on and off by using a compiler switch and if your compiler performs inlining automatically.

You may wish to defer the use of inlining until late in the development of a program. The reason is that recompilation of a package *body* containing an inlined subprogram may require recompilation of every unit that depends on the package *specification*, even if the subprogram body was not modified §10.1.4(7).

15.2 Compilation and the environment of compilation*

The language specifies that every compilation takes place within an environment of compilation. This environment includes, among other things, the predefined units of the language, as described in Annex §A: the package `Standard`, and packages for strings, input-output, numeric computations, containers, etc.

The environment has another function: it ensures that when an executable file is created by compiling a main program and all the units on which it semantically depends (transitively), the resulting executable is consistent, that is, no portion of that executable contains code that originates from a source file that is out of date. In other languages, this consistency may be ensured by a *make* tool, which is not defined by the language. In Ada, consistency is a formal requirement of the software that manages the environment. When compiling a single unit, say some package P, all that needs to be present in the environment are the declarations for the units P1, P2, ... on which it depends; these are the specifications of the packages that are mentioned in the context clause of P. This requirement ensures that the legality of P can be verified even before the bodies of P1, P2, ... are written.

As noted in the previous section, if P specifies that calls to some subprogram defined in P1 are to be inlined, then P also depends on the *body* of P1, and that body must be present as well when compiling P. The same applies if P contains an instance of a generic unit declared in P1.

The requirement that compilation be done in the context of an environment (Section 6.2.1, §10.1.4(1)) does not require that the environment be implemented as a place to store the results of compilations, such as the symbol tables that result from parsing package specifications. The only important concept is that of semantic dependences: when a package body or a client of the package is compiled, there must be a legal package specification in the environment.

An alternate method of implementation is used, for example, by the GNAT compiler. There is no environment other than the file system of the operating system that stores the source and object files. Whenever a package body is compiled, its package specification is compiled also. Similarly, whenever a unit is compiled, the specifications of *all* the packages in its with_clauses are read and analyzed. There is no need to explicitly compile package specifications.

Normally, the implementation of the environment is transparent to the programmer, because the compiler will decide by itself what units must be compiled or re-compiled, taking into account the semantic dependences and the time-stamps of the source files.

15.3 Subunits*

If a unit becomes very large, it is possible to "break off" enclosed bodies into *subunits* §10.1.3. Subunits are transparent in terms of visibility §10.1.3(16–17). A subunit is created by writing a *stub* in place of a body, and then creating additional compilation_units for the bodies. The case study in the following subsection shows some of the rules that apply to subunits.

Subunits may have their own context clauses §10.1.1(3), so they can be used to reduce the dependences of a unit. A subunit depends semantically on its parent §10.1.1(26), so any change in the parent requires recompilation of all subunits. The GNAT compiler simply copies the text of the subunit into its parent so any change to the subunit requires that the parent be recompiled. In such implementations, there is no advantage to subunits in terms of reduced compilation time.

Child units are a superior way of structuring programs and have made subunits almost obsolete.

15.3.1 *Case study: subunits*

The body of package `P` has two stubs, one for the body of procedure `Proc1` and one for the body of package `Inner`:

subunit

```
package P is
  procedure Proc1;
end P;

package body P is
  S: String := "Global variable";

  package Inner is
    procedure Proc2;
  end Inner;

  procedure Proc1 is separate;
  package body Inner is separate;
end P;
```

The subunit for `Proc1` has its own context clause with a with_clause for `Ada.Text_IO` that was not needed in the enclosing unit:

```
with Ada.Text_IO; use Ada.Text_IO;
separate(P)
procedure Proc1 is
begin
  Put_Line(S & " visible from Proc1");
  Inner.Proc2;
end Proc1;
```

`Proc1` was declared after the specification for package `Inner`, so `Inner.Proc2` is visible.

The package body of `Inner` is also a subunit, and it, in turn, declares the procedure `Proc2` whose body is a subunit:

```
separate(P)
package body Inner is
  procedure Proc2 is separate;
end Inner;
```

The body of `Inner` cannot be placed within `P`, because it contains a stub and stubs must appear immediately within a compilation unit body §10.1.3(13).

Although `Proc2` is a subunit of a subunit, the global variable `S` remains visible:

```
with Ada.Text_IO; use Ada.Text_IO;
separate(P.Inner)
procedure Proc2 is
begin
  Put_Line(S & " visible from Proc2");
end Proc2;

with P;
procedure Test_Subunit is
begin
  P.Proc1;
end Test_Subunit;
```

15.3.2 Summary of package organization

There are four ways of organizing packages:

- Root library packages
- Nested packages
- Child packages
- Subunits

A root library package, one that is a child only of `Standard`, achieves maximum compilation independence, but it can only access declarations in the visible part of another package, and then only after a with_clause is given. A nested package can be used to reduce name-space clutter by encapsulating declarations, but the package is still part of the unit's compilation so neither independence nor compilation time is improved. A child package has visibility of the declarations in the entire package specification including its private part, but not of the declarations in the body. The compilation of a child is relatively independent from that of its parent, because it only depends on its parent's specification, not its body. A subunit has visibility of the declarations in its parent's body, but it is tightly coupled to the parent. Although an implementation may support separate compilation of subunits, any change in the parent requires recompilation of all its subunits. In practice, nested packages and subunits are of little use; programs should be structured as a small number of root library packages, together with child packages to the depth that is needed.

15.4 Pragmas

Pragmas are directives to the compiler §2.8. Special rules apply to the placement of certain pragmas §10.1.54.

Configuration pragmas apply to an entire program. The pragma declaration is itself a compilation unit §10.1.5(8–9), which is normally the first unit that is compiled. For example, pragma `Restrictions` §13.12 is a configuration pragma used to inform the compiler that you intend to restrict the use of the language. For example, if:

```
pragma Restrictions(No_Allocators);
```

is given, the use of an allocator anywhere within the program would be diagnosed as an error.

A *program unit pragma* §10.1.5(2–6) applies only to a single program unit. Such pragmas can be placed either within the unit they apply to or after the unit. If the pragma is the first entity within a unit, you can sometimes omit the name of the unit. A program unit pragma is called a *library unit pragma* if it applies only to library units. In the next section, you will see two possible placements of the library unit pragma `Elaborate_Body`.

A list of language-defined pragmas can be found in Annex §L.

15.5 Elaboration*

Elaboration §3.1(11) is the process by which a declaration has its run-time effect (Section 2.9.1). Declarations are elaborated in the order in which they appear. We now ask: when are library units elaborated? The answer is that they are considered to be declared local to an *environment task* §10.2(8) whose execution is initiated by the operating system. The units are elaborated in any order that is consistent with their semantic dependences §10.2(9). However, semantic dependence is not always strong enough to resolve dependences that are relevant to elaboration, and, occasionally, stronger control over the elaboration order is required, as we now demonstrate. Section 22.2.5 discusses the interaction between elaboration and concurrency.

15.5.1 Case study: elaboration order

Package `P` declares the function `Func` that encapsulates a "complicated" computation:

elab

```
package P is
   function Func return Integer;
end P;
```

In our program, the computation is represented by a single return statement:

```
package body P is
  function Func return Integer is
  begin
    return 10;
  end Func;
end P;
```

The function is used to initialize the variable `N` in the specification of package `Q`:

```
with P;
package Q is
  N: Integer := P.Func;
end Q;
```

The main program uses the value of this variable that was declared in package `Q`:

```
with Q; with Ada.Text_IO;
procedure Elab is
begin
  Ada.Text_IO.Put_Line(Integer'Image(Q.N));
end Elab;
```

The semantic dependences require that the body of package `P` be elaborated after the specification of `P`, and that the specification of `P` be elaborated before the specification of `Q` because of the with_clause for `Q`. However, the *body* of `P` may be elaborated *before* or *after* the specification of `Q`. If the specification of `Q` is elaborated before the body of `P`, then the call to the initialization function `Func` will be a call to a subprogram that does not yet exist! `Elaboration_Check` will fail and `Program_Error` will be raised §11.5(19–20).

15.5.2 *Case study: table package*

A similar problem occurs when the package specification consists of a variable whose initial value is set by a complicated computation during the initialization of the package:

table

```
package Table is
  Translate: array(1..10) of Character;
end Table;

package body Table is
begin
  Translate := (others => 'X');
end Table;
```

A library package is not allowed to have a body unless one is actually needed §7.2(4), usually to contain the bodies of subprograms declared in the specification. This rule simplifies configuration management. The above package body containing the initialization is illegal because the specification is legal without the body.

15.5.3 *Elaboration pragmas*

Elaboration pragmas can be used to solve the above problems. **pragma** `Elaborate_Body` specifies that the body of the package must be elaborated immediately after its specification §10.2.1(19–26). It is a library unit pragma §10.2.1(24), so it can be placed either within the package declaration:

```
package P is
  pragma Elaborate_Body;
  function Func return Integer;
end P;
```

or immediately following the declaration §10.1.5(4):

```
package Table is
  Translate: array(1..10) of Character;
end Table;
pragma Elaborate_Body(Table);
```

Alternatively, we could use **pragma** `Elaborate(P)` in the context clause of package `Q` of the first example to specify that `P` be completely elaborated before `Q`. The **pragma** `Elaborate_All(P)` is a transitive version of `Elaborate(P)` and specifies that all units upon which `P` depends must be elaborated before `Q`. The advantage of this pragma over `Elaborate` is that `Q` does not have to know about the dependences of `P`.

Elaboration checks can be very expensive because the code for the check is executed for *every* call of a subprogram declared in a package specification, even though it is only relevant during the first call. If you are satisfied that you have solved every possible elaboration problem (using elaboration pragmas, if necessary), you may want to suppress the check.

15.5.4 *Elaboration control*

pragma `Pure` §10.2.1(13–19) declares that a library unit is *pure*. This means that it has no state at run-time; note that any variable declared in the unit gives rise to state. Since it has no state, a pure unit can be replicated in a distributed system (Section 22.1).

pragma Preelaborate §10.2.1(2–12) declares that a unit is *preelaborable*. Such a unit contains no executable statements, so the elaboration can be done as part of the construction of the executable program. A unit with the following declaration:

```
V: T := F;
```

is not preelaborable unless the function F itself is computable at compile-time. An implementation should be able to store the elaborated unit in ROM so that its initialization need not be performed each time the system is reset.

pragma Preelaborable_Initialization §10.2.1(11.1–11.8) is used with a private *type* to indicate that a unit that uses that type can be preelaborable. Examples are the types implemented by the container libraries; for example, Ada.Containers.Doubly_Linked_Lists declares §A.18.3(6):

```
type List is tagged private;
pragma Preelaborable_Initialization(List);
```

The default initialization of an object of type List can be done at compile-time, so:

```
with DLL;                    -- some instantiation of doubly-linked lists
package P
  Max: Natural := 1000;
  L:   DLL.List;
end P;
```

is preelaborable.

All pure units are elaborated before all preelaborable units, which, in turn, are elaborated before a unit to which neither of the pragmas applies §10.2(13–17).

Package Ada §A.2 and some of its children are declared pure. Other children are preelaborable, while some, such as Ada.Text_IO, are neither.

Ada 95

Preelaborable_Initialization is new to Ada 2005.

15.6 Renamings

Objects, exceptions, packages, subprograms, and generic units and instances can be renamed §8.5. Renaming can be used to declare an additional, shorter, name for an entity, especially if you do not want to employ a use_clause:

```
package LEF renames Ada.Numerics.Long_Elementary_Functions;
```

In the quaternion case study (Section 6.8.1), renaming was used to change the implementation in one place without otherwise modifying the program.

Object renamings can be used to improve readability and (depending on the optimizer) run-time efficiency when accessing complex data structures:

```
for N1 in A1'Range loop
  for N2 in A2'Range loop
    declare
      V: Integer renames A1[N1].Field1.A2[N2].Field2.all;
    begin
      V := (V + K1) * (V - K2) / 4*V;
    end;
  end loop;
end loop;
```

Subprogram renamings §8.5.4 come in two flavors: *renaming-as-declaration* and *renaming-as-body*. The former gives a new name (and new parameter names and default expressions if needed) to a subprogram or entry. We used renaming-as-declaration in the case study in Section 11.3 to obtain a function `Trim` with a default value for the parameter `Side`.

Renaming-as-body completes the declaration of a subprogram with an existing subprogram so you don't have to write a trivial subprogram to call it. Renaming-as-body makes it easy to export a different or partial view of an abstraction, as shown in the following case study.

15.6.1 Case study: renaming

Package `Java_IO` exports string output procedures from `Ada.Text_IO` with the names expected by a Java programmer:

renam

```
package Java_IO is
  procedure print(S: in String);
  procedure println(S: in String);
  procedure println;
end Java_IO;
```

`Ada.Text_IO.Put_Line` and `Ada.Text_IO.Put` can be exported by renaming-as-body to complete the subprogram declarations in the package specification:

```
with Ada.Text_IO;
package body Java_IO is
  procedure print(S: in String)   renames Ada.Text_IO.Put;
  procedure println(S: in String) renames Ada.Text_IO.Put_Line;
```

For Ada.Text_IO.New_Line, however, this cannot be done, because the subprogram has a parameter Spacing §A.10.5(2). Although the parameter has the default value 1 that we want, nevertheless, renaming-as-body requires that the renamed subprogram fully conform §8.5.4(5) to the declaration it completes. Therefore, we have to write a body to call it:

```
   procedure println is
   begin
      Ada.Text_IO.New_Line;
   end println;
end Java_IO;
```

15.7 Use type clause

Is the following program legal?

question

```
package P is
   type T is (A, B, C, D);
end P;

with P;
procedure Question is
   V: P.T;
begin
   if V = P.A then null; else null; end if;
end Question;
```

The answer is no! The problem is with the expression in the condition of the if-statement. V and P.A are both of type P.T, but the operator "=" for the type is not directly visible. A use_clause for the package P would, of course, make it directly visible, but many Ada programmers prefer to minimize the number of use_clauses. It would also be possible to use prefix notation: P."="(V,P.A), but this syntax is unnatural. A better solution is furnished by the use_type_clause:

```
use type P.T;
```

The *primitive operators* of the type, but not other entities of the package, become visible §8.4(8). More exactly, they become potentially use-visible, as described in the next section.

15.8 Visibility rules*

Visibility of entities in Ada has been informally discussed throughout the text. The rules in §8.1–§8.4 are among the most difficult in the *ARM*, but fortunately you can usually write correct programs without understanding them in detail. Here we will survey the terminology used in case you need to study the rules; in addition, we will point out a few details worth knowing.

15.8.1 Declarative regions and scope

A *declarative region* §8.1 is a portion of the program text that can contain other declarations. Most declarative regions are declarations: packages, procedures, records and so on, but so is a for-loop statement that declares its loop parameter. The declarative region of a package includes its body, children and subunits.

The *scope* §8.2 of a declaration is the portion of a program text where it is legal to refer to the declared entity. The scope includes the *immediate scope*, which extends from the declaration itself until the end of the *immediately enclosing* declarative region. For example, the immediate scope of a type declared in a package specification comprises the remainder of the package specification, as well as the package's body, children and subunits. The *scope* of the type includes its immediate scope and extends to include the scope of the package itself §8.2(10) and of its semantic dependents §8.2(3).

The following diagram shows the scope of the declaration of the variable `N` declared in the *visible part* of package `P`. The scope includes the rest of the specification, the body (including subunits), child packages and other units that have a with_clause for the package. The thick arrows below show the scope, while the thin arrows show the dependences:

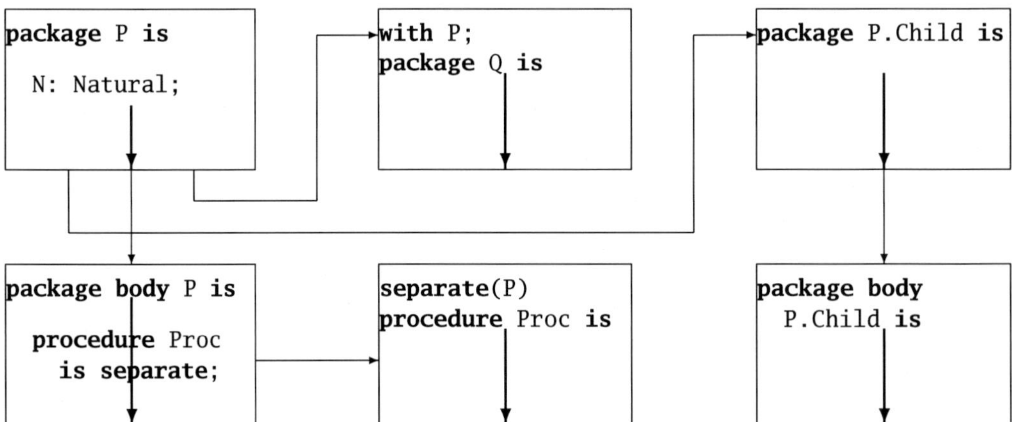

If the declaration is in the *private part* of the package, its scope does not include the visible part of child packages (although it does include the private parts and the bodies), nor does it include units that have a with_clause for the package:

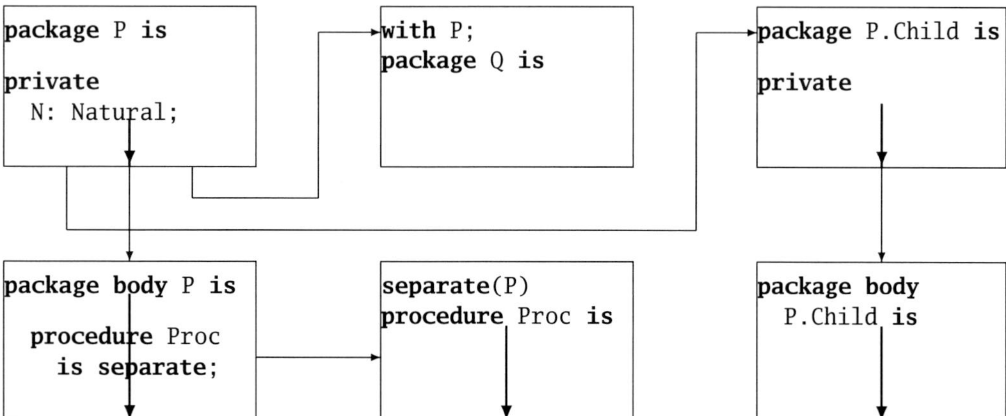

The scope of a declaration in the private part includes the visible part of *private* child packages:

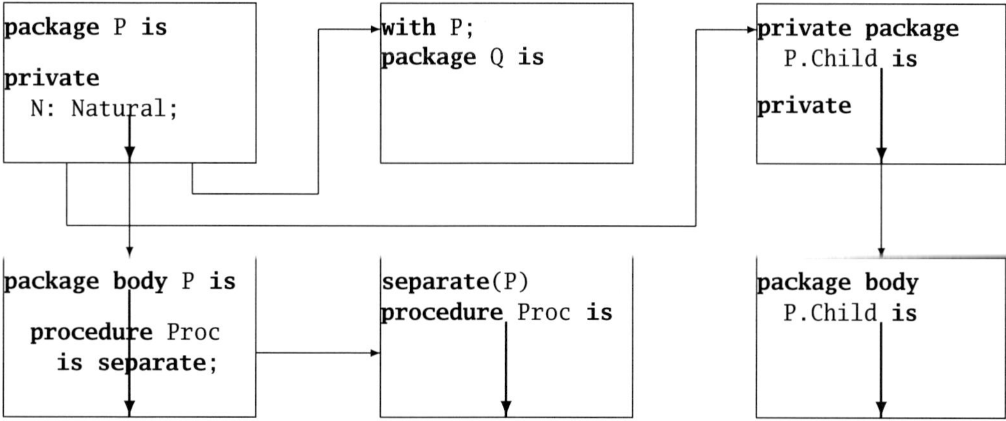

15.8.2 *Visibility*

Within its immediate scope, a declaration is normally *directly visible* so it can be referred to by using its direct name alone. A declaration can be directly visible because it is *immediately visible*, or because it is *use-visible*. For example, a type declared in a package specification is immediately visible within the package itself; outside the package, it is directly visible only if a use_clause has been given for the package. Within its scope but not its immediate scope, selector syntax `P.T` must be used to access an entity.

A use_clause only makes the names in a package specification *potentially use-visible* §8.4(8). Name conflicts—use_clauses for two packages that both declare the same name, or a local declaration with the same name as one in a package mentioned in a use_clause—will prevent direct visibility, and you will have to use selector syntax.

§8.3

> 8 Two declarations are *homographs* if they have the same defining name, and, if both are overloadable, their profiles are type conformant. An inner declaration hides any outer homograph from direct visibility.
>
> 9 Two homographs are not generally allowed immediately within the same declarative region unless one *overrides* the other ...

Are the following two declarations homographs?

```
procedure Proc(A: Integer);
procedure Proc(B: Positive);
```

The answer is yes because: (a) they have the same defining name Proc, (b) as procedures they are overloadable, and (c) they are type-conformant because Positive is a subtype of type Integer. Since they are homographs, they cannot appear in the same declarative region. If Positive were changed to Float, the second declaration would no longer be type-conformant, and the overloaded declarations could appear in the same declarative region.

A declaration can be *hidden* by an inner homograph; in this case, it is *hidden from direct visibility*, but not *hidden from all visibility*, and can be accessed using selector syntax:

```
procedure P is
  X: Integer;
  procedure Q is
    X: Integer;    -- Local declaration hides the outer declaration
  begin
    X := 2;        -- The local declaration is directly visible
    P.X := 3;      -- The global declaration is visible, but not directly
  end Q;
begin
  Q;
end P;
```

Some declarations are *hidden from all visibility* §8.3(4–20); in particular, once an inherited declaration is overridden, there is no way to name it.

There are special visibility rules for context clauses §10.1.6.

15.9 Overloading

The rules for overloading are described in §8.6. As with the visibility rules, they are quite complex, but you will rarely need to understand the details. At worst, the compiler will be unable to disambiguate the use of a name, and you can supply additional syntax such as an expanded name or a qualification.

Overloading resolution is done within each *complete context* §8.6(4–6) such as a declaration or a statement. An *interpretation* of the context is determined by first using the syntax and the visibility rules to list the *possible interpretations*. A possible interpretation is *acceptable* if it obeys the overloading rules, that is, if the interpretation fits the *expected type* or *profile* defined in the Name Resolution Rules. The concept of expected type must be extended to consider the cases of class-wide, universal and access types; see §8.6(25) for details. Overloading is also affected by the preference for root numeric types §8.6(29) as discussed in Section 13.11.

15.9.1 Case study: overloading

Consider the following program:

over

```
1 procedure Over is
2   function F(A: Integer) return Boolean is
3   begin
4     return False;
5   end F;
6
7   function F(A: Integer) return Integer is
8   begin
9     return 1;
10  end F;
11
12  function F(A: Long_Integer) return Boolean is
13  begin
14    return False;
15  end F;
16 begin
17   if F(1) then null; else null; end if;
18 end Over;
```

The syntax rules of the if-statement ‡17 require that the condition be an expression §5.3(3). Therefore, all three functions are *possible interpretations*. However, the Name Resolution Rule

§5.3(4) specifies that the condition must be of a boolean type. Therefore, only the first and third functions are *acceptable interpretations*. Since there must be only one acceptable interpretation §8.6(28, 31), the call to F is ambiguous and the program illegal. If the third function were not declared, overloading resolution would succeed, choosing the first function as the only acceptable interpretation. Alternatively, you could write the parameter as a qualified expression F(Long_Integer'(1)) to disambiguate the call.

Projects

1. Experiment with **pragma** Inline and see how it affects running time and memory requirements.
2. Extend the case study in Section 15.6 and implement as many of the methods of the Java class System as you can; use renaming wherever possible.
3. Develop a package that uses table lookup to compute sine, cosine and tanget for each degree in the range 0..90. Modify the package so that it works for any value, positive or negative, and use interpolation for fractions of a degree.

Quizzes

Quiz 1:

```
procedure Proc1(I: in Integer) is
begin
  Put(I);
end Proc1;
procedure Proc2(I: in Positive) renames Proc1;

Proc2(0);
```

Quiz 2:

```
package P is
  Mode: Integer;
end P;

package body P is
begin
  Mode := 777;
end P;

with P; use P;
procedure Main is
begin
  Put(Mode);
end Main;
```

Quiz 3:

```
package P is
  procedure Proc1(I: in Positive);
  procedure Proc2(I: in Natural);
  procedure Proc3(I: in Natural) renames Proc1;
end P;

package body P is
  procedure Proc1(I: in Positive) is
  begin
    null;
  end Proc1;
  procedure Proc2(I: in Natural) renames Proc1;
end P;
```

Quiz 4:

```
  N: Integer := 5;
  procedure Proc is
    N: Integer := 10;
  begin
    Put(N);
    Put(Main.N);
  end Proc;

  Proc;
```

Quiz 5:

```
procedure Proc(X: in Integer; Y: in Integer := 2) is
begin
  Put(X*Y);
end Proc;

procedure Proc(Z: in Integer; Y: in Float := 3.0) is
begin
  Put(Z*Integer(Y));
end Proc;
procedure Proc(X: in out Integer) is
begin
  Put(X);
end Proc;

Proc(Z => 4);
Proc(X => 5);
```

Quiz 6:

```
package P is
  procedure Proc;
end P;

package body P is
  procedure Proc is
  begin
    Put_Line("Hi from Proc in the package");
  end Proc;
end P;

with P; use P;
procedure Main is
  procedure Proc is
  begin
    Put_Line("Hi from Proc in the main subprogram");
  end Proc;
begin
  Proc;
end Main;
```

Quiz 7:

```
package P is
  type T is tagged null record;
  procedure Proc(X: T);
end P;

package body P is
  procedure Proc(X: T) is
  begin
    Put_Line("Parent");
  end Proc;
end P;

with P; use P;
package Q is
  type T1 is new T with null record;
private
  procedure Proc(X: T1);
end Q;

package body Q is
  procedure Proc(X: T1) is
  begin
    Put_Line("Derived");
  end Proc;
end Q;

with Q; use Q;
procedure Main is
  A: T1;
begin
  Proc(A);
end Main;
```

Quiz 8:

```
function F return Integer is
begin
  return 1;
end F;
function F return Float is
begin
  return 1.0;
end F;

Put(F);
Put(Integer(F));
```

Quiz 9:

```
package Names is new Ada.Strings.Bounded.Generic_Bounded_Length(16);
Hello:  String := "Hello";
use type Names.Bounded_String;

Put_Line(Names.To_String(2 * Hello));
Put_Line(2 * Hello);
```

Quiz 10:

```
with Ada.Text_IO;
package P is
  procedure Proc(N: Ada.Text_IO.Count);
end P;

use Ada.Text_IO;
package body P is
  procedure Proc(N: Ada.Text_IO.Count) is
  begin
    for I in 1..N loop
      Put_Line("*");
    end loop;
  end Proc;
end P;
```

Chapter 16
Containers

The Ada library contains packages for data structures called *containers* §A.18. The containers are generic packages that can be instantiated for any nonlimited type. There are separate packages for definite and indefinite types, because indefinite types must be implemented using pointers and thus are less efficient. The container library also includes generic procedures for sorting arrays §A.18.16 (see Section 9.4).

The subprograms in the container packages are required to be *reentrant*, as are all subprograms in Annex A §A(3). The containers are not "thread-safe," so subprograms that operate on a single object should not be called from different tasks without additional synchronization.

The description of the container library takes over 50 pages of the *ARM*. In this chapter, we limit the presentation to the concepts that you need to know in order to use containers; a case study using containers was given in Section 11.3.

There are six containers. Two are encapsulations of physical data structures: `Vector` implements extensible arrays, and `Doubly_Linked_List` implements what its name says it does. A *map* is a data structure that associates values with keys. The container `Hashed_Maps` uses a hashing function on the keys to efficiently store and retrieve the values, while `Ordered_Maps` maintains a data structure that enables efficient sequential access. A *set* is a data structure that contains only values with no duplication. Here, too, there are two containers: `Hashed_Sets` and `Ordered_Sets`.

Ada 95

There are several open source container libraries for Ada 95:

- Ada 95 Booch Components
  `http://sourceforge.net/projects/booch95`;
- Ada Structured Library
  `http://sourceforge.net/projects/adasl`;
- Charles Container Library
  `http://home.earthlink.net/~matthewjheaney/charles/index.html`.

16.1 Concepts

16.1.1 *The root package*

The root package `Ada.Containers` declares two types: a modular type `Hash_Type` for defining the result returned by a hash function, and an integer type `Count_Type` for parameters and results representing the number of elements in a container or the number of elements to insert into a container or to delete from it.

16.1.2 *Comparing elements and keys*

Each of the container packages has a generic formal function parameter for equality of elements of the container:

§A.18.2

> 83 The actual function for the generic formal function "=" on Element_Type values is expected to define a reflexive and symmetric relationship and return the same result value each time it is called with a particular pair of values. . . .

Ordered maps have a generic formal function parameter for comparing keys:

§A.18.6

> 56 The actual function for the generic formal function "<" on Key_Type values is expected to return the same value each time it is called with a particular pair of key values. It should define a strict ordering relationship, that is, be irreflexive, asymmetric, and transitive. . . .

and there is a similar parameter for comparing elements of ordered sets §A.18.9(79).

Hashed maps have a generic formal function parameter for computing the equivalence of keys:

§A.18.5

> 42 Two keys *K1* and *K2* are defined to be *equivalent* if Equivalent_Keys (*K1*, *K2*) returns True.
>
> 44 The actual function for the generic formal function Equivalent_Keys on Key_Type values is expected to return the same value each time it is called with a particular pair of key values. It should define an equivalence relationship, that is, be reflexive, symmetric, and transitive.

and there is a similar parameter for for computing the equivalence of elements in hashed sets §A.18.8(64,66).

The distinction between *equal* keys and *equivalent* keys is that unequal keys can have the same hash values if different representations of the same key are allowed. For example, two strings might be hashed to the same value if one is the same as the other except for case ("Current_Value" is equivalent to "current_value"), and dates could be in different formats ("11/12/1948" is equivalent to "11.12.1948").

To facilitate changing the data structure in a program from a hashed container to an ordered container, the ordered containers declare (non-generic) functions for computing equivalence defined in terms of the generic formal function for "<". For ordered maps, the definition is:

§A.18.6

> 55 Two keys *K1* and *K2* are *equivalent* if both *K1* < *K2* and *K2* < *K1* return False, using the generic formal "<" operator for keys. Function Equivalent_Keys returns True if Left and Right are equivalent, and False otherwise.

There is a similar definition for `Equivalent_Elements` in ordered sets §A.18.9(78).

16.1.3 Cursors

Cursors are used to "point to" elements of a container:

§A.18

> 2 ... Each container includes a *cursor* type. A cursor is a reference to an element within a container. Many operations on cursors are common to all of the containers. ...

All container packages declare functions `First` and `Last` which return values of type `Cursor`:

Many subprograms take a parameter `Position` of type `Cursor`. The concept is a generalization of an index into an array or an access value that points to a node in a linked list. When deleting an element from a container, a value of type cursor must be supplied to indicate which element to delete, and, similarly, a value of type cursor indicates the place to insert a new element.

16.1.4 Iterators

An *iterator* is a procedure that receives as parameters a container and an access to a procedure with a parameter of type `Cursor`; it automatically invokes the procedure with the parameter pointing to each element of the container. For ordered containers, the cursor will reference the elements in the natural order of the elements. Iterators were demonstrated in the case study in Section 11.3.

16.1.5 Copying vs. in-place processing

The container packages all declare the function:

```
function Element(Position: Cursor) return Element_Type;
```

for returning an element of a container, and a procedure:

```
procedure Replace_Element(
  Container: in out Vector; Position: in Cursor; New_Item: in Element_Type);
```

for replacing an element of a container with a new value.

Both of these subprograms involve *copying* an element. Sometimes, we may wish to avoid this; for example, suppose that the element of a container is:

```
type Data_Type is
  record
    Empty: Boolean;
    Data:  String(1..4095);
  end record;
```

Evaluating the expression `Element(Position).Empty` is very inefficient because entire record will be copied just to read a single component.

The following procedures perform in-place read and write of the values of an element:

```
procedure Query_Element(
  Position: in Cursor;
  Process:  not null access procedure(Element: in Element_Type));

procedure Update_Element(
  Container: in out Vector;
  Position:  in Cursor;
  Process:   not null access procedure(Element: in out Element_Type));
```

Their use is somewhat complicated, because `Query_Element` has no provision for returning the element and `Update_Element` cannot be called with new components to update the element. Instead, nested subprograms are used, as shown in the following program.

First, we declare the type and a container:

query

```
with Ada.Text_IO, Ada.Containers.Doubly_Linked_Lists;
procedure Query is
  type Data_Type is
    record
      Empty: Boolean;
      Data:  String(1..4095);
    end record;

  package Data_Lists is
    new Ada.Containers.Doubly_Linked_Lists(Element_Type => Data_Type);
  List: Data_Lists.List;
```

Next, a function is defined that takes a cursor and returns the value of the component `Empty`:

```
  function Is_Empty(Position: in Data_Lists.Cursor) return Boolean is
    Empty_Element: Boolean;

    procedure Is_Element_Empty(D: Data_Type) is
    begin
      Empty_Element := D.Empty;
    end Is_Element_Empty;

  begin
    Data_Lists.Query_Element(Position, Is_Element_Empty'Access);
    return Empty_Element;
  end Is_Empty;
```

`Query_Element` is called with an access to the nested procedure `Is_Element_Empty`, which copies the value of the component to the variable `Empty_Element` that is global to the nested procedure. When `Query_Element` returns, this value is then returned by the outer function.

This technique is called *downward closure*: the closure—the procedure `Is_Element_Empty`, together with its context, the variable `Empty_Element`—is passed "down" into the procedure `Query_Element` as a parameter of access-to-subprogram type.

The main program inserts two elements and then queries the `Empty` components:

```
begin
  List.Append(Data_Type'(True,  (others => ' ')));
  List.Append(Data_Type'(False, "Hello World" & (12..4095 => ' ')));
  Ada.Text_IO.Put_Line(Boolean'Image(Is_Empty(List.First)));
  Ada.Text_IO.Put_Line(Boolean'Image(Is_Empty(List.Last)));
end Query;
```

16.1.6 *Tampering with cursors and elements*

Some subprograms of the container libraries take parameters that are of access-to-subprogram type; for example, `Iterate` applies the subprogram to all elements of a container. It is important that a procedure passed as a parameter not *tamper with the cursor* of the container, in the sense of modifying the cursor when the container implementation does not expect it to be done. Similarly, some subprograms require that the subprogram passed as a parameter not *tamper with the elements* of the container. For each of the containers, the precise meaning of "tamper with" is defined.

The procedures `Query_Element` and `Update_Element` for reading and writing elements in-place do not tamper with elements.

16.2 Vectors

§A.18.2

> 1 ... A vector container allows insertion and deletion at any position, but it is specifically optimized for insertion and deletion at the high end (the end with the higher index) of the container. A vector container also provides random access to its elements.
>
> 4 A vector container may contain *empty elements*. Empty elements do not have a specified value.

A vector is similar to an array, allowing both sequential and random access to its elements:

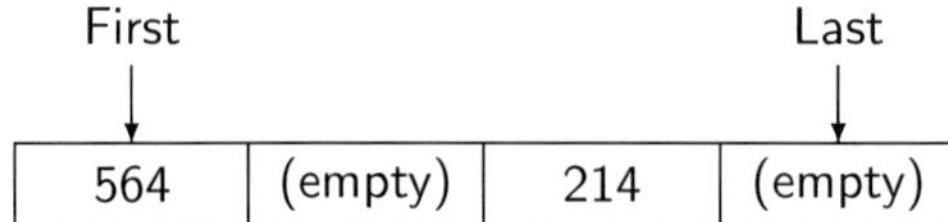

The main difference between a vector and an array is that a vector can expand automatically, so we don't have to choose a maximum size when an object is declared.

§A.18.2

> 2 A vector container behaves conceptually as an array that expands as necessary as items are inserted. The *length* of a vector is the number of elements that the vector contains. The *capacity* of a vector is the maximum number of elements that can be inserted into the vector prior to it being automatically expanded.

When using vectors it is important to be aware of the overhead associated with the expansion of the data structure. One way to implement expansion is simply to allocate a new, larger, array and to copy the elements of the smaller array to the new one:

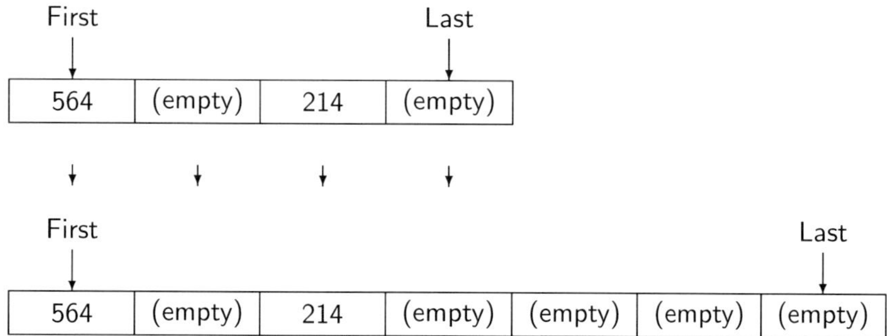

This retains the efficiency of accessing individual elements, but will be inefficient for large arrays; furthermore, the processing required to copy the array elements can occur at an unpredictable time, which can make vectors inappropriate for real-time systems.

`Ada.Containers.Vectors` is a generic package with the following formal parameters:

§A.18.2

```
6 generic
     type Index_Type is range <>;
     type Element_Type is private;
     with function "=" (Left, Right : Element_Type) return Boolean is <>;
  package Ada.Containers.Vectors is ...
```

The package defines the private type `Vector` (with deferred constant `Empty_Vector`), the private type `Cursor` (with deferred constant `No_Element`), a generic package for sorting, and numerous subprograms for manipulating vectors. When a position in a vector is required—for example, `Replace_Element` needs a parameter telling it which element to replace—it may be given either as an index value or as a cursor value.

16.3 Doubly-linked lists

The doubly-linked list is a familiar data structure:

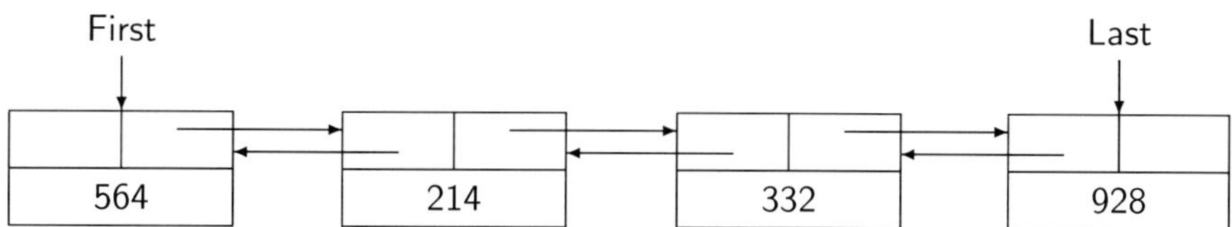

Compared with arrays and vectors, lists have a number of important disadvantages: significant overhead for the pointers and the inefficiency of locating a specific element since there are no indices. The advantages of the list data structure are:

- Memory is allocated only for elements that are created; there are no "empty" elements.
- It is possible to insert and delete arbitrary elements of the list very efficiently by just copying a few pointers.

Since there is no index type, there are only two generic formal parameters:

§A.18.3

```
5  generic
      type Element_Type is private;
      with function "=" (Left, Right : Element_Type) return Boolean is <>;
   package Ada.Containers.Doubly_Linked_Lists is ...
```

16.4 Maps

Maps are used when there is a many-one relationship between *keys* and *elements*; that is, every key maps into exactly one element, but many keys may map into the same element.

§A.18.4

> 5 A map contains pairs of keys and elements, called *nodes*. Map cursors designate nodes, but also can be thought of as designating an element (the element contained in the node) for consistency with the other containers. There exists an equivalence relation on keys, whose definition is different for hashed maps and ordered maps. A map never contains two or more nodes with equivalent keys. The *length* of a map is the number of nodes it contains.

Definitions and subprograms common to hashed and ordered maps are given in §A.18.4.

16.4.1 Hashed maps

In a hashed map, an element is stored at a location based upon the result of a hash function that is computed from the key associated with the element. An array can be used to store the key-element pairs and the value returned by the hash function is used as an index into the array. However, it is possible for two different keys to result in the same hash value, in which case we say that the two keys *clash*. One way of to handle clashes is for the array to hold pointers to linked lists for key-element pairs that hash to the same value:

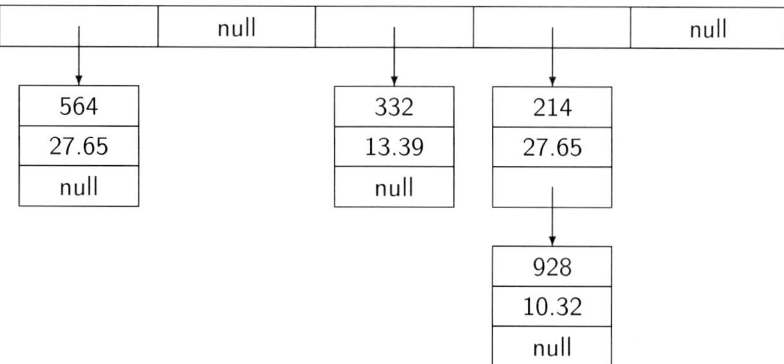

If the hash function results in few clashes, the data structure is very efficient, because most elements can be retrieved in a constant amount of time: the time needed to compute the hash function plus the time required to check the key that the hash array points to. If the number of clashes is large, the data structure is less efficient, because the correct key must be found by a linear search of the keys that hash to the same value.

The *range* of values of the keys can be much larger than the number of "slots" in the data structure. For example, if the keys are long strings, the range of values is extremely large, but the number of slots needed for efficient hashing is a small multiple of the number of key-element pairs to be stored.

The hash function is given as a generic actual parameter, so different functions can be used in different instantiations:

§A.18.5

2
```
generic
   type Key_Type is private;
   type Element_Type is private;
   with function Hash (Key : Key_Type) return Hash_Type;
   with function Equivalent_Keys (Left, Right : Key_Type) return Boolean;
   with function "=" (Left, Right : Element_Type) return Boolean is <>;
package Ada.Containers.Hashed_Maps is ...
```

For strings, there is a predefined library hash function `Ada.Strings.Hash`:

§A.4.9

1 The library function Strings.Hash has the following declaration:

2
```
with Ada.Containers;
function Ada.Strings.Hash (Key : String) return Containers.Hash_Type;
```

Similar functions exist for bounded and unbounded strings, as well as for the wide and wide-wide types.

Writing good hash functions is not an easy task, especially since the performance of a hash function depends on the data that is stored in the hashed data structure.

16.4.2 *Ordered maps*

In an ordered map, the elements are stored in a data structure that allows efficient retrieval of the elements in the order of the value of their keys. An ordered map could be stored as a sorted array, as we did in our first implementation of priority queues in Chapter 5, but that would be inefficient because inserting a new element would require that an arbitrary number of elements be moved. A better implementation is to use a linked list whose elements are maintained in sorted order:

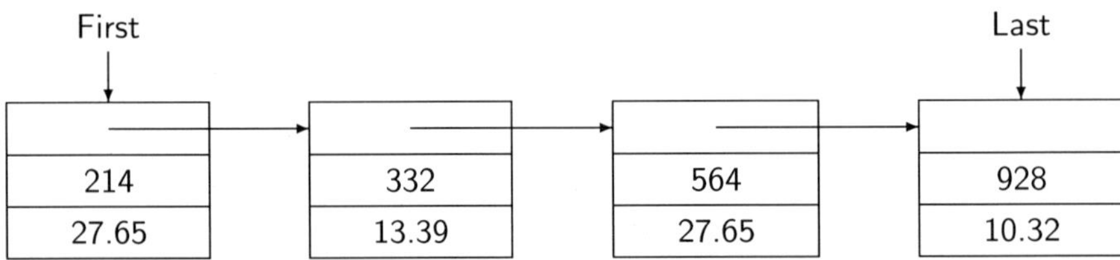

The smallest element can be retrieved in contstant time, but inserting a new element requires a linear search of the list. For that reason, trees are the preferred implementation of ordered maps. If balanced trees (such as red-black trees) are used, inserting a new element can be done in time proportional to the logarithm of the number of elements in the tree.

The generic formal part is as expected:

§A.18.6

```
2  generic
      type Key_Type is private;
      type Element_Type is private;
      with function "<" (Left, Right : Key_Type) return Boolean is <>;
      with function "=" (Left, Right : Element_Type) return Boolean is <>;
   package Ada.Containers.Ordered_Maps is ...
```

16.5 Sets

§A.18.7

> 1 ... A set container allows elements of an arbitrary type to be stored without duplication. ...

There are hashed and ordered sets; see §A.18.7 for the common definitions and declarations. Hashed sets are like hashed maps except that values are stored without separate keys:

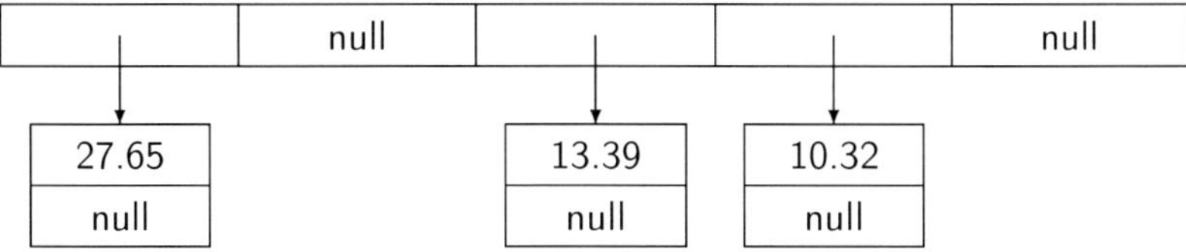

The element `27.65` appeared twice with different keys in the hashed *map* above, but here only the value is of interest.

The hash function is from elements to hash values:

§A.18.8

```
2  generic
      type Element_Type is private;
      with function Hash (Element : Element_Type) return Hash_Type;
      with function Equivalent_Keys (Left, Right : Key_Type) return Boolean;
      with function "=" (Left, Right : Element_Type) return Boolean is <>;
   package Ada.Containers.Hashed_Sets is ...
```

Ordered sets can be stored as linked lists ordered by the values of the elements:

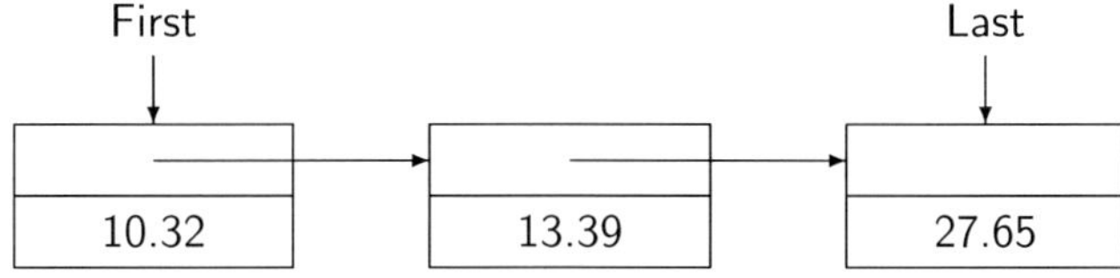

As for ordered maps, balanced trees should be used for an efficient implementation.

The generic formal part is very simple:

§A.18.6

```
2 generic
     type Element_Type is private;
     with function "<" (Left, Right : Element_Type) return Boolean is <>;
     with function "=" (Left, Right : Element_Type) return Boolean is <>;
  package Ada.Containers.Ordered_Sets is ...
```

16.6 Indefinite containers

For each container `Ada.Containers.X`, there is a container `Ada.Containers.Indefinite_X`. The generic formal parameter:

```
type Element is private;
```

is declared with unknown discriminants:

```
type Element(<>) is private;
```

so that it can be instantiated with indefinte types, such as unconstrained arrays like `String` or discriminated records with no defaults. For the map containers, the type `Key_Type` is similarly defined to be indefinite. The subprograms for indefinite containers are almost exactly the same as those for the definite containers.

Indefinite containers require an extra level of indirection, so they require more processing time and memory than definite containers:

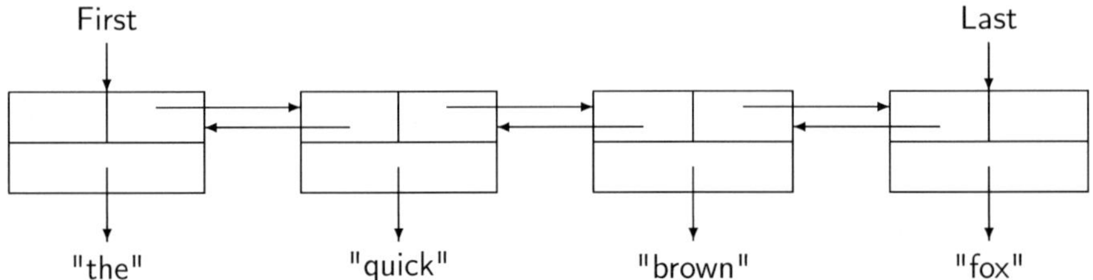

16.6.1 *Case study: simulation with containers*

The rocket simulation can use an indefinite ordered set to store the events:

rocketcon

```
with Ada.Containers.Indefinite_Ordered_Sets;
with Root_Event;
package Event_Queue is new
  Ada.Containers.Indefinite_Ordered_Sets(
    Root_Event.Event'Class, Root_Event."<", Root_Event."=");
```

The main program must be modified to call the subprograms of the container library instead of the previous implementations of priority queues:

```
with Event_Queue;
with Root_Event.Engine, Root_Event.Telemetry, Root_Event.Steering;
use Root_Event;
procedure RocketCon is
  Q:        Event_Queue.Set;
  Position: Event_Queue.Cursor;
begin
  for I in 1..15 loop
    Event_Queue.Insert(Q, Engine.Main_Engine_Event'(Engine.Create));
    ...
  end loop;

  while not Event_Queue.Is_Empty(Q) loop
    Position := Event_Queue.First(Q);
    Root_Event.Simulate(Event_Queue.Element(Position));
    Event_Queue.Delete(Q, Position);
  end loop;
end RocketCon;
```

Language Comparison

The Ada library is based upon the *Charles Container Library*, which, in turn, was based on the *Standard Template Library (STL)* of C++. This library, originally designed by Alex Stepanov and influenced by the earlier *Booch Components* for Ada, includes sequential and associative structures, all of which are templates parameterized by component type (like Ada's generic units).

Language Comparison

Since Java uses reference semantics, all containers are indefinite with the extra time and space overhead. Since the elements of definite containers in Ada can be of elementary types like `Integer`, there is no need for "autoboxing" that is used in Java to facilitate the use of containers containing primitive types. There is no universal type in Ada comparable to the type `Object` in Java, so truly heterogenous containers whose elements are of any type are not possible in Ada. However, closely related types like discriminated and class-wide types can be used as elements of indefinite containers, as was demonstrated in the simulation case study (Section 7.1).

Projects

1. Modify the simulation case study in Section 7.1 to use an ordered map container instead of an ordered set.
2. An indefinite container can be used even if the elements are definite like fixed strings. Measure the time and space overhead of using indefinite instead of definite containers.
3. Write a program to demonstrate the difference between equal keys and equivalent keys in hashed containers.

Quizzes

Quiz 1:

```
package Float_Vector is new Ada.Containers.Vectors(Natural, Float);
V: Float_Vector.Vector;

Put_Line(Ada.Containers.Count_Type'Image(V.Length));
```

Quiz 2:

```
package Float_Map is
  new Ada.Containers.Ordered_Maps(Natural, Float);
V: Float_Map.Map;
P: Float_Map.Cursor;
B: Boolean;

V.Insert(1, 1.0, P, B);
V.Insert(1, 2.0, P, B);
V.Insert(1, 3.0);
```

Quiz 3:

```
subtype Name is String(1..8);
package Name_Set is
  new Ada.Containers.Hashed_Sets(Name, Ada.Strings.Hash, "=");
S: Name_Set.Set;

S.Insert("Goodbye ");
S.Insert("Earth   ");
S.Insert("Hello   ");
S.Insert("World   ");
Put_Line(Name_Set.Element(S.First));
```

Chapter 17
Interfaces and Multiple Inheritance

A derived type *inherits* the components and primitive subprograms defined in its ancestor types; it can add new components and subprograms, as well as override the inherited subprograms. Dynamic dispatching within a derivation class can be efficiently implemented using dispatch tables (Section 8.13).

Suppose that we wish to derive a type from more than one parent type; for example:

```
type Root_Event is tagged
  record
    Time: Simulation_Time;
  end record;
procedure Simulate(E: Root_Event);

type Thermodynamic_Model is tagged
  record
    Temperatures: Temperature_Array;
  end record;
procedure Update(M: in out Thermodynamic_Model);

type Engine_Event is new
  Root_Event and Thermodynamic_Model with ...   -- ???
```

This is called *multiple inheritance (MI)* and is supported by languages like C++ and Eiffel.

It is not easy to give a clear definition of the semantics of multiple inheritance. The problems arise when the same component is inherited from more than one ancestor:

```
type T1 is tagged record A: Integer; end record;
type T2 is tagged record A: Integer; end record;

type T3 is new T1 and T2 with ...   --- ???
```

Which component A is inherited?

The same problem can occur if a concrete subprogram is inherited from two ancestors.

To avoid these semantic difficulties, Ada supports a limited form of MI that is well known from Java. *Components* can only be inherited from a single ancestor called its *parent*, while *subprograms* can be inherited from its parent (including subprograms that were inherited from the parent's parent and so on), as well as from other ancestors called its *progenitors* that are not related to the parent. More precisely, progenitors declare abstract or null subprograms that the derived type must implement.

An object of a derived type can be used in any context where the progenitor type is expected:

```
type Derived_Type is new Parent_Type and Progenitor_Type;

procedure Proc(P: Progenitor_Type'Class) is
begin
  P.Any_Operation;     -- Any primitive operation for Progenitor_Type
end Proc;

D: Derived_Type := ...

Proc(D);               -- OK, because Derived_Type is derived from
                       -- Progenitor_Type
```

Since `Progenitor_Type` is a progenitor of `Derived_Type`, we are assured that `Any_Operation` is either null or overridden by the derived type.

Ada has a construct called *interfaces* for declaring types to be used as progenitors of derived types. The first part of this chapter presents the rules for interfaces, followed by two case studies; then interfaces for concurrent programming are discussed. The final part of the chapter presents generic formal private and tagged types that can be used—at some inconvenience—to implement a form of MI.

Ada 95

Interfaces are new in Ada 2005. Generics can be used for MI as shown in Sections 17.5–17.6.

17.1 Interfaces

The declaration of an *interface type* consists of the reserved word **interface**, optionally preceeded by a reserved word that characterizes the interface, and optionally followed by a list of other interface types:

§3.9.4

> 2 interface_type_definition ::=
>   [**limited** | **task** | **protected** | **synchronized**] **interface** [**and** interface_list]
>
> 3 interface_list ::= *interface*_subtype_mark { **and** *interface*_subtype_mark }

An interface type is an *abstract* tagged type §3.9.4(4) with the following limitations:

§3.9.4

> 8 An interface type has no components.
>
> 10 All user-defined primitive subprograms of an interface type shall be abstract subprograms or null procedures.

Since an interface type is a tagged type, the normal rules for defining primitive operations hold.

A derived type must be derived from a single tagged type, but it can also be derived from an arbitrary number of interface types.

§3.4

> 2 derived_type_definition ::=
>   [**abstract**][**limited**] **new** *parent*_subtype_indication
>   [[**and** interface_list] record_extension_part]
>
> 3 The *parent*_subtype_indication defines the *parent subtype*; its type is the *parent type*. The interface_list defines the progenitor types (see 3.9.4). A derived type has one parent type and zero or more progenitor types.

The derived type *inherits* the primitive operations of each of its progenitor types §3.4(17); since the operations are primitive they can, of course, be overridden. In fact, operations that are not null procedures are abstract and must be overridden, unless the derived type is itself abstract.

As can be seen from the syntax in §3.9.4(2–3), an interface type can itself have progenitors:

§3.9.4

> 9 An *interface*_subtype_mark in an interface_list names a *progenitor subtype*; its type is the *progenitor type*. An interface type inherits user-defined primitive subprograms from each progenitor type in the same way that a derived type inherits user-defined primitive subprograms from its progenitor types (see 3.4).

This can be used to "group" sets of operations from several interfaces into one interface.

17.1.1 *Limited interfaces*

An interface type can be declared to be limited, meaning, as usual, that predefined equality and copying are not defined for the type. While a type that is derived from a limited type is automatically limited, this is not true for a type derived from a limited interface type §7.5(6):

```
type Parent            is tagged ...
type Limited_Interface is limited interface;

type Derived           is Parent and Limited_Interface;
```

If an object of type `Derived` is used in a context that expects `Limited_Interface`, predefined equality and copying are simply not used.

Conversely, however, a type that implements a nonlimited interface must be non-limited, because it can be used in a context where predefined equality and copying are expected to be available.

17.2 Case study: displayable events

We define an interface `Displayable` that is intended for types that can be displayed, perhaps by a graphical user interface:

inter

```
package Display is
  type Displayable is interface;
  function  Format(D:   Displayable) return String  is abstract;
  procedure Set_Size(D: in out Displayable; N: Natural) is abstract;
  function  Get_Size(D: Displayable) return Natural is abstract;

  procedure Display_Item(D: in Displayable'Class);
end Display;
```

A type implementing this interface is required to supply a function `Format` that returns a string representation of the type. Since an interface cannot have components, the implementing type must contain a component for the size of a displayed object; the display software can access this components through the subprograms `Set_Size` and `Get_Size` that must also be supplied by the implementing type.

The display software itself is represented by the subprogram `Display_Item`. Its parameter is of type `Displayable'Class` so it is not primitive and thus need not be null or abstract. It can be called with an actual parameter that is of any type that implements `Displayable`. In the case study, this subprogram simply prints the object and its size using the subprograms that are guaranteed to be implemented:

```
with Ada.Text_IO;
package body Display is
  procedure Display_Item(D: in Displayable'Class) is
  begin
    Ada.Text_IO.Put_Line(
      "Size = " & Integer'Image(D.Get_Size) & ", " & D.Format);
  end Display_Item;
end Display;
```

Since Format and Get_Size are declared abstract, these calls need to be dispatching. Distinguished receiver syntax (Section 8.1) is used; alternatively, we could have written:

```
    Ada.Text_IO.Put_Line(
      "Size = " & Integer'Image(Get_Size(D)) & ", " & Format(D));
```

This syntax clarifies that the call is dispatching: the actual parameter D is class-wide ‡11, while the formal parameters of the two subprograms are of specific types ‡27,41.

To demonstrate the use of the interface, we naturally turn to the discrete event simulation, and declare a type Displayed_Event with parent Event and with one progenitor Displayable:

```
with Display;
package Root_Event is
  type Event is abstract tagged private;
  -- Primitive operations for Event

  type Displayed_Event is abstract
    new Event and Display.Displayable with private;
  procedure Set_Size(D: in out Displayed_Event; N: Natural);
  function  Get_Size(D: Displayed_Event) return Natural;
```

Since Displayed_Event is declared abstract, the function Format is inherited as an abstract function. The other subprograms are overridden with concrete subprograms.

The private tagged type Displayed_Event is completed with a record containing the component Size that is needed to implement the subprograms Set_Size and Get_Size:

```
private
  type Event is abstract tagged record ... end record;

  type Displayed_Event is abstract
    new Event and Display.Displayable with
      record
        Size: Natural := 10;
      end record;
end Root_Event;
```

The implementation of the package body can be found in the software archive.

We can now derive concrete event types from `Displayed_Event`; for simplicity, the implementation is limited to the engine event types:

```
package Root_Event.Engine is
  type Engine_Event is new Displayed_Event with private;
  function  Create return Engine_Event;
  procedure Simulate(E: in Engine_Event);
  function  Format(D: Engine_Event) return String;

  -- Declare Main_Engine_Event and Aux_Engine_Event as usual
private
  ...
end Root_Event.Engine;
```

In the package body, `Format` is represented by a function that returns the external tag of its parameter. The other modification is to include a value for the component `Size` when creating an object of type `Displayed_Event`.

The main program creates events and sets their sizes before putting them on the queue:

```
with Priority_Queue; with Root_Event.Engine;
use Root_Event;
with Display;
procedure Inter is
  package Event_Queue is new Priority_Queue(Event'Class);
  Q: aliased Event_Queue.Queue;
begin
  for I in 1..5 loop
    declare
      M: Engine.Main_Engine_Event :=
           Engine.Main_Engine_Event'(Engine.Create);
      A: Engine.Aux_Engine_Event  :=
           Engine.Aux_Engine_Event'(Engine.Create);
    begin
      Set_Size(Displayed_Event(M), 100+I);
      Event_Queue.Put(M, Q);
      Set_Size(Displayed_Event(A), 200+I);
      Event_Queue.Put(A, Q);
    end;
  end loop;
```

When the events are removed from the queue, the primitive operation `Simulate` of the parent type `Root_Event` is called, followed by the subprogram `Display_Item`. This subprogram takes a class-wide parameter so a type conversion must be done:

```
   while not Event_Queue.Empty(Q) loop
     declare
       EC: Event'Class := Event_Queue.Get(Q'Access);
     begin
       Root_Event.Simulate(EC);
       Display.Display_Item(Display.Displayable'Class(EC));
     end;
   end loop;
 end Inter;
```

The conversion to `Displayable'Class` succeeds because the object is of a type derived from `Displayable_Event`, which has as a progenitor the interface `Displayable`. We are also assured that it implements the primitive operations of the interface needed by the procedure `Display_Item`.

17.3 Case study: storable interface*

The section contains a large case study that demonstrates that entirely different types can implement the same interface. We implement a *store* that can hold values of any type and then use it to store values of two quite different types.

17.3.1 *The store*

Values can be stored if they are of a type that implements the interface `Storable`:

store

```
package Store is
  type Storable is interface;
  function  Default(S: Storable) return Storable'Class is abstract;
  procedure Copy(From: in Storable; To: out Storable)  is abstract;
```

Any type that wishes to be stored must implement the procedure `Copy` to copy elements to and from the store. The function `Default` returns a value of class-wide type that is of the same type as the formal parameter and initialized to a default value. It is used for technical reasons discussed below.

The store is defined in this package as the private type `Table`. The elements that are placed in the store will be identified using a fixed string type `Handle_Type`:

```
  type Table (Size: Natural) is private;
  subtype Handle_Type is String(1..8);

  procedure Insert(
    Handle: in Handle_Type; S: in  Storable'Class; T: in out Table);
  procedure Remove(
    Handle: in Handle_Type; S: out Storable'Class; T: in out Table);
  function  Has_Element(
    Handle: in Handle_Type; T: Table) return Boolean;

  Table_Overflow, Copy_Error: exception;
```

The store is an array of records, where each record contains a handle and a reference to the value it stores. Indirect allocation has to be used because `Storable'Class` is not definite:

```
private
  Blanks: constant Handle_Type := (others => ' ');
  type Item is
    record
      Handle:    Handle_Type := Blanks;
      Reference: access Storable'Class;
    end record;

  type Item_Array is array(Natural range <>) of Item;
  type Table(Size: Natural) is
    record
      Contents: Item_Array(0 .. Size);
    end record;
end Store;
```

The function `Has_Element` searches for a matching handle:

```
package body Store is
   function  Has_Element(
     Handle: in Handle_Type; T: Table) return Boolean is
   begin
     for I in T.Contents'Range loop
       if Handle = T.Contents(I).Handle then
         return True;
       end if;
     end loop;
     return False;
   end Has_Element;
```

Remove and Insert use the procedure Copy to copy values to and from the store. Remove is simple, because we assume that Handle identifies an element of Table that matches the concrete type supplied for the formal parameter S. If not, Constraint_Error will be raised and propagated to the caller:

```
41    procedure Remove(
42      Handle: in Handle_Type; S: out Storable'Class; T: in out Table) is
43    begin
44      for I in T.Contents'Range loop
45        if Handle = T.Contents(I).Handle then
46          T.Contents(I).Handle := Blanks;
47          Copy(From => T.Contents(I).Reference.all, To => S);
48          return;
49        end if;
50      end loop;
51    end Remove;
```

Inserting a value is more difficult. Once we find the index I of an unused table entry, we have to allocate an object whose access is assigned to T.Contents(I).Reference ‡57, and then copy the value in S to that object using Copy ‡58:

```
52    procedure Insert(
53      Handle: in Handle_Type; S: in Storable'Class; T: in out Table) is
54    begin
55      for I in T.Contents'Range loop
56        if T.Contents(I).Handle = Blanks then
57          T.Contents(I) := (Handle, new Storable'Class'(Default(S)));
58          Copy(From => S, To => T.Contents(I).Reference.all);
59          return;
60        end if;
61      end loop;
62      raise Table_Overflow;
63    end Insert;
64  end Store;
```

We must ensure that the allocated object is of the same concrete type as the type of the actual parameter supplied for the class-wide formal parameter S. The function Default is overridden for each type that implements Storable. Since the formal parameter S of Insert is of class-wide type, when used as an actual parameter to Default, it dispatches to the overriding subprogram for its type. The function returns a value of the same type and this is used in the allocator to allocate an object of the correct type. This is not dispatching on a function result as described in Section 8.10, because the dispatching is determined by the parameter S of Default.

Let use now turn to implementing two types whose values can be stored. The first type will be our events, while the second will be matrices of two representations. The next subsection presents a program for the matrices. Following that we will show the modifications needed so that the two types can implement the interface `Storable`.

17.3.2 Matrices

Two common representations of matrices are *dense matrices* and *sparse matrices*. The former are stored as two-dimensional arrays:

$$\begin{bmatrix} 1.0 & 0.0 & 0.0 \\ 0.0 & 4.0 & 0.0 \\ 0.0 & 0.0 & 9.0 \end{bmatrix}$$

For a sparse matrix, a record is defined for each *non-zero* element of the matrix:

```
type Item is record
  Value: Float;
  X, Y:  Natural;
end record;
```

and these elements are stored in a data structure like a one-dimensional array or a linked list. Clearly, if there are very few non-zero elements in the matrix, even very large matrices can be stored using little memory, although the time required for reading and writing elements of the matrix will be larger than for a two-dimensional array, where elements can be read and written in constant time by indexing. Regardless of the representation chosen, the set of subprograms used to work with a matrix is uniform, so we declare an interface:

store

```
package Matrices is
  type Matrix is interface;
  function  Element(M: Matrix; X, Y: Natural) return Float is abstract;
  procedure Set_Element(
    M: in out Matrix; X, Y: in Natural; Value: in Float) is abstract;

  function  Rows(M: Matrix) return Natural is abstract;
  function  Cols(M: Matrix) return Natural is abstract;
  procedure Zero(M: in out Matrix) is abstract;
  function  "="(M1, M2: Matrix) return Boolean is abstract;
end Matrices;
```

The visible part of the package specification of the implementation for dense matrices is:

```
with Matrices;
package Dense_Matrices is
  type Dense_Matrix(Rows, Cols: Natural) is new Matrices.Matrix with private;

  function Element(M: Dense_Matrix; X, Y: Natural) return Float;
  procedure Set_Element(
    M: in out Dense_Matrix; X, Y: Natural; Value: Float);
  procedure Zero(M: in out Dense_Matrix);

  function Rows (M: Dense_Matrix) return Natural;
  function Cols (M: Dense_Matrix) return Natural;
  function  "="(M1, M2: Dense_Matrix) return Boolean;
private
  ...
end Dense_Matrices;
```

The interface is implemented by a private extension Dense_Matrix, while the subprograms are non-abstract subprograms with the same profiles except for the type name. For sparse matrices, the visible part of the package specification is exactly the same except that Dense is replaced by Sparse. The representations of the types in the private parts and the implementations of the subprograms can be found in the software archive.

A package of matrix operations can be implemented using only the subprograms provided by the interface Matrix. Here are a few examples:

```
with Matrices;
package Matrix_Operations is
   function Trace(M: Matrices.Matrix'Class) return Float;
   function "="(M1, M2: Matrices.Matrix'Class) return Boolean;
   procedure Display(M: Matrices.Matrix'Class);
end Matrix_Operations;
```

These operations are implemented by dispatching the class-wide formal parameter to the specific subprograms for Element, Set_Element and so on:

```
package body  Matrix_Operations is
  function Trace(M: Matrices.Matrix'Class) return Float is
    Result : Float := 0.0;
  begin
    for J in 1 .. M.Rows loop
      Result := Result + M.Element (J, J);
    end loop;
    return Result;
  end Trace;
```

```
  function "="(M1, M2: Matrices.Matrix'Class) return Boolean is ...

  procedure Display(M: Matrices.Matrix'Class) is ...
end Matrix_Operations;
```

17.3.3 *Deriving the types from* `Storable`

The matrix and event packages must be modified so that the types are derived (also) from the interface `Storable` and implement the abstract subprograms `Default` and `Copy`. For dense matrices, the package specification is:

```
with Matrices, Store;
package Dense_Matrices is
  type Dense_Matrix (Rows, Cols: Natural) is
    new Matrices.Matrix and Store.Storable with private;

  -- Override the primitive subprograms of the interface Matrix
  ...

  -- Override the primitive subprograms of the interface Storable
  procedure Copy(From: in Dense_Matrix; To: out Dense_Matrix);
  function  Default(S: Dense_Matrix) return Store.Storable'Class;
private
  -- as before
end Dense_Matrices;
```

The implementation of `Copy` for two-dimensional arrays is very simple:

```
package body Dense_Matrices is
  -- Other subprograms as before

  procedure Copy(From: in Dense_Matrix; To: out Dense_Matrix) is
  begin
    if From.Rows /= To.Rows or From.Cols /= To.Cols then
      raise Store.Copy_Error;
    else
      To.Contents := From.Contents;
    end if;
  end Copy;
```

The function Default builds an aggregate with zero content whose number of rows and number of columns are taken from the formal parameter. The value is converted to Storable'Class before returning:

```
   function  Default(S: Dense_Matrix) return Store.Storable'Class is
   begin
     return Store.Storable'Class(
       Dense_Matrix'(S.Rows, S.Cols, Contents => (others => (others => 0.0)))
     );
   end Default;
end Dense_Matrices;
```

The modifications to Sparse_Matrices are similar, although the implementation of Copy is no longer a simple assignment; see the software archive for details.

Events are now derived from Storable_Event which has Event as its parent and Storable as its progenitor:

```
with Store;
package Event_Package is
   type Event is abstract tagged record ... end record;

   type Storable_Event is
     abstract new Event and Store.Storable with null record;

   type Engine_Event is new Storable_Event with
     record
       Fuel, Oxygen: Natural := 0;
     end record;
   function  Create return Engine_Event;
   procedure Simulate(E: in Engine_Event);
   function  Default(S: Engine_Event) return Store.Storable'Class;
   procedure Copy(From: in Engine_Event; To: out Engine_Event);

   -- Other types and primitive operations
end Event_Package;
```

Each event type must override the primitive subprograms of Storable as well as those of Event. The implementation of these subprograms is straightforward and can be found in the software archive. The archive also contains two main programs, one for testing the matrix implementations, and another that tests that the store can hold both matrices and events.

17.4 Synchronized interfaces

This Section depends on the concepts and case studies in Chapter 18.

Synchronized, task, and protected interfaces are intended to group families of types that share run-time behavior in a concurrent program.

§3.9.4

> 5 An interface with the reserved word **limited**, **task**, **protected**, or **synchronized** in its definition is termed, respectively, a *limited interface*, a *task interface*, a *protected interface*, or a *synchronized interface*. In addition, all task and protected interfaces are synchronized interfaces, and all synchronized interfaces are limited interfaces.

Task interfaces must be implemented by task types, protected interfaces by protected types, while synchronized types can be implemented by either tasks or protected types §3.9.4(13–15).

For a task interface, the primitive operations of the progenitors will be implemented by entries of a task type:

§9.1

> 9.2 For a task declaration with an interface_list, the task type inherits user-defined primitive subprograms from each progenitor type (see 3.9.4), in the same way that a derived type inherits user-defined primitive subprograms from its progenitor types (see 3.4). If the first parameter of a primitive inherited subprogram is of the task type or an access parameter designating the task type, and there is an entry_declaration for a single entry with the same identifier within the task declaration, whose profile is type conformant with the prefixed view profile of the inherited subprogram, the inherited subprogram is said to be *implemented* by the conforming task entry.

Similarly, for a protected interface, the primitive operations will be implemented by protected subprograms or entries of a protected type §9.4(11.1).

17.4.1 Case study: synchronized buffer

In this case study, we declare a `Buffer` as an interface type and show how it can be implemented by either a task type or a protected type; the implementations are adapted from the case studies in Chapter 18. Let us start with a protected interface:

protectpc

```
package Buffer_Interface is
  type Buffer is protected interface;
  procedure Append(B: in out Buffer; N: in  Integer) is abstract;
  procedure Take  (B: in out Buffer; N: out Integer) is abstract;
end Buffer_Interface;
```

As with all interfaces, the subprograms must be abstract (or null procedures).

This interface is the progenitor of a protected type:

```
with Buffer_Interface;
package Protected_Buffer is
  type Index is mod 8;
  type Buffer_Array is array(Index) of Integer;

  protected type Buffer is new Buffer_Interface.Buffer with
    entry Append(I: in  Integer);
    entry Take  (I: out Integer);
  private
    B: Buffer_Array;
    In_Ptr, Out_Ptr, Count:  Index := 0;
  end Buffer;
end Protected_Buffer;
```

The body of the package simply encapsulates the body of the protected type taken from the source code of the case study in Section 18.1.1.

To use the protected type, a protected object is allocated:

```
with Ada.Text_IO; use Ada.Text_IO;
with Buffer_Interface, Protected_Buffer;
procedure ProtectPC is
  Buffer: access Buffer_Interface.Buffer'Class :=
            new Protected_Buffer.Buffer;
  task Producer;
  task body Producer is
  begin
    for N in 1..200 loop
      Put_Line("Producing " & Integer'Image(N));
      Buffer.Append(N);
    end loop;
  end Producer;
  ...
end ProtectPC;
```

`Buffer` is of type `Buffer_Interface.Buffer'Class`, so the call to Append is a dispatching.

Alternatively, the buffer can be declared as a task interface:

taskpc

```
package Buffer_Interface is
  type Buffer is task interface;
  procedure Append(B: in out Buffer; N: in  Integer) is abstract;
  procedure Take  (B: in out Buffer; N: out Integer) is abstract;
end Buffer_Interface;
```

and implemented by a task type:

```
with Buffer_Interface;
package Task_Buffer is
  task type Buffer is new Buffer_Interface.Buffer with
    entry Append(I: in  Integer);
    entry Take  (I: out Integer);
  end Buffer;
end Task_Buffer;
```

Of course, the best design is to declare the interface as a synchronized interface that can be implemented by either a task type or a protected type:

syncpc

```
package Buffer_Interface is
  type Buffer is synchronized interface;
  procedure Append(B: in out Buffer; N: in  Integer) is abstract;
  procedure Take  (B: in out Buffer; N: out Integer) is abstract;
end Buffer_Interface;
```

The choice of implementation can be made at run-time and the call will be dispatched:

```
with Ada.Text_IO; use Ada.Text_IO;
with Buffer_Interface, Protected_Buffer, Task_Buffer;
procedure SyncPC is
  use Buffer_Interface;
  function Get_Buffer return access Buffer'Class is
  begin
    if ... then
      return B: access Buffer'Class := new Protected_Buffer.Buffer;
    else
      return B: access Buffer'Class := new Task_Buffer.Buffer;
    end if;
  end Get_Buffer;
```

```
  Buffer: access Buffer'Class := Get_Buffer;
  ...
end SyncPC;
```

17.5 Generic formal tagged private types*

A generic formal private type can be declared as tagged §12.5.1(2):

```
generic
  type Item is tagged private;
```

The category of types for the actual parameter is the category of all nonlimited tagged types. As with ordinary formal private types, limited may be specified in the formal parameter §12.5.1(17), in which case any tagged type may be the actual parameter. What can you do with *any* tagged type? Obviously, you cannot call any of its primitive operations, since these will be different for different tagged types, but any tagged type can be extended.

17.5.1 Case study: generic tagged types

In the following program, an arbitrary tagged type `Item` is extended to define a new type `Displayed_Item` with an additional component and primitive subprograms:

mixin1

```
generic
  type Item is tagged private;
  with function Format(D: Item) return String is <>;
  with function Create return Item is <>;
package Display is
  type Displayed_Item is new Item with private;
  function  Create return Displayed_Item;
  procedure Display_Item(D: in Displayed_Item);
  procedure Set_Size(D: in out Displayed_Item; N: Natural);
  function  Get_Size(D: Displayed_Item) return Natural;
private
  type Displayed_Item is new Item with
    record
      Size: Natural := 10;
    end record;
end Display;
```

The new subprograms are implemented in the package body:

```
with Ada.Text_IO;
package body Display is
  function Create return Displayed_Item is
  begin
    return (Item'(Create) with Size => <>);
  end Create;

  procedure Display_Item(D: in Displayed_Item) is ...
  procedure Set_Size(D: in out Displayed_Item; N: Natural) is ...
  function  Get_Size(D: Displayed_Item) return Natural is ...
end Display;
```

`Display` is instantiated with `Root_Event.Event`:

```
with Display;
with Root_Event; use Root_Event;
package Displayed_Event is new Display(Event);
```

The package declaration `Root_Event` must be modified so that the type and subprograms are no longer abstract because the parameters of the generic package are not abstract. The events themselves are now derived from the type in the instantiation `Displayed_Event`:

```
with Displayed_Event;
package Root_Event.Engine is
  type Engine_Event is new Displayed_Event.Displayed_Item with private;
  ...
end Root_Event.Engine;
```

The functions `Create` use extension aggregates:

```
with Ada.Text_IO; use Ada.Text_IO;
with Root_Event.Random_Time;
package body Root_Event.Engine is
  G: Random_Time.Generator;
  function Create return Engine_Event is
  begin
    return (Displayed_Event.Create with
            Fuel =>   Random_Time.Random(G) mod 100,
            Oxygen => Random_Time.Random(G) mod 500);
  end Create;
  ...
end Root_Event.Engine;
```

The main subprogram is similar to that used in the interface case study and can be found in the software archive.

This programming paradigm is a form of MI called *mixin inheritance*. We have no intention of creating objects of type `Display.Displayed_Item`; instead, we "mix in" the properties of this type with an existing parent type (here `Event`) to derive a new type (here `Displayed_Event.Displayed_Item`).

17.6 Generic formal derived types*

A generic formal derived type can be declared §12.5.1(3):

```
with Root_Event;
generic
  type Item is new Root_Event.Event with private;
```

The actual parameter can be `Event` or any type descended from it. According to the contract, within the generic unit any primitive operation of `Event` can be used, since any descendant of `Event` is certain to supply that operation, either by inheritance or by overriding. Additional operations that were declared for the descendants upon extension are of course not available, since they are different for each type.

17.6.1 Case study: generic derived types

We now give another version of the mixin program where the generic formal parameter is derived from `Event`, rather than from an unspecified tagged type:

mixin2

```
with Root_Event;
generic
  type Item is new Root_Event.Event with private;
package Display is
  type Displayed_Item is new Item with private;
  function  Create return Displayed_Item;
  procedure Display_Item(D: in Displayed_Item);
  procedure Set_Size(D: in out Displayed_Item; N: Natural);
  function  Get_Size(D: Displayed_Item) return Natural;
private
  -- as before
end Display;
```

The primitive operations of the tagged type are copied into the instance §12.3(16), so `Create` can be used directly in the generic package body, and need not be supplied as an additional generic parameter.

Projects

1. Implement sparse matrices using a two-dimensional list structure.

```
type Element;
type Element_Ptr is access all Element;
type Element is record
  Value: Float;
  X, Y:  Natural;
  Next_In_Row, Next_In_Col: Element_Ptr;
end record;

type Row_Or_Col is array (Natural range <>) of Element_Ptr;
type Sparse_Matrix (Rows, Cols: Natural) is
  new Matrix and Storable with record
    Row_Array: Row_Or_Col(0 .. Rows);
    Col_Array: Row_Or_Col(0 .. Cols);
end record;
```

2. Implement the store as a hash table. The function `Hash` will be a primitive operation of the interface `Storable` and each type implementing the interface must override it with a concrete function.
3. Implement a Linda tuple space [2, Chapter 9] using a synchronized interface.

Quizzes

Quiz 1: The equality operation from `Matrix_Operations` is called with an expanded name in the main program of the storable case study:

```
MD: Dense_Matrices.Dense_Matrix(3,3);
MS: Sparse_Matrices.Sparse_Matrix(3,3);

IO.Put(Matrix_Operations."="(MD1, MS1));
```

Can a use_type_clause be given so that it can be called in infix notation: `MD1 = MS1`?

Quiz 2:

```
package Buffer_Interface is
  type Buffer is task interface;
  procedure Append(B: in Buffer; N: in  Integer) is abstract;
  procedure Take  (B: in Buffer; N: out Integer) is abstract;
end Buffer_Interface;
```

Quiz 3:

```
type T is limited interface;

protected type P is new T with
  procedure Proc;
end P;

protected body P is ...

Put_Line(P'External_Tag);
```

Quiz 4:

```
type T is task interface;
type P is protected interface;
type G is tagged null record;
type D is new G and T and P with null record;
```

Chapter 18
Concurrency

An Ada program contains one or more *tasks* that execute *concurrently*. (Tasks are called *processes* or *threads* in other languages; the distinctions are not important in this context.) We use the term concurrent in preference to "parallel" to emphasize that the parallelism is conceptual, not necessarily physical. A correct *multitasking* Ada program will produce the same result, whether it is run on a multiprocessor system or on a time-shared single processor, though the multiprocessor system will (hopefully) be significantly faster.

For convenience, the material on concurrency is divided into two chapters, with more advanced material in Chapter 19. Multitasking programs are frequently written for embedded computer systems where hardware interfaces and program performance are critical; the constructs in Ada that support embedded systems are discussed in Chapters 20–21.

Chapters 18–21 are not an introduction to concurrent programming, for which the reader is referred to the author's textbook [2]. The software archive accompanying that book contains implementations in Ada of many concurrent and distributed algorithms. More advanced textbooks are [4] on concurrent and real-time programming in Ada 2005, and [5] on algorithms for building real-time systems.

A task is like a subprogram because it has data declarations, a sequence of statements and exception handlers; the difference is that a *thread of control* is associated with each task. The thread is implemented using a data structure containing pointers to the task's current instruction and to local memory such as a stack segment. If each task is assigned a processor, the processors will execute the instructions of the tasks simultaneously. If there are more tasks than processors—at worst, if there is only one processor—a *scheduler* will assign processors to tasks according to some scheduling algorithm.

In Ada, there are three main constructs for writing concurrent programs:

- Load and store of shared variables (Section 20.7); these are usually too low-level.
- Protected objects for asynchronous sharing of resources.
- Rendezvous for direct task-to-task synchronous communication.

(See Sections 21.11–21.12 for other, low-level, constructs defined in the Real-Time Annex.)

The term *asynchronous* means that different tasks need not access the protected object at the same time. In fact, a task can insert data into a protected object and then terminate, while a second task later extracts the data from the object. The rendezvous is *synchronous* because both tasks must participate in the synchronization and communication at the same time. In the next two sections we will solve a simple problem, once using protected objects and once using rendezvous so that we can compare the constructs.

18.1 Tasks and protected objects

The problem that we will solve is called the *producer–consumer problem*. One or more tasks produce data elements which must be transferred to one or more consumer tasks. An example is a network interface that "produces" data downloaded from the net and a web browser that "consumes" the data. A *buffer* is used for data structure transformation (the data may arrive in large blocks, which must be stored in a data structure so that the browser can process one element at a time), and for flow control (the browser must be blocked if no data is currently available, and, similarly, the interface must not download data if the data structure is full).

18.1.1 Case study: producer–consumer (protected object)

The following program solves the producer–consumer problem. For simplicity, the data elements are integer values and the array data structure can hold 8 elements:

protectpc

```
with Ada.Text_IO; use Ada.Text_IO;
procedure ProtectPC is
   type Index is mod 8;
   type Buffer_Array is array(Index) of Integer;
```

Buffer is a *protected object*. Syntactically, a protected unit (which can be either a single object, or a type that can be used to declare objects §9.4(1)) is like a package, with a declaration divided into a visible part and a private part, and a body §9.4(2–9).

```
   protected Buffer is
      entry Append(I: in  Integer);
      entry Take  (I: out Integer);
   private
      B: Buffer_Array;
      In_Ptr, Out_Ptr, Count:  Index := 0;
   end Buffer;
```

A protected unit cannot contain type declarations, so the data types used to implement the buffer have been declared in the enclosing procedure. The visible part of the protected object contains the declaration of two *entries* Append and Take. The private part contains the declaration of the components belonging to the protected object. Components can only be declared in the private part, while operations such as entries can be declared anywhere in the protected unit declaration §9.4(4–6).

The bodies of the entries are contained within the body of the protected unit:

```
12  protected body Buffer is
13    entry Append(I: in  Integer) when Count < Index'Last is
14    begin
15      B(In_Ptr) := I;
16      Count := Count + 1;
17      In_Ptr := In_Ptr + 1;
18    end Append;
19
20    entry Take(I: out Integer) when Count > 0 is
21    begin
22      I := B(Out_Ptr);
23      Count := Count - 1;
24      Out_Ptr := Out_Ptr + 1;
25    end Take;
26  end Buffer;
```

The statements in the entries are the usual ones used to append data to a buffer and to take data from a buffer. The boolean-valued expressions after the word **when** are called *barriers* and are used to ensure that data will not be appended to a full buffer or taken from an empty buffer. The synchronization of calls to the entries and subprograms of a protected object is described in detail in the next subsection.

Protected objects are passive and just "sit there" waiting for their entries and subprograms to be called. Threads of control are associated with *tasks*. In this case study, there is one producer task which produces 200 integer values and appends them to the buffer:

```
27  task Producer;
28  task body Producer is
29  begin
30    for N in 1..200 loop
31      Put_Line("Producing " & Integer'Image(N));
32      Buffer.Append(N);
33    end loop;
34  end Producer;
```

A task body is syntactically like a procedure body §9.1(6). The task declaration ‡27 must be present even if it is empty §9.1(8).

For the consumers, we declare a task *type* so that more than one consumer can be declared:

```
35    task type Consumer(ID: Integer);
36    task body Consumer is
37      N: Integer;
38    begin
39      loop
40        Buffer.Take(N);
41        Put_Line(Integer'Image(ID) & " consuming " & Integer'Image(N));
42      end loop;
43    end Consumer;
```

The task type ‡35 has a discriminant §9.1(2,16), which is used for configuring the tasks with ID numbers when they are declared. The consumer tasks contain infinite loops: as long as there is data that can be taken from the buffer, they will do so. When the producer task terminates after appending 200 values to the buffer, the consumer tasks will be blocked.

We can now declare the two consumer tasks `C1` and `C2`:

```
44    C1: Consumer(1);
45    C2: Consumer(2);
46  begin
47    null;
48  end ProtectPC;
```

The main program has just the **null** statement, because all the execution is performed by the threads of control associated with the other three tasks. These tasks are activated just after the **begin** of the main subprogram, which must wait until the tasks have terminated. Since the consumer tasks do not terminate, make sure that you know how to break the execution of a program on your computer (usually `ctrl-c`) before running this example. See Section 19.1 for details on task activation and termination.

Task units and protected units are *not* compilation units; they must be declared within a compilation unit such as a subprogram or a package. However, a task or protected *body* can be separately compiled as a subunit §10.1.3(10).

18.1.2 Protected actions

How is a protected unit different from a package? The subprograms of a package can be called concurrently from multiple tasks §6.1(35), possibly leading to race conditions. The operations of a protected unit are *mutually exclusive*, meaning that only one will be executed at a time.

§9.5.1

> 4 A new protected action is not started on a protected object while another protected action on the same protected object is underway, unless both actions are the result of a call on a protected function. This rule is expressible in terms of the execution resource associated with the protected object:
>
> 5 • *Starting* a protected action on a protected object corresponds to *acquiring* the execution resource associated with the protected object, either for concurrent read-only access if the protected action is for a call on a protected function, or for exclusive read-write access otherwise;
>
> 6 • *Completing* the protected action corresponds to *releasing* the associated execution resource.

The statements of `Append` in the producer task and those of `Take` in a consumer task should not be executed simultaneously so that they will not try to update `Count` simultaneously. In fact, this will not occur, because one of the tasks will acquire the lock ("execution resource") granting it exclusive read-write access. The other task must wait until the entry body is complete and the lock released.

Functions allow multiple read-only access to the data of a protected object, provided that no subprogram or entry has access to the protected object. See Section 18.6 for more on protected subprograms.

In addition to mutual exclusion, a protected object can also provide flow control.

§9.5.3

> 7 • An entry of a protected object is open if the condition of the entry_barrier of the corresponding entry_body evaluates to True; otherwise it is closed. ...
>
> 8 For the execution of an entry_call_statement, evaluation of the name and of the parameter associations is as for a subprogram call (see 6.4). The entry call is then *issued*: For a call on an entry of a protected object, a new protected action is started on the object (see 9.5.1). The named entry is checked to see if it is open; if open, the entry call is said to be *selected immediately*, and the execution of the call proceeds as follows:
>
> 10 • For a call on an open entry of a protected object, the corresponding entry_body is executed (see 9.5.2) as part of the protected action.
>
> 12 If the named entry is closed, the entry call is added to an *entry queue* (as part of the protected action, for a call on a protected entry), and the call remains queued until it is selected or cancelled; there is a separate (logical) entry queue for each entry of a given task or protected object (including each entry of an entry family).

The barrier `when Count > 0` ‡20 closes the `Take` entry when the buffer is empty; a consumer calling `Take` will be enqueued on the entry queue for `Take`. Similarly, the barrier `when Count < Index'Last` ‡13 closes the `Append` entry when the buffer is full. Suppose that the buffer is empty and that one or more calls from consumer tasks are enqueued on the queue for `Take`. In this state, only the producer will now succeed in passing its barrier and commencing the execution of its protected action `Append`.

Since the completion of a protected operation can potentially change the value of a barrier, the barriers are reevaluated, so that if one of them is now open, its entry queue can be serviced:

§9.5.3

> 13 When a queued call is *selected*, it is removed from its entry queue. Selecting a queued call from a particular entry queue is called *servicing* the entry queue. An entry with queued calls can be serviced under the following circumstances:
>
> 15 • If after performing, as part of a protected action on the associated protected object, an operation on the object, other than a call on a protected function, the entry is checked and found to be open.

To continue with the example, when `Append` completes, the value of `Count` is now `1`, the barrier `**when** Count > 0` evaluates to true, and the entry queue for the `Take` operation will be serviced as part of the same protected action. `Count` will become 0 again, closing the barrier, so that additional calls from consumer tasks that are on the queue remain blocked. The protected action is now completed.

18.1.3 Preference for servicing queues

Consider the following scenario, where we assume that there are multiple producer tasks. First, a consumer task attempts to `Take` an element from an empty buffer and blocks on the entry queue; then, several producers attempt to `Append` elements to the buffer. One will acquire the lock and be allowed to execute the entry, appending its element to the buffer. When the entry body is completed, there are two ways to continue:

- Another producer can be allowed into the entry body to append its element.
- The queue can be serviced so that a call from the enqueued consumer can take the newly appended element.

§9.5.3

> 18 For a protected object, the above servicing of entry queues continues until there are no open entries with queued calls, at which point the protected action completes.

An entry call (here from a producer) will not begin a new protected action until the ongoing protected action is completed; in other words, there is a *preference* for servicing calls already enqueued on an entry queue.

Figure 18.1 shows how protected objects should be viewed: an outer shell protecting access to the resources, and an inner set of operations and entry queues. Entry calls, represented by parallelograms with arrows, may be in one of three places: (i) executing an entry body (such as `Append`), (ii) blocked in an entry queue (the one for `Take`), or (iii) attempting to enter the protected object. Calls that have already passed the outer shell are considered part of the "club" and have preference over calls that have not yet been commenced.

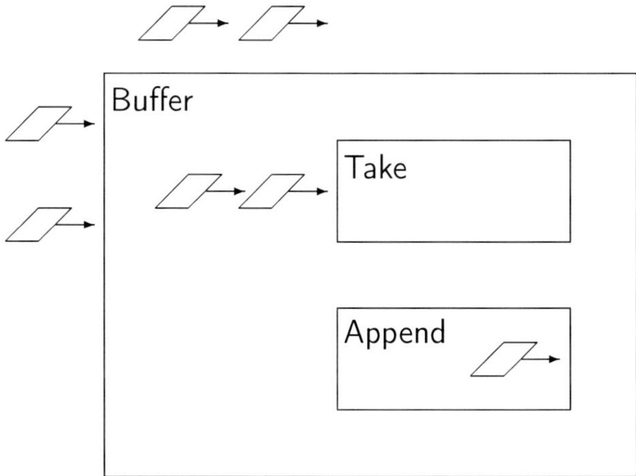

Fig. 18.1 Protected object

The preference for serving entry queues implements *immediate resumption* of blocked tasks. This is done for two reasons:

- If one task modifies a variable that will open the barrier for a blocked task, the awakened task can assume that no third task will intervene and change the state. Therefore, the condition need not be checked again.
- Blocked tasks will not be starved by a stream of new entry calls.

There is no queue associated with the mutual exclusion on the access to the protected object itself. This will not be a problem if protected entries and subprograms are kept very short, so that a call either quickly executes the entry body or is quickly enqueued because its barrier is false; in either case the mutual exclusion is released.

> **Language Comparison**
>
> A protected object is similar to a Java class, all of whose methods are **synchronized**. A synchronized method cannot be executed unless the caller has obtained the lock associated with an object, just as the execution of a protected entry or subprogram requires that the calling task obtain the "associated execution resource." In Java, however, there are no queues, no barriers and hence no immediate resumption of an unblocked process. `java.util.concurrent` (added to version 5 of Java) is an extensive library of constructs for implementing synchronization of concurrent programs.

18.2 Rendezvous

Let us examine more closely the body for the entry `Append`:

```
entry Append(I: in  Integer) when Count < Index'Last is
begin
  B(In_Ptr) := I;
  Count := Count + 1;
  In_Ptr := In_Ptr + 1;
end Append;
```

The parameter `I` and the assignment of its value to a component of the buffer `B` are used to communicate—to pass data—between the calling task and the protected object. But incrementing the values of `Count` and `In_Ptr` is solely concerned with updating the internal data structure of the protected object. Nevertheless, the calling task is responsible for executing these statements, so there is less potential for concurrent execution. There would be no point in utilizing the extra concurrency for two short instructions, but one can imagine that the buffer is stored in a data structure that requires significant internal processing between insertions and extractions.

Additional concurrency can be implemented by making the buffer itself a task:

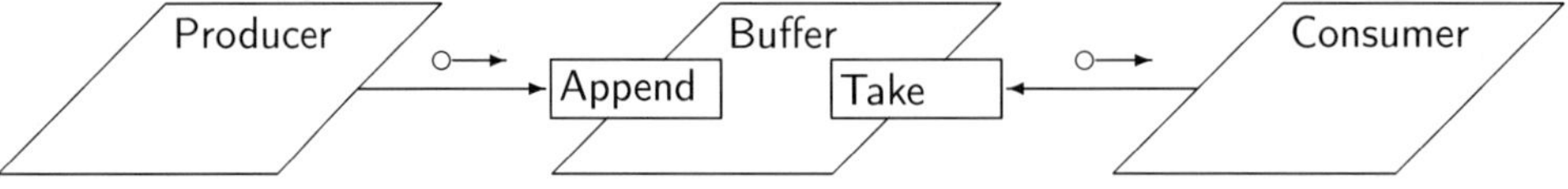

Synchronization and communication is done directly with the buffer task. The producer and consumer both initiate calls on entries of the buffer task, but in the case of the consumer, the direction of the data flow (denoted by the small arrow) is opposite the direction of the call.

18.2.1 *Case study: producer–consumer (rendezvous)*

The following program solves the producer–consumer problem using a buffer task, whose declaration contains the declaration of the two entries Append and Take:

taskpc

```
with Ada.Text_IO; use Ada.Text_IO;
procedure TaskPC is
  type Index is mod 8;
  type Buffer_Array is array(Index) of Integer;

  task Buffer is
    entry Append(I: in  Integer);
    entry Take  (I: out Integer);
  end Buffer;
```

Unlike protected units, the declaration of a task can contain only entries and representation clauses §13.1(2), even in the private part §9.1(4–5).

A task is an active entity and its body contains declarations and a sequence of statements just like a procedure. The body of the task consists of a single nonterminating loop statement:

```
  task body Buffer is
    B: Buffer_Array;
    In_Ptr, Out_Ptr, Count:  Index := 0;
  begin
    loop
      select
        when Count < Index'Last =>
          accept Append(I: in Integer) do
            B(In_Ptr) := I;
          end Append;
        Count := Count + 1;
        In_Ptr := In_Ptr + 1;
      or
        when Count > 0 =>
          accept Take(I: out Integer) do
            I := B(Out_Ptr);
          end Take;
        Count := Count - 1;
        Out_Ptr := Out_Ptr + 1;
      end select;
    end loop;
  end Buffer;
```

Synchronization and communication with the buffer task are done using a selective accept statement that is described later in this section.

The producer and consumer tasks are unchanged from the previous solution.

18.2.2 Accept statements

The task `Producer` calls the entry Append of the task `Buffer`. The calling task and the called task must execute a *rendezvous* at an accept_statement.

§9.5.2

> 3 accept_statement ::=
>   **accept** *entry*_direct_name [(entry_index)] parameter_profile [**do**
>   handled_sequence_of_statements
>   **end** [*entry*_identifier]];
>
> 24 For the execution of an accept_statement, the entry_index, if any, is first evaluated and converted to the entry index subtype; this index value identifies which entry of the family is to be accepted. Further execution of the accept_statement is then blocked until a caller of the corresponding entry is selected (see 9.5.3), whereupon the handled_sequence_of_statements, if any, of the accept_statement is executed, with the formal parameters associated with the corresponding actual parameters of the selected entry call. Upon completion of the handled_sequence_of_statements, the accept_statement completes and is left. ...
>
> 25 The above interaction between a calling task and an accepting task is called a *rendezvous*. After a rendezvous, the two tasks continue their execution independently.

(Entry indices are discussed in Section 18.5).

The basic principle of a rendezvous is that the first party to reach the rendezvous point must wait until the second party arrives. The semantics of a rendezvous are illustrated by the time lines below, where solid lines indicate intervals during which the process is ready or executing and dashed lines indicate intervals when the process is blocked on the statement written within parentheses.

Let us ignore the selective_accept statement for now and consider the following diagram, where task `Buffer` executes until it reaches the accept statement for Append ‡17, at which point it is blocked:

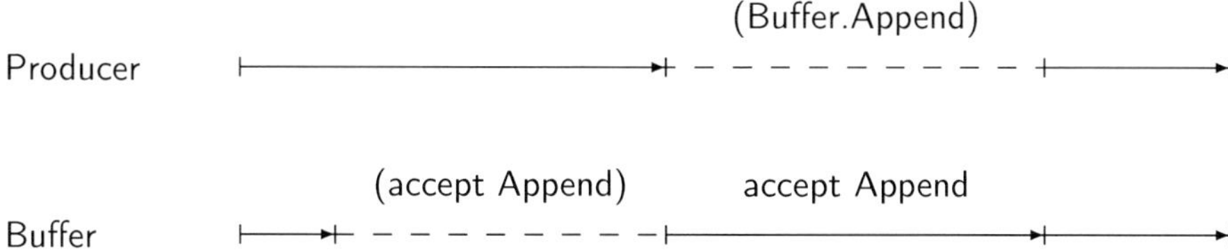

The task `Producer` executes concurrently until it reaches the entry call `Buffer.Append`. Now the producer is blocked and the buffer executes the sequence of statements within the accept statement. When the rendezvous is completed, both tasks are made ready; in a single-processor system, the scheduler will have to choose one of them.

The following diagram shows another possibility. Here the producer task blocks when it calls the entry, because the buffer task has not yet reached the accept statement. The producer task is made ready again only when the accept statement has been completed.

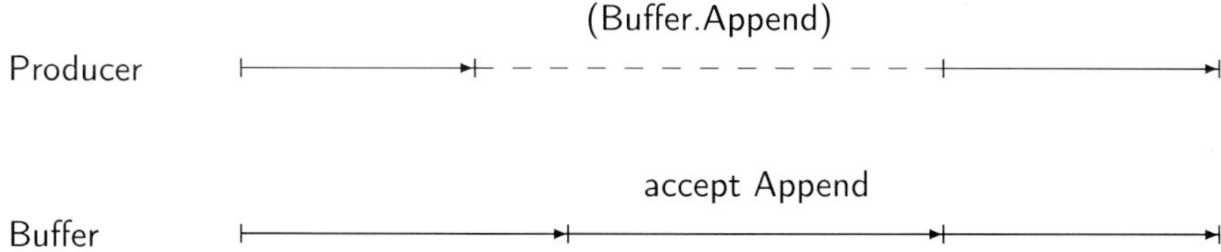

Before commencing the rendezvous, **in** and **in out** parameters are transferred to the accepting task; upon completion, **out** and **in out** parameters are transferred back to the calling task. Data transfer is bidirectional even though the entry call is unidirectional. Furthermore, the call is asymmetrical: the calling task knows the name of the accepting task but not conversely.

When the rendezvous is complete, both tasks can proceed independently, so the producer is not blocked while the internal data structure is updated ‡20–21. The increased concurrency has been obtained at the price of additional overhead associated with the extra task, and additional *context switches* to block the caller and then resume it.

18.2.3 Selective accept

Suppose that the task `Buffer` arrives at the rendezvous, but neither producers nor consumers have yet issued a call. We would like `Buffer` to serve the *first* task that calls one of its entries; however, a task body is just a sequence of statements that have to be executed one after another. If we had written:

```
loop
  accept Append do ...
  accept Take   do ...
end loop;
```

the `Buffer` would block pending a call from a producer, even if there were waiting consumers and data in the buffer.

The selective accept statement enables a task to carry out a rendezvous with any waiting calling task, or, if there are none, to wait simultaneously for calls to multiple entries.

§9.7.1

```
2 selective_accept ::=
      select
         [guard] select_alternative
      { or
         [guard] select_alternative }
      [ else
         sequence_of_statements ]
      end select;
3 guard ::= when condition =>
4 select_alternative ::= accept_alternative | delay_alternative | terminate_alternative
5 accept_alternative ::= accept_statement [sequence_of_statements]
```

(The delay_alternative, terminate_alternative, and the **else**-part are discussed in Section 19.3.)

The semantics of the selective accept statement are as follows:

§9.7.1

> 14 A select_alternative is said to be *open* if it is not immediately preceded by a guard, or if the condition of its guard evaluates to True. It is said to be *closed* otherwise.
>
> 15 For the execution of a selective_accept, any guard conditions are evaluated; open alternatives are thus determined. ... Selection and execution of one open alternative, or of the else part, then completes the execution of the selective_accept; the rules for this selection are described below.

The entry `Append` is guarded by `Count < Index'Last` ‡16, which is true only if the buffer is not full; if so, the alternative is open. Similarly, the entry `Take` is guarded by `Count > 0` ‡23, which is true only if the buffer is not empty; if so, the alternative is open. If the buffer is neither full nor empty, both guards are true and both alternatives are open.

§9.7.1

> 21 The exception Program_Error is raised if all alternatives are closed and there is no else part.

Show that it is impossible for both alternatives to be closed; therefore, `Program_Error` will not be raised in this program.

Once the set of open alternatives is determined, the execution of the selective accept statement proceeds as follows:

§9.7.1

> 16 Open `accept_alternative`s are first considered. Selection of one such alternative takes place immediately if the corresponding entry already has queued calls. If several alternatives can thus be selected, one of them is selected according to the entry queuing policy in effect (see 9.5.3 and D.4). When such an alternative is selected, the selected call is removed from its entry queue and the `handled_sequence_of_statements` (if any) of the corresponding `accept_statement` is executed; after the rendezvous completes any subsequent `sequence_of_statements` of the alternative is executed. If no selection is immediately possible (in the above sense), and there is no else part, the task blocks until an open alternative can be selected.

The buffer task will select one of the open alternatives with enqueued calls, if any, and perform a rendezvous. If there are no enqueued calls it will block, waiting for either a producer or a consumer to call an entry. If one alternative is closed (say, the buffer is full, so the `Append` alternative is closed), the buffer task will rendezvous with a task blocked on the entry for the open alternative `Take`, if any, or it will block pending an entry call on that open alternative. A new call by a producer to `Append` will be ignored because the alternative is closed.

The default entry queuing policy is `FIFO_Queuing` §D.4(7), so if there are two consumer tasks waiting on the entry `Take`, they will be accepted in the order that they arrived. Other queuing policies are discussed in Section 21.5.

18.3 Implementation of entry calls

Paragraph §9.5.3(13) (see page 350) talks about servicing a queued *entry call*, not a queued *task*.

§9.5.3

> 22 An implementation may perform the sequence of steps of a protected action using any thread of control; it need not be that of the task that started the protected action.
> ...

Assume that the producer in the program using protected objects attempts to append an item to a full buffer. The entry call `Buffer.Append` will be enqueued, the producer task will be blocked and a consumer task will be allowed to execute. Eventually, the consumer task will take an item from the buffer. Upon completion of the body of `Take`, servicing of the entry queue can be done by the *consumer task*, as shown in the following diagram:

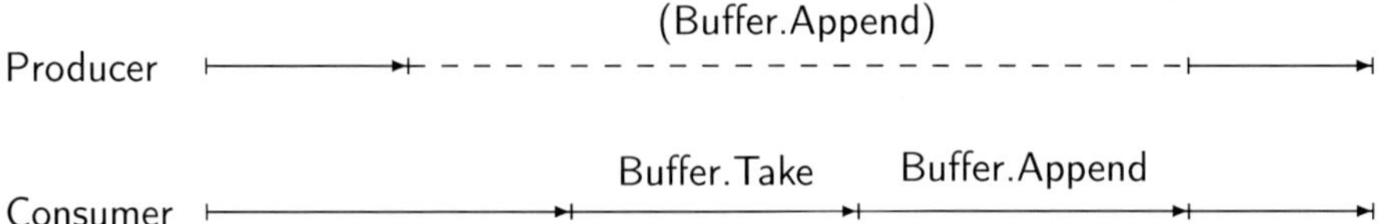

In effect, appending an item is executed by the consumer on behalf of the producer. Upon completion of the entry call, both tasks become ready.

In contrast, a rendezvous normally requires context switches:

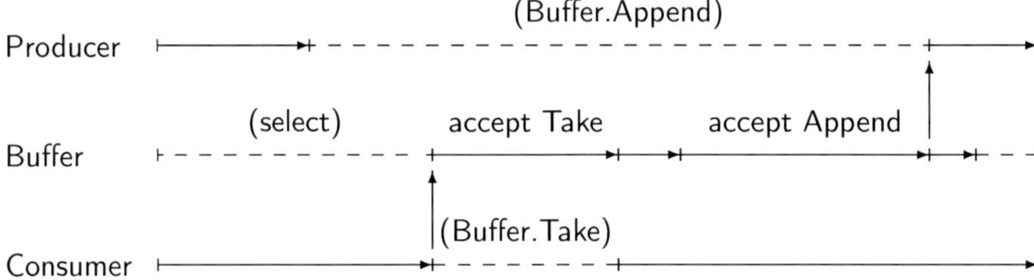

Assume that the buffer task is blocked on the selective accept statement and that the alternative for `Append` is closed because the buffer is full. The producer task blocks on the entry call `Buffer.Append`. When the consumer task executes the call `Buffer.Take`, the rendezvous takes place, removing an item from the buffer. When the selective accept is executed again, the alternative for the entry `Buffer.Append` is now open and the entry call can be accepted. Two extra context switches are needed (vertical arrows): one for the buffer task to execute its accept statement and another to switch either to the producer or to the consumer task.

18.4 Case study: synchronization with rendezvous and protected objects

The concurrent program presented in this section employs both rendezvous and protected objects for synchronization. The case study will be used to present important constructs in Ada tasking: entry families, the requeue statement and the abort statement. The problem is to implement a synchronization scheme described by the following story:

> The CEO (Chief Executive Officer) of a company likes to play golf. He does not allow himself to be interrupted by single employees with problems; instead, they must form themselves into groups before coming to consult him. The size of the group depends on the department to which the employee belongs: engineering, marketing, finance. A waiting group from finance has precedence over a group from marketing, which has precedence over an engineering group.

Let us look first at the structure of the program (Figure 18.2). There will be one task for the CEO and one task for each employee: engineers, salespersons in the marketing department,

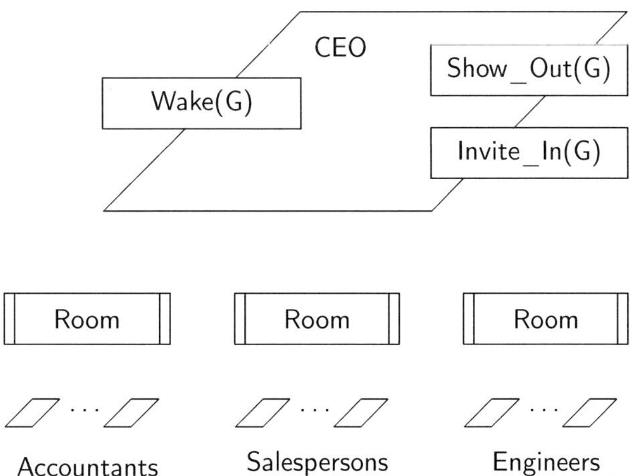

Fig. 18.2 The CEO program

and accountants in the finance department. These are declared as task types, and the tasks themselves are dynamically allocated in the main subprogram. Protected objects of type `Room` are used to synchronize the groups.

The program is contained within a main procedure; we start with the global declarations:

ceot

```
pragma Queuing_Policy(Priority_Queuing);
with Ada.Text_IO; use Ada.Text_IO;
procedure CEOT is
  type Departments is (Engineering, Finance, Marketing);
  type ID_Numbers  is range 0..10;
  Group_Size: constant array(Departments) of
                ID_Numbers range 2..ID_Numbers'Last := (
                  Engineering => 5, Finance => 3, Marketing => 2);
```

The enumeration type `Departments` declares the groups and the integer type `ID_Numbers` is used for the size of the groups. **pragma** `Queuing_Policy` is discussed Section 21.5.

The declaration of the CEO task contains three entry families: `Wake` to awaken the CEO task, `Invite_In`, which each employee task calls to enter the CEO's office, and `Show_Out`, upon which employee tasks block until the consultation is finished:

```
  task CEO is
    entry Wake(Departments);
    entry Invite_In(Departments)(ID: ID_Numbers);
    entry Show_Out (Departments)(ID: ID_Numbers);
  end CEO;
```

Groups are synchronized in a waiting room that is implemented by a protected type. Its body is placed in a subunit (Section 15.3) which will be explained later:

```
type Door_State is (Open, Closed);
protected type Room(Department: Departments; Size: ID_Numbers) is
  entry Register;
  procedure Open_Door;
private
  entry Wait_for_Last_Member;
  Waiting:   ID_Numbers := 0;
  Entrance:  Door_State := Open;
  Exit_Door: Door_State := Closed;
end Room;
protected body Room is separate;
```

The protected type has two discriminants that are used to specify the department and the size of the group. Entry Register is called by an employee task wishing to join a group. Once the correct number of employees for a group of this department is in the room, the Entrance is closed and the group waits for the CEO to receive them. Procedure Open_Door is called by the CEO to reset Entrance to True so that a new group can register.

The protected type has a private entry Wait_for_Last_Member that is used to block registering tasks until the last member of the group has arrived, at which point Exit_Door will be opened. The component Waiting counts the number of waiting employee tasks.

The room for each department is an object of the protected type Room:

```
Engineering_Room: Room(Engineering, Group_Size(Engineering));
Finance_Room:     Room(Finance,     Group_Size(Finance));
Marketing_Room:   Room(Marketing,   Group_Size(Marketing));
```

The task body for the CEO is straightforward, consisting of a selective accept with an alternative for each of the three departments. The body of the accept statement for Wake is empty because it serves simply as a synchronization point; no processing is done and no data is exchanged with the caller:

```
task body CEO is
  I: ID_Numbers;
begin
  loop
    select
      accept Wake(Finance);
```

The sequence of statements following the accept statement implements the CEO's algorithm: the employees are invited in, consult with the CEO and are then shown out. The syntax of the selective accept statement is such that a (possibly guarded) accept statement must *immediately* follow **select** and each **or**, but an arbitrary sequence of statements may be included in the alternative following the **accept** §9.7.1(5–6):

```
34         for N in 1..Group_Size(Finance) loop
35           accept Invite_In(Finance)(ID: ID_Numbers) do
36             I := ID;
37           end Invite_In;
38         end loop
39         -- Consult
40         for N in 1..Group_Size(Finance) loop
41           accept Show_Out(Finance)(ID: ID_Numbers) do
42             I := ID;
43           end Show_Out;
44         end loop;
45         Finance_Room.Open_Door;
```

For the other groups, the guards ‡47,51 in the selective accept statement use the Count attribute: E'Count gives the number of tasks currently waiting in the queue for entry E §9.9(4–5):

```
46       or
47         when Wake(Finance)'Count = 0 =>
48           accept Wake(Marketing);
49           -- As above with Marketing replacing Finance
50       or
51         when Wake(Finance)'Count = 0 and Wake(Marketing)'Count = 0 =>
52           accept Wake(Engineering);
53           -- As above with Engineering replacing Finance
54       or
55         terminate;
56       end select;
57     end loop;
58   end CEO;
```

This is used to implement the precedence requirement: if the CEO finds that more than one group is attempting to wake him, he will rendezvous with Wake(Marketing) only if there are no tasks waiting in the queue for Wake(Finance). The guard for Wake(Engineering) is correspondingly more complex. (There is a subtle race condition that prevents the precedence requirement from being fulfilled without the use of **pragma** Queuing_Policy as explained in Section 21.5.)

The employee tasks are very simple: an employee who needs to consult with the CEO registers at the department waiting room, waits until invited in and then consults with the CEO until shown out. Each task declaration has a discriminant, which is used to give the task its ID number. Delay statements of different durations are used to introduce some asymmetry into the execution of the program:

```
59  task type Finance_Task(ID: ID_Numbers);
60  task body Finance_Task is
61  begin
62    loop
63      delay 4.0;
64      Finance_Room.Register;
65      CEO.Invite_In(Finance)(ID);
66      CEO.Show_Out(Finance)(ID);
67    end loop;
68  end Finance_Task;
69
70  task type Marketing_Task(ID: ID_Numbers);
71  task body Marketing_Task is
72    -- As above with Marketing replacing Finance
73  task type Engineer_Task(ID: ID_Numbers);
74  task body Engineer_Task is
75    -- As above with Engineering replacing Finance
```

The tasks are allocated dynamically in loops so that each employee receives a distinct ID as a discriminant constraint in the allocator.

```
76  type Finance_Ptr   is access Finance_Task;
77  type Marketing_Ptr is access Marketing_Task;
78  type Engineer_Ptr  is access Engineer_Task;
79  Accountants:       array(1..5) of Finance_Ptr;
80  Salespersons:      array(1..8) of Marketing_Ptr;
81  Engineers:         array(1..7) of Engineer_Ptr;
82 begin
83  for I in Accountants'Range loop
84    Accountants(I) := new Finance_Task(ID_Numbers(I));
85  end loop;
86  -- Similarly for Salespersons and Engineers
```

Accesses to the tasks are stored in arrays so that the employees can be fired by using the **abort** statement. The CEO task will terminate because it has a **terminate** alternative ‡55. These constructs are explained in Section 19.1.

```
87  delay 15.0;
88  for I in Engineers'Range loop
89    abort Engineers(I).all;
90  end loop;
91  -- Similarly for Salepersons and Accountants
92 end CEOT;
```

18.5 Entry families

Entry families are used to declare sets of related entries:

```
task CEO is
  entry Wake(Departments);
  entry Invite_In(Departments)(ID: ID_Numbers);
  entry Show_Out(Departments)(ID:  ID_Numbers);
end CEO;
```

§9.5.2

> 2 entry_declaration ::=
> [overriding_indicator]
> **entry** defining_identifier [(discrete_subtype_definition)] parameter_profile;

(On overriding indicators see Section 8.6; overriding of entries is discussed in Section 17.4.)

§9.5.2

> 20 An entry_declaration with a discrete_subtype_definition (see 3.6) declares a *family* of distinct entries having the same profile, with one such entry for each value of the *entry index subtype* defined by the discrete_subtype_definition. A name for an entry of a family takes the form of an indexed_component, where the prefix denotes the entry_declaration for the family, and the index value identifies the entry within the family. The term *single entry* is used to refer to any entry other than an entry of an entry family.

Each entry of the family is a distinct entry with its own queue. Entry families are somewhat like arrays of entries: calls and accept statements for an entry of a family use indexed notation as shown, for example, in ‡33, 35, 41, 65, 66. The index need not be constant, but it is not possible to write an accept statement that will wait simultaneously on all the entries of a family. If `D` is a variable, **accept** `Wake(D)` waits for an entry call on the queue corresponding to the current value of `D`. This construct is used to perform a rendezvous sequentially with each member of the family ‡34–44. Of course you would only use this construct if you knew that each entry would actually be called; otherwise, the program could deadlock. See Section 19.3 for other polling techniques, and Section 18.8 for the rules for entry families of protected objects.

18.6 Protected subprograms

Let us now study the body of the protected object Room. The CEO task calls the *protected procedure* Open_Door to indicate that the waiting room for this group can be re-opened:

```
separate(CEOT)
protected body Room is
  procedure Open_Door is
  begin
    Entrance := Open;
  end Open_Door;
```

§9.5.1

> 2 Within the body of a protected function (or a function declared immediately within a protected_body), the current instance of the enclosing protected unit is defined to be a constant (that is, its subcomponents may be read but not updated). Within the body of a protected procedure (or a procedure declared immediately within a protected_body), and within an entry_body, the current instance is defined to be a variable (updating is permitted).

Unlike entries, protected procedures have no queues associated with them and a call is not blocked once it passes the outer exclusion "shell" of the protected object.

Several tasks can execute protected functions concurrently provided that no other task is executing a protected procedure or entry §9.5.1(4–5). The current instance of a protected unit is a constant §9.5.1(2), so a function cannot modifying its components and no race conditions can result. Protected functions are used to return a value that depends on the private components:

```
function Crowded return Boolean is
begin
  return Waiting >= Group_Size / 2;
end Crowded;
```

An access to a protected subprogram §3.10(11) can be declared.

18.7 The requeue statement

As employee tasks call the entry Register to enter the Room, the calls will be enqueued upon the private entry Wait_for_Last_Member until the last member of the group has entered. At that point, it closes the Entrance door and opens the Exit_Door:

```
108     entry Register when Entrance = Open is
109     begin
110       Waiting := Waiting + 1;
111       if Waiting < Size then
112         requeue Wait_for_Last_Member with abort;
113       else
114         Waiting := Waiting - 1;
115         Entrance  := Closed;
116         Exit_Door := Open;
117       end if;
118     end Register;
```

The barrier of Wait_for_Last_Member is initially closed so that the tasks will be blocked until the last task of the group has registered and opened the barrier:

```
119     entry Wait_for_Last_Member when Exit_Door = Open is
120     begin
121       Waiting := Waiting - 1;
122       if Waiting = 0 then
123         Exit_Door := Closed;
124         requeue CEO.Wake(Department) with abort;
125       end if;
126     end Wait_for_Last_Member;
127   end Room;
```

The implementation of the protected object Room is based on the concept of *cascaded wakeup* and uses the **requeue** statement to move calling tasks from one entry to another. Initially, tasks calling Register are requeued on the entry Wait_for_Last_Member ‡112. The barrier of this entry Exit_Door=Open is false, so the calls will be enqueued. When the last member of the group executes Register, it will set Exit_Door to Open ‡116, making the barrier of Wait_for_Last_Member true. As each task completes its execution of this entry, the barrier is re-evaluated and since it remains true, another waiting task will be unblocked. This cascade of awakened tasks continues until all tasks enqueued on Wait_for_Last_Member are released and their protected actions completed. The last released task will close Exit_Door ‡123 and awaken the CEO by requeuing itself on the entry CEO.Wake for its department ‡124.

§9.5.4

> 2 requeue_statement ::= **requeue** *entry*_name [**with abort**];
>
> 8 For the execution of a requeue on an entry of a target task, after leaving the enclosing callable construct, the named entry is checked to see if it is open and the requeued call is either selected immediately or queued, as for a normal entry call (see 9.5.3).
>
> 9 For the execution of a requeue on an entry of a target protected object, after leaving the enclosing callable construct:
>
> 10 • if the requeue is an internal requeue (that is, the requeue is back on an entry of the same protected object—see 9.5), the call is added to the queue of the named entry and the ongoing protected action continues (see 9.5.1);

(**with abort** is discussed in Section 19.1.3.)

Room contains examples of requeue on both task entries ‡124 and protected entries ‡112.

Closing the entrance door ‡115 closes the barrier Entrance=Open of entry Register and prevents other employees of the same type from overtaking the group that has been formed.

Requeue is also essential to avoid overtaking when awakening the CEO. Suppose that a group of accountants has been formed, that is, the last task of the group has completed Wait_for_Last_Member. Without requeue, the last accountant task would have to complete the protected action and then call the entry CEO.Wake(Finance) from within the sequence of statements of its task body:

```
Finance_Room.Register;
if I_Am_Last_Member then
  CEO.Wake(Finance);
end if;
```

This task could be preempted—and a group of engineers could be formed and enqueued on CEO.Wake(Engineering)—*after* the protected action Finance_Room.Register completes, but *before* the call to CEO.Wake(Finance) is issued. With requeue, the protected action of the last accountant task is not *completed* until the task entry call has been made and immediately selected or enqueued. If it is enqueued, the guards on the accept statements of the selective accept prevent overtaking.

18.8 Additional rules for protected types*

The following subsections present addition rules for protected types.

18.8.1 *Formal parameters in barriers*

§9.5.2

> 18 A name that denotes a formal parameter of an entry_body is not allowed within the entry_barrier of the entry_body.

In the protected object `Buffer`, we cannot refuse to append negative numbers by writing:

```
entry Append(I: in  Integer)
  when Count < Index'Last and I >= 0 is
    -- Error, the barrier cannot use the formal parameter I
```

The reason is that all calls on the queue for an entry are considered to be waiting for the *same* event to occur. If you want calls to wait for distinct events, you should use different entries or an entry family. Furthermore, allowing formal parameters in barrier would make it inefficient to evaluate barriers, because the run-time system would have to scan the entry queue and re-evaluate the barrier *for each call*. With this rule, the code executed for each barrier is fixed regardless of how many calls are enqueued.

If blocking of a call really does depend on the formal parameters, call an entry with the barrier `True`, examine the formal parameters within the body and requeue on other private entries. For example, in the CEO case study, we might have considered passing a parameter to the `Register` entry so that last caller need not register:

```
entry Register(Is_Last: Boolean) when not Is_Last is  -- Error
```

Instead, all members of a group call this entry and a decision to requeue or not is made by performing the computation `Waiting < Size` on a component of the protected object and a discriminant.

18.8.2 *Potentially blocking operations*

A protected action is not allowed to invoke an operation that could result in blocking the calling task *within* the protected action.

§9.5.1

> 8 During a protected action, it is a bounded error to invoke an operation that is *potentially blocking*. ...

Potentially blocking operations are listed in §9.5.1(9–16); in particular, calling an entry is potentially blocking. The bounded error *need not* be detected by the implementation §9.5.1(17), though Annex §H High Integrity Systems contains **pragma** `Detect_Blocking` §H.5, which requires an implementation to to detect this error.

Ada 95

pragma `Detect_Blocking` is not in Ada 95.

18.8.3 Parameters of the requeue target

The requeue statement is restricted as follows:

§9.5.4

> 3 The *entry*_name of a requeue_statement shall resolve to denote an entry (the *target entry*) that either has no parameters, or that has a profile that is type conformant (see 6.3.1) with the profile of the innermost enclosing entry_body or accept_statement.
>
> 12 If the new entry named in the requeue_statement has formal parameters, then during the execution of the accept_statement or entry_body corresponding to the new entry, the formal parameters denote the same objects as did the corresponding formal parameters of the callable construct completed by the requeue. In any case, no parameters are specified in a requeue_statement; any parameter passing is implicit.

In the case study, both requeues are to entries without parameters. The entry family index in **requeue** `CEO.Wake(Group)` is not a parameter.

18.8.4 Internal and external requeues

A call or requeue can be to the same protected object—an *internal call or requeue*—or it can be to a subprogram or entry of a different object—an *external call or requeue* §9.5(2–7). (A call must be to a subprogram, because a call to an entry is potentially blocking, as noted previously). An external call or requeue uses the syntax of a selected component to distinguish it from an internal call or requeue: **requeue** `Wait_for_Last_Member` is internal and correct, but

requeue `Room.Wait_for_Last_Member` is an external call to the same protected object and thus incorrect because it is potentially blocking §9.5.1(15).

There is an important difference between the semantics of internal and external requeues:

§9.5.4

> 10 • if the requeue is an internal requeue (that is, the requeue is back on an entry of the same protected object—see 9.5), the call is added to the queue of the named entry and the ongoing protected action continues (see 9.5.1);
>
> 11 • if the requeue is an external requeue (that is, the target protected object is not implicitly the same as the current object—see 9.5), a protected action is started on the target object and proceeds as for a normal entry call (see 9.5.3).

An external call or requeue will initiate a new protected action so it may have to wait to obtain exclusive access to the protected object. An internal requeue is immediately enqueued on the existing queue; then, as part of the completion of the protected action, the barriers will be re-evaluated. The requeued task will receive no precedence over tasks already enqueued on entries, but we are assured that if some entry is open, a protected action will be immediately executed for some task.

18.8.5 Families of protected entries

An entry family can be declared in a protected unit; like an entry family for a task, it can be considered as if it were an array of entries, but the syntax of the entry body is more flexible. One entry body with an entry_index_specification defines the common code for processing all entries in the family.

§9.5.2

> 6 entry_body_formal_part ::= [(entry_index_specification)] parameter_profile
> 7 entry_barrier ::= **when** condition
> 8 entry_index_specification ::= **for** defining_identifier **in** discrete_subtype_definition

In the following declarations, `E1` is a family of entries each with one formal parameter, while `E2` a single entry with two formal parameters:

```
entry E1(Departments)(I: in Integer);
entry E2(D: in Departments; I: in Integer);
```

There is a *separate* queue for each member of the family `E1`, but only one queue for `E2`. The barrier of `E1` can depend on its entry index `D`, but, as we have seen, the barrier of `E2` cannot depend on its formal parameter `D`.

Projects

1. Implement a solution to the problem of the Readers and Writers using protected objects. In this problem, exclusive write-access to a resource is required although multiple tasks can have read-only access. This is trivial to implement using a protected object (a function is used for reading and a procedure for writing) as long as there are no requirements for preventing starvation. State the requirement that your solution fulfils.
2. Write a program that demonstrates that the preference for serving entry queues is essential for the correctness of the case study in Section 18.1.1.
3. If the Real-Time Annex is not included in an Ada implementation, the entry queuing policy `Priority_Queuing` may not be available. Modify the CEO case study so that it works even if `FIFO_Queuing` is in effect.
4. Write a program to demonstrate how to work around the limitation that barriers cannot depend on formal parameters (Section 18.8).

Quizzes

Quiz 1:

```
procedure Main is
  task T is
    entry E1(N: Integer);
    entry E2;
  end T;
  task body T is
  begin
    accept E1(N: Integer) do
      select
        when N > 0 => accept E2;
      end select;
    end E1;
  exception
    when Ex: others =>
      Put_Line("Task T " & Exception_Name(Ex));
  end T;

  task A;
  task body A is
  begin
    T.E1(0);
  exception
    when Ex: others =>
      Put_Line("Task A " & Exception_Name(Ex));
  end A;

begin
  T.E2;
exception
  when Ex: others =>
    Put_Line("Main " & Exception_Name(Ex));
end Main;
```

Quiz 2:

```
task type T is
  entry E;
end T;

task body T is
  procedure P is
  begin
    accept E;
  end P;
begin
  begin
    accept E do
      accept E;
    end E;
  end;
end T;
```

Quiz 3:

```
protected P is
  entry E1;
  entry E2;
end P;
procedure Proc renames P.E1;
protected body P is
  entry E1 when True is
  begin
    null;
  end E1;
  entry E2 when True is
  begin
    Proc;
    requeue Proc;
  end E2;
end P;
```

Quiz 4:

```
procedure Main is

  protected PO is
    entry E;
  private
    C: Character := Character'First;
  end PO;
  protected body PO is
    entry E when Character'Pred(C) < 'A' is
    begin
      null;
    end E;
  end PO;

begin
  PO.E;
exception
  when Ex: others =>
    Put_Line("Main " & Exception_Name(Ex));
end Main;
```

Quiz 5:

```
  task type T;
  type Ptr is access T;

  function F return Ptr is
  begin
    return new T;
  end;

  task body T is
    X: Ptr := F;
    Y: Ptr := new T;
  begin
    null;
  end T;

  Z: Ptr := new T;
```

Chapter 19
Concurrency (Continued)

19.1 Activation and termination

Tasks must be activated and terminated. It is important to specify what happens if an exception is raised during activation and to define when a task can participate in a rendezvous. We have to specify what happens if a task is terminated during the execution of a protected action or a rendezvous. Finally, the termination of a task must take into account the tasks that it activated.

§9

> 10 Over time, tasks proceed through various *states*. A task is initially *inactive*; upon activation, and prior to its *termination* it is either *blocked* (as part of some task interaction) or *ready* to run. While ready, a task competes for the available *execution resources* that it requires to run.

19.1.1 Activation

It is important to distinguish between the elaboration of a task and its activation. Elaboration is performed as part of the elaboration of the enclosing package, subprogram or task. Elaboration of the task declaration can set its priority §D.1 and the amount of storage allocated for the task §13.3(61); elaboration of the task body essentially does nothing §9.1(13). Activation creates the task and allows it to begin execution, or at least to compete for the available execution resources. The rules for task activation §9.2 can be summarized as follows:

- Task that are declared within a unit (such as the producer and consumer tasks) are activated before the enclosing unit begins executing its statements §9.2(3). The task executing the enclosing unit waits at the **begin** until all its tasks have been activated §9.2(5).
- Task created by allocators (such as the employee tasks in the CEO program) are activated as part of the evaluation of the allocator §9.2(4).

The rationale for these rules is that during the activation of a task, the elaboration of the declarations in the task body §9.2(1) may raise an exception; similarly, the enclosing unit may raise an exception after elaborating the task §9.2(5–6). The rules ensure that in such cases the task is not activated, but instead the exception is propagated to the enclosing unit.

19.1.2 Termination

Termination of tasks is defined in terms of a dependence tree. Each task *depends* on one or more *masters* §9.3(1), which are the enclosing dynamic constructs such as subprograms or tasks §7.6.1(3). The main subprogram is called by an anonymous *environment task* §10.2(8). Tasks declared in library packages are considered to be dependent on this master. The producer, consumer and buffer tasks in the case studies were declared within the main subprogram and depend upon it.

Tasks created by allocators (such as the employee tasks) depend on the master containing the declaration of the access *type* §9.3(2). The reason is that the task can live as long as the type lives; it can even become a garbage task:

```
E := new Engineer_Task(7);
E := null;
```

A task cannot terminate until all its dependent tasks have terminated.

§9.3

> 5 A task is said to be *completed* when the execution of its corresponding task_body is completed. A task is said to be *terminated* when any finalization of the task_body has been performed (see 7.6.1). The first step of finalizing a master (including a task_body) is to wait for the termination of any tasks dependent on the master. The task executing the master is blocked until all the dependents have terminated. Any remaining finalization is then performed and the master is left.

The rules in §9.3(5) explain why we could write a null body for the main subprogram of the producer–consumer program. The main subprogram is a master, and the producer and consumer tasks depend on it, so the main subprogram cannot terminate until they do. The producer completes when it completes the statements of its task body. Since the consumer tasks never complete, the main subprogram waits indefinitely. The program is deadlocked and the execution must be stopped by an operating system command.

How can server tasks such as `Buffer` and `CEO` be terminated? Almost by definition, a server task does not know when it has finished serving all potential clients. One possibility is to declare a special entry that can be used to signal the server:

```
loop
  select
    accept Append(I: in Integer) do ...
  or
    accept Take(I: out Integer) do ...
  or
    accept Stop;
    exit;
  end select;
end loop;
```

A better solution is to use the terminate alternative §9.7.1(7) on the selective accept statement (‡55 of the CEO program). If every task that could possibly call the entries of the server task is completed (or also waiting on a selective accept statement with a terminate alternative), the server task becomes completed §9.3(6).

A protected object is not a task and therefore it is meaningless to ask about its termination. However, tasks can be executing protected actions and they can be blocked on entry queues. Protected actions will always complete, either normally or by **requeue**, but it is possible that a task will be enqueued indefinitely on an entry queue. This happens, for example, in the case study of the producer–consumer in Section 18.1.1: the producer task produces a finite number of items, but the consumer tasks call the Take entry in a non-terminating loop.

19.1.3 Aborting a task

Any task, including one blocked on an entry queue, can be terminated with an abort statement.

§9.8

> 1 An abort_statement causes one or more tasks to become abnormal, thus preventing any further interaction with such tasks. ...
>
> 2 abort_statement ::= **abort** *task*_name {, *task*_name};

In the CEO program, we abort all the employee tasks because they contain infinite loops. Task CEO need not be aborted, because it contains a selective accept statement with a terminate alternative. Once the employee tasks are terminated and the main subprogram is completed, there are no longer any potential callers, so the CEO task will terminate.

The semantics of the abort statement ensure—as far as practicable—that the overall consistency of the tasks in a program is maintained.

§9.8

> 5 When the execution of a construct is *aborted* (including that of a task_body or of a sequence_of_statements), the execution of every construct included within the aborted execution is also aborted, except for executions included within the execution of an *abort-deferred* operation; the execution of an abort-deferred operation continues to completion without being affected by the abort; the following are the abort-deferred operations:

Abort-deferred operations are listed in §9.8(6–11). In particular, protected actions and rendezvous are abort-deferred.

The implementation need not perform the abort immediately; instead, it can defer the abort to places that actually affect the synchronization of the program.

§9.8

> 15 If the execution of an entry call is aborted, an immediate attempt is made to cancel the entry call (see 9.5.3). If the execution of a construct is aborted at a time when the execution is blocked, other than for an entry call, at a point that is outside the execution of an abort-deferred operation, then the execution of the construct completes immediately. For an abort due to an abort_statement, these immediate effects occur before the execution of the abort_statement completes. Other than for these immediate cases, the execution of a construct that is aborted does not necessarily complete before the abort_statement completes. However, the execution of the aborted construct completes no later than its next *abort completion point* (if any) that occurs outside of an abort-deferred operation; the following are abort completion points for an execution:

Abort completion points are listed in §9.8(16–19); examples are the start or end of an entry call or accept statement.

A task that is in an entry queue is immediately aborted, because the task has yet to affect the accepting task or protected object. The question now arises: what about a task that has executed a **requeue**? On the one hand, the task has already started a protected action and should be allowed to complete it. On the other hand, the task could be indefinitely blocked and presumably we had a good reason to abort it. The Ada language standard does not attempt to choose between these alternatives; instead, when you write a requeue statement, you can choose whether to allow the abort to cancel the call, or whether the call should be protected from cancellation §9.5.4(13–16). In the CEO program, the abort statement is used when all employees are being fired and the company shut down, so we choose to allow cancellation by specifying **with abort** on the requeue statement ‡112,124.

19.1.4 *Task attributes*

The attribute `T'Callable` §9.9(2) can be used to check if an entry of task `T` can be called, that is, if the task is not completed or abnormal. `T'Terminated` §9.9(3) checks if `T` is terminated or not.

19.2 Exceptions

There are special rules for exceptions that occur in multitasking programs. An exception in one task should not affect another task:

§11.4

> 3 When an exception occurrence is raised by the execution of a given construct, the rest of the execution of that construct is *abandoned*; that is, any portions of the execution that have not yet taken place are not performed. The construct is first completed, and then left, as explained in 7.6.1. Then:
>
> 4 • If the construct is a task_body, the exception does not propagate further;

If two tasks are engaged in a rendezvous, the accepting task is given the opportunity to handle the exception *within the accept statement*; if the exception propagates outside the statement, the calling task is also notified:

§9.5.2

> 24 ... When an exception is propagated from the handled_sequence_of_statements of an accept_statement, the same exception is also raised by the execution of the corresponding entry_call_statement.

The predefined exception `Tasking_Error` is used to signal inconsistencies in the tasks of a program; in particular, calling a task that has already completed or become abnormal raises `Tasking_Error` §9.5.3(21). The exception is also raised in case of problems during task activation; see §9.2(5) for details. Certain catastrophic errors cause `Program_Error` to be raised, for example, an exception in the evaluation of a barrier §9.5.3(17), and a selective accept statement with no open alternatives §9.7.1(21). You should keep barrier and guard expressions very simple so that you can prove that these problems will not occur.

Every task body should include an exception handler. In the absence of a handler, an exception will cause the task to terminate silently while the rest of the program continues to execute.

19.3 Time

So far we have discussed concurrency in terms of synchronization constructs (protected actions and rendezvous) that do not take time into account. However, many programs, in particular, real-time systems, will have timing constraints. In this section, we present the core concepts of time in Ada; extensions for real-time programming are discussed in Section 21.8.

There are two concepts that must be clearly distinguished: a *point* in time and an *interval* between two points in time. Points of time are declared to be of the private type `Time` in package `Ada.Calendar` §9.6(8,10), while intervals are declared to be of the predefined fixed point type `Duration` §A.1(43) and §9.6(7):

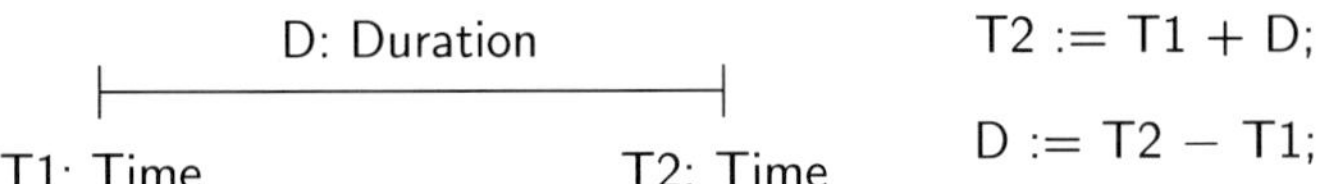
D: Duration
T1: Time
T2: Time
T2 := T1 + D;
D := T2 − T1;

`Duration` is in seconds so the value `0.000_001` of the type represents one microsecond.

Function `Clock` §9.6(12,23) returns the current time, and the package `Ada.Calendar` contains subprograms §9.6(13–15, 24–25) for decomposing a value of type `Time` into year, month, day and seconds, and conversely for creating a value of type `Time` from these values. The package also has the expected arithmetical and relational operations on values of the types `Time` and `Duration` §9.6(16–17); for example:

```
function "-"(Left: Time; Right: Time) return Duration;
```

returns the interval between two points of time.

Values of types `Time` and `Duration` are used to specify delays.

§9.6

> 1 A delay_statement is used to block further execution until a specified *expiration* time is reached. The expiration time can be specified either as a particular point in time (in a delay_until_statement), or in seconds from the current time (in a delay_relative_statement). The language-defined package Calendar provides definitions for a type Time and associated operations, including a function Clock that returns the current time.
>
> 2 delay_statement ::= delay_until_statement | delay_relative_statement
> 3 delay_until_statement ::= **delay until** *delay*_expression;
> 4 delay_relative_statement ::= **delay** *delay*_expression;
>
> 21 The task executing a delay_statement is blocked until the expiration time is reached, at which point it becomes ready again. If the expiration time has already passed, the task is not blocked.

A task is unblocked upon expiration of the delay, but there is no guarantee that the task is scheduled immediately; other, higher-priority, tasks can be scheduled instead. In other words, the delay is a lower bound on the interval that the task will not be running. Even if the task is not blocked—because the delay is zero or negative—the delay statement is meaningful; it is an abort completion point §9.8(18), and it can cause a context switch. In fact, **delay** 0.0 is a convenient way to call the scheduler.

19.3.1 *Case study: periodic task with delay*

Control algorithms that are implemented by periodic tasks can use delay statements to execute subprograms at predetermined time intervals. The following program prints '*' 50 times, once every 0.2 seconds; in addition, it prints the Start and Stop times so that we can check that it executes for about $50 \times 0.2 = 10$ seconds:

period

```
1 with Ada.Text_IO; use Ada.Text_IO;
2 with Ada.Calendar; use Ada.Calendar;
3 procedure Period is
4   Start, Stop: Time;
```

The periodic task calls Clock to obtain the current time; then the Interval of type Duration is added to obtain the time of the Next execution of the periodic task ‡8. The program executes a delay_until_statement with this time ‡12:

```
5   task Periodic;
6   task body Periodic is
7     Interval: constant Duration := 0.2;
8     Next: Time := Clock + Interval;
9   begin
10    Start := Clock;
11    for N in 1..50 loop
12      delay until Next;
13      Put('*');
14      Next := Next + Interval;
15    end loop;
16    Stop := Clock;
17  end Periodic;
```

Upon expiration of the delay, the "algorithm" of the task (to put a character) is executed ‡13 and the Next wakeup time is computed ‡14.

The main program checks for the termination of the periodic task. Additional computation could be done in the meantime (perhaps by additional tasks), but we have simply used a **delay** statement to ensure that the scheduler can be allowed to schedule the periodic task:

```
begin
   loop
      exit when Periodic'Terminated;
      delay 0.01;
   cnd loop;
   Put_Line("Elapsed time = " & Duration'Image(Stop-Start));
end Period;
```

Do not replace the delay_until_statement with a delay_relative_statement:

```
delay Interval;
```

The periodic task will then be executed once every `Interval` seconds *plus* the number of seconds it takes to execute the computation *plus* the number of seconds that the task is ready but not scheduled! It is less obvious, but you also don't want to write:

```
delay Next - Clock;
```

because a race condition could occur. Suppose that the task were preempted *after* evaluating `Clock`, but *before* evaluating the subtraction. The interval during which the task was blocked would not be taken into account in the computation of the delay.

The delay_until_statement ensures that the program is self-synchronizing, regardless of the variability of the computation represented by the `Put` statement.

19.4 Time formatting and time zones*

Global software systems like reservation systems need to take account of the time zone in which a program is executing. The package `Ada.Calendar.Time_Zones` §9.6.1(2–7) declares a function `UTC_Time_Offset` §9.6.1(6), which returns a value of type `Time_Offset` §9.6.1(4), the number of minutes between the local time and *Coordinated Universal Time (UTC)*. *Greenwich Mean Time (GMT)* is sometimes used in place of UTC, but the term GMT is outdated.

The package `Ada.Calendar.Arithmetic` §9.6.1(8–14) extends the arithmetic capabilities of `Ada.Calendar` to include arithmetic on days in addition to arithmetic on seconds.

`Ada.Calendar.Formatting` §9.6.1(15–39) includes further utilities for working with time: procedure `Split` §9.6(29) extends `Split` in `Ada.Calendar` §9.6(14) and further breaks down a value into hours, minutes, the number of seconds in a day and "sub-seconds." Other subprograms can now take time zones into account. The functions `Image` and `Value` §9.6.1(35–38) support conversion between times and strings like the attributes of scalar types.

`Ada.Calendar.Arithmetic` and `Ada.Calendar.Formatting` both support *leap seconds*. Since 1960, time standards have been based upon atomic clocks, rather than on astronomical observations (*International Atomic Time (TAI)*). However, the rotation of the earth is slowing down, primarily because of tidal friction, so a day as measured by the rotation of the earth is always a bit longer than that measured by an atomic clock. To maintain synchronization between them, UTC is corrected by adding a leap second every year or two to the TAI year. Leap seconds are problematic to implement because it is impossible to predict when they will occur.

Ada 95

These packages are new for Ada 2005.

19.5 Representation of Time and Duration*

As with all fixed point types, there is a tradeoff between range and precision in the implementation of `Duration`. The requirements are as follows:

§9.6

> 27 The implementation of the type Duration shall allow representation of time intervals (both positive and negative) up to at least 86400 seconds (one day); Duration'Small shall not be greater than twenty milliseconds. The implementation of the type Time shall allow representation of all dates with year numbers in the range of Year_Number; it may allow representation of other dates as well (both earlier and later).
>
> 30 Whenever possible in an implementation, the value of Duration'Small should be no greater than 100 microseconds.

Twenty milliseconds is achievable using the 50–60 Hz frequency of ordinary alternating-current electricity. However, almost all computers have an electronic time base, so the 100 microsecond precision should be easy to implement. The subtype `Year_Number` requires that the type `Time` represent at least all dates between the years 1901 and 2399.

There is an additional tradeoff between efficiency and the rate at which the clock is updated. This is specified by the value `System.Tick`:

§9.6

> 23 The time base associated with the type Time of package Calendar is implementation defined. The function Clock of package Calendar returns a value representing the current time for this time base. The implementation-defined value of the named number System.Tick (see 13.7) is an approximation of the length of the real-time interval during which the value of Calendar.Clock remains constant.

§9.6

> 35 There is no necessary relationship between System.Tick (the resolution of the clock of package Calendar) and Duration'Small (the *small* of type Duration).

`Duration` might have enough precision to store time intervals down to single microseconds, but for efficiency, the clock may be "ticked" only once every 50 microseconds.

A time base is *monotonic* if the value of its clock never decreases, but this may not be true for the function `Clock` if the computer system clock is adjusted, for example, because of daylight savings time.

§9.6

> 31 The time base for delay_relative_statements should be monotonic; it need not be the same time base as used for Calendar.Clock.

`Time` and `Duration` have relatively large ranges with reasonable precision, and are sufficient for "ordinary" timing requirements, such as financial computations and tasks with periods in the tens of milliseconds. More precise timing is available if your system supports Annex §D Real-Time Systems (Chapter 21).

19.6 Timed and conditional entry calls*

When a task calls an entry of another task or a protected object, it risks being blocked indefinitely. An alternate programming technique is for a task to specify a time limit on how long it is willing to wait for an entry call to be accepted. The timed_entry_call cancels a entry call if it is not accepted by the time that a delay expires.

§9.7.2

```
2 timed_entry_call ::=
    select
      entry_call_alternative
    or
      delay_alternative
    end select;
```

A conditional_entry_call is equivalent to a timed_entry_call with a delay of zero.

§9.7.3

```
2 conditional_entry_call ::=
    select
      entry_call_alternative
    else
      sequence_of_statements
    end select;
```

Of course, it will take some time to determine if an entry call is ready, because the barriers will have to be evaluated and a check has to be made if the task or protected object is ready to accept the call. But if the entry can be called, the else-part or delay alternative will not be taken.

Conditional entry calls can be used to implement *polling*, where a task checks for the occurrence of an event and continues to execute if the event has not occurred.

Be careful not to confuse these constructs with the selective accept statement, which has a similar syntax (Sections 18.2 and 19.8). A timed or conditional entry call is used in the *calling task*, not the accepting task. There is no construct in Ada that enables a calling task to block waiting for one of several calls to be accepted.

The semantics of a timed_entry_call is defined as follows.

§9.7.2

4 For the execution of a timed_entry_call, the *entry*_name, *procedure*_name, or *procedure*_prefix, and any actual parameters are evaluated, as for a simple entry call (see 9.5.3) or procedure call (see 6.4). The expiration time (see 9.6) for the call is determined by evaluating the *delay*_expression of the delay_alternative. If the call is an entry call or a call on a procedure implemented by an entry, the entry call is then issued. Otherwise, the call proceeds as described in 6.4 for a procedure call, followed by the sequence_of_statements of the entry_call_alternative; the sequence_of_statements of the delay_alternative is ignored.

5 If the call is queued (including due to a requeue-with-abort), and not selected before the expiration time is reached, an attempt to cancel the call is made. If the call completes due to the cancellation, the optional sequence_of_statements of the delay_alternative is executed; if the entry call completes normally, the optional sequence_of_statements of the entry_call_alternative is executed.

The complexity of the rules in §9.7.2(4) is due to the possibility that a primitive procedure of a synchronized, task or protected interface may be implemented by an entry (Section 17.4).

Do not use a timed or conditional entry call if the guard of the entry uses the entry attribute `E'Count` §9.9(7–8). It is possible that between the time that the accepting task evaluates `E'Count` and the time it executes the accept statement, the task on the queue was cancelled. This can lead to deadlock.

19.6.1 *Case study: periodic task with conditional entry call*

The technique of polling is demonstrated in the following program that is a modification of the case study in Section 19.3. A task `User` waits for the user to enter a string and then accepts the entry `Trigger`:

cond

```
with Ada.Text_IO; use Ada.Text_IO;
with Ada.Calendar; use Ada.Calendar;
procedure Cond is
  task User is
    entry Trigger;
  end User;
  task body User is
  begin
    declare
      S: String := Get_Line;
    begin
      null;
    end;
    accept Trigger;
    Put_Line("User trigger");
  end User;
```

The periodic task (putting a character) now appears within a conditional entry call that attempts to call the entry `Trigger` of the task `User`:

```
  Period: constant Duration := 0.2;
  Next: Time := Clock + Period;
begin
  loop
    select
      User.Trigger;
      exit;
    else
      delay until Next;
      Put('*');
      Next := Next + Period;
    end select;
  end loop;
end Cond;
```

Until a string is entered, the call will not be *immediately* accepted so the sequence of statements following the **else** is executed. After a string is entered, the *next* entry call will succeed and the loop will be exited.

19.7 Asynchronous transfer of control*

In the case study in the previous section, the periodic task must explicitly poll the user task to check for the trigger. Another possibility is to have the user task interrupt the execution of the periodic task when the triggering event occurs. This can be done with an *asynchronous transfer of control (ATC)*.

§9.7.4

```
2 asynchronous_select ::=
     select
        triggering_alternative
     then abort
        abortable_part
     end select;
```

The first statement of the triggering_alternative is called the triggering_statement and it can be an entry call or a delay statement. As with a conditional entry call, if the entry call can be selected immediately or the delay is expired, then the abortable part is not executed. Otherwise, it begins it execution, there are now two possibilities.

§9.7.4

8 If the abortable_part completes and is left prior to completion of the triggering_statement, an attempt to cancel the triggering_statement is made. If the attempt to cancel succeeds (see 9.5.3 and 9.6), the asynchronous_select is complete.

9 If the triggering_statement completes other than due to cancellation, the abortable_part is aborted (if started but not yet completed—see 9.8). If the triggering_statement completes normally, the optional sequence_of_statements of the triggering_alternative is executed after the abortable_part is left.

19.7.1 Case study: periodic task with ATC

The periodic task can be written as an abortable_part:

async

```
with Ada.Text_IO; use Ada.Text_IO;
with Ada.Calendar; use Ada.Calendar;
procedure Async is
  task User is         -- as before
  task body User is    -- as before

  Period: constant Duration := 0.2;
  Next: Time := Clock + Period;
begin
  select
    User.Trigger;
  then abort
    for I in 1 .. 50 loop
      delay until Next;
      Put('*');
      Next := Next + Period;
    end loop;
  end select;
end Async;
```

When a string is entered, the entry call `User.Trigger` is accepted and the abortable part is aborted. The loop in this program is finite so that the abortable part can complete, after which an attempt is made to cancel the triggering statement, the entry call. While this will succeed, the task `User` will still be blocked waiting for input and must be terminated manually.

Asynchronous transfer of control can be used to implement a *watchdog* task that terminates a computation that has overrun the amount of time allocated for its execution. In a real-time system, ATC can be used to terminate an iterative computation when a time interval expires or an event occurs; the "best available" result is then used:

```
Result: Float := ...;         -- Initial estimate of the result
Needed: Time  := ...;         -- Time when the result is needed

select
  delay until Needed;         -- Use current Result
then abort
  loop
    Refine_The_Value(Result, Error);
    exit when Error < ... ;   -- Result is good enough
  end loop;
end select;
```

Section 21.9 describes other constructs that can limit the execution time of a task.

19.8 Alternatives for selective accept

In place of a terminate alternative, a selective accept statement may have a delay alternative or an else-part; these can be used to implement timeouts or polling in an *accepting task* §9.7.1(10–11). For example, we could modify the CEO task to include a delay alternative:

ceod

```
      select
        accept Wake(Finance_Group);
          ...
      or
        when Wake(Finance_Group)'Count = 0 =>
          accept Wake(Marketing_Group);
            ...
      or
        when Wake(Finance_Group)'Count = 0 and
             Wake(Marketing_Group)'Count = 0 =>
          accept Wake(Engineering_Group);
            ...
      or
        delay 1.0;
        ...
      end select;
```

If no group calls one of the Wake entries within one second, the CEO performs some other activity instead of being blocked waiting for entry calls.

A realistic application of this technique would be in an alarm system that receives periodic messages from a sensor. If no message is received within a given time interval, the system can assume that the line has been cut and can raise an alarm.

An else-part can be used to allow the accepting task to perform a computation if there are no calling tasks that can be immediately accepted. If all alternatives are closed and there is an else-part, Program_Error will not be raised §9.7.1(21).

The terminate alternative, one or more delay alternatives and the else-part are mutually exclusive §9.7.1(12).

19.9 Case study: concurrent simulation

This section presents a concurrent version of the discrete event simulation. Instead of creating all the events before running the simulation, separate tasks will create the events and simulate them. In fact, a separate task will be used to create events of each subsystem of the rocket.

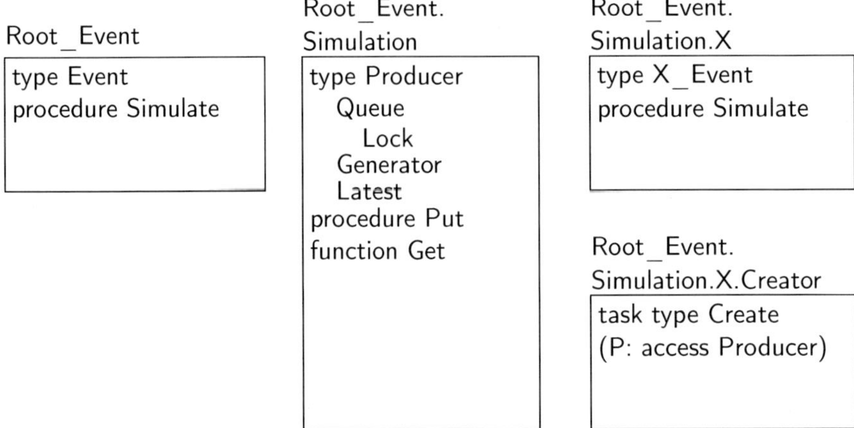

Fig. 19.1 Concurrent simulation framework

The program will be sufficiently general so that several independent simulations could be run within the same program.

Figure 19.1 shows the simulation framework. As before, package `Root_Event` provides the abstract tagged type `Event` and the abstract procedure `Simulate`. A simulation is defined by a child package `Root_Event.Simulation` that declares a `Producer` type. This type contains the data associated with a single simulation: a `Queue` with a protected component `Lock` to synchronize access between the event creators and the task doing the simulation, a random number `Generator`, and an indication of the `Latest` simulated time already used, so that a monotonic sequence of events can be created. The interface to the queue is through subprograms `Put` and `Get` that take parameters of type `Producer`, rather than of the encapsulated `Queue`.

For each subsystem `X` to be simulated, a child package `Root_Event.Simulation.X` is declared containing the derived events and the overridden `Simulate` procedure. A further child package declares a type for a task that `Create`'s events. This task takes an access discriminant (Section 12.7) to the `Producer` object where the task will enqueue its events.

We now specialize the simulation framework for the rocket. The usual derived types and simulation subprograms are declared, followed by package `Rocket_Simulation` (Figure 19.2). This package contains a `Producer` object and `Create` objects (tasks) for each derived type. The tasks create objects concurrently and enqueue them.

The main subprogram `Rocket` contains the standard simulation loop. It removes the events from the producer `R` one-by-one and dispatches them to the appropriate `Simulate` procedure. The creators have infinite loops with delay statements to regulate the rate of event creations; the simulation loop runs continuously, blocking on the queue's `Lock` if the queue is empty.

To generalize to more than one simultaneous simulation, another simulation package with a `Producer` object can be declared. Instead of a single loop directly within the main subprogram (which is executed by the environment task), each simulation loop would be placed in a separate task.

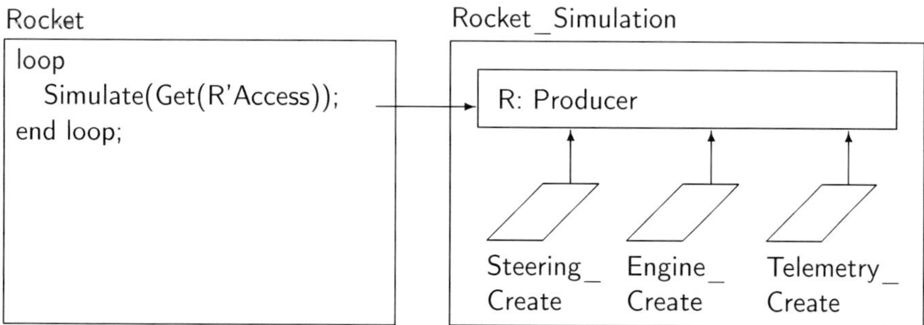

Fig. 19.2 Concurrent rocket simulation

We now present the essential part of the source code for the concurrent rocket simulation, starting with the package `Root_Event.Simulation`. The visible part of the package specification declares the type `Producer` and the two subprograms `Put` and `Get`:

rockett

```
with Heterogeneous_Priority_Queue;
with Ada.Numerics.Discrete_Random;
package Root_Event.Simulation is
  type Producer is limited private;

  procedure Put(E: in Event'Class; P: in out Producer);
  function  Get(P: access Producer) return Event'Class;
```

The rest of the declarations can be in the private part because they are used only by child packages. Type `Producer` has three fields: a `Queue` implemented by instantiating a generic package, a random number `Generator` obtained by instantiating the library package `Discrete_Random`, and the `Latest` time component:

```
private
  package Event_Queue is new Heterogeneous_Priority_Queue(Event'Class);
  package Random_Time is new Ada.Numerics.Discrete_Random(Natural);
  type Producer is
    record
      Queue:     aliased Event_Queue.Queue;
      Generator: Random_Time.Generator;
      Latest:    Simulation_Time := Simulation_Time'First;
    end record;
  function Random(P: Producer) return Natural;
  function Random_Update(P: access Producer) return Simulation_Time;
end Root_Event.Simulation;
```

The generic package Heterogeneous_Priority_Queue (not shown) contains, in addition to the binary tree, a protected type Lock. The private subprograms Random and Random_Update are used by the (grand-)child packages to create events.

The child packages that declare the event types are familiar except that they contain only the Simulate procedure:

```
package Root_Event.Simulation.Steering is
  type Steering_Event is new Event with private;
  procedure Simulate(E: in Steering_Event);
private
  -- as before
end Root_Event.Simulation.Steering;
```

Creation of events is done in a Creator child package, which exports a type Create that is implemented by a task type. The access discriminant P is used to pass the Producer object to the task:

```
package Root_Event.Simulation.Steering.Creator is
  type Create(P: access Producer) is limited private;
private
  task type Create(P: access Producer);
end Root_Event.Simulation.Steering.Creator;
```

The task itself simply executes a loop calling Create_Event to create a random event and placing the event on the queue encapsulated in the producer:

```
package body Root_Event.Simulation.Steering.Creator is
  task body Create is
    function Create_Event return Steering_Event is ...
  begin
    loop
      Put(Create_Event, P.all);
      delay 1.0;
    end loop;
  end Create;
end Root_Event.Simulation.Steering.Creator;
```

Package Rocket_Simulation declares and exports a Producer object R:

```
with Root_Event.Simulation;
package Rocket_Simulation is
  pragma Elaborate_Body;
  R: aliased Root_Event.Simulation.Producer;
end Rocket_Simulation;
```

The package body declares and hides the creators. An access to the producer object R is passed to each creator:

```
with Root_Event.Simulation.Telemetry.Creator;
with Root_Event.Simulation.Engine.Creator;
with Root_Event.Simulation.Steering.Creator;
package body Rocket_Simulation is
  use Root_Event.Simulation;
  T: Telemetry.Creator.Create(R'Access);
  E: Engine.Creator.Create(R'Access);
  S: Steering.Creator.Create(R'Access);
end Rocket_Simulation;
```

pragma Elaborate_Body is required because there are no declarations in the package specification that require completions in the body. The pragma forces the elaboration of the body.

Finally, the main subprogram just contains the simulation loop:

```
with Root_Event.Simulation, Rocket_Simulation;
procedure RocketT is
begin
  loop
    Root_Event.Simulate(
      Root_Event.Simulation.Get(Rocket_Simulation.R'Access));
  end loop;
end RocketT;
```

19.10 Tasks as access discriminants*

An access discriminant can be an access to a task type. The following program shows how access discriminants can be used to configure a set of tasks at run-time. A task of type Main_Task has two access discriminants Left and Right that will be initialized with accesses to tasks of type Worker_Task:

config

```
package Tasks is
  task type Worker_Task(ID: Character) is
    entry Input;
  end Worker_Task;

  task type Main_Task(Left, Right: access Worker_Task);
end Tasks;
```

Main_Task calls the entry Input of these two worker tasks in succession. Note the implicit dereferencing in the entry calls to the worker tasks:

```
with Ada.Text_IO;
package body Tasks is
  task body Main_Task is
  begin
    Left.Input;
    Right.Input;
  end Main_Task;

  task body Worker_Task is
  begin
    accept Input do
      Ada.Text_IO.Put_Line(ID & " called");
    end Input;
  end Worker_Task;
end Tasks;
```

In the main program, worker tasks are declared and used to initialize the main task:

```
with Tasks;
procedure Config is
  W1: aliased Tasks.Worker_Task('A');
  W2: aliased Tasks.Worker_Task('B');
  M:  Tasks.Main_Task(W2'Access, W1'Access);
begin
  null;
end Config;
```

The worker tasks are declared as **aliased** so that the attribute Access can be applied to them. In a realistic application, the tasks would be dynamically allocated and the worker tasks used to initialize each main task would be determined at run-time.

19.10.1 Simulating dispatching on entries

Access discriminants can be used to simulate dispatching on entry calls. An access value to a task can be obtained from a heterogeneous data structure and used to call an entry:

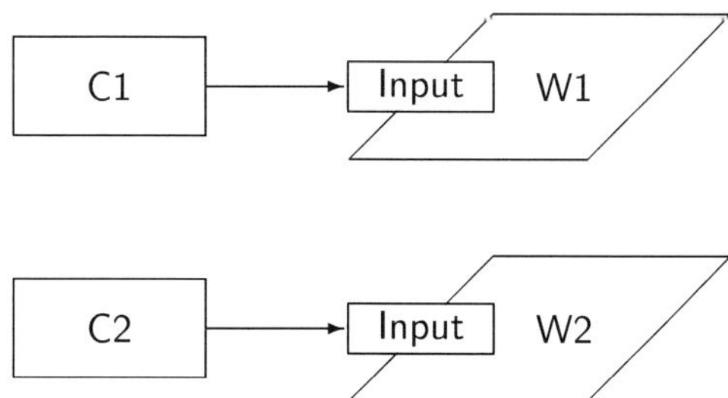

Two task types Worker_1 and Worker_2 are declared, together with their access types:

disptask

```
package Tasks is
  task type Worker_1 is
    entry Input;
  end Worker_1;
  type W1_Ptr is access Worker_1;

  task type Worker_2 is
    entry Input;
  end Worker_2;
  type W2_Ptr is access Worker_2;
end Tasks;
```

The task bodies just print their identifications and the source code is omitted here.

Dispatching will be done on the tagged type Channel by calling the subprogram Output:

```
package Channels is
  type Channel is abstract tagged limited null record;
  procedure Output(C: access Channel) is abstract;
  type Channel_Ptr is access all Channel'Class;
end Channels;
```

Types W1_Channel and W2_Channel are derived from abstract type Channel and contain an access discriminant to the respective task types:

```
with Tasks;
package Channels.Workers is
  type W1_Channel(W: access Tasks.Worker_1) is
    new Channel with null record;
  procedure Output(C: access W1_Channel);

  -- Similarly for W2_Channel
end Channels.Workers;
```

This overridden subprogram calls an entry of the task pointed to by the access discriminant:

```
package body Channels.Workers is
  procedure Output(C: access W1_Channel) is
  begin
    C.W.Input;
  end Output;

  procedure Output(C: access W2_Channel) is
  begin
    C.W.Input;
  end Output;
end Channels.Workers;
```

In the main subprogram, two workers W1 and W2 are dynamically allocated, as well as two channels—one for each worker task. The channels are stored in a heterogenous data structure; for simplicity, we use just two variables C1 and C2 of access to *class-wide* type:

```
with Tasks;
with Channels.Workers; use Channels;
procedure DispTask is
  W1: Tasks.W1_Ptr := new Tasks.Worker_1;
  W2: Tasks.W2_Ptr := new Tasks.Worker_2;
  C1: Channel_Ptr  := new Workers.W1_Channel(W1);
  C2: Channel_Ptr  := new Workers.W2_Channel(W2);
```

The variable Get_Channel is initialized by the value of one of the channels; this is intended to represent getting an arbitrary channel from the data structure. Procedure Output, whose formal parameters are of access to a tagged type, is called with an actual parameter of access to the class-wide type:

```
  Get_Channel: Channel_Ptr := C2;
begin
  Output(Get_Channel);
end DispTask;
```

By §3.9.2(2), this is a dispatching call on the designated type. Whichever version of Output that is dispatched to now calls the entry for the task pointed to by the channel, so in effect we have dispatched an entry call.

This technique is not needed in Ada 2005, which supports interfaces (Section 17.4).

Projects

1. Write a program that is correct only because of the rule for task activation that the main program does not begin executing until the enclosed tasks have been activated.
2. Write a program to demonstrate that timed or conditional entry calls can cause the `Count` attribute to be incorrect.
3. Modify the case study in Section 19.7.1 so that updating the value of `Result` is within an (abort-deferred) protected action; therefore, if the abort is executed the value is not destroyed.
4. Reimplement the case study in Section 19.10 using interfaces instead of access discriminants.

Quizzes

Quiz 1:

```
procedure Main is
  task type T(ID: Integer);
  task body T is
    N: Positive := ID;
  begin
    for I in 1 .. 4 loop
      Put_Line("Hi from task " & Integer'Image(ID));
    end loop;
  end T;

  T0: T(0);
  T1: T(1);

begin
  null;
exception
  when Tasking_Error => Put_Line("A task has died");
end Main;
```

Quiz 2:

```
procedure Main is

  task type T(ID: Integer);
  type Ptr is access T;
  task body T is
  begin
    for I in 1 .. 5 loop
      Put_Line("Hi from task " & Integer'Image(ID));
      delay 0.5*ID;
    end loop;
  end T;
begin
  Put_Line("Main subprogram");
  declare
    P: Ptr := new T(1);
--     type New_Ptr is access T;
--     New_P: New_Ptr := new T(2);
  begin
    null;
  end;
  Put_Line("Back from block");
end Main;
```

What would happen if the commented lines were added to the program?

Quiz 3:

```
procedure Main is

  task T1 is
    entry E;
  end T1;
  task body T1 is
  begin
    delay 0.2;
    accept E do
      Put_Line("Starting T1.E");
      delay 0.8;
      Put_Line("Finishing T1.E");
    end E;
  end T1;

  task T2 is
    entry E;
  end T2;
  task body T2 is
  begin
    delay 0.4;
    accept E do
      Put_Line("Starting T2.E");
      delay 0.1;
      Put_Line("Finishing T2.E");
    end E;
  end T2;

begin
  select
    T1.E;
    Put_Line("Finished triggering");
  then abort
    T2.E;
    Put_Line("Finished abortable");
  end select;
end Main;
```

Chapter 20
Systems Programming

20.1 Implementation dependences

Ada is rooted in the requirements of computer systems with their hardware and operating systems, and in the requirements of projects for performance, reliability and reuse. The design of a programming language for complex projects must cope with conflicting requirements:

- If the language is small, implementation-specific extensions and third-party add-ons will be needed, making the software non-portable. If the language is large, it may be too difficult to implement fully for important target computers and operating systems.
- If the language specification is too general, implementations will fill in the details as they see fit and the software developer will not be able to rely on a portable behavior. If the language specification is very detailed, there may be difficulty implementing the language as specified on a target architecture.

The Ada approach to implementation dependency can be summarized as follows: certain features in the language need not be implemented, but if you do implement them, it must be done as described in the standard. Where the standard leaves a decision up to the implementation, the decision must be documented. The standard specification of "optional" features means that programming techniques and even existing source code can be easily adapted to a new implementation. Furthermore, little retraining is necessary for software engineers moving from one implementation to another, because the concepts, the terminology, and even the type and subprogram declarations will be almost identical across all implementations. There are two levels of implementation dependency in Ada. First, there are six *Specialized Needs Annexes*:

- Annex C Systems Programming
- Annex D Real-Time Programming
- Annex E Distributed Systems
- Annex F Information Systems
- Annex G Numerics
- Annex H Safety and Security

An implementation need not provide any of these annexes. The marketing literature for an implementation will list which annexes are supported and which are not.

The second level of support for flexibility in an implementation are paragraphs entitled *Implementation Permissions* and *Implementation Advice* that appear throughout the *ARM*. In addition, the annexes contain paragraphs entitled *Documentation Requirements*, requiring an implmentation to supply information about individual constructs. A centralized list of this material appears in Annex §M Summary of Documentation Requirements. Once you have chosen candidate implementations that support the annexes your project requires, you can further compare the level of support for individual constructs.

In time-critical systems, you need to be able to predict the performance of the software. Paragraphs entitled *Metrics* require the implementation to document performance characteristics, mostly bounds on execution time in terms of processor cycles. This information will be useful when you are choosing the language constructs to be used. For example, you may want to compare the overhead of an entry call of a protected object with that of a task.

The Information Systems Annex was discussed in Section 13.8 and the Numerics Annex in Section 13.11. This chapter and the next will present the other Specialized Needs Annexes, as well as parts of Section §13 Representation Issues and Annex §B Interface to Other Languages.

Since the Annexes were introduced in Ada 95, you will want to read the chapters of the Ada 95 *Rationale* concerning the Annexes; they are quite extensive: discussing goals, justifications, tradeoffs, and examples.

20.2 Representation items

Basic information about the implementation is given in package `System` §13.7; the most important is the constant `System.Storage_Unit` §13.7(13), which gives the number of bits in the smallest addressable storage element such as an 8-bit byte or a 32-bit word, depending on the architecture. Type `Address` §13.7(12) represents actual machine addresses as opposed to language-defined access values. You can obtain the address of an object or a subprogram by using the attribute `Address` §13.3(10–12). Conversion between access values and machine addresses is supported by package `System.Address_To_Access_Conversions` §13.7.2.

Type `Storage_Element` §13.7.1(5) is defined in `System.Storage_Elements` §13.7.1:

```
type Storage_Element is mod implementation-defined;
```

together with operations for address arithmetic.

20.2.1 Representation attributes

Most representation characteristics are given as attributes §13.3 and can be specified using *attribute definition clauses* §13.3(2). The use of representation attributes was shown in the case study in Section 11.5:

```
type Byte is mod 2**System.Storage_Unit;
for  Byte'Size use System.Storage_Unit;
```

The modular type Byte is to be represented in the number of bits in one storage unit. These declarations are portable, though there is no assurance that the type is stored in 8 bits.

Similarly, the enumeration type Code is also represented in one storage unit:

```
type Codes is (M0, M1, M2, M3);
for  Codes'Size use System.Storage_Unit;
```

Of course, if there are more values in the type than there is space in a storage unit (256 for an 8-bit byte), the clause would be illegal §13.1(12) and the program would not compile.

An enumeration representation clause §13.4 can be used to specify the representation of enumeration literals in place of the default representation—the position numbers §13.4(8). The following clause specifies that each message code is assigned a separate bit:

```
for Codes use (M1 => 2#0001#, M2 => 2#0010#, M3 => 2#0100#, M4 => 2#1000#);
```

This construct is particularly useful for hardware interfacing.

Enumeration representation clauses do not change the position numbers that are returned by the attribute Pos, so if C is a variable of type Codes, the value of C'Pos is in the range 0..3.

For the record type Structured_Message an attribute definition clause is not given, because we are not interested in the details of its representation. Instead, **pragma** Pack §13.2, a *representation pragma*, is used to specify that storage for objects of type Structured_Message should be minimized:

```
pragma Pack(Structured_Message);
```

The meaning of "minimized" is implementation-defined; if you need a precise representation, use record layout clauses §13.5 as shown in Section 11.9.

The declaration of the type Raw_Message is interesting:

```
Max_Bytes: constant Integer :=
  Structured_Message'Size/System.Storage_Unit;
type Raw_Message is array(1..Max_Bytes) of Byte;
pragma Pack(Raw_Message);
```

Objects of the type should be represented as arrays with just enough memory to store a value of type Structured_Message. This can be computed using the Size attribute so the declaration is not only portable, but need not be changed if Structured_Message is modified.

20.3 Interfaces to other languages

Few software systems are developed in a vacuum. Your program will almost certainly have to call operating-system services and library subprograms; it may also need to be integrated with existing "legacy" code. To facilitate software development in such environments, Ada supports mixed-language programming. There are two technical problems that must be solved:

- The representation of similar types may differ from one language to another. Two well known examples are the use of null-terminated strings in C instead of storing the current length of the string as is common in other languages, and the storage of multi-dimensional arrays in Fortran in column-major order rather than in row-major order.
- There are many different subprogram naming and calling conventions. For example, C++ uses a language-specific encoding of the external names of subprograms called "name mangling" to perform type-safe linkage.

In Ada, there are two approaches to solving these problems:

- A *convention* can be specified for a type, object or subprogram, requesting that the representation of the entity be appropriate for the specified language.
- Language-specific child packages of package `Interfaces` §B.2 declare Ada types that are represented in the same way as types in other languages.

With these constructs, an Ada object that is a null-terminated C string can be declared, an Ada string converted to this object, and then the object passed to a system service that expects parameters in the C convention.

20.3.1 Interfacing pragmas

§B.1

> 2 A pragma Convention is used to specify that an Ada entity should use the conventions of another language. It is intended primarily for types and "callback" subprograms. For example, "**pragma** Convention(Fortran, Matrix);" implies that Matrix should be represented according to the conventions of the supported Fortran implementation, namely column-major order.

Predefined conventions, such as the default convention `Ada`, are defined in §6.3. An implementation may define other conventions, such as language-specific conventions.

§B.1

> 1 A pragma Import is used to import an entity defined in a foreign language into an Ada program, thus allowing a foreign-language subprogram to be called from Ada, or a foreign-language variable to be accessed from Ada. In contrast, a pragma Export is used to export an Ada entity to a foreign language, thus allowing an Ada subprogram to be called from a foreign language, or an Ada object to be accessed from a foreign language. The pragmas Import and Export are intended primarily for objects and subprograms, although implementations are allowed to support other entities.

pragma `Import` and **pragma** `Export` take two required parameters, the convention and the entity it applies to, as well as one of two optional parameters, either an `External_Name` §B.1(34) or a `Link_Name` §B.1(35):

```
pragma Import(C, CFunc, Link_Name => "_cfunc");
```

If the system can guess the link name of the imported entity from the local name, neither is needed; if not, the system may be able to deduce it from the external name in the foreign language; finally, you can give the exact name expected by the linker. Obviously, each option in this sequence is less portable than the previous one.

§B.1

> 22 A pragma Import shall be the completion of a declaration. . . .

For example:

```
package Fortran_Matrices is
  type Matrix is array(Integer range <>, Integer range <>) of Long_Float;
  pragma Convention(Fortran, Matrix);
  Identity: constant Matrix;
  function Determinant(M: Matrix) return Long_Float;
private
  pragma Import(Fortran, Identity);
  pragma Import(Fortran, Determinant);
end Fortran_Matrices;
```

An Ada subprogram can be exported and called from a foreign language; in fact, the main program may be in the foreign language. Implementations are advised to supply two subprograms `adainit` and `adafinal` that can be called from the foreign-language main program to perform elaboration of Ada library units and finalization of the environment task §B.1(39).

20.3.2 *Package Interfaces*

Package `Interfaces` §B.2 declares types and subprograms for interfacing to other languages. There are declarations of numeric types of all precisions directly supported by the target computer: signed `Integer_`*n* and modular `Unsigned_`*n* integer types, as well as floating point types. There are `Shift` and `Rotate` operations for each modular type. Clearly, using these types will tend to make the program non-portable and they should only be used to declare objects that are passed directly to the hardware.

An implementation may provide child packages of `Interfaces` §B.2(11) for interfacing to other languages; interfaces for C/C++, COBOL and Fortran are defined in Annex §B. The interfaces declare types corresponding to the types in the languages, as well as functions `To_`*Lang* and `To_Ada` for converting the types of language *Lang* to and from Ada.

20.3.3 *C and C++*

Package `Interfaces.C` §B.3 contains declarations of types corresponding to C's types such as `int` and `unsigned_char`. Type `char_array` is a character array, and the conversion functions `To_Ada` and `To_C` can deal with the null terminator §B.3(25–28). The correspondence between Ada subprograms and parameters and those of C is given in §B.3(63–71). For example, a C function that returns **`void`** corresponds to an Ada procedure, and a parameter of type `T*` corresponds to an **`in out`** parameter of type `T` in Ada.

String processing in C is usually done on dynamically allocated objects rather than on static arrays. The declarations:

```
char s1[ ] = "Hello world";
char *s2   = "Hello world";
```

give rise to the data structures shown in the following diagram:

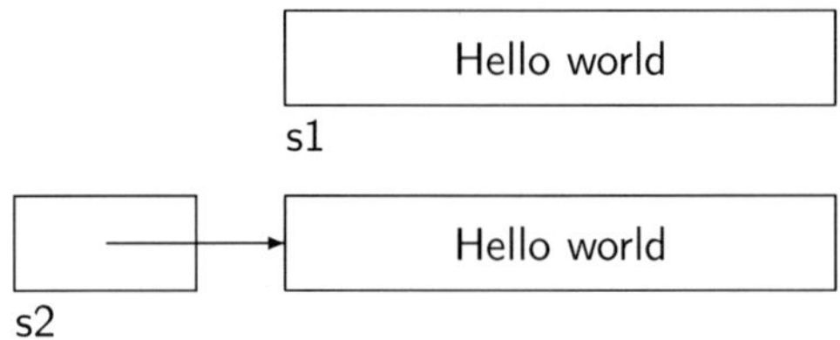

The declaration of `s1` corresponds to a value of type `char_array`.

Package `Interfaces.C.Strings` declares a private type `chars_ptr` for pointers to C strings of type `char*` such as `s2` in the diagram, and `chars_ptr_array` for arrays of pointers. The Ada program can manage the storage for these strings. Function `New_Char_Array` §B.3.1(9) and procedure `New_String` §B.3.1(10) allocate a C string initialized by an existing value of type `char_array` and `String`, respectively. The procedure `Free` §B.3.1(11) releases the storage.

Given an access to an object S of type `char_array`, `To_Chars_Ptr` §B.3.1(8) returns a value of the C type `chars_ptr` pointing to S. There are also subprograms for the reverse conversion and subprograms for directly updating C strings.

Generic package `Interfaces.C.Pointers` §B.3.2 declares type `Pointer` as an access to a generic formal parameter, and provides subprograms for pointer arithmetic and copying arbitrary arrays.

Ada 95

C++ was not mentioned in Ada 95, although implementations are allowed to provide interfaces for constructs of C++ that extend C. Ada 2005 added subprograms for converting the types `char16_t` and `char32_t` to and from Ada's `Wide_Wide_Character` and `Wide_Character`, respectively.

20.3.4 *Unchecked unions*

Variant records are similar to C's *union types*, except that variant records are required to store the discriminant, which does not exist in union types. *Unchecked unions* §B.3.3 create variant records without storing the discriminant so that they can be passed to C programs.

§B.3.3

> 5 The *first_subtype*_local_name of a pragma Unchecked_Union shall denote an unconstrained discriminated record subtype having a variant_part.

The type must be unconstrained with a default value for the discriminant.

Consider declaring the type `Structured_Message` as an unchecked union:

union

```
with Ada.Text_IO; use Ada.Text_IO;
procedure Union is
  type Codes is (M1, M2);
  type Structured_Message(Code: Codes := M1) is
    record
      case Code is
        when M1 => A: Integer;
        when M2 => B: Float;
      end case;
    end record;
  pragma Unchecked_Union(Structured_Message);
```

Both unconstrained and constrained objects of the type can now be declared:

```
   S1: Structured_Message     := (M1, 44);
   S2: Structured_Message     := (M2, 12.34);
   T1: Structured_Message(M1) := (M1, 44);
   T2: Structured_Message(M2) := (M2, 12.34);
```

What will happen when we try to read each of the components of these records?

```
begin
   -- Put the components A and B of each record
end Union;
```

For the unconstrained records `S1` and `S2`, all components except the discriminant can be read. `S1.A` and `S2.B` are read with their intended values. Reading the value of `S1.B` is erroneous, although if `Float` and `Integer` are the same size, the result is likely to be whatever floating point number corresponds to the bits representing the integer 44, and conversely for `S2.A`. The components `T1.A` and `T2.B` are read with their intended values, but `T1.B` and `T2.A` cause `Constraint_Error` to be raised. Even though the discriminants are not stored, since the records are constrained, the compiler knows that the "wrong" components cannot be accessed.

Ada 95

pragma `Unchecked_Union` is new in Ada 2005.

20.3.5 COBOL

Package `Interfaces.COBOL` §B.4 defines interfaces with the COBOL language. It includes `Interfaces.COBOL.Decimal_Conversions` §B.4(31), a generic package for converting between an Ada decimal type value and COBOL representations.

Recall that decimal fixed point arithmetic is supported in the Ada language (Section 13.8), and picture editing is supported in Annex §F Information Systems (Section 13.8), so you do not need to write COBOL code to obtain this functionality.

20.3.6 Fortran

Package `Interfaces.Fortran` §B.5 declares types corresponding to Fortran types such as `Double Precision` and `Logical`. There is very little functionality in the Fortran language that does not exist in Ada, so the primary use of this interface will be to access numerical and scientific libraries, and to integrate legacy software.

20.4 Annex C Systems Programming

Annex §B describes interface capabilities at the applications software level. Annex §C specifies capabilities needed to interface with the hardware and the underlying operating system (if any). Many of the features needed for hardware interface are specified in Section §13 Representation Issues, but the core language does not require §13.1(20) that the implementation actually support the features described in Section §13. This permission is not available if Annex §C is supported.

§C.2

> 2 The implementation shall support at least the functionality defined by the recommended levels of support in Section 13.

The recommended level is that specified in the *Implementation Advice* paragraphs of Section §13.

20.4.1 Discard_Names

Some Ada constructs have a string associated with them so that they can be displayed:

- The attributes `Image` and `Value`, and IO for enumeration types.
- `Ada.Exceptions.Exception_Name` §11.4.1(5).
- `Ada.Tags.Expanded_Name` §3.9(10).

pragma `Discard_Names` §C.5 allows the implementation to save storage by not storing these strings at run-time; if you do call these functions the result is implementation defined. This feature is important for saving memory in embedded computer systems that have no display device, or no use for the constructs listed above.

20.4.2 Preelaboration

Embedded computer systems need the ability to quickly restart a program in case of a failure such as loss of power. In Ada, the time to start a program includes the elaboration time, which may be significant. Elaboration time can be reduced by *preelaborating* as much of the program as possible (Section 15.5.4). An implementation may be able to store the constants of a preelaborated unit in ROM, further reducing startup time.

Paragraphs §10.2.1(2–12) specify restrictions that a library unit must satisfy for it to be preelaborable. Roughly, a unit can be preelaborated if no "code" need be executed at run-time. For example, tasks are illegal because they require run-time structures that must be initialized.

The core language does not specify what "privileges" a preelaborable unit has—only that it is elaborated after a pure unit and before an ordinary unit. Annex §C imposes requirements on the implementation of preelaborated units.

§C.4

> 2 The implementation shall not incur any run-time overhead for the elaboration checks of subprograms and protected_bodies declared in preelaborated library units.
>
> 3 The implementation shall not execute any memory write operations after load time for the elaboration of constant objects declared immediately within the declarative region of a preelaborated library package, so long as the subtype and initial expression (or default initial expressions if initialized by default) of the object_declaration satisfy the following restrictions. The meaning of *load time* is implementation defined.

The restrictions given in §C.4(4–11) are intended to ensure that expressions are static.

20.5 Machine code*

The architecture of most computers includes specialized instructions; use of these instructions can be essential when implementing time-critical algorithms. Of course, hardly anything makes a program less portable than the use of machine code!

§C.1

> 2 The implementation shall support machine code insertions (see 13.8) or intrinsic subprograms (see 6.3.1) (or both). Implementation-defined attributes shall be provided to allow the use of Ada entities as operands.
>
> 4 The interfacing pragmas (see Annex §B) should support interface to assembler; the default assembler should be associated with the convention identifier Assembler.

Suppose that the machine includes an atomic increment instruction, and that to implement a concurrent algorithm it is essential that this instruction be used to implement the statement `X:=X+1`. There are three ways in which this could be supported. The implementation could simply allow to program to call an assembly language subprogram. The problem with this method is that there may be significant overhead associated with subprogram call and return. A better method is to have the implementation simply supply an intrinsic subprogram: `Inc(X)`.

§6.3.1

> 4 The *Intrinsic* calling convention represents subprograms that are "built in" to the compiler. . . .

Intrinsic subprograms are probably the best solution when there are a few commonly used machine-code instructions. However, to access the full set of instructions and addressing modes, support for *machine code insertions* §13.8 is a better solution. The implementation supplies a package `System.Machine_Code` that defines types that allow qualified expressions to be written for each instruction and addressing mode. Attributes must also be defined for addressing ordinary objects of the Ada program. For example, if an object is addressed by a page number and an offset, the implementation could support a statement like:

```
Instruction'(Inc, X'Page, X'Offset);
```

20.6 Interrupts*

In this section, we describe a simple model for interrupts and the constructs that can be used to implement an interrupt handler. There is an extensive discussion in the *ARM* and the Ada 95 *Rationale* on adapting the constructs to support other architectures. Note in particular the extensive documentation requirements associated with interrupt support §C.3(12–22).

§C.3

> 2 An *interrupt* represents a class of events that are detected by the hardware or the system software. Interrupts are said to occur. An *occurrence* of an interrupt is separable into generation and delivery. *Generation* of an interrupt is the event in the underlying hardware or system that makes the interrupt available to the program. *Delivery* is the action that invokes part of the program as response to the interrupt occurrence. Between generation and delivery, the interrupt occurrence (or interrupt) is *pending*. Some or all interrupts may be *blocked*. When an interrupt is blocked, all occurrences of that interrupt are prevented from being delivered. Certain interrupts are *reserved*. The set of reserved interrupts is implementation defined. A reserved interrupt is either an interrupt for which user-defined handlers are not supported, or one which already has an attached handler by some other implementation-defined means. Program units can be connected to non-reserved interrupts. While connected, the program unit is said to be *attached* to that interrupt. The execution of that program unit, the *interrupt handler*, is invoked upon delivery of the interrupt occurrence.

In a common architecture, when an interrupt occurs, the hardware looks in a fixed memory location called a *vector* for the address of a subprogram called the *handler*:

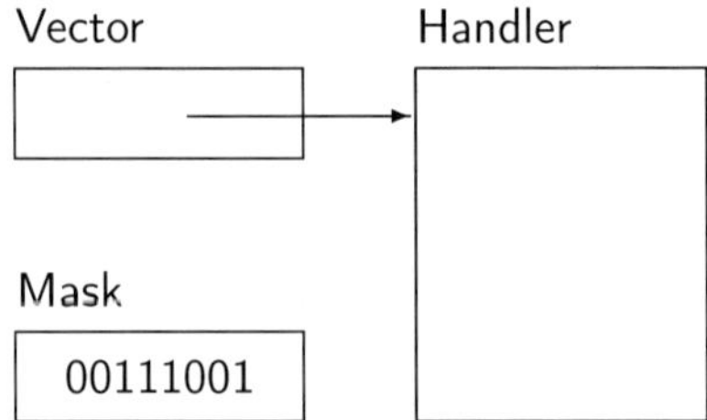

Delivery of the interrupt consists of preempting the currently executing task and executing the statements of the handler; any needed stack space is "borrowed" from the current task. Upon completion of the handler, a return-from-interrupt instruction restores the stack and registers of the preempted task. A bit may be set in a *mask* register to block a pending interrupt.

Interrupts implement a simple form of mutual exclusion: during the execution of the handler, software tasks are blocked because interrupts execute at a higher priority than any software task. If a task wishes to update a variable shared with an interrupt handler, it simply sets the mask register to block the interrupt.

This interrupt model maps onto procedures of protected objects. The interrupt is modeled as an anonymous hardware task executing a protected procedure, and mutual exclusion with other protected operations is implemented by masking the interrupt.

§C.3.1

2 **pragma** Interrupt_Handler(*handler*_name);
4 **pragma** Attach_Handler(*handler*_name, expression);

5 For the Interrupt_Handler and Attach_Handler pragmas, the *handler*_name shall resolve to denote a protected procedure with a parameterless profile.

9 If the pragma Interrupt_Handler appears in a protected_definition, then the corresponding procedure can be attached dynamically, as a handler, to interrupts (see C.3.2). Such procedures are allowed to be attached to multiple interrupts.

10 As part of the initialization of that object, if the Attach_Handler pragma is specified, the *handler* procedure is attached to the specified interrupt. ...

13 When a handler is attached to an interrupt, the interrupt is blocked ... during the execution of every protected action on the protected object containing the handler.

The difference between the two pragmas is that `Attach_Handler` attaches the interrupt handler when the protected object is initialized, whereas `Interrupt_Handler` simply notifies the compiler that a protected procedure is an interrupt handler. Subprograms in the package `Ada.Interrupts` §C.3.2 must be used to attach the handler. In this case, the handler may be dynamically attached and detached.

20.7 Shared variables*

If several tasks are declared within a subprogram or package, they can all read and write variables declared previously in the enclosing declarative region. Such variables are called *shared variables*. Similarly, sharing of variables can occur if a subprogram that reads or writes a global variable is called by several tasks. Normally, sharing variables is not considered a good programming technique, because the variables should be encapsulated in protected objects or tasks. For reasons of efficiency, low-level systems programming can require this capability. The problem is only in sharing variables; the executable code is assumed not to modify itself ("pure code") and can be executed concurrently by several tasks §6.1(35).

There are two potential problems that can arise from concurrent access to shared variables. First, the variable may not be atomic; this is likely to happen if more than one memory word is needed to store the variable, such as with high-precision floating point numbers and with arrays and records. Suppose that a task updates one word of a two-word variable and then it is preempted by another task that updates both words of the same variable. When the first task is resumed, it will update the second word, leaving the variable with a mixture of two values.

The second problem is that code generators, in particular optimizers, make assumptions that may not be valid in the presence of concurrency. For example, given the statements:

```
X := Y + 4;
Z := X + Y;
```

the code generator might not write to the memory word for X immediately after the first statement; instead, when computing the expression X+Y, it will use the value of Y+4 that was stored in a register. Then another task might use the old value in X.

An extreme case of this problem is shown by the sequence of instructions:

```
Mem := 16#F000#;
Mem := 16#000C#;
```

where the assignment is done solely for the side effect of issuing a command to a memory-mapped peripheral. An optimizer will simply discard the first assignment.

Clause §9.10 defines what it means for two actions to be *sequential*. Roughly, they are sequential if they are part of the same task, or if they are synchronized by a task rendezvous or protected action. Reading and updating an unprotected shared variable is erroneous unless the actions are sequential §9.10(11).

For systems programming, we may want to read and update shared variables without the overhead of rendezvous or protected actions. This is done by using pragmas to specify that an object or all objects of a type are *atomic* or *volatile*.

§C.6

> 15 For an atomic object (including an atomic component) all reads and updates of the object as a whole are indivisible.
>
> 16 For a volatile object all reads and updates of the object as a whole are performed directly to memory.
>
> 17 Two actions are sequential (see 9.10) if each is the read or update of the same atomic object.

pragma `Atomic` specifies that an object can be read and updated indivisibly, and thus can be accessed concurrently §9.10. If the implementation cannot ensure this, the program is illegal §C.6(10). **pragma** `Volatile` (which is also implied by `Atomic` §C.6(8)) specifies that no temporary copies of the variable are kept and that no reads or updates will be discarded. Volatile can be used on a compound object that cannot be accessed atomically; you will have to use other means to ensure that the object contains a consistent value.

It is possible to specify that the components of an array are atomic or volatile (even if the entire array is not) with **pragma** `Atomic_Compoments` §C.6(5) or **pragma** `Volatile_Compoments` §C.6(6). These pragmas can be applied to a constant object §C.6(13), provided that `Import` is also applied so that an external program (or perhaps the hardware) can modify it. The rules for passing atomic or volatile objects as parameters are discussed in §C.6(12,18,19).

20.8 Task identification and attributes*

Dynamic data structures containing tasks can be created by declaring a record or an array with a component of a task type. However, since tasks are typed, you cannot create a data structure that contains tasks of different types, as would be needed, for example, when writing an operating system. Package `Ada.Task_Identification` §C.7.1 declares a nonlimited private type `Task_ID` that can hold the identification of a task regardless of its type.

§C.7.1

> 5 A value of the type Task_ID identifies an existent task. The constant Null_Task_ID does not identify any task. Each object of the type Task_ID is default initialized to the value of Null_Task_ID.
>
> 8 The function Current_Task returns a value that identifies the calling task.

The function `Current_Task` §C.7.1(8) is not well-defined within a protected entry body. The reason is that when a blocked task is awakened, the entry body will probably be executed by the awakening task to avoid a context switch.

Several attributes are defined that return values of type `Task_ID`:

§C.7.1

12 T'Identity Yields a value of the type Task_ID that identifies the task denoted by T.
14 E'Caller Yields a value of the type Task_ID that identifies the task whose call is now being serviced. Use of this attribute is allowed only inside an entry_body or accept_statement corresponding to the entry_declaration denoted by E.

Data can be associated with a task by declaring discriminants; again, however, this is type-specific. Instead, we may need to add data items to the "task control block" that contains the data associated with each task, such as its priority. This is done instantiating the generic package `Ada.Task_Attributes` §C.7.2 one or more times to create user-defined attributes. The attributes can be written and read using the procedure `Set_Value` and the function `Value`, respectively. Task identification and attributes are demonstrated in the following case study.

20.8.1 *Case study: task identification and attributes*

The program in this case study models a server receiving requests from an arbitrary set of client tasks. At any point in time, the server stores the `Task_ID` of the two "most important" tasks, where importance is an attribute associated with each task. The most important tasks will be released before other tasks.

`Importance` is an instantiation of `Ada.Task_Attributes` with an attribute of type `Integer`:

id

```
with Ada.Numerics.Discrete_Random;
with Ada.Task_Identification; with Ada.Task_Attributes;
procedure ID is
  package Importance is new Ada.Task_Attributes(Integer, 0);
```

Clients will call entries `Request` and `Release` of the task `Server`:

```
  task Server is
    entry Request;
    entry Release;
  private
    entry Slow_Release;
  end Server;
```

The task stores the IDs and attributes of the two most important tasks:

```
task body Server is
  use Ada.Task_Identification;
  ID1, ID2:                   Task_ID;
  Importance1, Importance2: Integer := 0;
```

The attribute E'Caller is used to obtain the ID of the calling task. If it has a higher value of Importance than the currently stored tasks, its ID and importance replace existing ones:

```
begin
  loop
    select
      accept Request do
        if Importance.Value(Request'Caller) > Importance1 then
          Importance2 := Importance1;
          ID2   := ID1;
          ID1   := Request'Caller;
          Importance1 := Importance.Value(ID1);
        elsif Importance.Value(Request'Caller) > Importance2 then
          ID2   := Request'Caller;
          Importance2 := Importance.Value(ID2);
        end if;
      end Request;
```

When a client calls Release, its ID is compared with the stored ID to see if it is one of the two most important tasks. If so, the rendezvous is completed; if not, the entry call is requeued on the private entry Slow_Release, whose guard ensures that it is only executed if no important tasks are being served:

```
    or
      accept Release do
        if Release'Caller /= ID1 and Release'Caller /= ID2 then
          requeue Slow_Release;
        else
          -- Perform service
        end if;
      end Release;
    or
      when Release'Count = 0 =>
        accept Slow_Release do
          -- Perform service
        end Slow_Release;
```

Note that tasks, not just protected objects, can have private entries.

Finally, the server has a terminate alternative for its selective accept statement:

```
      or
        terminate;
      end select;
    end loop;
  end Server;
```

Clients set their own importance by calling a random number generator:

```
  subtype Numbers is Integer range 1..100;
  package Random_Numbers is new Ada.Numerics.Discrete_Random(Numbers);
  G: Random_Numbers.Generator;
```

We now declare two task *types*, which are used to declare ten client tasks; all of them, however, can use the same types for their IDs and importance attributes:

```
  task type Client1;
  task body Client1 is
  begin
    Importance.Set_Value(Random_Numbers.Random(G));
    Server.Request;
    -- Do something while waiting
    Server.Release;
  end Client1;

  task type Client2;
  task body Client2 is  -- similar

  C1: array(1..5) of Client1;
  C2: array(1..5) of Client2;
begin
  null;
end ID;
```

20.9 Detecting task termination*

We noted in Section 19.2 that exceptions raised in a task do not affect other tasks unless these tasks are in a rendezvous or on an entry queue for the task. Sometimes, however, a task does wish to be informed when another task terminates; package `Ada.Task_Termination` supports this capability.

A termination handler can be attached to a task. This is a protected procedure that will be executed when the task terminates:

§C.7.3

```
3  type Cause_Of_Termination is (Normal, Abnormal, Unhandled_Exception);
4  type Termination_Handler is access protected procedure
      (Cause : in Cause_Of_Termination;
      T : in Ada.Task_Identification.Task_Id;
      X : in Ada.Exceptions.Exception_Occurrence);
```

8 The type Termination_Handler identifies a protected procedure to be executed by the implementation when a task terminates. Such a protected procedure is called a *handler*. In all cases T identifies the task that is terminating. If the task terminates due to completing the last statement of its body, or as a result of waiting on a terminate alternative, then Cause is set to Normal and X is set to Null_Occurrence. If the task terminates because it is being aborted, then Cause is set to Abnormal and X is set to Null_Occurrence. If the task terminates because of an exception raised by the execution of its task_body, then Cause is set to Unhandled_Exception and X is set to the associated exception occurrence.

The handler shown here is called a *specific handler* that is called when the task it is attached to terminates. A handler can also be attached as a *fallback handler* §C.7.3(5,9), in which case it applies to the dependents of a task. When a task terminates, a search for a specific handler is made; if one is not found, a search commences for a fallback handler in the task's master (and recursively its master) §C.7.3(14).

Ada 95

This package is new for Ada 2005.

20.9.1 Case study: detecting task termination

Recall that in the case study for the producer–consumer problem (Section 18.1), the producer terminated but the consumers were blocked indefinitely. We now use `Ada.Task_Termination` to force termination if the producer terminates for any cause except `Normal`. To make the problem more realistic, we put the two task types in separate packages. This modification is straightforward and can be seen in the source code archive.

A package is declared that contains a protected object with a procedure having the profile required by §C.7.3(4):

```
with Ada.Task_Identification; with Ada.Task_Termination;
with Ada.Exceptions;
package Termination is
  protected Termination_Object is
    procedure Handle_Termination
     (Cause : in Ada.Task_Termination.Cause_Of_Termination;
      T     : in Ada.Task_Identification.Task_Id;
      X     : in Ada.Exceptions.Exception_Occurrence);
    entry Watchdog;
  private
    Unexpected_Termination: Boolean := False;
  end Termination_Object;
end Termination;
```

The protected object also has an entry Watchdog, which will be called by a task that wants to be notified when termination occurs. The variable `Unexpected_Termination` will be used as the barrier of this entry, and will be set by the termination handler if the cause of termination is not normal:

```
package body Termination is
  protected body Termination_Object is

    procedure Handle_Termination
     (Cause : in Ada.Task_Termination.Cause_Of_Termination;
      T     : in Ada.Task_Identification.Task_Id;
      X     : in Ada.Exceptions.Exception_Occurrence) is
      use Ada.Task_Termination;
    begin
      Unexpected_Termination := Cause /= Normal;
    end Handle_Termination;

    entry Watchdog when Unexpected_Termination is
    begin
      null;
    end Watchdog;

  end Termination_Object;
end Termination;
```

The procedure `Handle_Termination` is set to be the specific handler of the producer task and a fault is introduced into the code (a range error when assigning to `N`):

```
with Ada.Task_Identification; with Ada.Task_Termination;
with Buffer, Termination;
package body Producer is
  task body Producer_Task is
    subtype Value_Range is Integer range 1..20;
    N: Value_Range := 1;
  begin
    Ada.Task_Termination.Set_Specific_Handler(
      Ada.Task_Identification.Current_Task,
      Termination.Termination_Object.Handle_Termination'Access);
    loop
      Buffer.Buffer_Task.Append(N);
      N := N + 1;
    end loop;
  end Producer_Task;
end Producer;
```

The main program declares the producer and consumer tasks, and calls the entry `Watchdog` of the termination handler. When it returns, it aborts the three tasks:

```
with Consumer, Producer, Termination;
procedure TaskPC is
  C1: Consumer.Consumer_Task(1);
  C2: Consumer.Consumer_Task(2);
  P:  Producer.Producer_Task;
begin
  Termination.Termination_Object.Watchdog;
  abort P, C1, C2;
end TaskPC;
```

Run the program and check that it terminates. Next, add an exception handler to the task `Producer` and explain happens:

```
exception
  when Constraint_Error => null;
```

Projects

1. If your computer has a C compiler, check that you can call C functions from an Ada program. Check, also, that unchecked union works correctly.
2. Examine the machine code produced by your compiler to see the effect of using pragmas `Atomic` and `Volatile`.
3. Modify the case study in Section 20.8.1 so that a linked list of tasks is maintained by the server.

Quizzes

Quiz 1: Add the following declaration to the program `Union` in Section 20.3.4 and try to access its components `A` and `B`:

```
U: Structured_Message(M1) := (M2, 12.34);
```

Quiz 2:

```
pragma Preelaborate;
Strange: Float :=
  Ada.Numerics.Elementary_Functions.Sqrt(
    Ada.Numerics.Pi + Ada.Numerics.E);
```

Chapter 21
Real-Time Systems

21.1 Annex D Real-Time Systems

The essence of real-time systems is *predictability*. The software requirements of these systems include reactive time constraints: when an input event occurs, the system must react within a specified time by computing and sending the correct output. Real-time systems frequently need to be very *efficient*—reacting to a large number of events within a very short time—but there is no necessary relationship between the two concepts. Annex §D goes into great detail on two main topics: task scheduling and time. The Annex includes documentation requirements and metrics, which supply the systems engineer with information needed to design a real-time program using a specific implementation.

An implementation that implements Annex D is also required to implement Annex §C Systems Programming.

21.2 Scheduling and priorities

Recall (Section 19.1) that a *ready* task competes for resources such as processors that it needs to run. However, the core language does not specify how a ready task is chosen if there are more ready tasks than resources. Similarly, the language does not specify how a task blocked on an entry queue is chosen if there is more than one open protected entry §9.5.3(17) or selective accept alternative §9.7.1(16), although paragraph §9.5.3(17) does specify that any particular entry queue will be served in first-in, first-out (FIFO) order of the arrival of the calling tasks. There could also be more than one expired delay §9.7.1(18) to choose from.

§D.1 through §D.5 describe how priorities are used with scheduling rules. For portability, an implementation must support these rules, though it is free to support other scheduling rules needed by applications.

Ada is designed to be "multiprocessor-friendly," but for simplicity, we will describe the standard rules for a single processor and refer you to the *ARM* and the Ada 95 *Rationale* for the modifications needed for multiprocessors.

Each task has a priority and there is a queue of tasks for each priority:

§D.2.1

> 5 *Task dispatching policies* are specified in terms of conceptual *ready queues* and task states. A ready queue is an ordered list of ready tasks. The first position in a queue is called the *head of the queue*, and the last position is called the *tail of the queue*. A task is *ready* if it is in a ready queue, or if it is running. Each processor has one ready queue for each priority value. At any instant, each ready queue of a processor contains exactly the set of tasks of that priority that are ready for execution on that processor, but are not running on any processor; that is, those tasks that are ready, are not running on any processor, and can be executed using that processor and other available resources. A task can be on the ready queues of more than one processor.

The following diagram shows the conceptual queues of ready tasks:

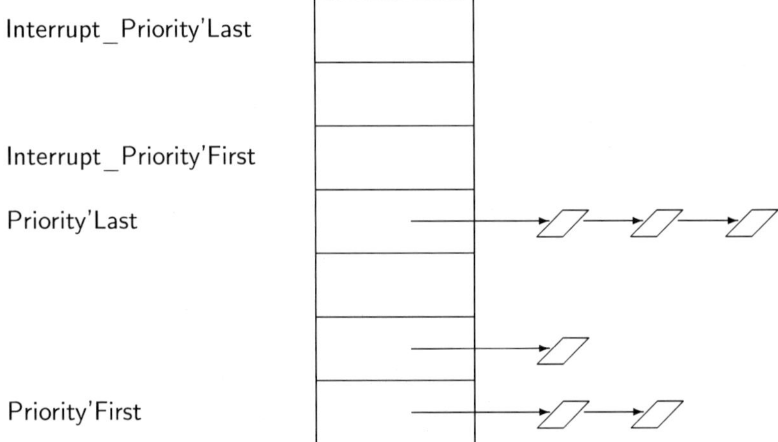

(The diagram is conceptual because the *ARM* does not specify the data structures that an implementation must use.)

Priority (more precisely, *base priority*) is specified by **pragma** `Priority` in the declaration of a task or protected unit §D.1(3–13). **pragma** `Interrupt_Priority` is usually used to specify the priority of an interrupt handler (Section 20.6) or the ceiling priority of a protected object (Section 21.7). Interrupts have higher priority than tasks. The priority is fixed when a task or protected object is declared, although it can be changed as explained in Section 21.6. The priority can depend on a discriminant §D.1(27), so different tasks of the same type can be assigned different priorities.

Priorities are used to control task dispatching.[1]

§D.2.1

> 6 Each processor also has one *running task*, which is the task currently being executed by that processor. Whenever a task running on a processor reaches a task dispatching point it goes back to one or more ready queues; a task (possibly the same task) is then selected to run on that processor. The task selected is the one at the head of the highest priority nonempty ready queue; this task is then removed from all ready queues to which it belongs.

Normally, a task will run until it reaches a task dispatching point such as an entry call.

§D.2.1

> 4 *Task dispatching* is the process by which one ready task is selected for execution on a processor. This selection is done at certain points during the execution of a task called *task dispatching points* is the process by which one ready task is selected for execution on a processor. This selection is done at certain points during the execution of a task called *task dispatching points*. A task reaches a task dispatching point whenever it becomes blocked, and when it terminates. Other task dispatching points are defined throughout this Annex for specific policies.

Tasks can also be *preempted* if a delay expires or if an interrupt causes some blocked task of a higher priority to become ready.

21.3 Task dispatching policies

A task dispatching policy specifies the transitions of tasks to and from the ready queues. The policy is specified by **pragma** `Tasking_Policy`; this is a configuration pragma (Section 15.4).

21.3.1 Preemptive dispatching

The default policy is implementation defined §D.2.2(6.1). A commonly used one is the preemptive scheduling policy *FIFO_Within_Priorities* §D.2.3 that can be specified by:

```
pragma Tasking_Policy(FIFO_Within_Priorities);
```

The policy is illustrated in Figure 21.1.

[1] This use of the term *dispatching* has nothing to do with the concept of dynamic dispatching of subprograms.

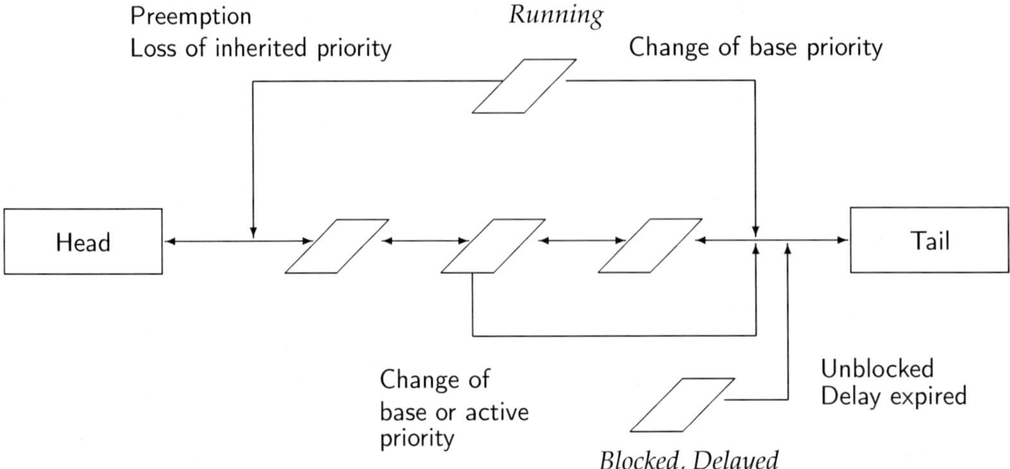

Fig. 21.1 `FIFO_Within_Priorities` policy

Let us first consider the transition in the lower right of the figure:

§D.2.3

> 4 • When a blocked task becomes ready, it is added at the tail of the ready queue for its active priority.

This is reasonable since there are other tasks of the same priority which have been ready, possibly for quite some time. The transition is also taken for a delay statement whose expiration time has already passed when it is executed §D.2.3(7), for example, if **delay** `0.0` is used by a task to voluntarily relinquish the processor.

The essence of preemptive scheduling is the replacement of the running task by a ready task of higher priority (the upper left of Figure 21.1):

§D.2.3

> 9 A task dispatching point occurs for the currently running task of a processor whenever there is a nonempty ready queue for that processor with a higher priority than the priority of the running task. The currently running task is said to be *preempted* and it is added at the head of the ready queue for its active priority.

If a task is preempted—say by an interrupt—there is no reason to "punish" it, so it goes back on the head of the queue. Of course, it may not become the next running task after the preempting task completes its execution, because a higher-priority task may have become ready in the meantime.

The other transitions show what happens when priorities are changed (Section 21.4).

21.3.2 Non-preemptive dispatching

The task dispatching policy *Non_Preemptive_FIFO_Within_Priorities* §D.2.4 is similar to the previous policy FIFO_Within_Priorities except that the running task is never interrupted just because a higher priority task becomes ready. If a task never becomes blocked, scheduling only occurs if it voluntarily executes a statement like **delay** 0.0.

§D.2.4

9 For this policy, a non-blocking delay_statement is the only non-blocking event that is a task dispatching point (see D.2.1).

21.3.3 Round robin dispatching

The task dispatching policy *Round_Robin_Within_Priorities* §D.2.5 is a modification of preemptive scheduling. In addition to the scheduling rules for FIFO_Within_Priorities, a task can be placed back on the ready queue if it takes "too long" to execute, where "too long" is defined by a *quantum* of time that can be set separately for each priority level §D.2.5(6). The subprograms for doing this are given in package `Ada.Dispatching.Round_Robin`. When a task becomes ready, it is given an *execution time budget* equal to the quantum for its priority level §D.2.5(11). The task is allowed to execute until its budget is reduced to zero, at which point the task is placed on the tail of the ready queue for its priority level §D.2.5(13–14). If the task is preempted by a higher priority task, it retains its budget §D.2.5(12).

21.3.4 Earliest deadline first dispatching

The task dispatching policy *EDF_Across_Priorities* §D.2.6 is an optimal policy in the sense that if it is at all possible to schedule a set of tasks, then it is possible to do so using *Earliest Deadline First (EDF)* scheduling. In EDF, there is no meaning to a fixed assignment of priorities to tasks, where a higher priority task is considered to be more important and preempts tasks of lesser importance. Instead, "priority" is assigned in terms of the time remaining until the deadline by which a task must complete its execution.

Consider two periodic tasks, T_1 and T_2. T_1 needs 2 seconds of execution time out of every 5 seconds of real time, while T_2 needs 1 second out of every 2 seconds. For simplicity, suppose that both tasks are released at time 0 when the system begins to run. According to EDF, since the deadline of T_2 is sooner ($2 < 5$), it is given priority over T_1, regardless of the "importance" of the tasks. It is easy to see that this assignment of priorities enables both tasks to execute by their deadlines.

Conceptually, EDF is like FIFO_Within_Priorities, except that there is only one priority level and one ready queue. When a task becomes ready, it is inserted into the ready queue at a position determined by its deadline. The EDF tasking policy is more complex than this because it must take into account interactions with priority ceiling locking (Section 21.7). This is described by the *preemption level control protocol* (also called the *stack-based priority-ceiling protocol*); see [4, Chapter 14] and [5, Chapter 8].

Types and subprograms for EDF scheduling can be found in package `Ada.Dispatching.EDF`.

Ada 95

The only standard task dispatching policy in Ada 95 is FIFO_Within_Priorities.

21.4 Base and active priorities

Suppose that task T_1 with priority 1 begins executing an entry E of a protected object PO, and suppose that T_1 is preempted by task T_2 with priority 2. Next, T_2 in turn is preempted by task T_3 with priority 3, which immediately calls the *same* entry E of PO:

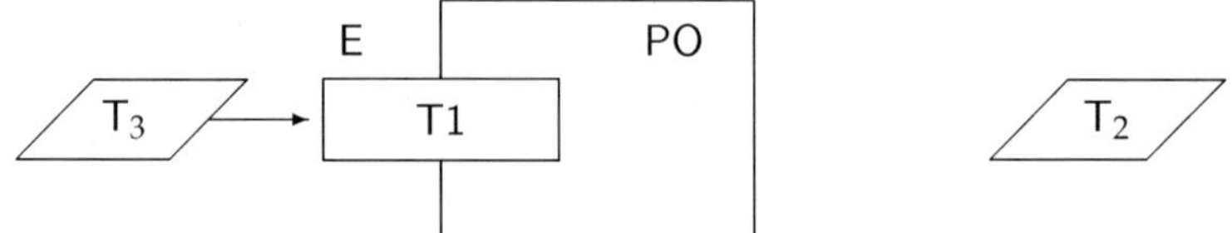

T_3 will be queued pending the completion of the entry body, but this will not occur as long as T_2 continues to execute because T_2 has a higher priority than T_1. Only when T_2 blocks, perhaps by calling an entry, will it relinquish the processor to T_1 and the entry will be completed. The state of the computation is that a high-priority task T_3 is waiting for a lower-priority task T_2 to block. This situation is called *priority inversion*. *Priority inheritance*, which distinguishes between the base priority and the active priority of a task, can be used to prevent priority inversion.

§D.1

15 A *task priority* is an integer value that indicates a degree of urgency and is the basis for resolving competing demands of tasks for resources. Unless otherwise specified, whenever tasks compete for processors or other implementation-defined resources, the resources are allocated to the task with the highest priority value. The *base priority* of a task is the priority with which it was created, or to which it was later set by Dynamic_Priorities.Set_Priority (see D.5). At all times, a task also has an *active priority*, which generally reflects its base priority as well as any priority it inherits from other sources. *Priority inheritance* is the process by which the priority of a task or other entity (e.g. a protected object; see D.3) is used in the evaluation of another task's active priority.

The active priority of a task is either its base priority or an inherited priority.

§D.1

20 At any time, the active priority of a task is the maximum of all the priorities the task is inheriting at that instant. For a task that is not held (see D.11), its base priority is a source of priority inheritance unless otherwise specified for a particular task dispatching policy. Other sources of priority inheritance are specified under the following conditions:

21 • During activation, a task being activated inherits the active priority that its activator (see 9.2) had at the time the activation was initiated.

22 • During rendezvous, the task accepting the entry call inherits the priority of the entry call (see 9.5.3 and D.4).

23 • During a protected action on a protected object, a task inherits the ceiling priority of the protected object (see 9.5 and D.3).

24 In all of these cases, the priority ceases to be inherited as soon as the condition calling for the inheritance no longer exists.

(Ceiling priority is discussed in detail in Section 21.7.)

In the example above, let us assume that the protected object has a priority such as 5 that is higher than any of the calling tasks. When the low priority task T_1 executes the entry, it *inherits* this priority, which becomes its active priority. Therefore, T_2 with priority 2 will not preempt T_1 when it is executing the protected action. Upon completion of the protected action, T_1 loses its inherited priority and returns to its low base priority. Since T_3 has a higher priority than T_2 it will now execute the entry call *before* T_2 is allowed to execute.

Priority inversion still occurs, but it is *bounded* by the maximum duration of the protected action. By analyzing all protected operations, a bound on the maximum duration of a priority inversion can be obtained and used to ensure that a real-time system meets its deadlines §D.2.3(11–13).

When a task's priority is reduced by the loss of the inherited priority (Figure 21.1, top left), the task goes to the head of the ready queue for its priority §D.2.3(5). This can prevent an additional context switch if no higher-priority tasks are ready.

21.5 Entry queuing policies

By default, the *queuing policy* is `FIFO_Queuing` §D.4(7), where entry queues are served in FIFO order. This can cause a form of priority inversion if a high-priority task is enqueued behind a long series of lower-priority tasks:

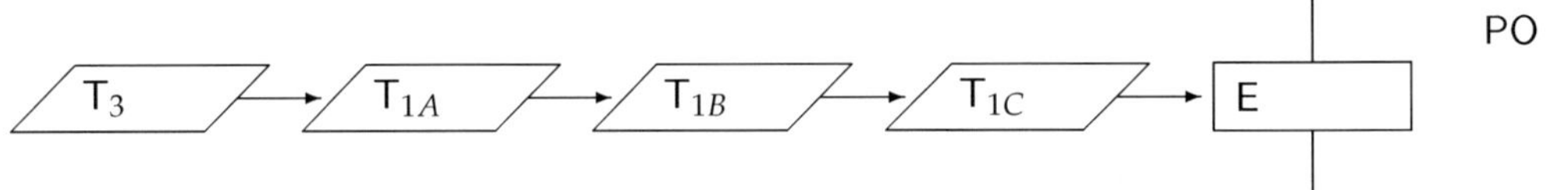

Priority inversion can also occur if there is more than one open alternative in a selective accept statement or more than one entry with an open barrier. Since the choice among the open alternatives or the entries is not specified by the language §9.5.3(17), a queue with a low-priority task could be served before a queue with a high-priority task. Annex §D specifies an additional queuing policy called `Priority_Queuing`, which can be chosen by using **`pragma`** `Queuing_Policy` §D.4(2–4). To define this policy, the priority of an entry call is first defined.

§D.4

> 9 • The calls to an entry (including a member of an entry family) are queued in an order consistent with the priorities of the calls. The *priority of an entry call* is initialized from the active priority of the calling task at the time the call is made, but can change later. Within the same priority, the order is consistent with the calling (or requeuing, or priority setting) time (that is, a FIFO order).

The rules for open alternatives and entry calls are now given.

§D.4

> 12 • When more than one condition of an entry_barrier of a protected object becomes True, and more than one of the respective queues is nonempty, the call with the highest priority is selected. If more than one such call has the same priority, the call that is queued on the entry whose declaration is first in textual order in the protected_definition is selected. For members of the same entry family, the one with the lower family index is selected.
>
> 14 • When more than one alternative of a selective_accept is open and has queued calls, an alternative whose queue has the highest-priority call at its head is selected. If two or more open alternatives have equal-priority queued calls, then a call on the entry in the accept_alternative that is first in textual order in the selective_accept is selected.

(The rule for delay_alternatives is given in §D.4(13).)

The rule that ties among priorities of entry calls are broken by the textual order of the entries or the accept statements may seem arbitrary, but it does ensure that the servicing of the queues is fully deterministic when using priority queuing.

In the CEO case study (Section 18.4), `Priority_Queuing` prevents the following race condition. The guard **when** `Wake(Finance)'Count = 0` of the alternative **accept** `Wake(Marketing)` is evaluated and found to be true; that is, there is no higher-priority accountant group waiting to wake the CEO. But before the CEO task can execute the accept statement, it is preempted and an accountant task is enqueued on `Wake(Finance)`. To ensure that the precedence specification is fulfilled, the rendezvous should be made with the accountant task, but this cannot be guaranteed with arbitrary selection of alternatives. `Priority_Queuing` ensures that the accountant task is accepted before the salesperson task, because it is waiting on an alternative that is textually before the other.

The queuing policy applies only to calls that are enqueued on an entry queue. If several tasks are trying to *start* a protected action, they are not queued and nothing can be said about the order in which they will begin the protected action §9.5.1(19).

Do not specify `Priority_Queuing` if you don't need it, because maintaining the entry queues in order of priority will be less efficient than simply adding a task to the tail of a FIFO queue.

21.6 Dynamic priorities*

Package `Ada.Dynamic_Priorities` §D.5.1 defines subprograms that set and return the *base priority* of a task. A change of the base priority will send the task to the tail of the ready queue for the new priority §D.2.2(9–10) (bottom center of Figure 21.1). The priority change is deferred during a protected action §D.5(10).

The attribute `Priority` §D.5.2 can be used to dynamically modify the ceiling priority of a protected object (see the following section).

Dynamic priority modification can be inefficient if `Priority_Queuing` is in effect, because the entry queues must be reordered. Furthermore, there are complications in the interaction between dynamic priority modification and protected objects.

21.7 Priority ceiling locking

Priority ceiling locking is an algorithm that enables priorities and preemptive scheduling to implement protected objects on a single processor without an additional locking construct. It is specified by **pragma** `Locking_Policy` with the argument `Ceiling_Locking` §D.3(3–4). In the absence of the pragma, the locking policy is implementation defined.

An implementation is required to support the specification of the ceiling locking policy together with all the task dispatching policies described in Section 21.3 §D.2.3(10), §D.2.4(10), §D.2.5(15), §D.2.6(10–11); in fact, ceiling locking must be specified if EDF scheduling is used.

A protected object is assigned a ceiling priority which is inherited by tasks executing protected actions of the object:

§D.3

8 • Every protected object has a *ceiling priority*, which is determined by either a Priority or Interrupt_Priority pragma as defined in D.1, or by assignment to the Priority attribute as described in D.5.2. The ceiling priority of a protected object (or ceiling, for short) is an upper bound on the active priority a task can have when it calls protected operations of that protected object.

12 • While a task executes a protected action, it inherits the ceiling priority of the corresponding protected object.

The following rule ensures that a task executing a protected object is not preempted by any task that could enter the protected object:

§D.3

13 • When a task calls a protected operation, a check is made that its active priority is not higher than the ceiling of the corresponding protected object; Program_Error is raised if this check fails.

Assume that task T_1 is executing a protected action with ceiling priority P_C. We show that another task T_2 cannot start a protected action of the same object, assuming that the task dispatching policy is FIFO_Within_Priorities:

- T_1 is executing a protected action at the inherited ceiling priority P_C §D.3(12).
- T_1 cannot block §9.5(8).
- T_2 cannot preempt T_1 to start the protected action: its priority must be less than or equal to P_C §D.3(13), but this is the priority of T_1, and a running task can only be preempted by a task of higher priority §D.2.3(9).

Therefore, T_1 cannot be directly preempted by T_2, but it is possible for T_1 to be preempted by a third task of priority higher than P_C, which could change the priority of T_2 to an arbitrary priority P_2. In that case:

- If $P_2 > P_C$, T_2 is not allowed to call the protected action §D.3(13).
- If $P_2 < P_C$, the scheduler will choose to run T_1, which has the higher, inherited, priority P_C.
- If $P_2 = P_C$, T_2 will be queued at the tail of the ready queue for this priority §D.2.3(5), but T_1 is at the head of the queue §D.2.3(9), so it will be chosen in preference to T_2.

21.8 Monotonic time

The package Ada.Real_Time §D.8 specifies a high-resolution monotonic clock. There is a private type Time and a function Clock that returns the current time. The unit of Time is an implementation-defined real number called Time_Unit.

Intervals of time are given by the private type Time_Span, rather than the predefined fixed point type Duration used in Ada.Calendar. The unit of Time_Span is called Time_Span_Unit and it represents the same interval as Time_Unit.

The type Time has no connection with astronomical or geographical time; instead, it is measured from an arbitrary point called the *epoch*:

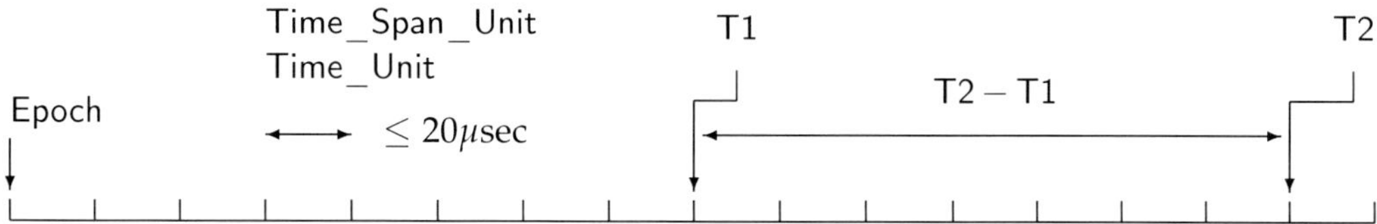

The epoch might be the time at which the system is switched on. Clock will return the *integral* number of Time_Units from the epoch until "just before now" §D.8(19). Intervals are measured in terms of the integral number of Time_Span_Units between two Times §D.8(20–23). In the diagram, at real times T1 and T2, the clock returns an integral number of units less than or equal to the time, so the time span T2-T1 is also integral. Subprograms are provided to do the usual arithmetical and relational operations on the private types.

The following table shows the required range and precision of time for both Ada.Calendar and Ada.Real_Time:

	Calendar	Real_Time
Range of time	500 years	50 years
Range of interval	1 day	± 1 hour
Precision	20 msec	20 μsec

It is recommended that the precision of calendar time be no less than 100 μsec and it is permitted that real time can have a smaller range and precision in implementations with a word size of less than 32 bits §D.8(46).

A value of type Time_Span can be converted to and from a value of type Duration §D.8(13), but there is no direct way to convert between Ada.Calendar.Time and Ada.Real_Time.Time. Instead, procedure Split §D.8(16) converts a value T of type Ada.Real_Time.Time measured in implementation-dependent Time_Units into SC of type Seconds_Count, which is the integral number of seconds since the epoch, and TS of type Time_Span, the remainder:

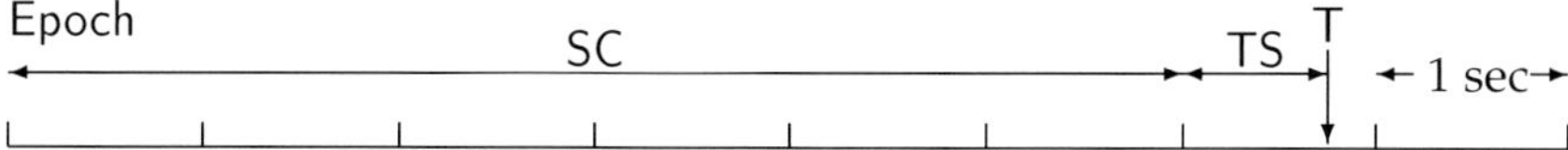

If you call Ada.Calendar.Clock once at the beginning of the program, you can use the seconds count to compute a calendar time based on real time.

Values of type Ada.Real_Time.Time can be used in a delay_until_statement §D.8(18), but to use values of type Ada.Real_Time.Time_Span in delay_relative_statements, delay alternatives or timed entry calls, they must be converted into values of type Duration.

21.8.1 *Timing events**

Computational requirements that take into account absolute or relative time can be programmed using delay statements (Section 19.3), delay alternatives (Section 19.8) and timed entry calls (Section 19.6). These constructs are used with tasks, but it can be useful to have *timing events* even in programs that do not use tasks. Timing events are supported by package Ada.Real_Time.Timing_Events §D.15.

Consider a long computation and suppose that we need to be notified if it takes more than one second. A timing event Watchdog is declared, and—before starting the computation—a handler for the event is set to be invoked in one second:

event

```
with Ada.Real_Time.Timing_Events;
with Watchdogs;
procedure Event is
  function Is_Prime(I: in Positive) return Boolean is ...

  Watchdog: Ada.Real_Time.Timing_Events.Timing_Event;
begin
  Ada.Real_Time.Timing_Events.Set_Handler(
    Event   => Watchdog,
    In_Time => Ada.Real_Time.Seconds(1),
    Handler => Watchdogs.Watchdog_PO.Watchdog_Handler'Access);
  if Is_Prime(179_424_673) then ... end if;
end Event;
```

The handler is an access to a protected subprogram:

```
with Ada.Real_Time.Timing_Events;
package Watchdogs is
  protected Watchdog_PO is
    procedure Watchdog_Handler(
      Event: in out Ada.Real_Time.Timing_Events.Timing_Event);
  end Watchdog_PO;
end Watchdogs;
```

The full program in the software archive simply prints a message if the handler is called.

Ada 95

Timing events are new for Ada 2005.

21.9 Execution time*

The constructs in `Ada.Calendar` and `Ada.Real_Time` measure the passage of "real" time; this is normally the output of a hardware counter that is transformed into points and intervals of time. *Execution time* is a measure of the time that a CPU is actually executing instructions of a *task*. The sum of the execution times of all the tasks of a partition (including the idle task) should more or less equal the passage of real time. Package `Ada.Execution_Time` §D.14 declares the type `CPU_Time` and subprogram `Clock` to measure execution time.

Package `Ada.Execution_Time.Timers` §D.14.1 declares a type `Timer` that can be used to handle timing events as in the previous case study, except that the time used is `CPU_Time` rather than `Ada.Real_Time.Time`. Package `Ada.Execution_Time.Group_Budgets` supports the creation of a *budget* of execution time that can be shared by a group of tasks. It declares the type `Group_Budget`, as well as subprograms for adding tasks to the budget and removing them, setting the budget, and defining a handler to call when the budget expires. These packages might not be implemented in an Ada implementation that runs on top of an operating system.

21.9.1 Case study: execution time

In this case study, worker tasks randomly receive computational tasks to perform; at the end of the program, the execution time for each task is printed, together with the total execution time for all the tasks. A worker task has two entries: `Input` to receive computational tasks and `Stop` to terminate the task and return its execution time:

total

```
with Ada.Real_Time;
package Worker is
  task type Worker_Task is
    entry Input(I: Positive);
    entry Stop(CPU: out Ada.Real_Time.Time_Span);
  end Worker_Task;
end Worker;
```

When the declarations in the task body are elaborated, `Ada.Execution_Time.Clock` §D.14.5 is called to obtain the initial CPU time which is stored in the variable `Start`:

```
with Ada.Execution_Time;
package body Worker is
  task body Worker_Task is
    Local: Natural;
    Start: Ada.Execution_Time.CPU_Time := Ada.Execution_Time.Clock;
    use type Ada.Execution_Time.CPU_Time;
```

When `Stop` is called, the task calls `Clock` again and returns the difference between it and `Start`:

```
  begin
    loop
      select
        accept Input(I: Positive) do
          Local := I;
        end Input;
        -- Compute computational task in Local
      or
        accept Stop(CPU: out Ada.Real_Time.Time_Span) do
          CPU := Ada.Execution_Time.Clock - Start;
        end Stop;
        exit;
      end select;
    end loop;
  end Worker_Task;
end Worker;
```

The type `CPU_Time` returned by `Ada.Execution_Time.Clock` is very similar to the type `Time` returned by `Ada.Real_Time.Clock`. It represents a point in time, rather than an interval of time as you might expect. To obtain the total execution time, we cannot add values of type `CPU_Time`; instead, the start and stop execution times are obtained and subtracted using the operator `"-"` §D.14(6) to give a value of type `Ada.Real_Time.Time_Span` that measures intervals ‡23.

An array `W` of `Worker` tasks is declared:

```
with Worker;
with Ada.Text_IO, Ada.Numerics.Discrete_Random, Ada.Real_Time;
procedure Total is
  subtype Group is Natural range 0..9;
  W: array(Group) of Worker.Worker_Task;
```

Generic package `Ada.Numerics.Discrete_Random` is instantiated with the subtype `Group` and `Ada.Text_IO.Fixed_IO` is instantiated with the predefined fixed point type `Duration` that will be used to print the values of the execution times:

```
  package Random_Numbers is new Ada.Numerics.Discrete_Random(Group);
  G: Random_Numbers.Generator;

  package Duration_IO is new Ada.Text_IO.Fixed_IO(Duration);
```

Two variables of type `Ada.Real_Time.Time_Span` are declared: `CPU` receives the CPU time from the task and `Total_CPU` is used to accumulate the CPU time:

```
  CPU:       Ada.Real_Time.Time_Span;
  Total_CPU: Ada.Real_Time.Time_Span := Ada.Real_Time.Time_Span_Zero;
  use type   Ada.Real_Time.Time_Span;
```

A use_type_clause is needed to make the subtraction operator visible.

The computational tasks are randomly allocated to worker tasks:

```
begin
  for I in 1 .. 100_000 loop
    W(Random_Numbers.Random(G)).Input(I);
  end loop;
```

Then, the system is shut down and the execution times are displayed:

```
  for I in Group loop
    W(I).Stop(CPU);
    Total_CPU := Total_CPU + CPU;
    Duration_IO.Put(Ada.Real_Time.To_Duration(CPU), Fore => 2, Aft => 5);
  end loop;
  Duration_IO.Put(Ada.Real_Time.To_Duration(Total_CPU), Fore => 2, Aft => 5);
end Total;
```

Ada 95

These packages are new for Ada 2005.

21.10 Preemptive abort*

Recall (Section 19.1.3, §9.8(15)) that the execution of the aborted construct completes no later than its next abort completion point. In a real-time system, it can be important that a task be aborted as soon as possible in order to release the resources it holds. Furthermore, a task in an infinite loop may never reach an abort completion point. §D.6(2) requires that an aborted construct be completed *immediately*, provided that it is not within an abort-deferred operation.

21.11 Synchronous task control*

A task that wishes to suspend itself can call a protected entry with a barrier that evaluates to false, and wait until another task changes the value of the variables in the barrier so that it evaluates to true. In §D.10, a lower-level primitive that can be used for this purpose is defined. Package `Ada.Synchronous_Task_Control` defines a limited private type `Suspension_Object` and subprograms that can be used to implement *two-stage suspension*: a task indicates that it is about to suspend on an object of the type and then it suspends itself. Another task will eventually release the suspension. The construct is equivalent to a binary semaphore with a queue of size one for blocked tasks. A suspension object is a very low-level, but very efficient construct. The use of suspension objects is demonstrated below in Section 21.14 on the Ravenscar profile.

21.12 Asynchronous task control*

Just as a task may want to suspend itself, it may need to suspend another task without its cooperation through an entry call. Package `Ada.Asynchronous_Task_Control` §D.11 declares the subprogram `Hold` for changing the priority of an arbitrary task to the *held priority*. This priority is defined to be lower than the priority of a conceptual *idle task*, which in turn is below the value of `System.Priority'First`. Such a task will never be scheduled until its priority is explicitly reset by calling `Continue`. The rules for held tasks follow naturally from this model as detailed in §D.11(14–19).

21.13 Tasking restrictions

There are no predefined limits to tasking in Ada: you can allocate an arbitrary number of tasks at run-time, any number of which can be blocked on a queue. Furthermore, the program text is not limited in terms of the number of select alternatives, nor in the number of task and protected entries. An implementation may need to use dynamic data structures to support this flexibility. In addition, certain features like abort can impose significant overhead on the algorithms that implement tasking. Full support of all the Ada constructs can conflict with the development of efficient run-time systems.

Tasking restrictions can be specified with **pragma** `Restrictions` (Section 22.2.4). Paragraphs §D.7(2–19) list restrictions that can be placed on the use of tasking in a program, for example:

```
pragma Restrictions(No_Task_Allocators, Max_Tasks => 10);
```

The implementation is required to enforce the restrictions, but the intention is that the restrictions be used to configure efficient run-time systems, although this is not required §D.7(20–21).

With the restrictions in the above pragma, the run-time system can use a static data structure to store task control blocks and this is likely to be more efficient than dynamic data structures. Even if your implementation does not create a more efficient run-time system when restrictions are requested, you may want to use the pragma to flag uses of features that you have decided to refrain from using in your design.

21.14 The Ravenscar profile

A *profile* enables a coordinated set of configuration pragmas to be concisely specified §D.13(5) by a single pragma:

```
pragma Profile(Ravenscar);
```

The one language-defined profile is the *Ravenscar profile*[2] §D.13.1 that is intended for use in building high integrity and high performance real-time systems. The profile includes the following three pragmas (see Sections 21.3.1, 21.7, 18.8.2):

```
pragma Task_Dispatching_Policy (FIFO_Within_Priorities);
pragma Locking_Policy (Ceiling_Locking);
pragma Detect_Blocking;
```

The first two enable task synchronization using the highly efficient ceiling locking protocol for synchronized objects, while the third ensures that a serious run-time error is actually detected.

In addition, the Ravenscar profile includes 23 restrictions on tasking §D.13.1(4), which facilitate the construction of small, efficient run-time systems. The inclusion of many of the restrictions such as No_Task_Allocators is obvious, because these constructs can seriously degrade performance or reliability. Others, however, will seem overly restrictive at first sight. Tasks can only be non-terminating loops with no entries, select statements, etc., because the rendezvous is considered to involve too much overhead and unpredictability. This leaves only protected objects and the very low-level *suspension objects* (Section 21.11, §D.10) for synchronization.

Protected objects are further restricted:

```
pragma Restrictions(
  Simple_Barriers,
  Max_Entry_Queue_Length => 1,
  Max_Protected_Entries  => 1);
```

This means that a protected object can have at most one entry §D.7(14), that at most one task at a time can be enqueued on that entry §D.7(19.1), and that the barrier on the entry must be a Boolean component of the protected object or a static Boolean expression §D.7(10.8):

[2] Ravenscar is the name of a village in Yorkshire, England, where the first meeting was held to define the profile.

```
protected PO is
  entry E;                    -- Only one entry
  procedure Proc;
private
  Signal: Boolean := False;
end PO;

protected body PO is
  entry E when Signal is      -- Simple barrier
  begin
    ...
  end E;

  procedure Proc is
  begin
    ...
  end;
end PO;
```

Synchronization algorithms have been developed that respect these restrictions. We give a series of case studies here and refer the reader to the Ravenscar guide [3] for further examples.

Ada 95

The Ravenscar profile is new to Ada 2005, but it is can be used to guide software development in Ada 95. The task dispatching policy FIFO_Within_Priorities and the locking policy Ceiling_Blocking were already defined in Ada 95, and an implementation is allowed to detect blocking with protected objects. The rest of the profile consists of restrictions that can be adhered to in Ada 95, whether or not your implementation enforces the restrictions.

21.14.1 *Case study: the Ravenscar profile*

We now present a sequence of case studies of algorithms for real-time systems in order to demonstrate what Ada constructs are consistent with the Ravenscar profile and how to work around those that are not.

A periodic task

A periodic task implemented with delay statements is consistent with the profile. The difference between the following program and the one in Section 19.3.1 is that we have used Ada.Real_Time instead of Ada.Calendar:

raven1

```
with Ada.Real_Time; use Ada.Real_Time;
procedure Raven1 is
  Interval: constant Time_Span := Milliseconds(200);
  Next:     Time := Clock + Interval;
begin
  loop
    delay until Next;
    -- Do something
    Next := Next + Interval;
  end loop;
end Raven1;
```

Sharing global data

Transferring simple data from one task to another can be done using global objects:

raven2

```
package Periodic is
  Data: Natural := 0;
  pragma Atomic(Data);
  task Periodic_Task;
end Periodic;
```

The **pragma** Atomic ensures that every read and write to Data is atomic and—since atomic also implies **pragma** Volatile—that accesses to the data are directly to memory.

Because of the restriction No_Task_Hierarchy, tasks cannot be declared local to the main subprogram; instead, tasks will be declared in library-level packages.

The task body is a periodic task that reads a value from a sensor and stores it in Data:

```
with Ada.Text_IO;
with Ada.Real_Time; use Ada.Real_Time;
package body Periodic is
  task body Periodic_Task is
    Interval: constant Time_Span := Milliseconds(200);
    Next:     Time := Clock + Interval;
  begin
    loop
      delay until Next;
      Data := ...
      Next := Next + Interval;
    end loop;
  end Periodic_Task;
end Periodic;
```

The main program is as before, except that it reads the variable `Data`.

Synchronization

Suppose now that the value from the sensor should not be saved in the variable `Data` until the previously value has been read. A suspension object (Section 21.11) can be used to implement this synchronization efficiently. A suspension object is added to the package specification:

raven3

```
with Ada.Synchronous_Task_Control;
package Periodic is
  Data: Natural := 0;
  pragma Atomic(Data);
  task Periodic_Task;

  S: Ada.Synchronous_Task_Control.Suspension_Object;
end Periodic;
```

The periodic task suspends itself on the suspension object until the main task sets it to true. If the delay has already expired by the time that the task is released from suspension, the delay statement will have no effect (except possibly to enable the task to be preempted):

```
with Ada.Text_IO;
with Ada.Real_Time; use Ada.Real_Time;
package body Periodic is
  task body Periodic_Task is
    Interval: constant Time_Span := Milliseconds(200);
    Next:     Time := Clock + Interval;
  begin
    loop
      Ada.Synchronous_Task_Control.Suspend_Until_True(S);
      delay until Next;
      Data := ...
      Next := Next + Interval;
    end loop;
  end Periodic_Task;
end Periodic;
```

The main task will release the suspension after it has read the variable `Data`:

```
with Ada.Real_Time; use Ada.Real_Time;
with Ada.Synchronous_Task_Control;
with Periodic;
procedure Raven3 is
  Interval: constant Time_Span := Milliseconds(400);
  Next:     Time := Clock + Interval;
begin
  loop
    delay until Next;
    ... := Periodic.Data;
    Ada.Synchronous_Task_Control.Set_True(Periodic.S);
    Next := Next + Interval;
  end loop;
end Raven3;
```

Protecting data

Leaving synchronization for now, suppose that we need to read and write multiword data, which cannot be accessed atomically just by using the pragma. The standard way to do this in Ada is to use protected objects, and this is consistent with the Ravenscar profile:

raven4

```
package Periodic is
  type Data_Type is array(0..1) of Natural;
  protected Protected_Data is
    procedure Write(D: in  Data_Type);
    procedure Read (D: out Data_Type);
  private
    Data: Data_Type := (others => 0);
  end Protected_Data;
  task Periodic_Task;
end Periodic;
```

The body of the protected object is straightforward:

```
with Ada.Real_Time; use Ada.Real_Time;
package body Periodic is
  protected body Protected_Data is
    procedure Write(D: in  Data_Type) is
    begin
      Data := D;
    end Write;
    procedure Read (D: out Data_Type) is
    begin
      D := Data;
    end Read;
  end Protected_Data;
```

The periodic task reads the individual input words and calls `Write` to transfer the data to the component of the protected object:

```
  task body Periodic_Task is
    Interval: constant Time_Span := Milliseconds(200);
    Next:     Time := Clock + Interval;
    Data:     Data_Type := ...;
  begin
    loop
      delay until Next;
      Data(0) := ...;
      Data(1) := ...;
      Protected_Data.Write(Data);
      Next := Next + Interval;
    end loop;
  end Periodic_Task;
end Periodic;
```

The main program calls Read to obtain the multiword data:

```
with Ada.Real_Time; use Ada.Real_Time;
with Periodic;
procedure Raven4 is
  Interval: constant Time_Span := Milliseconds(400);
  Next:     Time := Clock + Interval;
  Data:     Periodic.Data_Type;
begin
  loop
    delay until Next;
    Periodic.Protected_Data.Read(Data);
    -- Compute something with Data
    Next := Next + Interval;
  end loop;
end Raven4;
```

Protecting data with synchronization

Let us now add synchronization to the protected object. Suppose that the requirement is that data not be read until it is ready, although older data may be written with new data sampled from the sensor. The protected procedure Read now becomes an entry and a Boolean component is used to signal that data is ready:

raven5

```
package Periodic is
  type Data_Type is array(0..1) of Natural;

  protected Protected_Data is
    procedure Write(D: in  Data_Type);
    entry     Read (D: out Data_Type);
  private
    Data:       Data_Type := (others => 0);
    Data_Ready: Boolean := False;
  end Protected_Data;

  task Periodic_Task;
end Periodic;
```

The task body is the same except that procedure Write sets Data_Ready to true and this component is used in a barrier for entry Read:

```
with Ada.Text_IO;
with Ada.Real_Time; use Ada.Real_Time;
package body Periodic is
  protected body Protected_Data is
    procedure Write(D: in  Data_Type) is
    begin
      Data := D;
      Data_Ready := True;
    end Write;

    entry Read (D: out Data_Type) when Data_Ready is
    begin
      D := Data;
      Data_Ready := False;
    end Read;
  end Protected_Data;

  task body Periodic_Task is  -- as before
end Periodic;
```

This is consistent with the Ravenscar profile since there is only one entry, its barrier is simple and only one task can be queued on the entry.

Working around the limitations on protected objects

Suppose that requirements are modified so that the two words of the data are obtained from two different sensors, sampled in separate tasks. Furthermore, the sampling tasks are to overwrite `Data` only after its value has been read. It is not at all difficult to implement this algorithm in Ada (raven6 in the software archive), but the natural implementation violates the restrictions of the Ravenscar profile just mentioned:

```
entry Write(D: in Natural; ID: in Natural) when not Data_Ready is
entry Read (D: out Data_Type);
```

There are now two entries, the barrier is not simple (though this is easy to fix by changing `Data_Ready` to `Data_Not_Ready`), and two tasks can be queued on an entry.

The workaround is to use protected objects only for protecting data (as in raven4) and to implement the synchronization of the sampling tasks using suspension objects (as in raven3). The synchronization of the main task can still be done using an entry (as in raven5).

For each word of the data (and periodic task), a suspension object is declared:

raven7

```
with Ada.Synchronous_Task_Control;
package Periodic is
  type Data_Type is array(0..1) of Natural;
  type SO_Type   is
    array(Data_Type'Range) of Ada.Synchronous_Task_Control.Suspension_Object;
  S: SO_Type;
```

A component is added to the protected object to count the number of `Updates` to words of data:

```
  protected Protected_Data is
    procedure Write(D: in  Natural; ID: in Natural);
    entry     Read (D: out Data_Type);
  private
    Data:       Data_Type := (others => 0);
    Data_Ready: Boolean := False;
    Updates:    Natural := 0;
  end Protected_Data;

  task type Periodic_Task(ID: Natural);
  T0: Periodic_Task(0);
  T1: Periodic_Task(1);
end Periodic;
```

The protected procedure `Write` counts the number of updates and opens the barrier of the entry Read when the writing is completed:

```
with Ada.Real_Time; use Ada.Real_Time;
package body Periodic is
  protected body Protected_Data is
    procedure Write(D: in Natural; ID: in Natural) is
    begin
      Data(ID) := D;
      Updates := Updates + 1;
      if Updates = Data_Type'Length then
        Data_Ready := True;
        Updates := 0;
      end if;
    end Write;
```

Entry Read releases all the sampling tasks once it has read the data:

```
    entry Read (D: out Data_Type) when Data_Ready is
    begin
      D := Data;
      Data_Ready :- False;
      for I in SO_Type'Range loop
        Ada.Synchronous_Task_Control.Set_True(S(I));
      end loop;
    end Read;
  end Protected_Data;
```

The periodic tasks suspend until released when the data is read. Initially, the suspension objects are released to enable initial samples to be written:

```
  task body Periodic_Task is
    Interval: constant Time_Span := Milliseconds(200);
    Next:     Time := Clock + Interval;
    D:        Natural := 0;
  begin
    Ada.Synchronous_Task_Control.Set_True(S(ID));
    loop
      Ada.Synchronous_Task_Control.Suspend_Until_True(S(ID));
      delay until Next;
      D := (D + 1) mod 10;
      Protected_Data.Write(D, ID);
      Next := Next + Interval;
    end loop;
  end Periodic_Task;
end Periodic;
```

Clearly, this algorithm is less elegant and requires more work than the direct use of protected objects, but it demonstrates how concurrent algorithms for high integrity systems can be developed within the restrictions of the Ravenscar profile.

Projects

1. Study the Extended Example of the use of the Ravenscar Profile [3, Chapter 7].
2. Write a program that demonstrates each of the transitions that are shown in Figure 21.1 on the `FIFO_Within_Priorities` tasking policy.

Quizzes

Quiz 1:

```
procedure Main is
  function F return Natural is
  begin
    return 4;
  end F;
  pragma Priority(F);

  task T is
    pragma Priority(F);
  end T;
  task body T is ...
begin
  null;
end Main;
```

Quiz 2:

```
pragma Priority_Specific_Dispatching(
  FIFO_Within_Priorities, 5, 10);
pragma Priority_Specific_Dispatching(
  Round_Robin_Within_Priorities, 10, 15);
```

Quiz 3:

```
pragma Profile(Ravenscar);
package Pack is
  protected P is
    entry E;
  private
    Flag: Boolean := False;
  end P;
end Pack;

package body Pack is
  protected body P is
    entry E when not Flag is
    begin
      null;
    end E;
  end P;
end Pack;
```

Quiz 4:

```
SO: Ada.Synchronous_Task_Control.Suspension_Object;

task type T;
task body T is
begin
  Ada.Synchronous_Task_Control.Suspend_Until_True(SO);
end T;

A: array(0..1) of T;
```

Chapter 22
Distributed and High Integrity Systems

22.1 Distributed systems

A distributed system consists of several computers running their own programs that communicate with each other over a network. The terms used in Ada are:

§E

> 2 A *distributed system* is an interconnection of one or more *processing nodes* (a system resource that has both computational and storage capabilities), and zero or more *storage nodes* (a system resource that has only storage capabilities, with the storage addressable by one or more processing nodes).
> 3 A *distributed program* comprises one or more partitions that execute independently (except when they communicate) in a distributed system.
> 4 The process of mapping the partitions of a program to the nodes in a distributed system is called *configuring the partitions of the program*.
> 5 The implementation shall provide means for explicitly assigning library units to a partition and for the configuring and execution of a program consisting of multiple partitions on a distributed system; the means are implementation defined.

What is normally called a "program" is called a *partition* §10.2 in Ada, while a program is a set of partitions that can be assigned to the nodes of a distributed system. One or more or all (active) partitions may be assigned to a (processing) node. The versions of the units of a distributed system must be consistent, as defined in §E.3.

22.1.1 Categorization

A central problem that arises in the development of a distributed system is to establish the semantic connections between units assigned to different active partitions §E.1(2). If a type `T` is declared in a package P, and the package is used in more than one active partition, is one type defined for all partitions, or does each partition define its own type which may not be consistent with the others? The solution in Ada is to *categorize* library units §E.2(1–2). A categorization pragma restricts the entities that can be declared within a unit; more restrictive categories can be used to maintain consistency across partitions.

There are five categories that are specified by pragmas:

- **pragma** Pure §10.2.1(14): A pure unit has no state so it can be consistently replicated in more than one partition.
- **pragma** Shared_Passive §E.2.1: A shared passive unit has only passive data (variables) and subprograms, but not tasks or protected objects with entries. A *passive partition* can contain only pure and shared passive units, and can be assigned to a storage node.
- **pragma** Remote_Types §E.2.2: Remote types units are used to contain declarations of access-to-subprogram types or access-to-class-wide types that are used as encodings for communications between active partitions. They can also be consistently replicated in more than one partition. Variables cannot be declared in the visible part of the unit.
- **pragma** Remote_Call_Interface §E.2.3: RCI units are split across partitions: all partitions share the package *specification*, but the package *body* is assigned to one partition. If a visible subprogram of an RCI unit is called from a partition not containing the body, the call is transparently forwarded to the partition containing the body. Variables cannot be declared in the visible part of the unit.
- Normal: No restrictions. A type declaration in a normal unit gives rise to distinct types in each partition containing the unit.

A unit can only depend on units of categories that appear above it in the hierarchy.

22.1.2 *Remote subprogram calls*

§E.4

> 1 A *remote subprogram call* is a subprogram call that invokes the execution of a subprogram in another partition. The partition that originates the remote subprogram call is the *calling partition*, and the partition that executes the corresponding subprogram body is the *called partition*. Some remote procedure calls are allowed to return prior to the completion of subprogram execution. These are called *asynchronous remote procedure calls*.

The mechanics of a remote subprogram call—also known as a *remote procedure call (RPC)*—are described in §E.4(9–20) and illustrated in Figure 22.1. The calling partition (on the left side of the Figure) contains the specification of an RCI package P that contains a procedure Proc. Replacing the body of the package is a *calling stub*. The stub is the interface between the calling

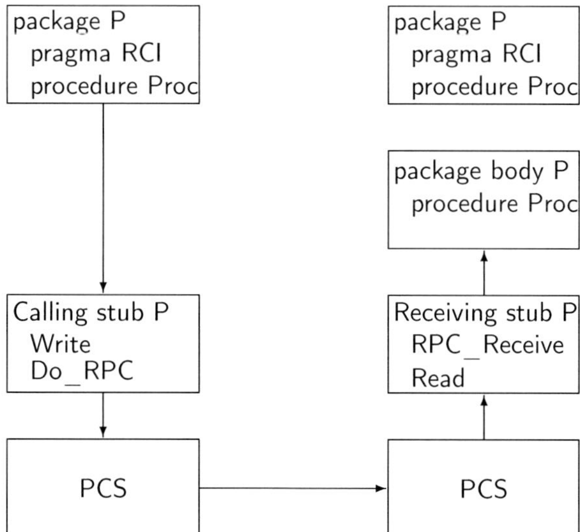

Fig. 22.1 Remote procedure call

partition and the underlying *partition communication subsystem (PCS)* §E.5. The calling stub *marshals* the parameters of the procedure call, that is, it translates them into stream elements using the attribute `Write`, as was described in Section 14.3. The stream is passed to the PCS by calling `Do_RPC` (or `Do_APC` for a non-blocking asynchronous call) declared in package `System.RPC` §E.5(17–20).

When the call is received by the PCS of the called partition, the *receiving stub* is notified by calling an *RPC_Receiver* procedure §E.5(21) and the parameters are *unmarshalled* from the stream. Finally, the receiving stub calls the subprogram body in the package body. If the RPC has **out** or **in out** parameters, they are returned to the calling partition in a similar manner.

This processing is transparent to the programmer; you only have to declare the units with pragmas such as `Remote_Call_Interface` (respecting the restrictions, of course), and configure the units into partitions using an implementation-supplied tool. The stubs, streams and PCS are the responsibility of the implementation. Only the PCS is non-portable, since it must implement the transmission of a stream over a physical communications channel.

§E.4

> 2 There are three different ways of performing a remote subprogram call:
> 3 • As a direct call on a (remote) subprogram explicitly declared in a remote call interface;
> 4 • As an indirect call through a value of a remote access-to-subprogram type;
> 5 • As a dispatching call with a controlling operand designated by a value of a remote access-to-class-wide type.
> 6 The first way of calling corresponds to a *static* binding between the calling and the called partition. The latter two ways correspond to a *dynamic* binding between the calling and the called partition.

We now give an example demonstrating the third technique.

22.1.3 *Case study: distributed simulation*

Suppose that our rocket simulation can no longer be run on a single computer; we redesign it for a system with a separate node (computer) for simulating each event type (here limited to telemetry and engine events) and an additional node to create the scenario:

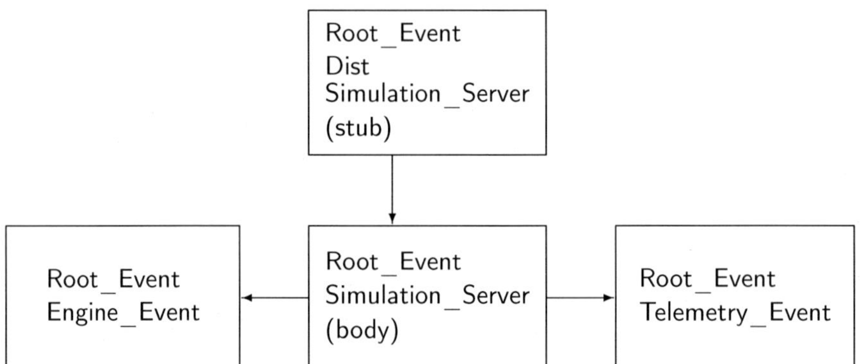

A remote types package `Root_Event` is shared by all partitions. Package `Simulation_Server` is a remote call interface package assigned to another partition and is responsible for dispatching calls from the client `Dist` to the `Simulate` subprogram.

The normal declarations of a tagged type and primitive subprograms are declared in the remote types package `Root_Event`:

dist

```
package Root_Event is
  pragma Remote_Types;
  type Event     is abstract tagged limited private;
  type Event_Ptr is access all Event'Class;
  procedure Simulate(E: in Event) is abstract;
private
  type Event is abstract tagged limited null record;
end Root_Event;
```

pragma Remote_Call_Interface is specified in the Simulation_Server to enable it to be split between the partition containing the client Dist and its own partition:

```
with Root_Event;
package Simulation_Server is
  pragma Remote_Call_Interface;
  procedure Go_Simulate(E_Ptr: Root_Event.Event_Ptr);
end Simulation_Server;

package body Simulation_Server is
  procedure Go_Simulate(E_Ptr: Root_Event.Event_Ptr) is
  begin
    Root_Event.Simulate(E_Ptr.all);
  end Go_Simulate;
end Simulation_Server;
```

The child packages of Root_Event for each subsystem are as before.

Function Get_Event, which returns a pointer to the class-wide type, stands for the Get function of the heterogeneous priority queue. It prompts you to enter a character, which is used to decide which specific type to return:

```
-- with's as needed
procedure Dist is
  function Get_Event return Root_Event.Event_Ptr is
    C: Character;
  begin
    Put(" Choose system ");
    Get(C);
    if C = 'e' then
      return Root_Event.Engine.Create( ... );
    else
      return Root_Event.Telemetry.Create( ... );
    end if;
  end Get_Event;
```

The value returned is sent to the `Simulation_Server`, which derefences the pointer and dispatches the call to one of the derived classes on another partition:

```
begin
   Simulation_Server.Go_Simulate(Get_Event);
end Dist;
```

22.2 High integrity systems

Annex §H and parts of Section §13 address support in Ada for high integrity systems.

SPARK [1] is an Ada-based language designed for the development of high integrity systems. It extends a subset of Ada with annotations for static analysis that can be analyzed by software tools.

22.2.1 *Program validation*

Annex §M summarizes implementation-defined characteristics that must be documented. Annex §H imposes additional documentation requirements.

§H.2

> 1 The implementation shall document the range of effects for each situation that the language rules identify as either a bounded error or as having an unspecified effect. If the implementation can constrain the effects of erroneous execution for a given construct, then it shall document such constraints. . . .

pragma `Reviewable` §H.3.1 requires that an implementation produce an object code listing, and information on memory requirements and error situations; these documents should be human-readable, as well as machine-readable so that they can be processed by automated tools §H.3.1(19).

A valuable tool for testing and debugging programs is a hardware analyzer that—with little or no effect on the behavior of the computer—can save some or all of the state of a computation for later analysis. **pragma** `Inspection_Point` §H.3.2 can be used within a sequence of declarations or statements to require the implementation to make some or all objects available for inspection. The pragma is not just a documentation requirement telling you where to find each object; it can modify code generation by requiring that a value be stored in memory rather than retained in a register when an inspection point is reached.

22.2.2 *Abnormal objects*

When you create and initialize an object, it is in a *normal* state §13.9.1(4). An object can become *abnormal* in certain circumstances; for example, if an assignment is interrupted by an abort statement, a discriminant might be updated but not a variant that depends on the discriminant. It is erroneous to use an abnormal object §13.9.1(8).

22.2.3 *Invalid representations*

A *scalar* object can have an *invalid representation* §13.9.1(9). Consider:

```
subtype Index is Integer range 0..200;
```

The unit of memory allocation is at least one byte, so variables of the subtype `Index` can hold values like 231 that do not represent values of the subtype. Sources of invalid data are primarily input data and the results of `Ada.Unchecked_Conversion`; for example, a byte received from a communications line might have any of the 256 bit patterns, although it is intended to contain values of a subtype like `Index` with fewer values. You can explicitly check the validity of a scalar object by using the attribute `Valid` §13.9.2. The attribute never raises an exception.

Many languages and compilers automatically zero uninitialized variables. This can actually reduce reliability, because zero is often a valid, though unintended, value of the subtype! **`pragma`** `Normalize_Scalars` §H.1 requests the compiler to set uninitialized objects to a predictable, possibly invalid, representation. The idea is to "flush out" the error as soon as possible by increasing the likelihood that `Constraint_Error` will be raised, rather than continuing the computation with an incorrect value.

22.2.4 *Restrictions*

Validation of a program requires validation not just of your code, but also of the code of the run-time system and standard libraries. By restricting the language features in a program, an implementation can support a smaller run-time system and set of libraries, greatly reducing the validation effort. Furthermore, a program that is guaranteed not to use a construct (like dynamic allocation) need not be checked for problems that can occur if it is used (storage leaks).

`pragma` `Restrictions` §13.12 specifies the restrictions that a program can take upon itself. Paragraph §13.12.1 defines four language-defined pragmas in the core language:

- `No_Implementation_Attributes`
- `No_Implementation_Pragmas`
- `No_Obsolescent_Features`
- `No_Dependence`

The first three are intended to ensure greater portability of the program. `No_Dependence` is used to specify that the program does not depend on a certain library unit.

An implementation that supports Annex §H is required to support certain restrictions such as `No_Allocators` §H.4. In addition, the restrictions described in §D.7 must be supported, in particular, restricting `Max_Tasks` to zero §H.4(2). This allows an implementation to remove support for tasking from the run-time system, making its validation significantly easier. Check your implementation's documentation to see what effect restrictions have on a program §13.12(9). Much of the Ravenscar Profile §D.13.1 (Section 21.14) for developing real-time systems with predictable performance consists of about two dozen restriction pragmas.

Ada 95

The four restrictions in §13.12.1 are new to Ada 2005. See §H.4 for the changes in the restrictions for high integrity systems. The Ravenscar Profile is also new.

22.2.5 *Elaboration policy*

As discussed in Section 15.5 and in §10.2, the order of elaboration is implementation-dependent as long as it respects the semantic dependences of the library units. When a task is declared in a library unit, it begins to execute as soon as the package body is elaborated (Section 19.1) and this can give rise to race conditions. Library-level tasks are common in real-time systems and, in fact, the Ravenscar profile (Section 21.14) includes the restriction `No_Task_Hierarchy`.

pragma `Partition_Elaboration_Policy` §H.6 can be used to specify an alternate policy for the order of elaboration of library-level tasks.

§H.6

> 8 If the partition elaboration policy is Sequential, then task activation and interrupt attachment are performed in the following sequence of steps:
>
> 9 • The activation of all library-level tasks and the attachment of interrupt handlers are deferred until all library units are elaborated.

The default policy is `Concurrent`.

Projects

1. Many algorithms for distributed systems are presented in [2] and the software archive for that book contains implementations where each node is represented as a task. Implement some of these algorithms on a distributed system using the constructs in Annex §G.

Appendix A
Glossary of ARM Terms

The *ARM* is written in a precise style, with specialized terms defined and then used consistently throughout the document; this glossary collects the definitions of these terms. For brevity, the glossary does not include well known terms like *procedure* and terms from the Annexes. Source code examples will help you understand and remember the definitions. The following declarations will be used in the examples:

```
type Piece is (Pawn, Knight, Bishop, Rook, Queen, King);
type Matrix (Integer range <>, Integer range <>) of Piece;
type Game_Board(Size: Positive) is
  record
    B: Matrix(1..Size, 1..Size);
  end record;

type Node;
type Ptr is access Node;
type Node is
  record
    Key: Integer;
    Next: Ptr;
  end record;

package P is
  type Parent is tagged null record;
  procedure Primitive(X: Parent);
  type Derived is new Parent with null record;
  procedure Primitive(X: Derived);
end P;
```

abandoned §11.4(3) See *exception*.

abort-deferred §9.8(5) When an abort statement is executed, if a task is executing one of the operations listed in this section, the operation is allowed to complete before the abort takes effect. For example, a protected action is abort-deferred and will be allowed to complete.

abnormal completion §7.6.1(2) The execution of a task completes abnormally if an exception is raised and not handled, or if a task is aborted.

abnormal object §13.9.1(1) If an assignment statement is interrupted by an abort statement or if a non-scalar object is returned from an imported subprogram, the bits representing the object might not form a value of the object's type. The object is abnormal and certain uses are *erroneous*. A scalar object that does not contain a value of its subtype is said to have an *invalid representation*. For example, an uninitialized variable of subtype `Natural` has an invalid representation if the initial contents of the variable represent a negative number.

accessibility §3.10.2(3) Accessibility is defined by the nesting levels of *masters* at run-time. They are used to prevent dangling pointers when general access types are used. It is illegal to apply the `Access` attribute to an object that has a *deeper* accessibility level *than* the access type. Usually, accessibility levels are known at compile-time, in which case one level can be determined to be *statically deeper than* another §3.10.2(4). A library unit is at *library level* §3.10.2(22).

```
type Pointer is access all Integer;
                              -- General access type
function F return Ptr is
  N: Integer;                 -- Statically deeper than Pointer
begin
  return N'Access;            -- Error !
end F;
```

actual subtype §3.3(23) See *nominal subtype*.

adjust §7.6(15–16) The operation performed on the target object of a *controlled* type after the new value is copied during assignment. Procedure `Adjust` can be overridden.

ambiguous §8.6(30) See *overloading*.

ancestor §3.4.1(10) See *derived type*.

ancestor §10.1.1(11) See *unit*.

anonymous type §3.2.1(7) Single arrays, tasks and protected objects are objects of anonymous type. Since the type has no name, you cannot declare other objects of the type; however, you can convert an anonymous array to a named array type §4.6(9–12).

applicable index constraint §4.3.3(10) This is an index constraint that is used to determine the bounds of an array aggregate with **others**. In the following declaration, the index constraint `(1..100)` is the *applicable index constraint* for the aggregate used as its initial value:

```
S: String(1..100) := (others => '*');
```

aspect clause §13.1 An *aspect clause* is used to specify a representation item or an operational item. A *representation item* is used to specify an object's run-time representation, such as the size, alignment and placing of the object. An *operational item* specifies an aspect of a type such as the external tag (string representation) of a tagged type §13.3(13.1) and stream attributes §13.13.2(1).

base range §3.5(6) Scalar types are usually implemented in a larger range than that needed to store values of the type; this range is called the *base range* of the type. Computations involving predefined operators are done in the base range. The attribute `S'Base` gives the *base subtype* of the type of S.

```
type     My_Integer is range 0..10_000;
K1, K2: My_Integer       := 8_000;
K:       My_Integer       := K1 + K2;
B:       My_Integer'Base  := K1 + K2;
```

The computation `K1 + K2` will not cause an error in any implementation that represents integers with at least 16 bits. `Constraint_Error` will be raised when the result is assigned to `K`, though not when assigned to `B`.

bounded error §1.1.5(7–8) See *error*.

by copy §6.2(2–3) Parameters of elementary types must be passed by copy, that is, by creating a local object and copying the actual parameter in and/or out. The types listed in §6.2(5–9) must be passed *by reference*; a reference to the entity is passed rather than a copy of the entity's contents. By-reference types include types such as tagged types and task types that have data structures (jump tables and task control blocks) associated with them. An implementation may choose to pass types such as records and arrays either by copy or by reference.

by reference §6.2(4) See *by copy*.

callable §6(2) A *callable entity* is a subprogram or entry. A *callable construct* defines the action taken when the entity is called; it is a subprogram or entry body, or an accept statement.

category of types §3.4(1.1) The term *category of types* is includes *classes* of types, and, in addition, sets of types with similar characteristics that are not necessarily related by derivation; examples are limited and abstract types. When instantiating a generic unit, an actual type must be in the category determined by the formal generic type §12.5(7). (This term is not used in Ada 95.)

check §11.5(2) A language-defined *check* such as `Index_Check` can *fail*, raising an exception.

class §3.4(1.1) A *class* of types is a set of types that is closed under derivation; for example, if we derive the type `My_Integer` from `Integer`, the two form a class. Classes derived from a tagged type are particularly important because class-wide types can be defined.

class-wide type §3.4.1(4) A type whose values are the union of the values of all the *specific types* within a *derivation class*.

compatible §3.2.2(12) See *constraint*.

compilation §10.1(2) See *unit*.

complete context §8.6(4) See *overloading*.

completely defined §3.11.1(8) See *full type*.

completion §3.11.1 Some declarations can be written in two parts: the first part is said to *require a completion*. An example is a subprogram that is declared in a package specification; it requires a completion (subprogram body) in the package body.

completion §7.6.1(2) The end of the execution of an entity. *Completion* may occur either by executing the last statement, or by a transfer of control caused by raising an exception or executing a statement such as return statement. After completion, a construct is *left* §7.6.1(3), meaning that execution continues with the next action. Before leaving a master, *finalization* §7.6.1(4) must be performed: waiting for a dependent task, and—for *controlled types*—execution of the `Finalize` procedure. A *master* §7.6.1(2) is the execution of certain constructs such as a subprogram or a task body.

composite type §3.2(4) Composite types are types that can have components: record types and their extensions, array types, task types and protected types. Private types and their extensions are also considered to be composite types. Composite types (except for arrays) may have discriminants.

conformance §6.3.1 Two subprogram *profiles* conform to each other in one of four ways, each one adding additional requirements:

- *type conformant* The number and types of the parameters are the same. Two subprogram declarations are *homographs* if they are type conformant §8.3(8); they cannot be overloaded.

  ```
  procedure Proc(X: in Integer := 5);
  procedure Proc(Y: out Positive);       -- Error
  ```

  The parameter `Y` has a different mode and *subtype* than `X`, but the declarations are type conformant and overloading is not legal.
- *mode conformant* The profiles have identical modes. Mode conformance is sufficient for generic instantiation §12.6(8).

  ```
  generic
    with procedure Formal(X: in Integer);
  procedure Gen;

  procedure Actual(Z: in Positive);
  procedure Instance Gen(Formal => Actual);
  ```

  The call `Formal(-1)` is legal within the body of `Gen`, although it will raise `Constraint_Error` in the instantiation `Instance`.
- *subtype conformant* Subtypes of the profile must *statically match*. Subtype conformance is sufficient for overriding §3.9.2(10). The declaration of `Primitive` for `Derived` overrides the parent's subprogram even though the formal parameter name has changed:

```
type Parent is tagged null record;
procedure Primitive(X:   Parent);
type Derived is new Parent with null record;
procedure Primitive(XXX: Derived);
```

- *fully conformant* The formal parameter names must be identical and the default expressions must be fully conformant §6.3.1(19–22). A completion must be fully conformant §6.3(4):

```
package P is
  procedure P1(X: Integer; Y: Integer);
  procedure P2(X: Integer := 5);
  procedure P3(X: Integer := 5);
end P;

package body P is
  procedure P1(XX: Integer; YY: Integer) is ...   -- Error
  procedure P2(X: Integer := 10)         is ...   -- Error
  procedure P3(X: Integer := 2#101#)     is ...   -- OK
end P;
```

constant §3.3(13) See *object*.

constraint §3.2(7) A restriction on the possible values of a type. A value *satisfies* a constraint if it satisfies the restriction. A constraint applied to a subtype must be *compatible* with the subtype. There are three types of constraints:

- *range constraint* §3.5(2)

```
subtype Moves_Far  is Piece     range Knight..Queen;
subtype Important1 is Piece     range Queen..King;
subtype Important2 is Moves_Far range Queen..King;
    -- Error, the constraint is not compatible with the subtype
```

- *index constraint* §3.6.1(2)

```
Rectangle: Matrix(1..4, 1..8);
```

- *discriminant constraint* §3.7.1(2)

```
Board: Game_Board(Size => 8);
```

constrained subtype §3.2(9) See *unconstrained subtype*.

controlled type §7.6(2) A controlled type is a type descended from the abstract tagged type `Controlled` or `Limited_Controlled` declared in `Ada.Finalization`. These types have primitive procedures `Initialize`, `Adjust` and `Finalize`, which are called when a value of the type is elaborated, assigned or finalized, respectively. The procedures are declared **null** and can be overridden if needed.

controlling formal parameter §3.9.2(2) If T is a tagged type and S is a primitive subprogram of T, then the formal parameters of S of type T are *controlling*. A call will be statically bound or dynamically dispatched depending on the corresponding *controlling operands* (actual parameters) of the call (see the glossary entry for *dynamically tagged*). A function may also have a *controlling result*. If the following declaration is placed after the declaration of the tagged type Parent, then P1 and P3 are controlling, but P2 is not:

```
procedure S(P1: in Parent; P2: out Integer; P3: in out Parent);
```

convention §6.3.1(2) A *convention* defines how a callable entity is invoked at the machine-code level. *Ada* is the convention for subprograms defined in Ada and *Intrinsic* is the convention for built-in operations. Protected operations have their own convention. Conventions are also used to specify the interfaces with other programming languages §B.1(2). Some language rules refer to the convention of a subprogram; for example, you cannot use the Access attribute on a subprogram of Intrinsic convention §3.10.2(32), such as predefined "+" on type Integer.

convertible §4.6(4) A type—the *operand type*—is convertible to another type—the *target type*—if type conversion can be performed according to the rules in §4.6. The conversion may be either a *value conversion*, which creates a new value of the target type, or a *view conversion*, which denotes the same object as the operand.

cover §3.8.1(9–12) A *discrete choice* such as 5..10 or **others** is said to *cover* a set of values of a subtype. In contexts such as aggregates, variant records and case statements, a *discrete choice list* must cover all the values of the subtype. The term is also used for exception choices §11.2(6).

cover §3.4.1(9) A class-wide type is said to *cover* all the types in the class, while a specific type covers only itself. Membership tests such as E **in** Main_Engine'Class are defined in terms of covering §4.5.2(2).

current instance §8.6(17–18) In contexts such as task types, protected types and generic units, the name of a type denotes a value or an object of the type rather than the type itself. This object or value is the one currently being executed. In the following protected type, the call PT.E refers to the entry of the *current instance* of the protected object:

```
protected type PT is
  procedure P;
  entry E;
end PT;

protected body PT is
  procedure P is
  begin
    PT.E;
  end P;

  entry E ...
end PT;
```

declaration §3.1(5) A declaration *defines a view* of an entity and associates a name with the view; it usually *defines the entity* itself. *Entity* is a general term used for "things" like objects, subprograms, exceptions, etc. A declaration may be *explicit* or *implicit*:

```
type Piece is (Pawn, Knight, Bishop, Rook, Queen, King);
  -- Explicitly defines the type Piece and the enumeration literals
  -- Piece'First is an implicitly declared attribute
function EOL return Boolean renames Ada.Text_IO.End_Of_Line;
  -- EOL is a new view of an existing subprogram
```

declarative region §8.1(1) A place where a nested declaration can occur; examples are declarations of subprograms and record types. A for-loop statement is also a declarative region, because the loop parameter is nested within. The declarative region of a package includes its body and children.

deeper than §3.10.2(3) See *accessibility*.

deferred constant §7.4(2) A constant can be declared before the full type is declared. The value of the constant must be completed following the full type declaration:

```
package P is
  type ID  is private;
  Null_ID: constant ID;
private
  type ID  new String(1..5);
  Null_ID: constant ID := "*****";
end P;
```

defining name §3.1(10) The occurrence of a name where it is defined is its *defining name*. Subsequent occurrences of the name are called *usage names*. Syntactic categories for defining names start with defining_, while categories for usage names are direct_name and selector_name.

definite subtype §3.3(23) See *indefinite subtype*.

definition §3.1(7) See *declaration*.

dereference §4.1(8) A *dereference* of an access value returns a view of the designated object or subprogram. A dereference may be either *explicit* or *implicit*:

```
Head:    Ptr     := new Node;
N:       Node    := Head.all;    -- Explicit dereference
I:       Integer := Head.Key;    -- Implicit dereference
```

derivation class §3.4.1(1) See *class-wide type*.

derived type §3.4 A *derived type* is a new type derived from an existing *parent type*. It is said to be a *descendant* of its parent type, which is the derived type's *ancestor*. These terms are extended transitively: if a type is derived from a descendant of a parent type, it is also a a descendant of the parent type. An "ancestor" that is an interface (not a tagged type) is called a *progenitor*.

descendant §3.4.1(10) See *derived type*.

descendant §10.1.1(11) See *unit*.

designate §3.10(1) An access value *designates* the object or subprogram that it points to. The subtype of a designated object is called the *designated subtype* §3.10(10), and the profile of a subprogram that is designated is called the *designated profile* §3.10(11). If `P` is an access object, then `P.all` is the object it designates.

determined class §12.5(6) A generic formal parameter determines a class of types; a matching generic actual parameter must be in this class. For example, the class determined by **private** is the class of all nonlimited types §12.5.1(17).

```
generic
  type T is private;
procedure Gen;

with Gen;
with Ada.Exceptions;
package Instance is new Gen(Ada.Exceptions.Exception_Id);
```

By §11.4.1(2), `Exception_Id` is a private type so the actual parameter is legal even though we do not know how the type is implemented. `Exception_Occurrence` is limited private §11.4.1(3) and would not be a legal actual parameter for an instantiation of `Gen`.

direct name §4.1(3) See *name*.

directly visible §8.3(2) See *scope*.

discrete choice §3.8.1(5) A *discrete choice* is a range of values in a case statement, array aggregate or variant record declaration:

```
type Values (Piece) of Integer;
V: Values :=
  ( Pawn           => 1,    -- Discrete choice is an expression
    Knight..Bishop => 3,    -- Discrete choice is a discrete range
    Rook           => 5,    -- Discrete choice is an expression
    others         => 10);  -- Discrete choice is others
```

discrete type §3.2(3) The *discrete types* are the integer types and the enumeration types (including `Character` and `Boolean`). Discrete types are used for loop parameters §5.5(4) and array index types §3.6(5).

dynamically tagged §3.9.2(5) A controlling operand of class-wide type is said to be *dynamically tagged* and causes dispatching at run-time. If the operand is of a specific type, it is said to be *statically tagged* and the subprogram can be statically bound at compile-time. If the operand is a function call that returns a class-wide type (and no operands of the function call are either statically or dynamically tagged), the operand is said to be *tag indeterminate*.

elaboration §3.1(11) See *execution*.

elaboration dependences §10.2(9) See *semantic dependences*.

elementary type §3.2(3) The *elementary types* are the *scalar* types and the *access* types. Elementary types are *definite* §3.3(23) and are passed *by copy* §6.2(3). The scalar types are the *discrete* types and the *real* types (*floating point* and *fixed point*). Scalar types are ordered §3.5(1) and can have *range constraints* §3.5(7).

environment §10.1.4(1) The *environment* of a compilation is the context in which the compilation takes place.

environment task §10.2(8) The execution of a partition takes place within an *environment task*, which elaborates all the library units and the main subprogram.

erroneous §1.1.5(9–10) See *error*.

error §1.1.5 A violation of a language rule. Errors are classified into four categories:

- Errors that must be detected prior to run-time:

```
procedure Proc(X: out Integer);
Proc(17);                        -- Illegal, must be a variable 6.4.1(5)
```

- Errors that must be detected at run-time; these errors will raise exceptions.
- *Bounded errors* need not be detected by the implementation, but the range of possible effects is limited. For example, it is a bounded error to access a formal parameter by an alias such as a global variable §6.2(12):

```
S: String := "Hello world";
procedure Proc(T: in String) is
begin
  S(1..5) := "Bye  ";
  Put(T);                        -- Is T a reference to S or a copy of S?
end Proc;

Proc(S);
```

  The possible effects are: read the old value, read the new value, and raise `Program_Error`.
- *erroneous execution* An error that need not be detected and whose effect is unspecified. Examples are: dereferencing a dangling pointer, unsynchronized access to a shared variable, and suppressing a check that can fail.

evaluation §3.1(11) See *execution*.

exception §11(1) An exception has a *name* (predefined or user-defined). Each time that an exception is raised, it creates a new *occurrence* of the exception and the execution of the enclosing construct is *abandoned* §11.4(3). The occurrence may be *handled* or *propagated*.

execution §3.1(11) A construct achieves its run-time effect when it is executed. Execution of an expression is called *evaluation* and execution of a declaration is called *elaboration*.

expanded name §4.1.3(4) A selected_component of the form prefix.selector_name denotes a component of an object or of a value of composite type such as a record, or an operation of some task or protected object. The same syntax is also used for an *expanded name*, in which case the prefix denotes a named construct such as a package and the name denotes an entity declared in the package. See §4.1.3(10–13) for a list of constructs that the prefix can denote in an expanded name.

```
R: Ada.Strings.Maps.Character_Range;    -- expanded name
R.Low := R.High;                        -- prefix.selector_name
```

expected type §8.6(20) The *expected type* appears in the Name Resolution Rules for a construct and is used for overload resolution. See §8.6(21–25) for the definition of expected type when class-wide types are concerned. Similarly, a context can have an *expected profile* §8.6(26) for a *callable entity*.

```
function F return Duration;
function F return Float;

delay F;          -- Delay expects Duration so the first F is chosen
```

expiration time §9.6(1) The time at which a delay will expire.

external call §9.5(4) An external call is a call on a task entry or protected operation that explicitly mentions the target object. An *internal call* §9.5(3) is also allowed, in which case the call is to the current task or protected object. The meanings of *external requeue* and *internal requeue* are similar §9.5(7). An external requeue on the same protected object is a bounded error, because it is a *potentially blocking* operation §9.5.1(15).

external effect §1.1.3(8) The effect of an Ada program on its external environment. Optimizations are permitted §11.6(3) provided that they don't change the external effect of the program.

fail §9.2(1) The activation of a task can fail, in which case the task becomes *completed*.

finalization §7.6.1(4) See *completion*.

first subtype §3.2.1(6) Types are not considered to have names; instead, types that are not *anonymous* are called *named* types and have *nameable subtypes*. A type declaration declares both the type and the name of a *first subtype*. Informally, the name is also the name of the type. In the following declaration, `Vector` is the name of the first subtype of the named array type:

```
type Vector is array(Integer range <>) of Float;
```

freezing §13.14 An entity is *frozen* at a point when its representation must be fully determined; constructs that freeze entities are listed in §13.14. For example, a tagged type is frozen by an extension and after it is frozen primitive operations cannot be added.

full type §3.2.1(8) Some type declarations do not define a type; for example, a private type declaration just declares a *partial view* of the corresponding full type declaration. The type is *completely defined* after the *full type definition*.

full type declaration §3.2.1(3) See *incomplete type declaration.*

full view §7.3(4) See *partial view.*

global §8.1(15) See *immediately within.*

hidden §8.3(5) See *scope.*

homograph §8.3(8) Two declarations are *homographs* if they have the same name, and, for callable entities (subprograms, entries and enumeration literals), if they have type conformant parameter profiles. One homograph can hide or override another; otherwise, it is usually illegal for two homographs to be immediately within the same declarative region. The following declarations are illegal because types and variables are not overloadable:

```
type T is ...
T: Integer;
```

immediately within §8.1(13) A declaration is *immediately within* the innermost enclosing declaration. For example, an accept statement must be immediately within a task body §9.5.2(14):

```
task body T is
  procedure Proc is
  begin
    accept E;      -- Error, not immediately within task body T
  end Proc;
begin
  accept E;        -- OK
end T;
```

A declaration D1 that is immediately with a declarative region D2 is *local* to D2; otherwise—if it is immediately within some other declaration region D3—it is *global* to D2 §8.1(14–15).

implementation-defined §1.1.3(18) A rule may specify a set of possible effects that a construct may have, and an implementation may choose any of these possible effects. For example, an implementation may supply predefined integer types in addition to `Integer` §3.5.4(25). *Unspecified* is the same as implementation-defined, except that the choice need not be documented. For example, it is unspecified if an array parameter is passed by copy or by reference §6.2(11).

incomplete type declaration §3.10.1 Recursive type definitions such as `Node` are implemented by declaring just the type name (and the discriminants, if any). This *incomplete type declaration* must eventually be completed by a *full type declaration.*

indefinite subtype §3.3(23) There are three categories of indefinite subtypes:

- Unconstrained array subtypes, for example, `Matrix`.
- Unconstrained discriminated record subtypes without defaults, for example, `Game_Board`.
- Subtypes with unknown discriminants (including class-wide types):

```
type Data_Structure(<>) is private;
```

All other subtypes, in particular, all elementary types, are *definite*.

If you declare an object of an indefinite subtype, you must supply a constraint either explicitly, or implicitly from an initial value or an actual parameter.

internal call §9.5(3) See *external call*.

intrinsic §6.3.1(4) See *calling convention*.

invalid representation §13.9.1(2) See *abnormal object*.

left §7.6.1(3) See *completion*.

library unit §10.2 See *unit*.

limited type §7.5 A type for which neither copying nor predefined equality is allowed. The reserved word **limited** can be used to explicitly denote that a record or private type is limited; in addition, task and protected types are limited.

```
task type Producer;         -- Limited type
type R is                   -- Limited type because ...
  record
    P: Producer;            -- ...this component is limited
  end record;
```

local §8.1(14) See *immediately within*.

master §7.6.1(3) See *completion*.

mode §6.1(18) An indication of the direction of the data flow from the actual parameter to the formal parameter and back. There are three modes: **in**, **out** and **in out**, which allow the subprogram to read from the actual parameter, write to the actual parameter, or both, respectively.

name §4.1(2) A name denotes a declared entity such as a variable or a component of a record. A *direct name* is either an identifier or an operator symbol such as "+". A name can also be a *prefix* of another name. An implicit dereference can also be a prefix.

```
N:     Node;
Head: Ptr := new Node;
```

`N` and `Head` are direct names. `Head.all` is a name that is an explicit dereference. In the name `N.Key`, `N` is a prefix that is a name, while in the name `Head.Next`, `Head` is a prefix that is an implicit dereference.

named number §3.3.2 See *object*.

nominal subtype §3.3(23) A *nominal subtype* is the subtype specified for (a view of) an object when the view is defined. The *actual subtype* of the object is determined when the object is created:

```
type Vector (Integer range <>) of Float;
procedure Proc(Parm: in Vector);
V: Vector(5..10);

Proc(V);
```

The nominal subtype of the formal parameter `Parm` is `Vector`, but during the call `Proc(V)`, the actual subtype is `Vector(5..10)`.

numeric type §3.5(1) The *numeric types* are the integer types and the real types. Real types can be either fixed point types (ordinary or decimal) or floating point types.

object §3.3 An *object* is an entity created at run-time to contain a value. A list of objects in Ada is given in §3.3(2-12). Objects may be *variable* objects, or *constant* objects whose value cannot be changed. A list of constants is given in §3.3(16–22). A *named number* §3.3.2 is not a constant object; it is just a compile-time name for a static value of universal type. A view of an object may also be constant, even if the object isn't:

```
Length:     Natural  := 100;           -- A variable object
Max_Length: constant Natural := 100;   -- A constant object
Max:        constant := 100;           -- A named number, not a constant

procedure P(X: in Parent) is ...
  -- Within P, X is a view conversion which is a constant
```

operational item §13.1(1.1) See *aspect clause*.

operator §6.6 An *operator* is a function whose name is one of the symbols listed in §4.5(2–7) such as "+" and "=". The words **in**, **not in**, **and then** and **or else** do not denote operators and cannot be overloaded.

overloading §8.3(6) A set of declarations is *overloaded* if they have the same name and are directly visible at some place in the program. Name Resolution Rules are used to resolve a reference, that is, to choose one of the possible interpretations §8.6(10–15). Preference can be given to *root* types §8.6(29). Overload resolution is done by examining a *complete context* §8.6(4). A complete context should have only one acceptable interpretation; otherwise it is ambiguous §8.6(30). For example, the procedure call statement `Ada.Text_IO.Put("Hello world")` is a complete context, and the possible interpretations are the `Put` procedures for characters and for strings. The interpretation of the statement as a call to `Put` for strings is chosen because `String`, the type of `"Hello world"`, is the *expected type* §8.6(20) for that procedure.

overriding §8.3(9) A declaration of a subprogram with the same name as the implicit declaration of an inherited primitive subprogram *overrides* the implicit declaration.

parent type §3.4(1) See *derived type*.

part §3.2(6) See *subcomponent*.

partial view §7.3(4) The declaration of a private type declares a *partial view* of the type; its *full view* is given by the full declaration in the private part.

```
package P is
  type Parent is private;
  type Not_Derived is new Parent with null record;    -- Error
private
  type Parent is tagged null record;
  type Derived is new Parent with null record;        -- OK
end P;
```

The partial view of Parent is not tagged, so the extension in the declaration of Not_Derived is illegal, even though Parent "really" is tagged as shown in the full view.

partition §10.2(2) An Ada program consists of a set of *partitions*, which can be executed in a distributed environment by assigning each partition to a node.

per-object constraint §3.8(18) A constraint in a component of a discriminated record is a *per-object constraint* if it *depends on a discriminant*. If so, it is evaluated only when the object is created, not when the type declaration is elaborated. In the following example, the discriminant D is a *per-object expression*:

```
G: Integer := 11;

type Rec(D: Integer) is
  record
    Field1: String(1..G);     -- Not a per-object constraint
    Field2: String(1..D);     -- Per-object constraint
  end record;

R: Rec := (10, "Hello world", "Hello world");
```

The constraint of Field1 is elaborated when the type declaration is elaborated and is (1..11) for all objects. The per-object constraint of Field2 is elaborated when an object is elaborated. For the object R, the constraint (1..10) will cause Constraint_Error to be raised.

pool-specific §3.10(8) See *storage pool.*

potentially blocking §9.5.1(8) It is a bounded error for a protected action to invoke an operation such as a call to an entry that could cause the task executing the action to block.

prefix §4.1(4) See *name.*

primitive operation §3.2.3 The primitive operations on a type include the predefined operations on the type, as well as user-defined *primitive subprograms*, which are subprograms that have a formal parameter or result of the type and are declared along with the type. Inherited and overriding subprograms are primitive operations.

private part §7.1(6) See *visible part.*

profile §6.1(22) The profile of a callable entry such as a subprogram or entry is defined by the declaration of the formal parameters. For a function, the profile includes the result type.

progenitor §3.9.4(9) See *derived type*.

protected action §9.5.1(3) The execution of a protected subprogram or entry, including acquiring and releasing the lock.

range §3.5(4) A *range* is subset of a *scalar type* defined by a lower and an upper bound. A *discrete range* or *discrete subtype indication* is specified by giving either a range or a subtype indication of a discrete subtype:

```
for P in Piece loop ...          -- subtype indication
for P in Knight..Rook loop ...   -- discrete range
```

representation clause §13.1 This term was used in Ada 95. In Ada 2005 the term has been changed to *aspect clause* because these clauses are used to define more than just representations.

representation item §13.1(1) See *aspect clause*.

root type §3.4.1(8) See *universal type*.

root library unit §10.1.1(1) See *unit*.

scalar type §3.2(3) See *elementary type*.

scope §8.2 The scope of a declaration is the portion of the program where the declaration might be *visible* §8.3. A declaration is *directly visible* §8.3(4) either because it is *immediately visible* and can be referred to by a direct name, or because it is *use-visible* §8.4(9). A declaration is use-visible if it has been made *potentially use-visible* by a use_clause §8.4(8) and there are no name conflicts §8.4(10–11). Within its scope, a declaration may be *hidden* §8.3(5), either from direct visibility or from all visibility.

```
type Index is Integer range 1..100;
type T(D1: Index := 10; D2: Index := D1) is ...
    -- Error, D1 is hidden from all visibility 8.3(19)

Head:  Ptr     := new Node;
First: Integer := Head.Key;
    --  Key is visible but not directly visible 8.3(2)
```

semantic dependence §10.1.1(24) One compilation unit may depend on another; this dependence is used to determine the correctness of a unit and the visibility of declarations. *Elaboration dependences* include semantic dependences, but they can be changed by using pragmas §10.2(9). For example, a package body depends on the corresponding package declaration. Elaboration dependences are used to determine the possible orders in which units can be elaborated at run-time.

short-circuit control form §4.5.1(1) The constructs **and then** and **or else** do not evaluate their second operand if the value of the form can be determined from the first one:

```
while P /=  null and then P.Key /= Value loop
  -- If P is null, P.Key is not evaluated
```

specific type §3.4.1(3) See *class-wide type*.

stand-alone object §3.3.1(1) An object (a constant or a variable) declared in an object declaration is a *stand-alone object*. Paragraph §3.3.1(23) lists objects that are not stand-alone, such as the loop parameter of a for-loop and parameters of subprograms.

static §4.9 A *static* expression is one whose value can be determined at compile-time. Similarly, a subtype whose constraint can be determined at compile-time is called a *static subtype* §4.9(26). The choices of a case statement must be static §5.4(5).

```
procedure Proc(Parm: Piece) is
  subtype R1 is Piece range Pawn..Bishop;    -- Static
  subtype R2 is Piece range Pawn..Parm;      -- Not static
begin
  case P is
    when Pawn  => ...;    -- OK
    when Parm  => ...;    -- Error
    when R1    => ...;    -- OK
    when R2    => ...;    -- Error
  end case;
end Proc;
```

statically match §4.9.1 Certain language constructs require that a pair of subtypes or constraints *statically match* so that the compiler can determine that they are the same: either they are both static and equal, or they are both derived from the same definition. For example, array type conversion is permitted only if the subtypes of the components statically match §4.6(12) (and the index subtypes are convertible).

```
procedure P(N: in Positive) is
  subtype R is Integer range 1..N;
  type AT1 is array(1..10) of R;
  type AT2 is array(1..10) of R;
  type AT3 is array(1..10) of Integer range 1..N;
  A1: AT1 := ...;
  A2: AT2 := AT2(A1);    -- OK
  A3: AT3 := AT3(A1);    -- Error
```

Although AT1 and AT2 are not static, they statically match because they are derived from the same subtype R. AT3 is structurally the same, but does not statically match the other two.

statically tagged §3.9.2(4) See *dynamically tagged*.

storage element §13.3(8) A storage element is an addressable element of memory. Although on most computers, storage elements are eight-bit bytes, it is best to use `System.Storage_Unit` to obtain the number of bits in a storage element:

```
for Ptr'Storage_Size use 1000 * (Node'Size / System.Storage_Unit);
          -- Storage pool for 1000 nodes
```

storage pool §13.11(2) Allocation of memory using **new** is done from an area of memory called a *storage pool*. A storage pool can be associated with a *pool-specific* access type §3.10(8). Normally, all storage is allocated from one or more *standard pools*, but the user can define other pools and memory allocation schemes. An object of a *general access type* can contain a value of any access type that has the same designated type.

stub §10.1.3(1) See *subunit*.

subcomponent §3.2(6) A subcomponent is a *component* of an object of composite type, or, recursively, a component of a subcomponent. A *part* is an entire object or any set of its subcomponents.

subsystem §10.1(3) See *unit*.

subtype §3.2(8) A *subtype* is a type together with a *constraint* on the values of the type. The subtype of an entity is determined at run-time and violations of subtype matching cause `Constraint_Error`.

```
subtype  Strong is Piece range Knight..Queen;
Current: Strong := Pawn;     -- Compiles OK, raises Constraint_Error
```

subunit §10.1.3 A *subunit* is a separately compiled unit that is a body corresponding to a *stub* in the parent unit.

```
package body P is
  Title: constant String := ...;
  procedure Display is separate;   -- Stub
end P;

with Ada.Text_IO;                  -- A subunit can have a context clause
separate(P)
procedure Display is
begin
  Ada.Text_IO.Put(Title);          -- A subunit retains visibility
end Display;
```

syntactic category §1.1.4(15) A *syntactic category* is a nonterminal appearing in the BNF grammar notation under the heading Syntax. The term is sometimes used in *ARM* rules; for example, §8.3(3) states that the syntactic category direct_name is used whenever direct visibility is required.

tag indeterminate §3.9.2(6) See *dynamically tagged*.

target object §9.5(2) The task or protected object called in an entry or protected subprogram call is the *target object*.

terminated §9.3(5) A task is in the *terminated* state after it has been *completed* and *finalized*.

type §3.2(1) A *type* is a set of values and a set of *primitive operations* on these values. The type of an object is determined at compile-time.

unconstrained subtype §3.2(9) An *unconstrained subtype* is a subtype that allows constraints, but for which no constraints have been defined:

```
type Game_Board(Size: Positive) is ...    -- Unconstrained subtype
subtype Chess_Board is Game_Board(8);     -- Constrained subtype
```

Subtypes with unknown discriminants are also unconstrained §3.7(26). `Integer'Base` and discriminated records with defaults are examples of unconstrained subtypes that are not *indefinite*, so uninitialized objects of these types can be declared.

unit §10.1(1) Ada programs (more exactly, *partitions*) are composed of (possibly nested) units such as packages, tasks and subprograms. A *compilation* consists of a set of one or more *compilation units*, which are either *library units* or *subunits*. A library unit is a unit not physically nested within another (except `Standard`). Library units that are not children of another package except `Standard` are called *root* library units §10.1.1(1). A unit may be a *parent unit* or a *child unit* §10.1.1(1), and the terms *ancestor* and *descendant* §10.1.1(11) are used transitively for this relation. A root library unit and its descendants form a *subsystem* §10.1(3).

universal type §3.4.1(6) A *universal type* is the conceptual class-wide type for a class of numeric types. The conceptual specific type at the root of a universal type is called a *root type* §3.4.1(8).

unspecified §1.1.3(18) See *implementation defined.*

usage name §3.1(10) See *defining name.*

use-visible §8.4(9) See *scope.*

view §3.1(7) A declaration defines a *view*, which is a way of "looking at" an entity. There may be several views for the same entity:

- A private type is a partial view of the full type whose definition is given in its completion §7.3(4).
- A formal parameter that is passed by reference is a view of the actual parameter §6.2(2).
- A type conversion to a tagged type is a view of the object §4.6(5,26).

visible §8.3 See *scope.*

visible part §7.1(6) The declarations in a package specification before the reserved word **`private`** form the *visible part* of the specification. Declarations following **`private`** (if any) form the *private part* of the specification.

Appendix B
Hints

2.1. §3.5.1(7), §3.5.4(15), §3.5.5(6)
2.2. §4.4(2–7)
2.3. §2.4.1(6), §2.4.2(7–8)

3.1. §6.1(21)
3.2. §6.6(5)
3.3. §6.6(6)

4.1. §4.3.3(3–4), §4.3.1(4-6)
4.2. §4.3.3(19)
4.3. §4.1.2(7)
4.4. §4.3.3(27), §4.3.3(26,29)
4.5. §4.3.3(17)

5.1. §3.6(10), §3.3(23)
5.2. §4.3.1(15), §4.5.2(22)
5.3. §5.2(7,13)
5.4. §4.3.1(17), §4.9(6,21–22)

6.1. §7.3(5)
6.2. §3.10.1(3)
6.3. §7.3.1(3,5)

7.1. §4.3(4), §3.9(29)
7.2. §3.4(17), §4.5.2(14)
7.3. §4.5.2(24)
7.4. §7.3.1(8–9)

8.1. §13.14(7,16), §3.9.2(13)
8.2. §3.3(12), §4.6(5), §5.2(5)
8.3. §3.9.3(4,6)
8.4. §3.9.2(11)
8.5. §13.14(6)

9.1. §12.5.3(3)
9.2. §12.1(10), §12.3(20)
9.3. §3.4(6), §12.5.1(11–14)
9.4. §12.7(10)
9.5. §12.3(16–17)
9.6. §12.6(9)

10.1. §11.4.1(12)

11.1. None
11.2. §3.8(12)
11.3. §8.5.1(5)
11.4. §3.7(11)
11.5. §3.7(9.1)
11.6. §4.6(43)
11.7. §13.1(10)

12.1. §6.4.1(12–15)

12.2. §3.10.2(6,22), §10.2(8)
12.3. §3.4(18), §6.1(27)
12.4. §4.1(12)
12.5. §3.3(9)
12.6. §9.5.2(13)
12.7. §3.10.2(28)
12.8. §3.10(4,10), §4.6(24.11,12,18)

13.1. §3.5(9),§3.4(26)
13.2. §3.5.3(1), §5.3(4)
13.3. §3.5(6), §3.5.4(21)
13.4. §4.5(9)
13.5. §4.5.1(5)
13.6. §3.5.9(13)
13.7. §3.3.1(2), §3.3(24)
13.8. §3.5.5(3), §5.4(8)
13.9. §3.4(19)
13.10. §3.4(6,19,34)
13.11. §4.5.5(19.1–19.3)

14.1. §A.10.1(3)
14.2. §A.10.1(10–11), §3.3(17), §6.4.1(5)
14.3. §A.13(4), §A.10.1(85)

15.1. §8.5.4(7)
15.2. §7.2(4)
15.3. §8.5.4(4–5)
15.4. §8.3(22), §4.1.3(4)
15.5. §6.4(6,9), §6.4.1(5), §8.6(2,14)
15.6. §8.4(10)
15.7. §3.2.3(7), §8.1(9)
15.8. §8.6(7,27)
15.9. §8.4(8), §3.2.3(1,6), §A.4.4(76)
15.10. §10.1.6(3)

16.1. §A.18.2(85)
16.2. §A.18.4(44–49)
16.3. §A.18.8(68)

17.1. §8.4(8), §3.2.3(6)
17.2. §9.4(11.9)
17.3. §3.9.4(6)
17.4. §3.9.4(16)

18.1. §9.7.1(21), §9.5.2(24), §9.5.3(21)
18.2. §9.5.2(14–15), §5.6
18.3. §8.5.4(7)
18.4. §9.5.3(7)
18.5. §8.6(17)

19.1. §9.2(1,5), §9.3(5)
19.2. §9.3(2)
19.3. §9.7.4(6,9), §9.5.3(20)

20.1. §B.3.3(16,18)
20.2. §10.2.1(7,8)
21.1. §D.1(7–8)
21.2. §D.2.2(4.1)
21.3. §D.13(4), §D.7(10.8)
21.4. §D.10(10)

Appendix C
Answers

2.1. Prints an asterisk that is at position 42 in the enumeration type `Character` and then prints zero. The position of an enumeration value is its position within the type, not the subtype, and the position of an integer is its value. `Val` returns a value of the *base* type.
2.2. Compile-time error. The declaration of `B1` is legal because repetitions of **and** (or **or**) are allowed by the syntax. The declaration of `B2` is illegal because combining operators requires the syntax of a parenthesized expression.
2.3. Compile-time error. The third statement is a parse error because the exponent must be decimal. With the third statement deleted, the program prints 2560 ($= 10 \cdot 16^2$) twice: exponent letters and hexadecimal digits can be of either case.

3.1. Compile-time error. A formal parameter cannot be used in the formal part.
3.2. Compile-time error. An explicit declaration of "/=" for predefined `Boolean` is illegal.
3.3. Prints `True` twice. Except for predefined `Boolean` type, there is no relationship between "=" and "/=".

4.1. Compile-time error. While record aggregates can have named associations after positional associations, array aggregates must be either positional or named (except for **others**).
4.2. Prints `S`. The bottom subaggregate can be a string literal if the component is of type `Character`.
4.3. Prints nothing. A null slice does not cause `Constraint_Error`.
4.4. Raises `Constraint_Error`. The declaration of `V1` is legal: the aggregate bounds are taken from the discrete choice list and then converted during the assignment (*sliding*). Because of the **others**, the bounds of the aggregate for `V2` are taken from the index constraint, and 6 is not within the bounds of the constraint. Aggregates with **others** do not slide.
4.5. Compile-time error. The second aggregate is illegal, because a choice may not be dynamic unless it is the only choice.

5.1. Compile-time error. A component must be of a definite subtype; an unconstrained array type is indefinite.
5.2. Prints `True`. Equality of a composite types returns true if there are no components.
5.3. Prints `HHell world`. There is no "overlap" because both sides of the assignment statement are evaluated *before* the target variable receives the value of the expression.
5.4. Compile-time error. The discrete choices must be static: `Character'Succ(Start)` is static, but `Stop` is not.

6.1. Compile-time error. An object cannot be declared before the full declaration of its type.
6.2. Compile-time error. The completion of an incomplete type declaration can be in the body only if the incomplete declaration is in the *private* part.
6.3. Compile-time error. The assignment of objects of limited type in the main progam is illegal. The package body is legal, because the completion of `T` by a nonlimited type is allowed to add equality and assignment. Of course, these are visible only within the declarative region of the package.

7.1. Compile-time error. Since an aggregate cannot be of class-wide type, a qualified expression like `T2'(I=>2, N=>4)` should be used to give the aggregate a specific type.
7.2. The first statement prints `True` because the first components 2 and 3 of `A` and `B` are equal by the overridden equality function, and the second components, which are both 4, are equal by predefined equality which is used on non-inherited components. The second statement prints `False` because 4 is not equal to 5 using predefined equality. We say that predefined equality is *incorporated*. Without the special rule, the second component `N` would be *ignored* by the inherited equality and both statements would print `True`.
7.3. Prints `True` then `False`. Predefined, rather than overridden, equality is used for untagged components of a composite type.
7.4. The specification is legal. Even though the partial view of `T` untagged, you can apply the attribute `T'Class` provided that the full view is tagged.

8.1. Compile-time error. The declaration of the extension `T2` freezes the type `T1`, and a primitive subprogram such as `Proc2` cannot be declared after the type is frozen.
8.2. Prints `1 3`. A type conversion to a tagged type is a view conversion, and a view conversion of a variable is a variable as required for the target of an assignment statement.
8.3. Compile-time error. The function must be overridden, otherwise the inherited function would return a value of type `T1`, which cannot be assigned to an object of type `T2`.
8.4. Compile-time error. A default expression must be tag indeterminate.
8.5. A deferred constant does not freeze a type, so the declaration of `Proc2` is legal.

9.1. Compile-time error. The index of a generic formal array type parameter must be a subtype mark.
9.2. Prints 100 then 200. Generic parameter associations are evaluated when the generic unit is instantiated, not when it is declared.

9.3. Compile-time error. The discriminated record `R` is unconstrained, but `S` is constrained by a discriminant constraint. Since `T` is a generic formal parameter with a known discriminant part, the instantiation of `Proc1` is legal because `R` is unconstrained and supplies a discriminant, while the instantiation of `Proc2` is not legal because `S` is constrained without a discriminant.

9.4. Prints `6 12`. The formal part of the formal package parameter (function `Formal`) is visible only if the formal package actual part is `(<>)`. If the actual part supplies parameters as in the commented instantiation, a compile-time error results because `Integer` and `"+"` are used, and the formals `T` and `Formal` are not visible.

9.5. Prints `Parent`, then `Actual`. The copied operations from `Formal` are the only ones visible within the instantiation. Outside the instantiation, the *whole new set* is visible and can be overridden.

9.6. An array parameter of a generic formal parameter is considered to be unconstrained. Therefore, in the subprogram `ProcG` the conversion of an array of type `TG` to type `P.T` is not illegal. However, at run-time, `Constraint_Error` will be raised.

10.1. Prints `P.INNER`. The function `Exception_Name` returns the fully expanded name of the exception even though the exception itself is not visible.

11.1. This might raise the exception `Storage_Error` if the implmentation allocates the maximum space that might be needed by any value of the discriminant subtype.

11.2. Compile-time error. A discriminant must be used directly in a constraint, not as part of a larger expression.

11.3. Compile-time error. The declaration of `C2` is illegal, because you can't rename something that might cease to exist.

11.4. Compile-time error. Default expressions are not allowed for discriminants of tagged type.

11.5. Compile-time error. Defaults must be given for all discriminants or for none.

11.6. The declaration of `D` raises `Constraint_Error`. When a discriminant of the target type corresponds to more than one discriminant of the operand, they must both be equal.

11.7. A compile-time error occurs in the main program. Changing the representation is a potentially expensive operation. It is not allowed when a subprogram is primitive and can be inherited so that the conversion is not easy to see.

12.1. `K` is uninitialized, so the first statement will print garbage or whatever the default initialization of an integer is. The second statement will print 5 because `P` is initialized to the actual parameter. The special rule exists so that uninitialized pointers will never exist, as this can break the type system.

12.2. Compile-time error. `Ptr` is at library level and `Main` is deeper than the master which calls it, namely, the library level environment task.

12.3. Compile-time error. The call to `Proc1` is a call to an unknown subprogram. `Parent_Ptr` is not of type `Parent`, so it is not inherited by the derived type. The call to `Proc2` is legal, because the profile of a subprogram includes the designated subtype of an access parameter.

12.4. Compile-time error. An implicit dereference is a prefix, thus `S(1..5)` returns a slice of a string, which is an acceptable parameter for `Put_Line`. However, there is no implicit dereference of `I` and a pointer is not an acceptable parameter for `Put`. The subprogram call `Put(I.all)` is legal.

12.5. Prints 5. The dereference is a variable, and it does not matter that the access object is returned by a function. However, you cannot assign directly to the function result, because it is a constant §3.3(21).

12.6. Compile-time error. An entry for task cannot have an access parameter, because implementation of accept statements would be too difficult. An entry for a protected object is not subject to this restriction.

12.7. Compile-time error. The view `D` of `N` is of the accessibility level of the main program, which is deeper than the library access level of the anonymous type of the discriminant.

12.8. Compile-time error. We do not want to be able to convert an access-to-constant to an access-to-variable, in order to prevent modification of constant; the reverse conversion makes sense. The rules are somewhat complex. A type that is an *access-to-constant* type is a *general access* type by §3.10(4,10). Therefore, by §4.6(24.11) the conversion `C := AC(P)` is permitted. The conversion `P := AV(C)` is not permitted, because the only type that can be converted to a *pool-specific access type* is *universal_access* §4.6(24.18) (of which null is the only value). If type `AV` were declared **`access all`** `Integer` so that it would be a general access type, then §4.6(24.11) would permit the conversion, but only if the rule in §4.6(24.12) holds; this is not the case since an access-to-constant type cannot be converted to an access-to-variable.

13.1. This is *not* a compile-time error; instead, `Constraint_Error` is raised at run-time.

13.2. Prints `Equal`. The descendant of `Boolean` is also a *boolean type* and the condition of an if-statement can be any boolean type.

13.3. Probably prints `4000`. Although 20_000 is not within the range of the type `Int`, the expression is evaluated using the *base range* of the type; there will be no error in any implementation that allocates at least 16 bits for the base range.

13.4. Prints `5`. The implicit parameter names of the predefined binary operators are `Left` and `Right`.

13.5. Prints `8` since 01010 **`xor`** 10101 = 11111 = 31 and 31 **`mod`** 23 = 8.

13.6. The program is correct even if it prints 10.0. The bounds of fixed point type are not necessarily values of the type.

13.7. Compile-time error. The first declaration declares an aliased object. The second declaration declares a named number, which is a value, not an object that is allocated storage and thus cannot be aliased.

13.8. Compile-time error. The attribute `Pos` returns a value of type *universal integer*. A case statement needs an **`others`** alternative if the expression is of universal type.

13.9. Prints `10 99`. The subtypes of the subprogram for the derived type are taken from the parent type.

13.10. Raises `Constraint_Error`. There is no way to call the inherited subprogram, because the parameters are constrained by `1..50`, while the derived values are constrained by `51..100`.

13.11. Compile-time error. `Special` is of type `Rates` and `Amount` is of type `Money`. There is no multiplication operator for types `Rates` and `Money`, so the only possibility is the standard multiplication for *universal_fixed* §4.5.5(19). There is no context for using the standard operator so the first sentence of §4.5.5(19.1) doesn't hold. The declaration of the operator for `Rates` means that the conditions in §4.5.5(19.2–19.3) hold, so the standard operator cannot be used without an explicit conversion.

14.1. Compile-time error. `Ada.Text_IO.File_Type` is limited.

14.2. Compile-time error. The `File` parameter of the subprograms is of mode **`in out`** and the actual parameter must be a variable, but the parameter `F` is of mode **`in`** and thus is a constant.

14.3. Prints `File not found`. The exception `Name_Error` is declared in `Ada.IO.Exceptions`, but it is renamed with the same same in `Ada.Text_IO` and thus visible by the use_clause for this package.

15.1. Prints `0`. The subtype is taken from the renamed procedure, not the renaming declaration.

15.2. A body is not allowed unless needed; if you delete the body, the result of the program depends on the implementation. It probably prints a garbage value. Use **`pragma`** `Elaborate_Body` §10.2.1(26) in the specification to require that the package have a body.

15.3. Compile-time error. The declaration of `Proc2` is a renaming-as-body which must be subtype conformant. The declaration of `Proc3` is correct because mode conformance is sufficient for a renaming-as-declaration.

15.4. Prints `10 5`. The homograph is hidden from direct visibility, but not from all visibility. An expanded name can be used to access the outer declaration.

15.5. Compile-time error. Overloading resolution can make use of the names in a named association §6.4(9), so the first call is unambiguous. However, the only way to disambiguate the second call is to note that the actual parameter of an **`out`** or **`in out`** formal parameter must be a variable. But this is a legality rule, *not* an overload resolution rule §6.4.1(5). §8.6(14) only requires that a possible interpretation satisfy the syntax rule—here §6.4(6). So overloading fails even before the legality is checked §8.6(2).

15.6. Prints `Hi from Proc in the main subprogram`. A use_clause will not cause ambiguity with a homograph declared directly in a declarative region.

15.7. Prints `Derived` even though the overridden subprogram is not visible. Overriding subprograms need not be declared in the visible part of the specification, only immediately within the same *declarative region* as the parent type, which includes the private part.

15.8. Compile-time error. The second call is ambiguous because a type conversion does not provide an expected type for overload resolution. The first statement by itself would print 1, because the call to Ada.Integer_Text_IO.Put is a context for overloading resolution.

15.9. Compile-time error on the second statement. There is no "*" operator declared for the operand types Natural and String in package Standard so that 2 * Hello would be always visible. The first statement is correct: there is an operator "*" that returns a bounded string, and the call to To_String provides a context. The operator returns a value of type Names.Bounded_String so it is primitive and the use_type clause makes it potentially use-visible.

15.10. Compile-time error. There are special visibility rules for context clauses; a use_clause can only be given for a package that appears in a with_clause within the same context clause.

16.1. Prints 0. The default initialization of a vector is the empty vector of length 0.

16.2. Raises Constraint_Error. A map cannot have more than one element associated with each key. There are two versions of the procedure Insert: one that returns a Boolean value if the insertion is successful or not, and another that raises an exception if the insertion in unsuccessful.

16.3. All sets and maps, not just ordered ones, have first and last elements, as well as subprograms Next defined on them. For hashed containers, the results are unspecified. The program obtained by compiling with GNAT prints Hello.

17.1. A use_type_clause clause makes *primitive* operations visible, but the "=" we want is declared in Matrix_Operations, not in Matrices where the type Matrix is declared, so it is not primitive.

17.2. Compile-time error. The first parameter of the inherited subprogram of a task, protected or synchronized interface is used for a task or protected object and must not be an **in** parameter, because the state of the task or protected object will probably be changed by the call.

17.3. Prints P. A task or protected type derived from an interface is a tagged type.

17.4. Compile-time error. A type cannot be derived from both a task and a protected interface.

18.1. Prints

```
Task T Program_Error
```

and then

```
Task A Program_Error
Main Tasking_Error
```

in some order.[1] The exception Program_Error is raised in T because there is no open alternative in the selective accept. The exception in the rendezvous between A and T is propagated to the caller A. Tasking_Error is raised in the main subprogram because the called task A completes before the call is accepted.

18.2. Compile-time error. An accept statement must be *immediately within* a task body, not within a nested subprogram body such as P. Furthermore, an accept statement cannot contain another accept for the *same* entry. Note that a block is a statement, not a body, so the outermost accept in the task body is legal.

18.3. Compile-time error. A renamed entry is a procedure, not an entry, so it cannot appear in a requeue statement.

18.4. Program_Error is propagated to the caller Main because an exception is raised when evaluating the barrier.

18.5. Compile-time error. The use of T within the declarative region of T denotes the *current instance*, not the type, so in the declaration of Y is not legal. The uses of T within the function F and the object declaration Z are legal because they are not within the declarative region of T.

19.1. Prints (in some order) A task has died and four times Hi from task 1. The exception in the elaboration of task T0 causes it to become completed and raise Tasking_Error in the main subprogram, but the main subprogram cannot terminate until *all* its dependents including T1 have terminated.

19.2. Prints Main subprogram and then Hi from task 1 five times and Back from block in some order. The termination of a dynamically allocated task depends on the master declaring the *access type*, in this case the main subprogram. The task is a *garbage task* which runs but is not accessible after the termination of the block. If the commented lines are added, the block becomes the master containing the declaration of the access type New_Ptr and will await the termination of T(2). Back from block will be printed only after the ten lines of output from the tasks.

19.3. Because of the delay 0.2 in the body of T1, the call T1.E is queued; thus the abortable part is started, calling T2.E. When the delay expires, T1.E is accepted and prints Starting T1.E. Because of the subsequent delay 0.8 within the accept statement, the call does not finish before the call to T2.E is started and finishes, printing the lines Starting T2.E and Finishing T2.E. When the call T2.E and the rest of the abortable part finishes (printing Finished abortable), an attempt is made to cancel T1.E, but, by §9.5.3(20), the attempt fails since the call is not on an entry queue. Thus the triggering statement is not cancelled §9.7.4(9), and the rest of the triggering alternative is eventually executed, printing Finishing T1.E and Finish triggering.

[1] The quizzes on tasking assume that the implementation ensures that a call to Put is executed in its entirety without a context switch; otherwise, the individual characters could be interspersed in the output.

20.1. The declaration is correct because the discriminant check is suppressed in an unchecked union. However, an attempt to access U.B raises `Constraint_Error`: because `U` is constrained by `M1`, the compiler knows that component `B` will not exist and emits code to raise the exception. An attempt to access `U.A` is erroneous; one possibility is that it interprets the floating point value as integer.

20.2. The declaration is legal because the initial value is static and can be computed at compile-time.

21.1. Compile-time error. A priority for a subprogram must be static. The pragma with a non-static priority for the task is legal.

21.2. Compile-time error. The priority ranges for priority-specific dispatching must not overlap.

21.3. Compile-time error. The barrier must be simple, not one which computes a non-static expression.

21.4. Only one task can be suspended on a suspension object. The first task to execute blocks on the suspension object, but the second one raises `Program_Error`. The program then blocks because the first task is still blocked.

References

1. J. Barnes. *High Integrity Software: The SPARK Approach to Safety and Security*. Addison-Wesley, Harlow, UK, 2003.
2. M. Ben-Ari. *Principles of Concurrent and Distributed Programming (Second Edition)*. Addison-Wesley, Harlow, UK, 2006.
3. A. Burns, B. Dobbing, and T. Vardanega. Guide for the use of the Ada Ravenscar Profile in high integrity systems. Technical Report YCS-2003-348, University of York, 2003. `http://www.sigada.org/ada_letters/jun2004/ravenscar_article.pdf`.
4. A. Burns and A. Wellings. *Concurrency and Real-Time Programming in Ada 2005*. Cambridge University Press, Cambridge, 2007.
5. J.W.S. Liu. *Real-Time Systems*. Prentice Hall, Upper Saddle River, NJ, 2000.
6. S.T. Taft and R.A. Duff, editors. *Ada 95 Reference Manual: Language and Standard Libraries. International Standard ISO/IEC 8652:1995(E)*, volume 1246 of *Lecture Notes in Computer Science*. Springer, 1997.
7. S.T. Taft, R.A. Duff, R.L. Brukardt, E. Ploedereder, and P. Leroy, editors. *Ada 2005 Reference Manual. Language and Standard Libraries. International Standard ISO/IEC 8652/1995(E) with Technical Corrigendum 1 and Amendment 1*, volume 4348 of *Lecture Notes in Computer Science*. Springer, 2006.

Index of ARM Sections

Subject Index

Printed by Books on Demand, Germany